Integrating Multiple Literacies
in K–8 Classrooms

Cases, Commentaries,
and Practical Applications

Integrating Multiple Literacies in K–8 Classrooms

Cases, Commentaries, and Practical Applications

JANET C. RICHARDS

and

MICHAEL C. MCKENNA

with

Linda D. Labbo
Donald J. Leu, Jr. and Charles K. Kinzer
Merryl R. Goldberg
Sharon Miller and Terri Austin
Peggy Albers
Ann Watts Pailliotet
Deborah Begoray
Kathryn Chapman Carr

 LAWRENCE ERLBAUM ASSOCIATES, PUBLISHERS
2003   Mahwah, New Jersey   London

Lawrence Erlbaum Associates, Inc., Publishers
10 Industrial Avenue
Mahwah, NJ 07430

Library of Congress Cataloging-in-Publication Data

Integrating multiple literacies in K–8 classrooms / [edited by]
Janet C. Richards and Michael C. McKenna
     p.   cm.
   Includes bibliographical references (p.   ) and index.
   ISBN 0–8058–3945–3 (pbk. : alk. paper)
   1. Literacy—Study and teaching. 2. Media literacy—Study
and teaching. 3. Interdisciplinary approach in education.
I. Richards, Janet C. II. McKenna, Michael C.
LC149 .I523 2003
372.6—dc21
        2002072498

Books published by Lawrence Erlbaum Associates are printed on acid-free paper,
and their bindings are chosen for strength and durability.

Printed in the United States of America
10 9 8 7 6 5 4 3 2 1

DEDICATION

In memory of Ann Watts Pailliotet—
a special, vibrant colleague, and a noteworthy contributor
to this book who understood the importance of including media
and popular culture instruction in K–12 curricula

Brief Contents

Foreword, *Jerome C. Harste*   xiii
Preface   xv
Acknowledgments   xviii
Notes to Readers   xxiii

Part I: Theoretical Perspectives   1

1 Writing and Analyzing Teaching Cases: A Process of Discovery   3
   and Reflection
   Janet C. Richards

2 The Symbol-Making Machine: Examining the Role of Electronic   10
   Symbol Making in Children's Literacy Development
   Linda D. Labbo

3 Toward a Theoretical Framework of New Literacies   18
   on the Internet: Central Principles
   Donald J. Leu, Jr. and Charles K. Kinzer

Part II: Integrating Multiple Literacies in K–8 Classrooms: 39
Applications to Teaching

4 Integrating Visual-Arts Literacy With Reading Lessons   41
   Overview: Janet C. Richards

5 Integrating the Literacies of Music and Dance   57
   With Reading Lessons
   Overview: Merryl R. Goldberg

6 Integrating Dramatic-Arts Literacy With Reading Lessons   80
   Overview: Janet C. Richards and Merryl R. Goldberg

7 Integrating the Literacies of Reading and Writing   101
   Overview: Sharon Miller and Terri Austin

8 Integrating the Literacies of Reading and Writing   125
   With Computer Technology
   Overview: Michael C. McKenna

9 Integrating a Semiotic View of Literacy   150
   Overview: Peggy Albers

10 Integrating Media and Popular-Culture Literacy   172
       With Content Reading
       Overview: Ann Watts Pailliotet

11 Integrating the Literacies of Viewing and Visually   190
       Representing With Content Reading
       Overview: Deborah Begoray

12 Integrating Multiple Literacies With Curriculum as Inquiry   210
       Overview: Kathryn Chapman Carr

       Glossary   235
       References   245
       About the Authors   263
       Author Index   265
       Subject Index   271

Contents

Foreword: *Jerome C. Harste*   xiii

Preface   xv

     Purpose of the Book   xv

     Inspirations   xv

     Overview and Features   xv

     Suggestions for Using the Text   xvii

     Acknowledgments   xviii

Notes to Readers   xxiii

Part I: Theoretical Perspectives   1

1   Writing and Analyzing Teaching Cases: A Process of Discovery   3
and Reflection
Janet C. Richards

     Teaching Cases and Teacher Preparation   4

       The Benefits of Case-Based Activities in Teacher Education   4

       Attributes of Good Cases   4

       Authoring Teaching Cases: A Process   5

       Guidelines for Authoring Teaching Cases   5

       Analyzing and Discussing Cases: Addressing Case Issues   7

       Summary   8

     Suggested Readings   8

2   The Symbol-Making Machine: Examining the Role of Electronic   10
Symbol Making in Children's Literacy Development
Linda D. Labbo

     Broadening Notions of Literacy to Include Multiple Sign Systems   11

     The Role of Computer-Related Multimedia and Multiple Sign Systems
in Children's Literacy Development   13

       Implications for Classroom Practice   16

     Suggested Readings   17

3   Toward a Theoretical Framework of New Literacies   18
on the Internet: Central Principles
Donald J. Leu, Jr. and Charles K. Kinzer

     If I Can Write It and Read It, I'm Literate!   18

So What Does It Mean to Be Literate Today?   19

The Need for New Theoretical Perspectives to Examine
New Literacies   21

What Are the New Literacies of the Internet?   23

Central Principles That Define the New Literacies of the Internet   25

If I Can Write It and Read It, I'm Literate! (Revisited)   35

Appendix: Summary of Central Principles That Help Define
the New Literacies of the Internet   36

Part II: Integrating Multiple Literacies in K–8 Classrooms: 39
Applications to Teaching

4   Integrating Visual-Arts Literacy With Reading Lessons   41
Overview: Janet C. Richards   41
Case #4.1: "Is It Time for Art Yet?"   45
Case #4.2: "Fear of Failure"   48
Case #4.3: "The Great Pyramid Mess!!"   52
Reflections and Explorations   54
Practical Applications   54
Suggested Readings   56

5   Integrating the Literacies of Music and Dance   57
With Reading Lessons
Overview: Merryl R. Goldberg   57
Case #5.1: "A Song That Never Was Finished"   62
Case #5.2: "Big Bear Disaster"   66
Case #5.3: "An Egyptian Pyramid Music and Dance Disaster!"   68
Case #5.4: "An Under-the-Sea Dance Dilemma"   72
Reflections and Explorations   75
Practical Applications   76
Suggested Readings   77
Appendix: Definitions and Examples of Poetry Forms   78

6   Integrating Dramatic-Arts Literacy With Reading Lessons   80
Overview: Janet C. Richards and Merryl R. Goldberg   80
Case #6.1: "Drama Needs Democracy"   83
Case #6.2: "Success at Last!"   87
Case #6.3: "What Did We Do Wrong?"   91
Case #6.4: "I Didn't Prepare"   94
Reflections and Explorations   98
Practical Applications   98
Suggested Readings   99

7   Integrating the Literacies of Reading and Writing   101
Overview: Sharon Miller and Terri Austin   101
Case #7.1: "What You See Is What You Talk About
and What You Dream at Night"   111
Case #7.2: "Confusion About Little Jack"   115

Case #7.3: "She Can Write About the Books We Read"   *118*
Reflections and Explorations   122
Practical Applications   122
Suggested Readings   123

8   Integrating the Literacies of Reading and Writing   125
       With Computer Technology
       Overview: Michael C. McKenna   125
          *Case #8.1: "Having Computers in Classrooms Isn't Always
             the Answer"*   *131*
          Case #8.2: "I Didn't Expect This!"   *135*
          Case #8.3: "Blank Screens"   *139*
          Case #8.4: "Cannot Reconnect—Server Failure"   *143*
       Reflections and Explorations   147
       Practical Applications   148
       Suggested Readings   149

9   Integrating a Semiotic View of Literacy   150
       Overview: Peggy Albers   150
          Case #9.1: "Who Is Cinderella, Really?"   *157*
          Case #9.2: "Well, This Didn't Work!"   *162*
          Case #9.3: "Too Many Sign Systems"   *166*
       Reflections and Explorations   170
       Practical Applications   170
       Suggested Readings   171

10 Integrating Media and Popular-Culture Literacy   172
       With Content Reading
       Overview: Ann Watts Pailliotet   172
          Case #10.1: " 'Hip-Hop' and All That Rock"   *177*
          Case #10.2: "Pokemon Problems"   *179*
          Case # 10.3: "Too Much Popular Culture for Me"   *184*
       Reflections and Explorations   188
       Practical Applications   188
       Suggested Readings   189

11 Integrating the Literacies of Viewing and Visually   190
       Representing With Content Reading
       Overview: Deborah Begoray   190
          Case #11.1: "What Visuals Can Do"   *195*
          *Case #11.2: "Where Is My Flashlight? and Stop Playing With the Bear!
             You Are Fifth Graders"*   *198*
          *Case #11.3: "Musical Chairs: Visual Representations That Went
             Awry"*   *202*
       Reflections and Explorations   206
       Practical Applications   207
       Suggested Readings   208

12 Integrating Multiple Literacies With Curriculum as Inquiry   210
    Overview: Kathryn Chapman Carr   210
      Case #12.1: "I Need the Time!"   215
      Case #12.2: "How Do You Incorporate All Subjects?"   219
      Case #12.3: "Less Is Probably More"   223
      Case #12.4: "Searching Everywhere for Nothing?"   226
    Reflections and Explorations   231
    Practical Applications   231
    Suggested Readings   233

    Glossary   235
    References   245
    About the Authors   263
    Author Index   265
    Subject Index   271

Foreword

Jerome C. Harste
Indiana University, Bloomington

The function of a foreword, like that of curriculum more generally, is to give perspective. When curriculum is at its best, all the parts fit together; even better, the parts send a bigger message than they do individually.

So one way to ask "What is this book about?" is to ask, "What is the curriculum being advocated in *Integrating Multiple Literacies in K–8 Classrooms: Cases, Commentaries, and Practical Applications?*" Interestingly, the answer to this question, no matter how you ask it, is that it is about learning. It's about prospective teachers trying out something new, getting feedback, and learning from the experience; at the most fundamental level it is education as inquiry and inquiry as education.

It's also, as the title suggests, about multiple literacies, about multiple ways of knowing, about sign systems like the visual arts, music, dance, drama, language, and more. These subtitles don't change anything. The book as a whole is still about learning. It is about using these sign systems to enhance student learning.

Without a doubt, the strongest feature of this book is that it focuses on preservice teachers' experiences in trying to implement a multiple-ways-of-knowing curriculum. Oh, they are not always successful, but here is where reflection and correction come in, because the second strongest feature of the book is that after each case study we hear from real teachers who have been there, done that, and have the T-shirt or, said differently, "learned from the experience."

One mistake often made when talking about a new way to teach literacy is telling only the success stories. There is in this sense something entirely refreshing in hearing about lessons that don't go so well and then hearing from experts that give advice on what might be done to improve the original lesson.

As an advocate of inquiry-based education, there is something very encouraging about this volume. In it we see inquiring teachers taking a risk, exploring the practical implications of adding art, music, drama, and computers to their curricula.

Because a good language arts curriculum expands communication potential, rather than shuts it down, forays in teaching using the arts are more than just cute. They provide access to kids whose ways of knowing are other than linguistic, whose cultures are different from ours, who, in the past, may not have found that schools serve them well.

Too often the arts are seen as ways to present what one has learned after a study is over, rather than as a tool for thinking about that topic. I can, for example, go on and on talking about topics about which I know lots, but if you asked me "to show what this topic would look like in art" or "what this topic would sound like in music," without a doubt, I would find the project a whole lot more challenging, a whole lot more generative, and a whole lot more interesting.

Furthermore, "thinking like an artist" or "thinking like a musician" would change me. I'd have new insights and new ways of interacting with people.

I might even start being known as "an artist," or "a musician," or "an inventor." In short, using the arts "to mean" positions me differently in the world. Not only do I have a new perspective, I have a new identity. I see curriculum as a metaphor for the lives you want to live and the people you want to be. I see the arts and a multiple-literacies curriculum as opening up classroom spaces for us to try on new identities, to engage in new literate practices, to expand our notions of literacy and what it means to be literate.

We often think about the arts as "soft," yet there is something urgent about a multiple-literacies curriculum when it comes to new literacies in new times. Popular culture probably teaches our kids more about what it means to be literate these days than anything we do in schools. Just watch the kids. It is this everyday, multimodal literacy that really matters. As new teachers we need to be able to build curriculum upon the literacy talents that today's kids bring with them to school.

So that, in a nutshell, is "the curriculum" *Integrating Multiple Literacies in K–8 Classrooms: Cases, Commentaries, and Practical Applications* offers. The authors of this volume, Janet C. Richards and Michael C. McKenna, know that the kinds of literate beings future teachers will create has everything to do with the kinds of social practices they engage in their teacher education classrooms. So watch out. You are about to be artistically engaged.

Preface

Purpose of the Book

We think this practical book differs considerably from most conventional reading/language arts texts. Its purpose is to inspire and prepare you to integrate **multiple literacies** in K–8 classrooms by weaving music, dance, visual arts, **popular culture media,** and computer technology with reading and writing lessons.

Inspirations

Our work with preservice teachers served as an inspiration for the book. In conjunction with their field-based literacy methods courses, the preservice teachers whose cases are presented in this text teach small groups of K–8 students. The students come from various cultures and home environments. Integrating multiple literacies into their teaching, the preservice teachers combine reading and writing lessons with other **semiotic systems** (e.g., music, drama, dance, popular-culture media, visual art, computer applications). Their case reflections show that they are well on their way toward becoming knowledgeable about the implications of today's technology, and they recognize that text "includes messages of all sorts" (Hobbs, 1997, p. 7). As classroom teachers, they will be well prepared to blend and integrate reading and writing instruction with other communication schemes.

OVERVIEW AND FEATURES

The text is organized into 12 chapters and is divided into two parts. The first part, entitled Theoretical Perspectives, consists of three chapters that support the Practical Applications part of the text. Because authentic teaching cases form the nucleus of the text, chapter 1 discusses the benefits of writing and analyzing cases. This chapter also provides information about the specific attributes of exemplary teaching cases. In addition, the chapter offers guidelines for authoring your own case narratives and lists some generic questions that provide a foundation for analyzing and discussing case issues with peers.

Chapter 2, authored by Linda D. Labbo, discusses the role of electronic symbol making and multiple sign systems in children's literacy development. This practical chapter explains how children use symbols and combinations of symbols to receive and express meaning.

Chapter 3, written by Donald Leu and Charles Kinzer, offers a theoretical framework that helps define the new literacies of Internet technology, and provides a strong rationale for expanding traditional definitions of literacy.

Part II of the text is entitled Practical Applications. Consisting of nine chapters, this pragmatic section is organized around pertinent issues associated with weaving the literacies of the arts and technology (e.g., visual arts, dramatic arts, the Internet, multiple texts, formats, genres, CD-ROM applications, music, and dance) with reading and writing. A chapter in this section of the text also focuses on how teachers and students might thoughtfully consider and include ideas communicated through a variety of popular-culture media.

In this second part of the text, we gradually lead readers toward a deeper understanding of how to conceptualize and structure more complex, integrated lessons; for example, communicating and learning through combinations of multiple sign systems; contemplating the influences of visual media, such as television and advertising images; using aspects of popular-culture texts to enhance literacy lessons; and organizing and integrating multiple communication forms into cohesive themed units of inquiry.

The chapters in this second part of the text also begin with relevant quotation excerpts that serve as advance organizers by activating prior knowledge and directing readers' attention to information that is provided in the chapter.

The quotation excerpts are followed by Overviews. Some chapter Overviews were authored by invited scholars who have written widely on various aspects of multiple literacies. The Overviews offer up-to-date information about the particular form of literacy discussed in each chapter, and include helpful sections entitled, "What Do You Need to Know and How Do You Begin?" These sections offer ideas and tasks for teachers who wish to nurture their artistic and technological aptitudes, expand their understanding of popular-culture media, and increase their knowledge about integrating diverse communication forms into cohesive themed units of instruction.

The chapter Overviews are accompanied by authentic cases authored by preservice teachers. Following Judy and Lee Shulman's (1992) descriptions of exemplary cases, the preservice teachers candidly describe their reflections, confusions, and concerns as they support K–8 students' reading and writing development through the visual and communicative arts. Commentaries written by skilled practitioners and university professors offer advice and sometimes supply contrasting solutions to the dilemmas described in the cases. The commentaries provide scholarly perspectives through which you might consider the issues presented in the cases. We urge you to to go beyond the commentary writers' ideas, and explore and consider as many issues as possible regarding each case.

Two questions follow each case. The case-specific questions encourage you to take an active part in analyzing, documenting, and talking about the particular issues portrayed in the case narratives. Responses to the questions can be discussed as a whole-class initiative, in small groups, or by individuals.

Activities designed to promote teachers' reflections and explorations are presented near the end of each chapter. These activities are intended to help teachers become more actively involved in thinking and learning about multiple literacies.

These chapters conclude with a set of questions crafted to enable teachers to optimize their planning by considering their own teaching environments and intent of their instruction as they integrate multiple literacy lessons into their curriculum.

Annotated bibliographies of suggested readings are provided at the end of each chapter to help teachers construct more in-depth knowledge about the multiple literacies discussed in the Overviews and the teaching cases.

Because assessment is reciprocally connected to teaching and learning (i.e., assessment informs teaching and learning; teaching and learning inform assessment), rather than addressing assessment issues in a separate chapter, an assessment thread runs throughout the text. For example, commentary authors pose questions that help teachers assess the results of their multiple literacy lessons, and each set of questions posed for teachers at the end of chapters contains student and teacher assessment considerations.

Footnotes direct readers to correlated readings for important or unusual concepts and terms mentioned in the chapter Overviews and the cases and commentaries. Suggested Readings also help readers make the connections between the integrated instructional activities discussed in the teaching cases and commentaries.

Finally, a glossary provides succinct definitions of special terms that are highlighted in bold print at first use throughout the text.

SUGGESTIONS FOR USING THE TEXT

We recommend that you become familiar with the ideas and theoretical perspectives presented in chapters 1–3 prior to reading subsequent chapters. Chapters 4–11 are not meant to be read in any particular order. Your teaching interests, concerns, and situations will guide your readings and discussions. We do strongly suggest, however, that you acquire a good understanding of the individual literacies described in chapters 4–11 before you read and discuss chapter 12. Chapter 12 provides insights into some of the problematic issues and concerns that may arise when teachers integrate multiple combinations of the visual and communicative arts (e.g., fiction and content literacy, computer technology literacy, music literacy, media/ visual literacy, and dramatic arts literacy) within comprehensive integrated curricula. Therefore, a good understanding of individual literacies is helpful before you consider the integration of the various combinations available.

ACKNOWLEDGMENTS

We offer heartfelt thanks to the following preservice teachers whose personal teaching cases serve as the nucleus of this text. They recognize that literacy has expanded far beyond "simply learning to read in a print-text format" (Rafferty, 1999, p. 2). Their candid narratives allow us to experience their concerns and accomplishments as they make the transition toward teaching multiple literacies.

Patti Alexander
Marci Andrews
Angelique Bathhurst
Karen Breland
Melinda Brown
Janice Clark
Victoria Cooper
Christina Cumbest
Kelly Daniels
Trudy Fore
Jennifer Green
Cecil Gregory
John Hall
Michael Harden
Eli Jacobs
Cassandra Lane
Beth LeBlanc
Brook Letort
Mariela Meneses
Cynthia Morales
Kristy Park
Bill Reagan
Alison Sconyers

Larisa Shaw
Patrice Sontag
Joni Spiers
Amy Stokes
Deneen Vanaman

We are also indebted to the following commentary writers—skilled class-room teachers and literacy teacher educators who work in diverse settings throughout the United States, Canada, Finland, Scotland, and Australia. Their thoughtful, encouraging advice and comments offer support and insights for 21st-century teachers who are eager to extend their curricula far beyond traditional reading and writing lessons. When viewed as a collective body of knowledge, their understanding of what it means to weave multiple literacies into K–8 curricula, and their sound recommendations and advice validate the wisdom comprised by literacy practitioners and scholars worldwide.

Terri Austin, Alaska
Deborah Begoray, Canada
Camille Blachowicz, Illinois
Patricia Bloem, Michigan
Kathryn Chapman Carr, Missouri
David Clarke, Louisiana
Mary Ellen Cosgrove, Georgia
Bruce Fischman, Pennsylvania
Margaret Humadi Genesio, Wisconsin
George Hunt, Scotland
Mary Gobert, Mississippi
Dana Grisham, California
Karen Parker Guillot, Louisiana
Susan Davis Lenski, Illinois
Carol Lloyd, Nebraska
Anita McClain, Oregon
Peggy McCullough, Mississippi
Kathleen McKenna, Illinois
Sharon Miller, Arizona
Timothy Morse, Mississippi
Barry Oreck, Connecticut
Jane Osterman, Kentucky
Carol Payne, Mississippi
Jane Percival, Massachusetts
Katherine Perez, California
Alice Quiocho, California
Timothy Rasinski, Ohio

Victoria Risko, Tennessee
Katherine Schlick Noe, Washington
Deborah Schussle, Tennessee
Ann-Sofie Selin, Finland
Patricia Smith, Australia
Jay Stetzer, New York
Paula Triche, Louisiana
Renee Useforge, Mississippi

A special thanks to Peggy Albers, Ann Watts Pailliotet, Kathryn Chapman Carr, Terri Austin, Sharon Miller, and Deborah Begoray, invited authors of some chapter Overviews. Because conceptions of literacy continue to transform at such a rapid pace, no single person can know everything there is to know about the unique characteristics of the individual or combined literacies described in the text (see Leu, 2000b). The particular expertise of these six contributors helps us better understand the broadened "educational focus that is reflected in multiple literacies" (Messaris, 1997, p. 3).

We also thank our colleagues who shared their special expertise with us. Merryl R. Goldberg at California State University, San Marcos, read the initial prospectus and graciously shared her considerable arts competence. Ramona C. Moore at Western Washington University zealously read first drafts of the text to uncover superfluous commas and numerous other mechanics-of-writing problems. Jamie Myers at Pennsylvania State University read the next-to-last draft of the text and offered his substantial knowledge about **semiotics** and **sign systems.**

We wish to recognize the astute reviewers of this text, Kathy Short, Professor at the University of Arizona, Peggy Albers, Associate Professor at Georgia State University, and Prisca Martin, Professor at Towson State University in Maryland. Their thorough scrutiny of the book's contents, and their forthright comments regarding the importance of semiotic systems as tools for learning, and student inquiry as the nucleus of curricula are greatly appreciated.

We are especially indebted to Jerry Harste, Distinguished Professor of Education at Indiana University. Jerry's seminal work in multiple ways of knowing served to inform us about semiotics and multiple sign systems when we needed to expand our thinking. Thank you, Jerry, for writing the Foreword to this text.

Chapter 2, authored by Linda D. Labbo, Professor at the University of Georgia, provides the theoretical underpinnings for this book. Because the text serves as a bridge between theory and practice, Linda's chapter is crucial to our understanding of semiotic systems and multiple literacies.

We are grateful to Donald Leu at the University of Connecticut and Chuck Kinzer at Vanderbilt University, whose chapter helps us clearly understand why teachers must expand and transform their teaching to include electronic literacies in order to prepare students for their literacy futures.

And we vigorously applaud Naomi Silverman, Senior Acquisitions Editor at Lawrence Erlbaum Publishers. Naomi is a masterful, dexterous mentor. As we slowly developed the book's prospectus over the course of a year, grappled with rapidly evolving ideas about integrating multiple literacies, and expanded our understanding of semiotic systems and curriculum as inquiry, Naomi astutely posed questions that helped to propel our thinking forward. Her expert scaffolding would have pleased and impressed Lev Vygotsky!

Notes to Readers

• It is beyond the scope of this text to provide in-depth information about what it takes to become literate in all of the multiple literacies (see Albers' comments in chap. 9, Overview). Therefore, this book does not offer specific details regarding what artists, musicians, authors, technology experts, and actors know, and what they do to become skilled in their craft (see Albers, 1997). Instead, the text serves as a bridge between research and practice for teachers who want to enhance students' chances for personal fulfillment and academic achievement by implementing a curriculum that views literacy in the broadest terms and provides opportunities for students to use "a full array of meaning-making systems" (Berghoff, Egawa, Harste, & Hoonan, 2000, p. 79).

• As you read each case in the Practical Applications section of the book, we think it is important for you to reflect carefully upon the dilemma(s) portrayed. All good teachers thoughtfully consider problematic issues pertinent to their teaching. In addition, identifying and reflecting on the case issues in this text will help prepare you to respond to teaching narratives presented in the practical applications section of the PRAXIS II teacher licensure examination. Beginning teachers in many parts of the United States are required to successfully complete this test.

• To help guide your contemplations about case issues, following each narrative we have placed two case-specific questions designed to inspire and activate your thoughtful reflections.

Part I

Theoretical Perspectives

Writing and Analyzing Teaching Cases: A Process of Discovery and Reflection

Janet C. Richards
University of Southern Mississippi

> My sixth-grade students were using the projector and an iBook computer to share interesting ideas they had encountered while reading on-line texts about the water cycle. It became clear that Timothy hadn't chosen very interesting sentences. In fact, the sentences he displayed gave very little information about accumulation, evaporation, condensation, or precipitation. Timothy is a good reader, so I don't know why he bombed out on this activity. Maybe I didn't explain the assignment correctly. Using on-line texts for content reading lessons is all new to me, and my computer technology skills are not that good. So, my question is this: Just how can I help students when their reading assignments entail using electronic text?
>
> —Preservice teacher's case excerpt

> When I found out we had to do a lot of art for these classes, I experienced anxiety and nervousness because I am not artistically inclined . . . I don't care what the National Standards say about integrating the arts with literacy lessons.
>
> —Preservice teacher's case excerpt

Teaching cases are not new to teacher education. "As early as 1920, case materials were . . . used in teacher education programs in New Jersey and Massachusetts" (Merseth, 1991, p. x). In response to the school reform movement in the early 1980s, interest in case methods expanded (Merseth, 1991), and by the early 1990s case books that focused on generic aspects of teaching and texts that described case methods became available (Doyle, 1990; Schon, 1991; J. Shulman, 1992; Welty, Silverman, & Lyon, 1991).

Recognizing that lectures and most textbooks do not allow future teachers to experience authentic lessons in contextually grounded, real-life-situations, in the past 5 years many teacher educators have added case writing and analysis to their curricula (Kinzer & Risko, 1998; Richards, 2000;

Richards, Moore, & Gipe, 2000; Richards, Risko, Camperell, Eanet, & Feldman, 1999). In addition, multimedia video cases that portray the myriad facets of instruction impacting students' learning in classrooms have become valuable resources to teacher education (Kinzer & Risko, 1998; Richardson & Kile, 1999).

Acknowledging the connection between case methods and an enhanced conceptual framework in teacher education, the newly developed Professional Development Section of PRAXIS II (formerly entitled the National Teachers Examination) now requires teacher candidates to respond to a series of teaching cases as part of certification and accreditation procedures (personal communication, Educational Testing Service, annual meeting of the American Association of Colleges for Teacher Education, Phoenix, Arizona, February 1997).

TEACHING CASES AND TEACHER PREPARATION

The Benefits of Case-Based Activities in Teacher Education

Though "no case can provide all of the contextual background and interactions that are part of a classroom" (Kinzer & Risko, 1998, p. 185), cases appear to have several advantages over other activities used in preservice and in-service teacher education. As with actual classroom experiences, "they allow teachers to explore the richness and complexity of genuine pedagogical problems" (Putnam & Borko, 2000, p. 8). Analyzing teaching cases also provides opportunities for stimulating teacher education students' abilities to identify, reflect upon, and make sound educational decisions about teaching dilemmas (Colberg, Trimble, & Desberg, 1996; Merseth, 1991; Richards & Gipe, 2000; Sykes & Bird, 1992). In addition, writing and analyzing cases have the potential to prepare future teachers for the contextual complexities and ambiguities of classrooms by promoting their dispositions toward critical thinking, encouraging their development of multiple versus single perspectives on teaching problems, and fostering their understanding of the consequences of their actions (Harrington & Hodson, 1993; Harrington, Quinn-Learing, & Hodson, 1996). Equally important because they are analogous to candid, poignant stories, cases have a high probability of relevance and practicality for both beginning and seasoned teachers because they document real, immediate teaching problems (Noddings, 2000).

Attributes of Good Cases

Although "there is not a consensus among educators as to what [exactly] constitutes a good case" (Merseth, 1991, p. 7), scholars agree that cases in teacher education are focused, engaging narratives varying in length from

1 to 30 pages (Sykes, 1992). They describe a "wide variety of situations, decisions, dilemmas, and difficulties that routinely confront teachers and teacher educators" (Sykes, 1992, p. ix) (e.g., multicultural issues, linking print-based literacy lessons with computer technology; connecting reading to narrative and expository writing lessons). Although context-dependent, the issues described in cases may be generalized to other teaching situations.

Usually written in the first person, cases tell one main story, "but embedded within that story are other problems that can be discussed" (L. Shulman, 1992, p. 2). Like all good stories, authentic cases portray characters that are real, contain dialogue and rich detail, present a problem or a series of related problems that unfold over time, and are "contextualized in time and place" (L. Shulman, 1992, p. 21). Good cases provide readers with sufficient contextual information to understand the conditions in which a teaching dilemma occurred (see Reinking, Mealey, & Ridgeway, 1993, for a discussion of **conditional knowledge**). At the same time, teaching cases do not burden readers with irrelevant details.

Authoring Teaching Cases: A Process

As holds true for all quality writing, authoring teaching cases takes time. Writing is a process that includes brainstorming and generating ideas for writing topics, composing first drafts, editing, and sharing completed pieces with peers. We have found that the following ideas help our preservice teachers organize their thinking, and serve as a guide as they work through the process of writing cases.

Guidelines for Authoring Teaching Cases

1. Begin by identifying some problems or a series of related problems that affect your teaching and your students' learning. It is important to note that all stories about teaching are not cases. Case dilemmas "merit more consideration than an amusing anecdote or vignette" (L. Shulman, 1992, p. 17), such as when your kindergarten students used their left hands to salute the flag or an eighth-grade student told an amusing joke in the middle of a spelling test.

2. Make a list of the problematic issues you have identified. For example, did you attempt to link a literacy lesson with computer technology and could not access the Internet? Did you offer a lesson that connected content text with a dramatic enactment and some students refused to take part because they considered the activity boring, or they wanted to play a specific character?

3. Read over your list of teaching concerns and choose *one* dilemma that is especially problematic to your teaching and your students' learning.

4. Discuss your teaching dilemma or achievement with one or two teaching colleagues. Encourage your colleagues to ask questions about your teaching case (e.g., "How many students are in the group?"; "What grade level do you teach?"; "How did you attempt to solve the problem?").

5. Remember that writing a teaching case is a process. Good writing takes time. Successful writers make many drafts of their teaching cases until they are satisfied with the final product.

6. Engage in some prewriting strategies to help you access and "discover" your ideas (e.g., a semantic map, a time line, speed-writing, small drawings, an outline).

7. Begin writing your case by giving a short explanation of your teaching context (e.g., kindergarten, an urban school; a group of three girls and one boy).

8. Provide sufficient contextual information, but do not provide information that is not relevant to the problem described in your case.

9. Write in the first person (i.e., "I").

10. Write in an informal "voice."

11. Include authentic dialogue (e.g., "So, I said to Jason, 'Do you know how to type?' Jason replied, 'No, we go to computer class everyday, but we play computer games.' ").

12. Write at least two, double-spaced pages.

13. Close your case by brainstorming some possible solutions to your teaching dilemma or success (e.g., "The first thing I did was ask the classroom teacher about Jason's typing abilities. I discovered that Jason was right. Fourth graders are not offered keyboarding lessons in this school. Then, I read chapter 3 in Debbie and Donald Leu's book, *Teaching With the Internet: Lessons From the Classroom* (1997). In this chapter the authors ask thought-provoking questions about keyboarding lessons for students (p. 61). Finally, I talked to my professor. She suggested that I visit Jason's computer lab teacher and ask him what he thought about keyboarding lessons for fourth-grade students. I have decided that it is important for my group of students to learn some keyboarding skills. Therefore, I intend to have Jason's group compose directly on the computer rather than write their stories and then copy them using a word-processing program.")

14. Title your case. Make sure that the title reflects the issues discussed in the case.

15. Read over your completed case. Put yourself in the place of a reader, not the writer of the case. Does the case make sense? Are all relevant parts of the case included? Have you employed appropriate mechanics of writing, including paragraphing, spelling, and punctuation?

16. When you are satisfied with your work, ask one or two teaching colleagues to read your case. Ask them for suggestions regarding how to modify and strengthen your writing.

Analyzing and Discussing Cases: Addressing Case Issues

The real power of cases develops from group discussions, "reflections and work that group participants do to learn from the case(s) and from one another" (Miller & Kantrov, 1998, p. vii). Initially, many education majors have difficulties analyzing and determining the specific issues portrayed in teaching cases (Welty et al., 1991). Therefore, their case discussions lack clarity and purpose. With some practice, however, they learn how to recognize case problems, and they become skillful in discussing case situations with teaching colleagues. The following questions help our preservice teachers address case issues:

1. What do you think is the purpose of this lesson or series of lessons?
2. How was the original plan interrupted or what surprised the teacher?
3. What actions did the teacher take in response to the interruption/ surprise?
4. Examine the consequences of the teacher's actions. What alternative action(s)/procedures would you suggest?
5. Identify the resources (e.g., outside readings, conversations with peers, teachers, or other professionals) used by the teacher in this case. What other specific resources might you suggest (e.g., titles of related articles or books, community agencies, etc.)?
6. From whose perspective is the case written?
7. What do you think are the students' perspectives?
8. Who are the players in the case other than those specifically mentioned (e.g., family, principal, other students)?
9. What seems to be working well in this case?
10. What needs to be improved?
11. Can you distinguish between the symptoms presented in the case and their causes?

These questions were adapted from Morine-Dershimer (1996), J. Shulman (1996), and Silverman and Welty (1996). (Also, see Richards & Gipe, 2000, for cases and accompanying workbook pages that help guide education majors in analyzing cases.)

Summary

Teaching cases have been employed in teacher education since the 1920s. In response to school reform movements, interest in case methods expanded in the 1980s, and by the early 1990s published case books became available. In the past 5 years, case writing and analysis and use of video cases have been added to many education methods courses.

Case discussions provide opportunities for education majors to explore genuine pedagogical problems and to make sound decisions about teaching dilemmas. Furthermore, writing and analyzing cases help prepare future teachers for the contextual complexities and ambiguities of the classroom.

Although there are no set guidelines regarding the specific attributes of good cases, experts agree that exemplary cases vary in length and discuss a genuine teaching problem that can be generalized to other teaching contexts. Sufficient contextual information and authentic dialogue are included. Good cases close with teachers brainstorming some possible solutions to the problem described.

Guidelines for authoring good cases include identifying a problem that warrants consideration, beginning the case with a short explanation of the teaching context in which the problem occurred, writing in the first person, including authentic dialogue, supplying a pertinent title for the case, and closing the case with some possible solutions to the problem portrayed.

SUGGESTED READINGS

Lundeberg, M., Levin, B., & Harrington, H. (1999). *Who Learns What From Cases and How?: The Research Base for Teaching and Learning With Cases.* Mahwah, NJ: Lawrence Erlbaum Associates.

Contributors to this text focus on many aspects of case-based pedagogy, including the benefits of writing and analyzing cases embedded within the context of authentic teaching, what constitutes a case, and how to facilitate case discussions.

Moje, E., & Wade, S. (1997). What case discussions reveal about teacher thinking. *Teaching and Teacher Education, 13*(7), 691–712.

This qualitative study discusses differences and similarities found in cases written by pre- and in-service teachers. Both groups viewed teaching as a technical act; however, in-service teachers were more aware of the constraints placed upon teachers. The authors found that case teaching has the potential to help teachers reflect upon practices, but they argue that case discussions must be carefully crafted to challenge teachers' assumptions.

Richards, J., & Gipe, J. (2000). *Elementary Literacy Lessons: Cases and Commentaries From the Field.* Mahwah, NJ: Lawrence Erlbaum Associates.

This practical book is organized into 12 chapters. Chapter 1 provides information about teaching cases. Chapters 2 through 12 include preservice teachers' teaching cases followed by commentaries that focus on aspects of literacy instruction in elementary schools, such as spelling, writing, reading comprehension, group management, meeting the needs of English-as-second-language students, and social factors affecting students' literacy. Workbook pages that guide readers in analyzing the cases and help prepare future teachers for the PRAXIS II examination follow each case.

Shulman, J. (Ed.). (1992). *Case Methods in Teacher Education.* New York: Teachers College Press.

The purpose of this book is to describe how to develop and use cases and to demonstrate the wide role of case-based teaching. Readers learn about the inseparability of teachers' thoughts, feelings, and actions.

Wasserman, S. (1994). Using cases to study teaching. *Phi Delta Kappan, 75*(8), 602–611.

This article tells us that when teacher education students read cases, they learn about life in classrooms and discover that there are no simple solutions to teaching problems. Real-life teacher education classroom scenarios are portrayed.

The Symbol-Making Machine: Examining the Role of Electronic Symbol Making in Children's Literacy Development

Linda D. Labbo
University of Georgia

> We are . . . expanding the definition of what literacy means. Students read and interpret not just words on a page, but also icons on a computer screen, images on TV, and graphs and charts in newspapers. But although we incorporate different kinds of literacies into the classroom, we do not eliminate any of the "old" literacies. We still expect students to read and write in the traditional way.
>
> —Tell (1999, p. 7)

> In the next generation, Americans will expect educated people to use several symbol systems.
>
> —Walker (1999, p. 19)

> From technology-related literacy to visual literacy to theater literacy to music literacy, understanding of these forms of representation also is key to successful school experiences and an enriched and fulfilling life.
>
> —Rasinski (2000, p. 2)

Stories about pets that died, lines of random letter strings, fire-station field-trip photos, lopsided paintings of toothy orange jack-o'lanterns, drawings of green pea pods growing in a weedy spring garden, video clips of a class play, storybook scenes that come alive with animation and mood music, and e-mail messages for chicken-pox-afflicted classmates are but a partial list of the jumbled parade of images, sounds, and messages that I have seen appear, disappear, and at times collide on the screen of a kindergarten class-room computer. After several years of observing classroom computer cen-ters and the work children do there, I have come to appreciate the com-puter as a learning environment, a screenland (Labbo, 1996), that provides youngsters with unique opportunities to use multiple sign systems to make meaning in dynamic and social ways that are often as fluid, transient, and natural as is their spoken language (Labbo, 1994; Labbo, Eakle, & Montero, 2002; Labbo & Kuhn, 2000).

On a fundamental level, sign systems may be understood as print and nonprint languages (symbols and how symbols combine to make meaning) that are used to receive and express meanings. When viewed from my researcher's perspective, I have come to realize that computers are "symbol machines" and "crossmodal canvases" (Char & Forman, 1994, p. 170) that allow children to negotiate a complex interplay of multiple sign systems (e.g., video clips, music, sound effects, icons, virtually rendered paint strokes, text in print-based documents), multiple modalities (e.g., linguis-tic, auditory, visual, artistic), and recursive communicative and cognitive processes (e.g., real-time and virtual conversations, cutting/pasting text, manipulating graphics, importing photographs).

The purpose of this chapter is to consider practical classroom impli-cations of relevant theoretical underpinnings that underscore the role of computer-related multimedia and multiple sign systems in fostering chil-dren's literacy development. I begin by briefly addressing the need to broaden definitions of literacy to include *electronic symbol making* (Labbo & Kuhn, 1998). Next, I discuss a theoretical framework that may shed light upon the uniqueness of children's computer-related opportunities to en-gage in powerful literacy development. I close with a brief discussion of implications for classroom practice.

BROADENING NOTIONS OF LITERACY
TO INCLUDE MULTIPLE SIGN SYSTEMS

When my great-grandparents were young children, their literacy education consisted of learning how to sign their names so they could engage in func-tional and economic activities (e.g., signing legal documents, registering homestead property deeds, ordering supplies from mail-order catalogues). When I was a young child, my literacy education included practice in auto-matically recognizing sight words, reading short passages that consisted of controlled vocabulary, and practicing how to form cursive letters during pen-manship lessons so I could use reading and writing to be a good, neat, and responsible citizen (e.g., able to read ballots during elections, writing busi-ness letters, reading bus schedules, and neatly filling out job applications).

My son and daughter developed literacy as they engaged in various types of communicative acts in whole-language-oriented classrooms so they could enter into various discourse communities for various purposes (e.g., poetry writing allowed them to discover their feelings about a topic; letters to the newspaper editor enabled them to have a voice for change; interviewing family members for oral-language histories that aligned with social studies topics empowered them to think like historians).

It is clear that definitions of what it means to be and to become literate have changed dramatically over the last century and a half from an ability to sign one's name for functional literacy activities to the abilities to read, write, speak, and listen for participation in various discourse communities. The shift in perspective from one literacy ability to four abilities takes into consideration the symbiotic and interdependent interactions that occur among the language arts (Flood & Lapp, 1997–1998). In other words, teachers and curriculum writers have come to understand that reading facilitates children's writing development; writing facilitates reading development; and when reading and writing are combined the result is likely to be empowered learners whose thinking processes and learning abilities are positively impacted (Harste, Short, & Burke, 1988; Rowe, 1994; Shanahan, 1990). This shift in perspective has profoundly impacted the type of literacy instruction that children have encountered as teachers have sought to design activities that integrate the arts of language.

Many educators, researchers, and theorists have suggested that with the recent infusion of computers and other technologies into classrooms and workplaces, the time has come for definitions of literacy to once again be broadened or reconceptualized to include communications that are expressed through multiple sign systems as they are encountered on computer screens (Flood & Lapp, 1997-1998; Gilster, 1997; Leu & Kinzer, 2000; Semali & Fueyo, 2001; Semali & Hammet, 1999; Tierney, 1990).

Communicative literacy refers to understanding how meaning is expressed in the communicative arts–sign systems "which include the language arts as well as the visual arts of drama, fine art, film, video, and television" (Flood & Lapp, 1997-1998). *New literacies* refers to the ability to read, analyze, interpret, evaluate, and produce communications in a variety of textual environments with multiple sign systems (Semali & Fueyo, 2001). *Digital literacy* refers to the ability to use information contained in various formats and sign systems as they are presented on computers (Gilster, 1997). Digital signals carry graphics, audio, video, animations, and text that are delivered for various interactive manipulations on computer screens. Thus, digital content can take on any shape or employ any sign system when it is transmitted as a sort of binary soup that moves, stores, and displays images, video, animations, voices, and links to documents or words on computer screens. In this way, various sign systems can link seamlessly, overlap each other, and be manipulated to effectively express various communicative goals.

For purposes of this chapter, I refer to the *electronic symbol making* as a perspective that expands the language arts of reading, writing, speaking, and listening to include multimedia symbol forms. The notion of electronic symbol making also aligns well with a conceptualization of the computer as a symbol machine. Electronic symbol making consists of the conceptual processes, strategies, and skills that children develop as they make meaning with digitally produced multimedia symbols. The shift in perspective from four abilities (language arts) to multiple abilities (digital arts) demands that we take into consideration the symbiotic and interdependent interactions that occur among the language and digital arts. As new technologies make it possible for us to broaden our notions of what it means to be literate, it becomes imperative for us to grapple with the impact that taking such a perspective has on classroom literacy learning and instruction. Thus, in this chapter, I argue that the nature of children's meaning-making cognitive processes is profoundly impacted by their interactions with combinations of symbol systems they encounter on computer screens.

THE ROLE OF COMPUTER-RELATED MULTI-MEDIA AND MULTIPLE SIGN SYSTEMS IN CHILDREN'S LITERACY DEVELOPMENT

Over a decade ago, Wright (1987) suggested that the educational field needed to wait until more was known about optimal formats for displaying and interacting with electronic texts before attempts were made to identify a relevant theory to guide computer-related instructional practices. At the onset of the 21st century, it seems clear that electronic symbol making involves digital literacies and multiple sign systems that may be best understood from a semiotic perspective.

Semiotics, the study of how meaning making is mediated through culturally known symbols, offers a productive framework for our consideration. The nature of semiotic acts may be easiest understood when viewed from the perspective of young children. Harry and Samantha are 5-year-olds who seem able to engage naturally in complex processes of semiotic mediation whereby thought, activity, and language are interwoven in their attempts to make meaning with the multiple symbol systems they encounter in their classroom. Stories the children hear during rug time evoke memories that are represented with words, gestures, and sound effects. Songs the children sing evoke interpretations that are represented through expressive movements and spontaneous dance steps (Eisner, 1998). Photographs of a field trip evoke dictations that employ the literary conventions of narrative and expository genres (Labbo et al., 2002). Painting a picture about a nature walk evokes reflective thinking and problem solving as they represent details of bird feathers with lines, textures, and colors (Greene, 1995). Playing on the playground provides occasions for dramatically enacting stories that are woven together and represented by connections to popular media, field trips, and storybooks (Gardner, 1991). Watching an animated story come to life on screen evokes singing, laughing, and moving (Labbo & Kuhn, 2000; Oklo & Hayes, 1996). These glimpses into young children's meaning-making experiences highlight the notion that moving among various symbolic representational systems is a generative act that children find motivational and rewarding (Eisner, 1998; Semali & Fueyo, 2001).

When working with creative computer applications at the classroom computer center, children like Harry and Samantha have unique opportunities to create meaning by drawing upon and elaborating upon their collective knowledge of multiple sign systems and multimedia symbol systems. The act of creating multimodal projects on the screen through electronic symbol making requires them to draw knowledge from various sign systems and use various types of symbols as *cognitive tools* that enrich their abilities to encounter, shape, and share meaning. Jonassen and Reeves (1996) suggested that computers are cognitive tools that serve as intellectual partners that are designed to support various types of meaning-making endeavors.

When Harry, a low-literacy-ability student, and Samantha, a high-literacy-ability student, are given the assignment to share what they have learned about community helpers during their computer center time, they follow a recursive, multimedia composing process that utilizes computer tools as intellectual partners in their cognitive, representational work.

Step 1: Using a Photograph Image as a Memory Link to a Relevant Experience. The children begin by selecting and importing a picture of a field trip to the fire station into a screen of a creativity software program. Their intent is to create a multimedia slide about firefighters. As they look over a collection of field-trip photographs the teacher had saved on the hard drive, they discuss some of the things they have learned about firefighters. Harry, who is a low-literacy-ability student, enjoys taking the lead in this activity because he is adept at navigating through computer applications that access, retrieve, and import photographs.

Step 2: Using an Interactive Letter-Stamp-Pad Tool to Compose a Description of the Photograph. Samantha selects a creativity computer tool that allows her to use *ABC* stamps to write a description. As she composes, she refers to details in the photograph to guide her word choices. Inventively spelled words begin to appear on the screen: Rd (red) - drk (truck) - Hlprzz (helpers). As she composes she utilizes a hunt-and-peck action scheme to select letters. When she clicks on an *ABC* stamp, a computer-synthesized voice pronounces the letter name. This tool capability scaffolds Samantha's ability to distinguish between the letters *b*, *p*, and *d*. The erasing tool allows her to recursively erase and restamp letters on the spot as she receives feedback.

Step 3: Using Sound Effects to Contextualize the Representation. Harry, who recalls how impressed he'd been when the fire chief had demonstrated turning on the siren during the field trip, selects a recording tool that allows him to add a sound effect. He places his mouth close to the computer's built-in microphone and wails a long screeching sound. When he is finished, Samantha suggests that they also use a string of letters to represent the sound of the siren on-screen. She helps Harry select letters. Harry stamps the letter string *eeeeeee-rrrrr-eeeeeeeee-rrrrrr* at the top of the screen in a large red font.

Step 4: Using Computer Features to Reflect on Symbolic Representations. The children decide to check their work to see if the sound effect will be activated when the screen is opened up, so they save, close, and then reopen the screen. Both of the children laugh when they hear Harry's voice screeching in a 3-second sound-effect siren that is automatically activated.

Step 5: Using Computer Drawing Tools to Add Additional Layers of Representation With a Sense of Audience. Harry and Samantha discuss the details of the photograph, reread their invented spelling, and listen to the siren sound effect again, but decide that they haven't yet adequately represented all of the things they have learned about firefighters. Samantha recalls some words she learned when the teacher read a book about fire trucks during rug time. The children decide to use drawing tools to create a labeled diagram of the fire truck in the picture. Their talk indicates that they are taking into consideration which particular symbols will serve to represent their learning to their audience, an audience that will be made up of their teacher, the teaching assistant, their peers, and the parents who will visit the school during upcoming parent conferences. Slightly shaky lines soon connect an image of a ladder with a corresponding label.

Step 6: Appreciating a Convergence of Media as the Most Effective Mode of Representation. Harry and Samantha viewed, reviewed, shared, and talked about their multimedia composition. The resulting process and product was definitely more valuable than the sum of its media parts. The children's knowledge base and abilities to represent meaning were enhanced as they came to understand that all of the media symbols worked together in a cohesive whole as presented on the computer screen (Lemke, 1998). In other words, Harry's sound effect enhanced the photograph by adding a dynamic sense of contextualized activity. The linguistic trace of the letter string on the screen represented a print version of sounds that further enhanced the experience for Samantha.

The example of Harry and Samantha's computer composing highlights the notion that computer applications include tools that augment and support learners' cognitive engagements as they solve problems of symbolic representation whereby they organize, reorganize, and represent meaning. The act of electronic symbol making and multimedia composing (use of action schemes, socially negotiated decision making, recursive revising, strategic navigation of tools) was empowering because exploring choices for electronic symbol making on a malleable computer screen provided Harry and Samantha with opportunities to extend their cognitive capabilities and to develop fluency across literacies.

Implications for Classroom Practice

Taking a semiotic perspective allows us to gain insights into cognitive processes involved in electronic meaning making that employs various sign systems. The following bulleted list highlights key implications for what teachers need to know about creating classroom environments that capitalize on the benefits of multimedia computer engagements that take place on classroom symbol machines:

- Teachers know that effective classrooms must not only be literacy-rich; they must also be multimedia-enriched. In an enriched multimedia classroom culture, computer use is not an end unto itself and computers are not used for isolated drill-and-practice exercises. Rather, multimedia technologies are seen as serving larger educational goals by inviting students to utilize multiple symbol systems to express their ideas and think critically (Labbo, 1996).
- Teachers provide children with ample time to recursively and collaboratively engage with electronic symbol-making activities as they compose with multimedia symbols (Labbo, 1996).
- Teachers create occasions for children to share their multimedia representations with authentic audiences. Indeed, children's multimedia work is celebrated, discussed, and woven into the classroom culture (Labbo, 1996).
- Teachers support children in their search for multimedia symbols and modalities that are most reflective of their preferred approach to learning (Veenema & Gardner, 1999).
- Teachers know that electronic symbol making may serve as a bridge to conventional literacy for some children (Labbo et al., 2002). Teachers expect that children are engaged in complex cognitive

work as they create multiple modes of symbolic representation on computers (Jonassen & Reeves, 1996).

- Teachers know enough about using computer applications to integrate computer-related, multimedia activities into the ongoing literacy curriculum.

In closing, it is important to note that there are very few ideas in education are brand-new (Gardner, 1991; Tierney, 1990). Indeed, at the previous turn of the century, my grandparents learned much about literacy through Bible stories, mail-order catalogues, and family letters from distant relatives. In addition, my own children's teachers brought multiple resources into the classroom environment in order to enhance learning a few years ago during an era when classroom computers were viewed primarily as drill-and-skill learning stations. However, it is my belief that by reconceptualizing computers as symbol machines and taking a semiotic perspective, teachers in classrooms at the current turn of the century may be drawn to create computer-related activities that are more likely to provide children with unique opportunities for motivating, cognitively engaging, and empowering electronic symbol making.

SUGGESTED READINGS

Berghoff, B., Egawa, K., Harste, J., & Hoonan, B. (2000). *Beyond Reading and Writing: Inquiry, Curriculum, and Multiple Ways of Knowing*. Urbana, IL: National Council of Teachers of English.
  Readers will find that this book is a must for their professional library. The authors explain semiotics and sign systems in easily understood terms, and motivate teachers to expand students' learning environment to include collaborative inquiry and multiple ways of knowing.

Kist, W. (2000). Beginning to create the new literacy classroom: What does the new literacy look like? *Journal of Adolescent & Adult Literacy, 43*(8), 710–718.
  The author suggests a rationale for teaching multiple literacies and describes characteristics of a new literacy classroom that include evidence of engaged students, a balance of individual and collaborative activities, and diversified expression.

Goldberg, M., & Phillips, A. (Eds.). (1995). *Arts as Education*. Cambridge, MA: Harvard Educational Review.
  The editors and contributors to this volume are dedicated to the arts and believe the arts are an essential aspect of human development and fundamental to education. Their stories inspire teachers to include painting, music, poetry, and dance throughout the curricula.

Toward a Theoretical Framework of New Literacies on the Internet: Central Principles

Donald J. Leu, Jr.
University of Connecticut

Charles K. Kinzer
Vanderbilt University

The purpose of this chapter is to develop a theoretical framework that helps us to define the new literacies of **Internet technologies.** We organize this theoretical framework around a set of central principles that inform our understanding of the new literacies emerging from Internet technologies. We argue that traditional definitions of literacy must be expanded if we are to understand the new literacies required to effectively use **information and communication technology (ICT),** such as the Internet, that continually changes. Along the way, we argue that multiple ways of understanding and communicating are blended in the new literacies of ICT. We also argue that both teaching and learning will need to be transformed if teachers wish to prepare students for their literacy futures. Finally, we argue that it is essential for every literacy researcher to bring their special insights to the study of literacy within Internet technologies if we are to fully understand literacy in our changing world.

IF I CAN WRITE IT AND READ IT, I'M LITERATE!

For five centuries, literacy has been largely defined by the skills and strategies required to effectively obtain information represented in books and other printed forms made possible by the invention of the printing press and other technologies. This definition is reflected in comments and questions we often hear from preservice education students who, when challenged to articulate a definition of literacy, make the statement, "It doesn't matter what form it's in. If I can write it and read it, I'm literate!"

Seemingly simple and intuitive, unpacking this view leads us to discover presuppositions and implicit definitions that both extend and hinder our understanding of literacy, technology, and their interaction. Consider, for example, these questions:

- What does it mean to write something? Does writing presuppose the use of alphabetic letters? Is an animation that clarifies alphabetic text a part of the composition, an extension, an add-on, or a distinct category of writing? If this animation stands alone, without text, should it be considered writing, composition, or what?

- Does reading mean comprehending any message in any form, or only in printed form on paper? Does reading an illustration constitute "reading"? Is "reading" a web page the same or different from reading a page in a textbook? How?

- Is one's response to the size of a thick book, to the illustration on a book's cover, or to a picture on a page a part of reading, or is only a response generated by printed letters a part of reading? Is one's response to the layout of a Web page and the structure of a Web site a part of reading?

- Does reading include the ability to process and interpret graphics, the use of color, sounds, streaming video, alphabetic characters, links to related screens, and other media forms? Is it important for a writer to use these aspects of communication, when necessary, to more completely communicate meaning?

These and other questions make clear the complex nature of trying to understand literacy in a world in which ICT plays an increasingly important part. They also point to the difficulty that we will continue to have in defining and studying aspects of literacy in the future.

Today, historic changes in ICT such as the Internet are fundamentally redefining what it means to be literate. New literacies, required to obtain and exchange information on the Internet, are rapidly emerging as this new technology for information and communication becomes important to our lives. These new literacies are central to our children's success in a world increasingly defined by information and global communication.

SO WHAT DOES IT MEAN TO BE LITERATE TODAY?

Though we have yet to obtain sufficient empirical data to adequately define these new literacies of the Internet, we can observe the psychological reality of their existence whenever we encounter individuals who can read a book or write a letter by hand but do not know how to access information or communicate with Internet technologies. Internet technologies generate new literacies required to effectively exploit their potentials and to fully and meaningfully communicate with others (Disessa, 2000; Karchmer, 2001; Leu & Kinzer, 2000; Reinking, Labbo, McKenna, & Kieffer, 1998; Topping, 1997; Warschauer, 1999). These technologies also make possible new instructional practices (Leu & Leu, 2000). Thus, traditional definitions of literacy and literacy education will be insufficient if we seek to provide students with the futures they deserve.

In an age of information and technology, reading and writing experiences on the Internet are increasingly becoming more authentic, and more common, than reading a book or writing with pencil and paper.[1] Yet many in the literacy community have not generally recognized the important changes taking place as literacy is being redefined by new technologies (Kinzer & Leu, 1997; Leu, 2002). From a practitioner's perspective, we find it surprising that despite the fact that 77% of K–12 classrooms in the United States possessed at least one Internet computer in the fall of 2000 (Cattagni & Farris, 2001) and despite the fact that school and university libraries are restructuring in ways that make traditional books less prevalent (witness, e.g., the number of e-journals and other materials replacing research journals and encyclopedias in libraries and the increase in audio books and e-books in public libraries), most of us have not yet begun the fundamental shift in focus necessary to ensure our students' success in a world where reading will take place more often within networked ICT than within the pages of a book.[2] From a researcher's perspective, we find it equally surprising that an infinitesimally small number of studies appearing in the major journals of the literacy research community explore central issues in the new literacies of Internet and other ICT (Kamil & Lane, 1998). A few efforts around general issues in literacy and technology are beginning to appear (Alvermann, Moon, & Hagood, 1999; Reinking et al., 1998), but little work has appeared that focuses specifically on the new literacies of Internet technologies.

Hofstetter (2001) pointed out that our future is shaped by individuals, it is not randomly determined; the future does not simply happen, but is

---

[1]By "more authentic and more common" we mean that increasing numbers of individuals read and write more text online, on a daily basis, than they read or write with traditional media. Using e-mail, Instant Messenger, web-newspapers, Internet research, and the like is more prevalent, and thus more authentic, than using traditional media forms such as a book for these populations.

[2]Though such a shift will not happen immediately, our argument is based on the belief that literacy researchers and practitioners must make efforts at change now, rather than waiting for full implementation of ICT and electronic literacies to occur. Waiting, rather than changing as society changes, runs the risk of missing important opportunities and, thus, becoming less relevant in the future.

constructed in the present. Engineers, software designers, and others are planning our futures even as we write and you read this chapter. They are constructing faster processors for computers, designing satellite systems that will take us increasingly into a wireless world, creating software that will be smarter and react to what we do in more complex ways. The future is being influenced by today's research and development, by our decisions and our research directions. It is ironic that those of us who have constructed our careers around the book may be among the last to recognize and thus to help shape needed research and pedagogy with regard to the fundamental changes taking place to literacy.

In this chapter, we argue that the future of our children's literacy and the future of literacy research will also be influenced by activities that are occurring today. If the literacy community does not react to changing conceptions of literacy and examine literacy processes and practices in ways that take into account emerging social practices that include technology, then we will be marginalized as the larger community comes to understand that we do not have much of significance to contribute. If our present (in)action leads to the teaching and learning of literacy as disconnected from societal literacy practices that use new forms of literacy, then researchers, practitioners, and theorists from other fields will supplant traditional literacy researchers and practitioners in society's views of who speaks with the most relevance to our children's futures.

Being aware of literacy's continued evolution and adapting our conceptions of literacy to this evolution benefits all of us by ensuring that we will teach, learn, and locate our research in relevant and important questions of the time. In making this argument, and in advocating for research and practice that incorporates changing technologies, we first examine where our definitions have come from. We then take a look at where we are, and conclude by examining the future of technology and its impact on literacy teaching, learning, and research. We do this by proposing and discussing 10 principles that can serve as an underpinning to a framework for examining the new literacies embodied in networked technologies and the Internet. Along the way, we hope to make clear that literacy is a multifaceted activity—one that requires teaching and learning of multiple literacies on a journey that has as its goal becoming a literate person.

THE NEED FOR NEW THEORETICAL
PERSPECTIVES TO EXAMINE NEW LITERACIES

As we begin to develop a systematic research agenda to explore the new literacies of the Internet, it is important to develop emerging theories to inform our initial inquiries. No single theoretical perspective has yet to explain the full range of the changes to literacy brought about by Internet technologies and ICT. Nevertheless, several useful perspectives are beginning to evolve from various quarters. We believe it is important to look to theoretical work on new literacies (Gee, 1996), **critical literacies** (A. Luke, 2000; Muspratt, Luke, & Freebody, 1998), multiliteracies (The New London Group, 1996, 2000), **media literacy** (Tyner, 1998) (see chap. 10, this volume), and others to provide us with insights about the new literacies of Internet technologies. Gee argued from a **sociocultural perspective** that literacy is not a single construct, but instead consists of many literate acts that are embedded in and develop out of the social practices of a culture. Combining work from linguistics, social psychology, anthropology, and education, Gee argued that many "new literacies" need to be recognized and valued in any discussion of literacy. Literacy, he suggested, is based on the various social practices cultures use to communicate. One might, for example, easily view reading, writing, and communication on the Internet as one of these new literacies emerging from cultures endowed with networked information technologies such as the Internet.

Others have argued that literacy needs to include new, critical literacies that enable students to adequately evaluate messages from individuals and corporations who shape the information they provide, depending on what they seek to accomplish (see, e.g., Muspratt et al., 1998). Muspratt et al. argued that it is impossible to discuss literacy without considering who is using it and for what purposes. They described the essential need to understand the stance of the person producing a message, the motive behind the message, and the need to critically evaluate these messages. They foregrounded the important need to develop critical literacies as an essential element of any instructional program, because new media forms, globalization, and economic pressures engender messages that increasingly attempt to persuade individuals to act in ways beneficial to an economic or political unit and not necessarily to the individual. As the Internet quickly becomes both an important source for information and an important commercial and political context, critical literacies become an important part of the new literacies of the Internet.

A third perspective that is useful comes from the work of the New London Group (2000). The New London Group has begun to use the construct "multiliteracies" to capture changes taking place in two dimensions central to literacy: the multiple modalities of communication in a world where many new communication technologies have appeared, and the increasingly apparent diversity of culture and language within an increasingly global community. Instead of a unitary construct, this group recognizes the inherent diversity that defines literacy in a world defined by new technologies of communication and new cultural and linguistic contexts that become more visible with globalization. Within this type of theoretical framework, one might view reading, writing, and communication on the Internet as including a set of multiliteracies, emerging as individuals from different cultural contexts encounter one another within different communication technologies.

Still, others (Silverblatt, Ferry, & Finan, 1999; Tyner, 1998) focus on the new literacies required from new media forms, taking a media literacy perspective. Media literacy perspectives are often closely aligned with critical literacy perspectives, though they focus more on media forms beyond text. Just as those who take a critical literacy perspective, media literacy perspectives point out the importance of analyzing the stance of the person producing a message, the motive behind the message, and the need to critically evaluate these messages. This perspective is important to include when considering literacy within Internet technologies because Internet technologies make possible a panoply of media forms within a single message, thus increasing the importance of understanding how each may be used by an author to shape a reader's interpretation. And, because locations on the Internet are often populated with commercial, political, and economic motives, it becomes essential to be able to carefully evaluate these while gathering information (Kinzer & Leander, 2002).

Other theoretical orientations, too, are possible when considering new literacies appearing on the Internet. These include feminist perspectives (Hawisher & Selfe, 1999), perspectives that draw upon **postmodernist interpretations of popular culture** (Alvermann et al., 1999), or perspectives that draw upon cultural transformations (Warschauer, 1999). Each has important insights to bring to understanding new literacies appearing on the Internet.

Although each of the aforementioned perspectives is useful, we do not see any one of them as attending sufficiently to an important point: The new literacies of the Internet encompass all of these views and add additional complexities not recognized by current theoretical work on "new literacies," "critical literacies," "multiple literacies," "media literacies," and other useful perspectives. We believe the new literacies of the Internet, because they are more encompassing and because they change more rapidly and in more profound ways than traditional print literacies, require their own theoretical framework in order to adequately understand them and the role they should play in a literacy curriculum.

WHAT ARE THE NEW LITERACIES OF THE INTERNET?

The new literacies of Internet technologies include the knowledge, skills, strategies, and insights necessary to successfully exploit the rapidly changing information and communication technologies continuously emerging in our world for personal growth, pleasure, and work (Leu, 2002). A more precise definition of the new literacies of the Internet may never be possible to achieve because their most important characteristic is that they regularly change; as new technologies for information and communication continually appear, still newer literacies emerge (Bruce, 1997; Leu, 2000a, 2000c; Reinking, 1998). Moreover, these changes often take place faster than we are able to completely evaluate them. Regular change is a defining characteristic of the new literacies.

Though continual change is inherent in the new literacies of the Internet, it is also quite clear that these new literacies might best be viewed in multiple, not unified, terms. Both Gee (1996) and the New London Group pointed out twin forces driving us to recognize multiple literacies: the many new modalities of communication forms that are now available and the increasingly global community in which we live with more widely encountered differences in languages and cultures. In addition, however, we believe that multiple literacy forms will rapidly emerge in our future because of a third force: New technologies for information and communication will repeatedly appear and new envisionments for exploiting these technologies will be continuously crafted by users. It is not just that new modalities of communication forms have generated new literacies; even more important is the fact that new technologies for information and communication will repeatedly appear in our future, generating even more literacies on a regular basis.

Consider, for example, the new writing skills required to effectively use a **word processor** like Microsoft's Word 5. Each time one upgrades to a new version (Office 98 and Word 6, Office 2001 and Word 2001, etc.), one must develop new composing and communication skills to effectively use them. Though one might have needed the ability to save documents in different formats in an earlier version of this program, the latest version includes the new composing skills associated with developing a web page, such as including hyperlinks within a document. Subsequent generations of this single program will require even newer literacies, perhaps the need to save documents in wireless versions that are readable by **PDAs** (such as the popular Palm Pilots® and Handspring Visors,® among others) as both new technologies and new communication and information potentials emerge.

The repeated changes taking place in the technologies of literacy continue to be embraced by individuals almost as quickly as they are announced. In our opinion, the rapid changes, together with the public's acceptance and use of these changes in their everyday lives, result in the most powerful force that affects the multiple literacies of our future. Because the central information and communication technology of our age—the Internet—is a network technology, there is also a multiplicative effect at work.[3] This mul-

---

[3]Though more linear technologies also change, they change within their own parameters. Making a given change within a networked technology, however, immediately affects something else in the network, which undergoes a change that recursively affects the originally changed item. This reciprocal effect partly explains the rapid and continuous change seen within networked systems.

tiplicative effect is speeding up the already rapid changes taking place to literacy and requires continual change to our view of, and definitions of, what "counts" as literacy and as literacy research and practice. The new literacies of the Internet permit the immediate exchange of even newer technologies and envisionments for their use, speeding up the already rapid pace of change in the forms and functions of literacy and generating multiple literacies on top of multiple literacies.

If change both drives and is driven by the technologies of literacy, critique has become central to the effective use of the content appearing within these technologies. It is also central to understanding this content. Both the critical literacy and the media literacy theorists remind us that our new world of ICT demands new critical literacies for an increasing variety of media forms. This is especially true of the Internet, where anyone may publish anything using a combination of powerful media forms. As a result, the information available on the Internet is useful only to the extent that a reader is able to navigate the social, political, economic, and ideological stances of authors that shape the nature of the information that they present to others.[4] This increases the central role that critical literacies will play in the new literacies of the Internet.

Thus, two major forces have coalesced to shape the nature of the new literacies of Internet technologies. First, rapid, continuously changing technologies of literacy, distributed by the networked information technologies themselves, generate rapid and continuous changes to the nature of literacy on the Internet. Second, the powerful media tools now at our disposal to communicate ideas to far greater numbers than ever before, in a far shorter period of time, generate the necessity for new means to critique the information appearing on the Internet. Multiple, critical literacies populate the new literacies of the Internet, requiring new skills, strategies, and insights to successfully exploit the rapidly changing ICT continuously emerging in our world and the information in the various media that these tools create.

CENTRAL PRINCIPLES THAT DEFINE THE NEW LITERACIES OF THE INTERNET

To begin to define the new literacies of the Internet, we believe that it is important to develop a theoretical framework grounded in these new technologies themselves. Perspectives from new literacies, critical literacies, multiliteracies, media literacy, and other sources are helpful, but insuffi-

---

[4]Similarly, authors who wish to shape readers must also be aware of the many media forms that can be used to write effective messages on the Internet, must be aware of how they interact to become more than the sum of their respective parts, and must also be facile in their uses.

cient on their own, to capture the essential nature of the new literacies of the Internet, which are more encompassing and change more rapidly and in more profound ways. We believe that a useful starting point for beginning to develop an adequate theoretical framework is to identify those central principles that operate to define the new literacies of Internet technologies.

Principle 1: *The new literacies of the Internet have initially emerged as a powerful force because of globalization, the restructuring of organizational and economic units, and the changing nature of the workplace.*

From a historical perspective, the forms and functions of literacy never spring from a vacuum. Instead, they are prompted by the cultural contexts in which they emerge. Understanding the cultural context in which the new literacies of the Internet are emerging is central to understanding both the challenges and the opportunities they present. Elsewhere (Leu & Kinzer, 2000), we have argued that the new literacies of the Internet have emerged because of global economic competition within a world economy based increasingly on the effective use of information and communication. It is not technological change that is the ultimate source of Internet literacies because technologies, like literacy, do not emerge from a vacuum. Instead, technological change and the new literacies that they prompt have emerged due to the globalization of markets and the restructuring of organizational and economic units that results from increased economic competition.

In some contexts, the nature of work has been defined by one's access to land, labor, or capital. Increasingly, however, we live in a world defined by intense global economic competition with economies based increasingly on the effective use of information and communication (Reich, 1992; Rifkin, 1995). As trade barriers have dropped, companies have been forced to compete within global, not national markets. Previously, a company competed with only one or two other companies producing the same goods or services within national boundaries. In a global economy, companies must compete with tens or hundreds of other companies around the world. This produces intense competition, with each looking for ways to accomplish their work more efficiently. The solution in many cases has been to restructure decision making, changing from a hierarchical organization with a top-down decision-making process to a horizontal organization, empowering units at all levels to make effective decisions and communicate their plans to everyone else within the organization (Leu, 2002; Mikulecky & Kirkley, 1998). Instead of decisions emanating from the top of an organization, teams within lower levels of organizations are increasingly encouraged to identify and solve important problems that lead to better ways of producing goods or providing services. Members of these teams must quickly identify important problems, gather useful information related to the problems they identify, use this information to solve the problems, and then communicate the solutions to others.

In a globally competitive information economy, everyone must be prepared to effectively use new information resources to solve important problems and communicate the solutions to others. Networked information technologies, including the Internet, have become central to this process because they assist individuals in identifying important problems, providing rapid access to enormous information resources, and allowing individuals to quickly communicate their solutions to an appropriate audience—from an individual supervisor to a large, global audience. In a global economy based increasingly on information and communication, our children's future depends on their ability to effectively use the new literacies of networked ICT such as the Internet (Bruce, 1997; Leu & Kinzer, 2000; Mikulecky & Kirkley, 1998). Indeed, this dynamic is a major factor driving the continued evolution of the new literacies of Internet technologies.

Several important implications may be derived from this first principle. First, if access to the new literacies of Internet technologies will be important to economic success, we must respond immediately in thoughtful and comprehensive ways to evidence of access differences, whether these differences appear within classrooms, national boundaries, or our community of nations. In each instance, these differences will deny individuals important access to life's opportunities. In considering access differences within the United States, some (D. L. Hoffman & Novak, 1998; National Telecommunications & Information Association, 1999) have referred to this as a "digital divide." However, it is important to keep in mind that important access issues also exist between nations (see, e.g., Brown & Jolly, 1999) as well as within individual classrooms (Kinzer & Leu, 1997). Local, national, and international policies must be aggressively developed to limit these differences and enable each student access to the important technologies of literacy that are central to an information age.

One must also keep in mind the powerful economic forces that will only become stronger as globalization occurs. These forces, while moving us in the direction of economic growth, may do so at the expense of individual freedom. We must continually work to ensure the freedoms that literacy and access to open information environments make possible and resist the tendency to restrict access to information for national economic advantage. We must also be aware of, and respond carefully to, the differential power relationships between students and their peers, and students and teachers, that new and emerging technologies can establish (see Bloome & Kinzer, 1999, for a discussion of these and similar issues). In addition, the growing use of networked information technologies in the workplace will require schools to provide a more balanced distribution of informational text experiences compared to narrative experiences that tend to dominate, especially in elementary-grade classrooms. If we seek to prepare children for the literacy opportunities of their future, we must begin to provide a more complete preparation in the variety of textual forms and genres, and provide adequate experiences in the text of information and communication.

Finally, in all of the emphasis that economies are placing on the restructuring of decision making, it seems to us somewhat ironic that the very units that shape our children for these more empowering workplace contexts appear to be the last to change. Instead of allowing teachers and local building teams to determine strategies for achieving instructional goals, for example, politicians at state and national levels in many nations are often determining the manner in which literacy instruction will take place. It seems that whereas economic units in many nations are moving from centralized, top-down structures for decision making, schools are moving in exactly the opposite direction: to state and national standards that reflect increasing regulatory requirements. Such decentralized and potentially coercive decision making can be seen even at the local school level, when schools must defer their instructional technology wishes in order to receive district funding (e.g., see Sellers, 2001). We should question the inevitability and the logic of these antipodal changes.

Principle 2: *Our limited focus on traditional literacies in the classroom must change to include the new literacies of Internet technologies.*

The Internet has entered our classrooms more rapidly than any previous technology of information and communication. In only 6 years (1994–2000), the percentage of instructional rooms in the United States possessing at least one Internet computer has gone from 3% to 77% (Cattagni & Farris, 2001), a rate that is unprecedented for any technology of literacy (e.g., books, pencils, television, radio, VCR, etc.). Similar changes are taking place in many developed nations around the world (Leu & Kinzer, 2000) as the Internet enters the classroom.

Few nations, however, are investing sufficiently in examining the effective use of these technologies, or to discover how to most effectively prepare students adequately for the new literacies they will require in their futures. In the United States, for example, a recent survey found that only about 20% of K–12 teachers felt well prepared to use technology in their classrooms (U.S. Department of Education, 1999b). This may be due, in part, to inadequate investment in staff development, because school districts in the United States spend, on average, only 20% of the recommended amount of their budgets on staff development in technology use (CEO Forum, 1999; U.S. Department of Education, 1999a). Though research is providing needed information about effective technology implementation, more resources must be provided to support the factors that facilitate effective technology integration in schools (Colburn, 2000a, 2000b).

The lack of teachers who can effectively teach the new literacies of Internet technologies is also due to the failure to adequately prepare new teachers. Only half of the states in the United States require a course in computer education for licensure (CEO Forum, 1999). Moreover, the major accreditation body in the United States for teacher education institutions has noted that the failure of professors to more rapidly integrate technology into their own classes limits their ability to adequately prepare new teachers for using technology in the classroom (National Council for the Accreditation of Teacher Education [NCATE], 1997). It should be noted, however, that not all nations have been as slow to respond to the challenge. Among other nations that are ahead of the United States in this area, Finland has been working since 1995 to integrate the use of information technologies into classrooms. Since 1998, a national policy initiative has provided all teachers with a 5-week, paid, release-time course in the effective instructional use of new information technologies in the classroom (R. Svedlin, personal communication, January 8, 1998).

The best evidence that schools largely ignore the new literacies of Internet technologies, at least in the United States, can be seen in the state assessment programs that purport to evaluate students' performance in reading and writing. In these state assessments, not a single state has students read anything on the Internet or another digital technology of literacy. This continues to occur even though there is general agreement that one's ability to locate, read, and evaluate information on the Internet is increasingly a part of our daily lives. Moreover, not a single state permits students to use anything other than paper-and-pencil technologies during state writing assessments. This continues to occur despite evidence such as from a recent Massachusetts state writing assessment indicating that, when children use word processors, 20% more students are able to pass the Massachusetts state writing assessment (Russell & Plati, 2000).

It seems clear that the limited focus on traditional literacies in many countries must change to include the new literacies of Internet technologies. Holding us back is the fact that we have little empirical work to demonstrate exactly what these new literacies might be and how each contributes to effective reading, writing, and communication. Clearly, an important research agenda is one that includes an exploration into the precise nature of the new literacies emerging from Internet technologies.

Principle 3: The new literacies build upon, but they do not typically replace previous literacies.

Though many new literacies will emerge from Internet technologies, traditional elements of literacy will continue to be important within these new literacies. Additional elements of reading and writing skills such as phonemic awareness, phonics knowledge, vocabulary knowledge, **syntactic** knowledge, discourse knowledge, metacognitive knowledge, interest and motivation, and social aspects of learning, among others, will remain important even as their function may change. In fact, it might be argued that traditional reading and writing skills will become even more essential. The ability to read text will become more important because it allows us to access information faster than listening, and speed counts in rich, complexly networked information environments. The ability to write text will become more important because written text can be easily stored and organized to generate new knowledge. Whereas reading and writing abilities become more important in the new literacies, they will also change in important ways (Eagleton, 1999; C. Luke, 2000a, 2000b). Reading and writing will take new forms as text is combined with new media resources and linked within complex information networks requiring new literacies for their effective use. The question that we must begin to investigate is, How do traditional literacies and literacy-related skills change and how do they contribute to the new literacies of the Internet? Understanding the answer to this two-part question will help us to more thoughtfully plan learning experiences for students.

Principle 4: The teacher's role becomes more important within the new literacies of the Internet, not less important.

It seems certain that Internet resources will increase, not decrease, the central role teachers play in orchestrating learning experiences for students as literacy instruction converges with Internet technologies (Leu & Kinzer, 2000). Teachers will be challenged to thoughtfully guide students' learning within information environments that are richer and more complex than traditional **print media,** presenting richer and more complex learning opportunities for both themselves and their students. This, alone, should make teacher education and staff development issues important priorities. In addition, however, we must recognize that as the new literacies continually change, new staff development and teacher education needs will emerge. It is safe to say that our educational systems have never before faced the professional development needs that will occur in our future. As teachers become more knowledgeable in new literacies and the Internet, there is also an opportunity for renewed respect by society for education as a profession and for the teacher's central role in children's futures. As teachers become acknowledged experts in these new literacies, they will be sought out as individuals who are important and who deserve increasing respect.

*Principle 5: Literacy becomes **deictic** in the new literacies of Internet technologies.*

Deixis is a term used by linguists to describe words whose meanings change quickly, depending on the time or space in which they are uttered (e.g., now, here, today, there, etc.). The term *literacy* is also deictic. Both the forms and functions of literacy have regularly changed over time. The current historical period is unique, however, because the forms and functions of literacy are changing so rapidly as new technologies for information and communication emerge and as new envisionments for their use are constructed. This will continue into the future at a rapid rate because these technologies, themselves, permit the rapid exchange of new technologies for information and communication.

Consider, for example, the new literacies acquired by students who graduated from secondary school this year. When these graduates started school, approximately 12 years ago, they began their literacy careers with the literacies required of paper, pencil, and book technologies. Since then, they have had to acquire the literacies of many new technologies, especially the new literacies of the Internet: e-mail, search engines, attachments, composing web pages, pdf, mp3, instant messaging, chat rooms, and many more. This observation makes obvious an important point: Never before have we been unable to accurately anticipate the literacy requirements expected at the time of graduation for students who will enter school this year. It also contains important consequences for thinking about the instructional applications of technology because most of our research, instruction, and policies still assume that the literacy of tomorrow will be the same as the literacy of today.

If literacy will regularly change in the years ahead, and we believe that it will, then it may be nearly impossible to anticipate all of the new literacies of the Internet that will appear. Thus, our instructional task may be defined as much by teaching students how to learn new literacies as by teaching each of the new literacies of the Internet as they emerge. Because new technologies and new envisionments for literacy will appear regularly, we will need to continually learn new ways to acquire information and communicate with one another. Increasingly, "becoming literate" will become a more precise term than "being literate," reflecting the continual need to update our abilities to communicate within new technologies that regularly appear. In fact, the ability to learn continuously changing technologies for literacy may be a more critical target than learning any particular technology of literacy itself.

> **Principle 6:** *Social learners, not monastic learners, become privileged in a world of rapidly changing new literacies.*

Because the technologies for information and communication are increasingly powerful, complex, and continually changing, no one person can hope to know everything about the technologies of literacy and teach these directly to others. As a result, literacy learning will be increasingly dependent on social learning strategies, even more so than traditional contexts for literacy learning. I may know how to edit digital-video scenes in the hope of including these within a web page, but you may know how best to compress my video so that it can function optimally in a web-based environment. By exchanging information, we both discover new potentials for literacy and enhance our literacy skills, our literacy knowledge, and our potential for effective communication.

If literacy learning will become increasingly dependent on social learning strategies, socially skilled learners will be advantaged; "monastic learners," students who rely solely on independent learning strategies, will be disadvantaged. This may be an important change in many classrooms, because individual learning has often been the norm, privileging children who learn well independently. Increasingly, we must support children who are unfamiliar or ineffective with social learning strategies.

Principle 7: *The new literacies of the Internet are increasingly dependent upon the ability to critically evaluate information.*

A central principle of the new literacies of Internet technologies is that they demand new forms of critical literacy and additional dependency on critical thinking and analysis as one encounters information. Open networks, such as the Internet, permit anyone to publish anything; this is one of the opportunities this technology presents. It is also one of its limitations; information is much more widely available from people who have strong political, economic, religious, or ideological stances that profoundly influence the nature of the information they present to others. As a result, we must assist students to become more critical consumers of the information they encounter (Alvermann et al., 1999; Muspratt et al., 1996). Although the literacy curriculum, and assessment programs, have always included items such as critical thinking and separating fact from propaganda, such skills have not always been emphasized in classrooms where textbooks and other traditional information resources are often assumed to be correct. As we begin to study the new literacies of the Internet, we will depend greatly on work from the communities of critical literacy and media literacy and will be informed by research that targets higher order thinking about what is being communicated.

Principle 8: *The new literacies of the Internet provide special opportunities to help us better understand the unique qualities in each of our cultural and linguistic traditions.*

The new literacies of the Internet provide us with access to new forms of cross-cultural learning experiences and enable us to discover new linguistic traditions. Conflicts around the world, often exacerbated by the inability of different cultural and religious groups to respect and understand one another, point to the importance of respecting and understanding diverse cultural traditions. An important aspect of the new literacies of the Internet is the opportunity they provide to increase multicultural understanding and celebrate the diversity that defines our lives. Understanding others and the cultural context from which they come is an increasingly important goal as we build a global village with this new technology, and the Internet provides special opportunities to help everyone better understand the unique qualities in each of our cultural and linguistic traditions. We have never had a tool for classroom learning that is as rich in its potential for developing an understanding and appreciation of the diverse nature of our global society. This is a double-edged blade, however.

As the Internet permits us to communicate with others throughout the world, and to access information from different cultural, linguistic, and regional groups, it also generates pressure for linguistic hegemony. In the past, languages and cultures have been dominated by nations possessing superior military and economic power. In our digital futures, languages and cultures will be dominated by nations possessing superior information resources on the Internet and superior vehicles for communication. We can already see this happening. Currently, the vast majority of Internet sites are located in the United States and the majority of Internet traffic takes place to and from locations in the United States (Brown & Jolly, 1999). One worries about the consequences of this for the rich heritage of diverse languages and cultures that characterize our world, which permit varied and unique interpretations of the reality we inhabit. Will the Internet mean that English will become the only language of international communication? Will the Internet provide a vehicle for the dominance of Western culture? One hopes not, but there is a possibility that we may quickly lose our linguistic and cultural diversity if we all inhabit the same information and communication space on the Internet, especially if economic pressures for Internet use shape the language and literacy-use conventions for communicating on the Internet.

Principle 9: *With the new literacies of the Internet, speed counts a lot.*

In a world of vast information resources, the new literacies of the Internet will be defined in important ways around the rate at which one can read, write, and communicate. Within competitive information economies where problem identification and solution are critical, the rate at which one can acquire, evaluate, and use information to solve important problems becomes central to success. The speed it takes to acquire information will become an important measure of success within various technologies. Quickly finding, evaluating, using, and communicating information will become central instructional issues. How can we help children learn to work with various information technologies efficiently? Which strategies, in which contexts, for which tasks allow us to acquire, use, and communicate information most efficiently? These and related questions will become important to our instructional futures.

As speed becomes essential for writing, reading, accessing, evaluating, processing, and responding/communicating via the new literacies of the Internet, it will be critical to solve the equity issues that result from children who process and communicate information at different rates. Slow readers and writers are challenged within traditional literacies; within the new literacies of the Internet these individuals will be left far behind. The gap between highly literate and literacy-challenged individuals will be exacerbated by the new literacies of the Internet. Highly literate individuals will skim web pages, link to other web pages, and generally sift through large amounts of information in a short time. Individuals who read slowly and haltingly will still be evaluating the first page of information by the time a more rapid individual has already completed the informational task. If we truly seek to enable every student to succeed in a society defined by information and the speed with which it may be accessed, we will need to devote important resources to discover solutions to this important issue.

Principle 10: *New forms of strategic knowledge are central*
to the new literacies of the Internet.

Mayer (1997) reminded us that each technology contains different contexts and resources for constructing meanings and requires somewhat different strategies for doing so. New technologies for networked information and communication are complex and require many new strategies for their effective use. Moreover, as we have argued, the technologies of the Internet will continue to regularly and rapidly change, presenting us with even newer technologies of literacy that demand more (and more sophisticated) strategies to effectively exploit them. Thus, the new literacies will be largely defined around the strategic knowledge central to the effective use of information within rich and complexly networked environments.

There will be many types of strategic knowledge important to the new literacies. We can be certain, though, that they will include the new forms of strategic knowledge necessary to locate, evaluate, and effectively use the extensive resources available within the Internet. The extent and complexity of this information is staggering. Moreover, these already extensive resources increase each day as new computers are connected to networks and as people create new information and publish it for others to use. The extensive information resources available on the Internet require new forms of strategic knowledge in order to exploit them effectively. How do we best search for information in these complex worlds? How do we design a web page to be useful to people who are likely to visit? How do we communicate effectively with video-conference technologies? How do we function in the virtual worlds that are being developed as social learning environments? What are the rules for participating on **listservs,** chat rooms, bulletin boards, and other electronic-communication environments? These questions highlight the central role that strategic knowledge will play for people who communicate using the new literacies of the Internet.

IF I CAN WRITE IT AND READ IT, I'M LITERATE! (REVISITED)

In the preceding sections of this chapter we have argued that the new literacies embodied in and exemplified by networked technologies such as the Internet require new conceptions of literacy and new conceptions of what it means to be literate. We also argued that research and pedagogy need to be expanded to include the new literacies that are being increasingly used and valued around the world. This is especially true if we are to adequately address important questions that are generated by the literacies embodied within networked technologies, including the Internet, and if we are to adequately prepare our children for their literacy futures.

As a community of literacy researchers and practitioners, we must all quickly turn our attention to the new literacies emerging from new technologies of information and communication. The literacy community has largely avoided recognizing the changes taking place to literacy as networked ICT becomes a reality. Instead of providing the leadership so critical to the insightful exploration of the new realities of ICTs, our field is one of the last to begin its journey into the literacies of our children's future. Professional organizations and research communities in most other areas of educational practice have moved faster and further into these new worlds of literacy than we have. Perhaps because members of the literacy community have built careers around the book, it is especially challenging to expand our definition of reading and writing to consider new media for literacy research, even ones so powerful as ICT. As a community, all of us must bring our special area of expertise to the study of literacy within the new worlds of ICT. The task is too large, involves literacy in such profound ways, and must be accomplished so quickly that it requires the brightest minds from every area of the literacy community, not solely those who have explored issues of literacy and technology (Leu, Mallette, & Karchmer, 2001).

To this end, we feel these 10 principles form the basis for a preliminary framework that allows us to begin carefully and systematically to examine new and rapidly changing literacies so that we can most effectively teach our future generations. These principles, restated in the Appendix following this chapter, are informed by work in the areas of new literacies, critical literacies, multiliteracies, and media literacy, and are presented as discrete items for discussion purposes. In fact, however, the principles are synergistic and interrelated, thereby adding to the complexity of the research and instructional issues that the literacy community must confront.

We began this chapter with a comment we often hear from preservice teachers who, when challenged to articulate a definition of literacy, make the statement, "It doesn't matter what form it's in. If I can write it and read it, I'm literate!" We argue, however, that "the form it's in" does matter; literacy in networked, electronic, Internet environments requires different conceptions and processes, by both the learner and the teacher, from those grounded in historical definitions of literacy. We would say to a student who makes this statement that his or her role, as a future teacher, is to carefully consider and to unpack their statement. She or he should carefully consider the form of literacy in networked environments along with the form of the medium in which literacy is located. Internet environments, for example, require much more than print to communicate. She or he should carefully consider what it means to read and to write in Internet environments, and consider also the skills and processes required to write a web page that includes, for example, text, color, video, audio, and links to other pages. And she or he should consider the underpinnings that need to be taught to students who need to be literate in these environments. That is, what would need to be taught, with regard to creating an audio file, or linking to another site, if we want students to be literate individuals in the future? And we would say that as they unpack their statement and learn how to teach the requisite new-literacy skills, they will be on the forefront of an exciting change in our field—a change that will make them increasingly valued and valuable in their chosen profession.

APPENDIX

Summary of Central Principles That Help Define the New Literacies of the Internet

Principle 1: The new literacies of the Internet have initially emerged as a powerful force because of globalization, restructuring, and the changing nature of the workplace.

Principle 2: Our limited focus on traditional literacies in the classroom must change to include the new literacies of Internet technologies.

Principle 3: The new literacies build upon, they do not typically replace previous literacies.

Principle 4: The teacher's role becomes more important within the new literacies of the Internet, not less important.

Principle 5: Literacy becomes deictic in the new literacies of Internet technologies.

Principle 6: Social learners, not monastic learners, become privileged in a world of rapidly changing new literacies.

Principle 7: The new literacies of the Internet are increasingly dependent on the ability to critically evaluate information.

Principle 8: The new literacies of the Internet provide special opportunities to help us better understand the unique qualities in each of
our cultural and linguistic traditions.

Principle 9: With the new literacies of the Internet, speed counts a lot.

Principle 10: New forms of strategic knowledge are central to the new
literacies of the Internet.

Part II

Integrating Multiple Literacies
in K–8 Classrooms:
Applications to Teaching

Integrating Visual-Arts Literacy
With Reading Lessons

I will continue to observe, question, and learn as my students paint
their words into their notebooks, write their pictures onto large
sheets of paper, and express their ideas through words and pictures.
—Ernst (1994, p. 51)

Children come into the classroom drawing pictures, even those who
do not yet know how to convey meaning through writing.
—Blecher & Jaffee (1998, p. 70)

One of the factors adversely affecting art education is the scant
amount of school time that is devoted to teaching art.
—Albers & Murphy (2000, p. 123)

OVERVIEW

Janet C. Richards
University of Southern Mississippi

Many teachers may not yet be familiar with the term "visual-arts literacy."
This is not surprising considering the arts were neglected in Goals 2000:
The Educate America Act (Greene, 1995). In addition, artistic pursuits
remain peripheral in many teacher education programs because K–8 teach-
ers are not required to teach the visual arts (Cornett, 1999; Fowler, 1988).
At this time, "few teachers have training in facilitating [students'] artistic
processes or in developing curricula that incorporate the arts" (Oreck,
Baum, & Owen, 1999, p. 2) (also see Eisner, 1995, and Oreck, 2000).

Despite such disheartening statistics, exciting new ideas about multiple
literacies and increased interest in semiotic systems (Berghoff et al., 2000;
Flood, Heath, & Lapp, 1997) coupled with Howard Gardner's conceptions
of **multiple intelligences** (1993) have begun to firmly establish the visual arts

as valid means of expression and learning. For example, new standards for instruction in the visual arts have been adopted in 47 states (National Standards for Arts Education, 1994; Oreck et al., 1999) (see http://www.menc.org). At the same time, convinced of the power of aesthetic pursuits for all learners, more teachers are incorporating the visual arts into their daily curricula (Burnaford, Aprill, & Weiss, 2001[1]; Cornett, 1999; Goldberg, 2000; Jacobs, Goldberg, & Bennett, 1999). Concurrently, some excellent examples of school-based arts programs have sprung up throughout the United States (e.g., Las Cruces, New Mexico; Miami, Florida; Milwaukee, Wisconsin; Vancouver, Washington). A few school districts even assess their students' competencies and familiarity with the arts in order to determine the strengths and shortcomings of their comprehensive arts programs (see Longley, 1999, for fuller descriptions of these schools[2]).

Certainly, the visual arts are primary forms of human expression and communication. Consider drawings on cave walls painted thousands of years ago; toddlers' innate drive and spontaneous enthusiasm for creating artistic scribblings; and urban youths' vivid, passionate, and intricate spray-painted portrayals of their emotions, and social, cultural, and political experiences on bridges, buildings, and thruway exits.

As these varied forms of human expression show, visual art, though manifesting itself in paintings, etchings, carvings, drawings, murals, designs, architecture, sculptures, and the like, is not only about products and artifacts. Visual art also is a method of knowing, a way of looking at the world, and a language that provides both artists and audiences an opportunity to imagine, question, and reflect—a chance to see things that are or that are not there (Merryl R. Goldberg, personal communication, August 2001).

Because visual art "has the potential to communicate ideas and feelings without words" (Cornett, 1999, p. 3), many teachers recognize that promoting students' visual-arts literacy development is helpful to both primary and elementary students who are learning to read and write. Students can collaborate in creating literature-based masks, **murals, mobiles,** and **dioramas.** They can illustrate their own books, draw concept maps of story events, paint their conceptions of characters' actions and goals, and construct **papier-mâché** or clay replicas of Snow White's[3] castle and the Three Little Pigs'[4] houses.

---

[1]Burnaford, G., Aprill, A., & Weiss, C. (2001). *Renaissance in the Classroom: Arts Integration and Meaningful Learning.* Mahwah, NJ: Lawrence Erlbaum Associates.

[2]Longley, L. (1999). Gaining the arts literacy advantage. *Educational Leadership, 52*(2), 71–74.

[3]Santore, C. (1996). *Snow White.* New York: Parker Lane Press.

[4]Galdone, P. (1984). *The Three Little Pigs.* New York: Houghton Mifflin.

Teachers also note that integrating **content-reading lessons** with the visual arts enhances middle school students' comprehension and recall. For example, some teachers ask students to read text passages through both the **efferent and aesthetic stances**[5] (Richards, 2003; Rosenblatt, 1978). Then, students work with a partner, sharing their ideas about the information they consider important and giving their thoughts and opinions about the important facts. When students complete the assigned reading, they collaborate with partners, creating an illustrated book, comic strip, or mural, linking significant facts presented in their textbooks with their own ideas. Partners present their visual-arts project to the class.

WHAT DO YOU NEED TO KNOW?
HOW CAN YOU BEGIN?

Because of the numerous benefits of integrating literacy lessons with the visual arts, as a good teacher you will want to connect reading and writing events with mural and mobile constructions, painting, drawing, torn-paper creations, and the like. You also will want to help students "develop a deeper more conceptual understanding of the power of art to communicate meanings, beliefs, ideologies, and experiences" (Albers, 1997, p. 348). **What do you need to know? How can you begin?** As a starting point, we suggest you read some excellent resources, such as chapter 5 in Claudia Cornett's book, *The Arts as Meaning Makers: Integrating Literature and the Arts throughout the Curriculum* (1999), and chapter 4 in Blecher and Jaffee's *Integrating in the Arts: Widening the Learning Circle* (1998). Read Wolf and Blalock's *Art Works! Interdisciplinary Learning Powered by the Arts* (1999) and Peggy Albers' article, "Art as Literacy" (1997). Read Albers and Murphy's text, *Telling Pieces: Art as Literacy in Middle School Classes* (2000), and contemporary essays and reviews on painting, sculpture, printmaking, and crafts (Wachowiak & Clements, 1997).

Enroll in a high-quality arts course. Become familiar with various visual-arts media, including tempera and finger paint, fabric, felt-nib watercolor markers, glitter, glue, pastels, and crayons. Develop sensitivity to length and width of lines; rough and smooth textures; warm and cool colors; contrasts in colors, texture, and shapes; the three-dimensional aspects of space that portray depth; emphasis or value; the volume and mass of forms, the

---

[5]A predominantly aesthetic role, generally adopted when readers interact with fiction, evokes readers' imaginations, stirs up feelings, and generates strong personal perceptions, opinions, and attitudes. A prevailing efferent stance occurs when readers concentrate on retaining facts and details commonly presented in informational text.

repetition or rhythm of visual movement, and the distribution of balance and shapes (Brommer, 1995; Wachowiak & Clements, 1997). Create some authentic works of art, using your special interests as a guide. For example, make **collages, frescoes,** box sculptures, clay figures, and ceramic vases.

Experiment with watercolor and paint still lifes, such as flowers and scenery. Cut a design in a potato, dip it in tempera paint, and print animals or free-form expressions on blank greeting cards. Using fine and broad markers, create comic strip wrapping paper for a friend's wedding or baby shower gift. Buy some wall paint and create a mural on your bedroom wall. Access the Internet to obtain a recipe for making papiermâché. Visit an art supply store and become familiar with tissue paper, construction paper, and paper especially manufactured for use with watercolors. Tour your local art museum with a **docent.** Compare two paintings and determine how they are similar and different. Concentrate on one painting and jot down what you notice about the colors, shapes, and focal points. Make a few quick sketches that illustrate what intrigues you most (Tammaro, 2001–2002).

Develop some insights about distinct styles of visual art (e.g., **pointillism, impressionism, postimpressionism**), and several artists' work (e.g., **Manet, Monet, van Gogh, Klee, Kandinsky, Picasso, Degas, Renoir, Chagall, Rothko, Diebenkorn**).[6] View Eric Carle's video, *Picture Writer* (2000b), in which he models the torn-paper methods he uses in his award-winning illustrations (http://www.eric-carle.com/pwriter.html). Read Eric Carle's, *You Can Make a Collage: A Very Simple How-to Book* (1998), and Jane Yolen's (1988) descriptions of Eric Carle's studio, routines, and illustrating techniques. Then, e-mail Eric Carle at fanclub@eric-carle.com (2000a) and ask him some questions about his prize-winning books, such as *The Grouchy Ladybug* (1996) and *The Very Hungry Caterpillar* (1984).

Recognize the difference between visual arts-and-crafts activities. Visual-arts products usually are not predetermined. Sometimes requiring special tools (e.g., a loom), the final products of crafts activities generally are known in advance (e.g., basket weavings and patterned fabrics). Read some books and articles about children's developmental stages of art (e.g., see Lowenfeld & Brittain, 1975) (also access information about Viktor Lowenfeld at http//www.ums.edu/~jbrutger/Lowenf.html).

Recognize that coloring books represent an adult's visual representations of the world and force children to color inside someone else's lines. Most of all, reflect upon the power of visual arts to support students' literacy and extend their abilities to communicate, explore, and understand their world.

---

[6]For more information on visual artists, see *The Grove Dictionary of Art* (1996). New York: Grove Dictionaries, Inc.

CASES AND COMMENTARIES

Case #4.1: Is It Time For Art Yet? (by Jennifer Green)

After about 30 minutes into every lesson, my third graders constantly asked, "Miss Jennifer, is it time for art yet? Are we going to have art?"

I always said, "Yes, look at our News of the Day. Art is listed on our chart." Then, worried that my students were losing interest in our reading lesson, I always asked them, "Don't you want to finish reading our story and doing our writing activity?"

Usually, the students would agree to finish the reading lesson, but I sensed that they saw reading and writing only as a way to get to our art activities. In other words, reading and writing were just a means to an end for them—art was really what they wanted to do. In fact, when they were involved in the arts, they always calmed down and concentrated the most.

During one lesson, after reading a collection of Shel Silverstein's poetry,[7] I asked my students to illustrate their favorite poem. As I walked around, interacting with my group, I noticed that Samantha was drawing a really fine picture of a little girl. "What a beautiful picture," I said. "Who is the little girl?"

Samantha proudly replied, "It's my sister."

"Your sister? What poem is that from?" I asked.

With a confused look on her face, Samantha said, "It's not from a poem. It's my sister."

I moved on and noticed that Rachel was filling her paper with hearts, flowers, and sentences that said, "I love you."

"Is this from a poem we read?" I asked her.

"Oh, no," Rachel replied. "I'm making this for you."

I tried to explain to the group what we were supposed to be doing. But, Rachel thought I didn't like her picture and she began crying.

I continued looking at my students' work and discovered that every single student was drawing whatever they felt like drawing. I suddenly realized that they had been drawing and painting whatever they liked the entire semester. They hadn't a clue that their artwork should be connected to our literacy lessons. They viewed art as "free time." I spoke to my professor about this dilemma and she said to make sure that my students always know why they are engaged in arts activities. I also recognized that I had contributed to my students considering art as "free time" by saying in each lesson, "Hurry through your reading and writing so we can get to art."

---

[7]Silverstein, S. (1964). *The Giving Tree*. New York: Harper & Row.

This reinforced my students' perceptions that our artwork was divorced from our literacy activities. I also caused problems by always handing out art supplies prior to giving directions. By the time I gave directions, my students were already drawing and painting and they didn't listen to me. Furthermore, I never engaged my students in productive discussions that would help them link our work in literacy with the arts (e.g., an exchange of ideas about their favorite Shel Silverstein poems).

1. What are the pertinent issues in the case? _____

_____

2. How might Jennifer solve her teaching problem(s)? _____

_____

Commentary #4.1A: "Is It Time for Art Yet?"
(by Jay Stetzer, Elementary and Middle School
Arts Teacher, Rochester, NY)

Dear Jennifer,

I find that, sadly, by the third grade, many students have already divided their world into separate and discrete disciplines, and art sits in a different zone from literacy because of what students have experienced in school. For too long, many teachers have neglected the arts or they have separated the arts from literacy lessons, which is a big mistake, especially considering the new National Standards for the arts and literacy. Because of this unfortunate, unnatural division between the arts and reading and writing, students sometimes need help to re-form the natural links you want them to experience between the two.

Do you know about **Ta'i Chi**? It's an ancient form of a meditation that incorporates slow body movements that have been practiced since ancient times in China. Part of the training involves learning how to "accept" the energy surrounding you. You can use your students' energy to get them to where you want them to go.

From what you wrote in your case, it sounds like you can use a little Ta'i Chi on your third-grade class yourself. It's clear that your students love to draw and paint. It's also evident that there was a breakdown in your communication concerning linking poetry and the visual arts. In the Ta'i Chi model I'm suggesting, why not start right off with a drawing exercise? First, model for your students by bringing in a piece of art of your own for which you have written a poem. Then, shape the exercise further by suggesting some titles for your students' drawings. This would give your students a specific direction to their work. Titles like "Night," "Storm," or "Laughter" tend to bring out a more abstract side of students. It encourages them to draw abstractly, too. After your students have completed their drawings, you may want them to talk a bit about their artwork, which would give them some verbal models for images and ideas to use in a poetry-writing exercise to follow.

As a footnote (although I absolutely adore Shel Silverstein—I actually met him in a school in Brooklyn, NY!), I would find his illustrations of his poems quite successful and a bit intimidating if I were a third grader. Also, his poetry is quite concrete and usually conveys a story rather than an image, mood, or feeling. Why not try a more abstract poem—a single poem for the whole class to try and illustrate? Perhaps you might offer work by **William Carlos Williams,** who often wrote poetry rooted in the details of his own life and the lives of those around him (see Williams, 1999). In closing, let me give you a big compliment! I admire your willingness to link visual-arts literacy with reading lessons and I know you will be a wonderful 21st-century teacher.

Commentary #4.1B: "Is It Time for Art Yet?"
(by Kathryn Chapman Carr, Teacher Educator
and Professor Emerita, Central Missouri State University)

Hello Jennifer,

Your students seem to have a misconception about the purposes of the visual arts. It might help to explain to them that there are different kinds of visual-arts activities. One activity, I call "free expression time," when students may draw and paint whatever they wish. The other type of activity is one for which teachers have certain goals and objectives—in your case, linking fiction with the visual arts. Objectives for this type of lesson are to: (a) enhance students' understandings of a story, and (b) provide opportunities for students to learn and express themselves through a form of communication other than oral and written language (i.e., **transmediation** through multiple sign systems) (Berghoff et al., 2000; Leland & Harste, 1994). I imagine this second type of visual-arts lesson is new to your students.

I suggest that you assure them that you will schedule many times when they may create anything they wish, and you will tell them clearly when those periods are. At other times there will be specific goals and objectives for the lessons; however, they will have free expression within those guidelines. Explain also that art is an expression of ideas, and that ideas can come from many areas, such as nature, stories (literature), music, body movement (dance), and their own imagination or mental images.

I have a few other teaching suggestions for you to consider. Before your students create visual-arts images, it is helpful for them to have rich material to provide those images. Choose a book that fosters rich imagery, such as Jane Yolen's *Owl Moon* (1987) or Dyan Sheldon's *Whale Song* (1997). Another choice would be one with hilariously funny scenes, such as *Thomas's Snowsuit* by Robert Munsch (1985). Ask your students to close their eyes as you read these books aloud and let the story ideas make pictures in their minds. Engage in teacher modeling by pausing to describe what you are picturing. Ask for volunteers to share what they envision. After the reading encourage students to illustrate a scene or their story characters from the book.

You also might ask students to fold drawing paper into four sections. Provide directions for them to illustrate what happened first in a story, next, in the middle, and what happened at the end. Accordion books also can be made for the story. Students fold long strips of paper so that one sheet is the first page and the others are folded accordion style behind it. Each page contains an illustration with a caption or longer paragraph so that pages are read sequentially when unfolded. Laminating the finished product adds stability to the book. This activity can be a prelude to writing a summary of the story, and it also ties artistic expression to literature.

Music and body movement could be a good way to help the class grasp the idea of artistic expression related to literature. Announce that you will play some music while your students listen. Let the music make pictures and stories in their minds. If classroom guidelines are well established and carefully explained (such as to stand as silently as a statue when you say, "Freeze!"), invite the students to move to the music. I suggest avoiding the term "dance" at first, as young and older students' concepts of dance may be related to the newest popular-culture dance fad, and not what you are looking for.

Afterwards, invite students to draw and use color the way the music makes them feel. Do this for several lessons, changing the type and tempo of the music. You can make the transition to literature by reading aloud a book, such as *Whale Song* (Sheldon, 1997) without sharing the illustrations, but while playing some peaceful, relaxing music. After the reading, play the music again while the students create illustrations that go with the text. All of these activities enhance students' listening abilities (i.e., **auding**), and reading comprehension, as well as foster integration of the visual arts with reading.

In closing, let me say that you are a motivated teacher—one who understands the benefits of linking literacy lessons with the visual arts. You will find that with some prior planning and organization, your students' visual-arts work and their understanding of the purposes of visual-arts activities will improve tremendously. As you continue teaching and learning, you will develop a deeper understanding of visual-arts literacy. You will recognize that being fully literate means not just being able to read and write. Being fully literate also means being able to learn and communicate through the visual arts.

Case #4.2: "Fear of Failure" (by Cynthia Morales)

My second graders recently constructed a mural based on the story *Charlotte's Web* (White, 1952). All of the students did a lovely job except Michael.

He is an excellent student who has to be perfect in everything. In fact, he can't do any visual-arts activities unless he has a ruler in his hand. He is so uptight about making a mistake that he detests art. For example, when we were doing the border for our mural, Michael stood back and let others in the group paint. I asked him, "Michael, don't you want to join in?"

Michael shook his head and replied, "Nope, I might mess up. I might make the border crooked."

I told Michael, "Even if the border is crooked, our mural will still be okay."

But Michael still refused to participate.

Michael also is insecure about writing creatively. Last week I reviewed the basic features of stories (i.e., characters, settings, problems, and solutions) and showed examples of other students' creative books. Then, I explained to my group that we would write and publish our own books. Michael immediately began to complain. "I don't know what to write about. I can't draw," he said.

No matter how I encourage him, he refuses to paint, write, or draw. I asked my professor about Michael and she said that some students have few opportunities to work with visual-arts media. Therefore, they don't know how to paint or draw. She also said that students may not enjoy writing because they have a fear of failure or they lack personal awareness of what steps to take to write. I know Michael is afraid to fail in the visual arts, but I don't know what to do about it.

1. Jot down three words that describe Cynthia's dilemma. _____

_____

2. Retitle this case and explain why you chose this new title. _____

_____

Commentary #4.2A: "Fear of Failure" (by Barry Oreck, Arts Teacher Educator, University of Connecticut)

Dear Cynthia,

When it comes to creative expression of any kind, we can all be our own worst enemies. That annoying critic in our heads can make it impossible to take even the first step. That ruthless editor saying, "What will it look like?"; "You're just going to mess it up"; "That's not original . . . it has already been done . . . better," never fully disappears and can be debilitating. It sounds like Michael has a particularly severe self-editor within himself.

There are a number of techniques you can try with Michael and with all students who need to be more spontaneous to quiet the internal critic and self-editor and to truly engage in the creative process rather than worry about the end product. With the strong product orientation of our society, process can easily get lost.

First, arts activities require a warm-up. The purpose of the warm-up is not just to get your body loose; it is to get your mind working in a different way, to connect with your materials, and with your own thoughts and feelings. The text *Creative Behavior* (Sagan & Sinton, 1993) offers a number of very effective warm-ups. Sagan and Sinton started by having students close their eyes and use large crayons or chalk to draw on very large sheets of paper. Sagan and Sinton advocated grasping chalk or crayon with a fist grip to encourage free, large movements. They also suggested drawing with the unaccustomed hand to make it impossible to worry about the perfection of the image, but instead, to direct the artist's attention to the movements, feelings, and ideas being expressed. Many of the opening activities in *Creative Behavior* are free drawing or experiments with lines, dots, or scribbles.

Michael might feel freer working in a medium that doesn't require pen/pencil/crayon and paper. Paper making and working with papier-mâché and clay sometimes free students who are insecure about their drawing abilities.

These explorations are valuable for their own sake and can also be used as a warm-up for further art or writing activities. In writing, many ideas can come from art warm-ups, movement, and dance explorations, theater games and improvisations, visualization, listening to or playing music, and brainstorming. We find much richer descriptive language, animated and interesting characters and relationships, and unique ideas as we cross disciplines and vary the experiences. Waking up the body and freeing the mind can break the block imposed by the blank page.

Another key to freeing students from embarrassment or self-criticism is to allow students to enter into the activity in ways in which they feel comfortable. Some students need to work by themselves. Others like working with a partner, and still others are most comfortable working in a large group. Some want to share their work immediately, whereas others take a long time, or never want to share. This is not to say you have to present every activity in all of these ways. Just be conscious that if you tend to set up visual-arts activities in groups of five, you should alter the structure often so that students can work in pairs, individually, or in larger groups. If you have students work alone, try assigned, random and self-selected groupings from time to time. At the end of the arts activity, encourage students to reflect on and support their peers' preferences for different working structures.

In order to encourage creativity, we need to educate our students as well as parents, administrators, and colleagues about the nature of the creative process. Everyone loves to see the products and every art project should have a goal of some kind to work toward. But the goal—be it exhibition, performance, anthology, bulletin board, portfolios, and so on—should not come at the expense of the open-ended discovery process that makes an artistic experience. I think of an incident I saw recently in a first-grade class. The class was working with clay with a visiting professional artist. The artist explained that they were going to use the shaping techniques they had learned to create animals. She told the students that they could keep any of the animals they liked or just put the clay back in the bag and start with a new piece at any time. As they worked, she showed them that if they overworked the clay it would dry out and would likely break when it dried so they should just smash it up and try again. Some students kept their animals but many did not. They just happily played with new shapes for the entire hour. The next day the teacher and the principal got phone calls from a few parents protesting that their child's sculptures had been destroyed and that they had nothing to bring home. "It is all part of a process," the teacher explained. The children had been happy just to participate in the process until they were expected to deliver a finished product to Mom. The process is about making mistakes, starting over, editing, experimenting. The more students experience that process and don't feel that they have to strive for a perfect product every time they start making something, the freer they become to try things and the more accepting they are of their own and their classmates' efforts.

Commentary #4.2B: "Fear of Failure" (by Terri Austin, Head Elementary Teacher, Fairbanks, Alaska)

Dear Cynthia,

I, too, have had students like Michael who were afraid of taking risks in creative pursuits. When I see that happening, I have learned to stop and take a look at what's going on in the classroom and reflect upon how I interact with students and what messages I am sending to them about visual art. I step back and observe. I look at student interaction patterns. Are students praising each other's endeavors or are they critical? I listen not only for spoken words, but also for subtle actions between students. Do students offer to help one another and do they reassure each other? Do they walk by a dropped crayon or do they pick it up? If I am not seeing kind, caring student behavior, then I set in motion an all-out plan of action to change negative thoughts and behaviors. For example, I model how to help others. As a class we talk about compassion and respect. We brainstorm ways to praise each other, and I plan activities where we all work together. When I look at myself, I analyze the type of messages I am sending students. What am I rewarding? Am I praising work that is perfect or am I praising risk taking in the visual arts? Is every visual-arts activity high-stakes and serious, or do we engage in enjoyable, happy art as well? By happy art, I mean low-key, fun, "we-just-have-to-be-together-and-paint" activities. I have found that when we can relax and have fun together, all of us are more likely to venture into visual-arts areas that might prove difficult—areas where we have to take some risks, which is what Michael needed to do.

I also look at what I am doing to build trust with each student. Do I have personal interactions with each student every day? Do I share my doubts and concerns with them? Do I feel confident enough to take risks in the visual arts? Do students trust me when I offer suggestions to enhance their paintings and murals? Are we honest with each other? This inner searching is hard sometimes, but I am never disappointed with the results. By examining my practices, I often find solutions.

Case #4.3: "The Great Pyramid Mess!!" (by John Hall)

My first graders were all painting three-dimensional pyramids described in the book *Emily Eyefinger and the Lost Treasure* (Ball, 1994). They loved painting and were really involved in their work. However, I didn't pay enough attention to what they were doing. When I glanced over at their work, they had mixed all the green, black, and white paint together until they formed a grayish-green color instead of the red and yellow we needed for our pyramids. Well, they certainly had a good time exploring how to mix and use paint, but I had to throw out all the paint and begin the lesson all over again.

I found some solutions to this pyramid/paint mess by reading *The Effective Teaching of Language Arts* (Norton, 1997). In this text, Ernst (1994) described an artists' workshop where students look at the work of other artists before they begin painting and drawing. This predrawing and -painting activity helps students become familiar with various types of media. Ernst also suggested that teachers provide minilessons that focus on techniques of painting and drawing before students engage in these activities. When students have opportunities to manipulate arts media, they learn how the media work. If I had presented some prearts lessons, we wouldn't have had such a mess. The problem is that I don't think I have enough time during each school day to allow my students to manipulate visual-arts media. How can I do everything that is expected of me as a primary teacher, find time to connect reading and writing with the visual arts, and also encourage my students to manipulate every type of arts media that we use throughout the year?

1. Try to answer John's question at the end of his case._____
_____
_____

2. From whose perspective is this case written (students? John's?)_____
_____

Commentary #4.3A: "The Great Pyramid Mess!!" (by Margaret Humadi Genesio, Teacher Educator, University of Wisconsin, Oshkosh)

Dear John,

Your caring concern for your students' literacy-based artwork is laudable. Please don't worry that you and your students are not doing a good job of integrating literacy activities with the visual arts. You and they are doing a great job! I think that your first graders were envisioning the total pleasure of what might have resulted when they mixed some very vibrant colors together. They probably imagined that their pyramids would be even wilder and more dynamic than the colors with which they started. I think they were optimistic and hopeful, and they probably loved what they got, even if it was not what they (or you) had planned.

Your students did a wonderful experiment that you can build on. They conducted an authentic test of mixing paint colors. I suggest that you revisit the lesson with them. Ask them to describe how they mixed the paint, what happened, and what they would do the next time they engage in paint mixing. You might even create a short, informal drama presentation about what happened. What a wonderful learning experience!

I appreciate what Ernst (1994) said about having students experiment with visual-arts media and studying artists' work in prearts lessons. But, you can't force students or adults into painting pyramids just the "right" color. Actually, we still aren't sure what color pyramids really were because of 3,000 years of erosion in Egypt. This makes me think of lesson extensions to "The Great Pyramid Mess." Collaborate with your students in researching the great pyramids of Egypt (see chap. 12, this volume). Use multiple ways of knowing to contrast and compare the data. This entire episode could turn into a great integrated study. The transfer of this type of learning will be everlasting for these first graders, and you won't have to worry that visual-arts activities are eroding valuable instructional time. In closing, I like gray-green pyramids done by first graders. Picasso never worried about what other people thought about his artwork and neither do first graders. Rejoice!

Commentary #4.3B: "The Great Pyramid Mess!!" (by Mary Gobert, Elementary Teacher, Hancock County Schools, Mississippi, and Instructor, University of Southern Mississippi)

Dear John,

Boy, I would love to paint 3-D pyramids with John's students! I paint along with my fourth graders all the time. It releases all my tensions and helps me discover my hidden talents. We turn on some classical music and really let our creative juices flow when we paint, sing, or dance. School can and should be fun, and the arts help to make learning fun and exciting. I bet John's students will never forget their adventure painting 3-D pyramids.

Now, how could John have handled this painting activity so it didn't turn into a dilemma? I too like the preart idea suggested by Ernst (1994). It really doesn't take very long to have students manipulate arts materials so they get a feel for how these materials work. My students and I keep a listing in our individual learning logs about various types of arts materials we use. We date our entries and jot down what we have discovered about tempera, water color, chalk, crayons, markers, glue, and so on. For example, chalk rubs off paper unless you use some sort of "fixident." Markers "bleed" through many types of paper. The water used for working with watercolors must be changed often. Glue should be used sparingly.

My advice to John is to relax and enjoy every learning experience in the classroom—and arts activities *are learning experiences*. Then he won't be concerned that arts activities take too much time. He should manipulate arts materials along with his students and connect these types of lessons to literacy events and student inquiry (e.g., list making, writing about arts experiments, making books, e-mailing to friends). John also might find ideas from Vygotsky useful (1986).

REFLECTIONS AND EXPLORATIONS

1. Reread Case #4.1 and think about how Jennifer might link visual-arts literacy with future reading lessons. Sketch your impressions of Jennifer's next visual-arts-literacy lesson with her third graders. Include dialogue for Jennifer and her students. Share your work with your teaching peers.

2. Assemble some water colors and tempera paint. Experiment with these materials. What are some good rules to follow when mixing paint to get a specific color or hue? What are the main differences between watercolors and tempera paint?

3. Conduct an ERIC (Educational Research Information Clearinghouse) document search (e.g., http://ericir.str.edu) to find and list some information that provides possible explanations for students' anxieties about participating in visual-arts endeavors. List the articles and their ERIC source numbers. E-mail the list to three of your teaching peers.

INTEGRATING VISUAL-ARTS LITERACY
IN YOUR CLASSROOM:
PRACTICAL APPLICATIONS

You will want to integrate visual arts literacy into your curriculum in a careful, thoughtful way to help ensure that your students will have rewarding, creative, personally meaningful experiences that enhance their visual-arts-literacy development. Responding to the following questions will help you contemplate your students' past experiences with the visual arts and their knowledge about artists and art media. Responding to the questions also will enable you to consider your teaching context as you organize and offer effective visual-arts lessons.

1. What do your students already know about the visual arts (e.g., artists' names and their work or famous works of art, such as van Gogh's *Starry Night*)?

2. What experiences have they had in the visual arts (e.g., explorations of various arts media, creating artistic pieces, or, visits to art museums)?

3. What visual arts materials do you and your students have or need?

4. Are your students familiar with the media they will use, or do they need to practice using paint, markers, and so on, prior to a lesson?

5. How long do you think a visual-arts activity will take? (An in-depth quality project may require three or four sessions, depending on students' ages and grade levels; Wachowiak & Clements, 1997.)

6. How will you keep students' clothing clean? (Large garbage bags with cut-out arm holes and head space make great aprons—so do old T-shirts.)

7. How will you keep the floor and tables clean? (Sheets of newspaper or plastic tablecloths make good table and floor coverings.)

8. How will you organize tables and chairs so that students have sufficient work space?

9. What policies have you and your students established for students' behavior? Experts note that "the quality of students' art diminishes as the rate of talking and socializing increases" (Wachowiak, 1985, p. 35).

10. What procedures have you established for students to share materials, and clean up after the lesson is over?

11. Will you model the arts activity or in some way prepare your students for the activity (e.g., by displaying slides, magazines, illustrated art books, examples of students' work, or examples of your own artwork)?

12. How will you motivate students who find it difficult to persevere and want to finish their work too quickly?

13. How will you challenge students who are gifted in the arts?

14. How will you encourage students from diverse cultures and heritages to enrich the classroom community by integrating their unique experiences with their drawing and painting?

15. Where will you store partially completed artwork?

16. Where will students clean their brushes, paint holders, and hands?

17. When will your students work on the project again, if necessary?

18. Where will you display your students' work?

19. How will you evaluate your own and your students' visual-arts efforts?

20. How will you create a classroom climate that encourages art as a process of meaning making, problem solving, and identity construction? (see Albers, 1997).

SUGGESTED READINGS

Cooke, G., Griffin, D., & Cox, M. (1997). *Teaching young children to draw: Imaginative approaches to representational drawing.* London: Falmer Press.

This illustrated handbook on teaching young children to draw has been developed using what the authors call the "negotiated drawing approach." Teachers learn how it works. Ideas for using the approach in classrooms are offered.

Olshansky, B. (1995, September). Picture this: An arts-based literacy program. *Educational Leadership, 53*(1), 44–46.

This short article describes an arts-based literacy program entitled Image-Making Within the Writing Process. The program transforms students' writing by integrating students' visual imagery at every stage of the writing process, from the earliest prewriting/idea formulation stage through rehearsal, drafting, revision, and preparation for publication.

Whitin, P. (1996). Exploring visual response to literature. *Research in the Teaching of English, 30*(1), 114–141.

This study describes a group of middle school students' experiences in learning to make and share meaning about literature through the creation of visual representations. This interpretive strategy, known as "sketch-to-sketch," involves learners in creating symbols, pictures, and other nonlinguistic signs to signify ideas generated through reading (see Berghoff et al., 2000).

5

Integrating the Literacies of Music and Dance With Reading Lessons

Education in music is most sovereign, because more than anything else, rhythm and harmony find their way to the inmost soul and take the strongest hold upon it.
—Plato (in Strunk, 1950, p. 8)

I think of dance as a constant transformation of life itself. In one way or another, what we'd thought we couldn't do was altogether possible, if only we didn't get the mind in the way.
—Cunningham (dancer and choreographer, 1991, p. 77)

Music is a reflection of our dreams, our lives, and it represents every fiber of our being. It's an aural soundscape, a language of our deepest emotions; it's what we sound like as people.
—Hart (drummer, Grateful Dead, performer, 1991, p. 7)

OVERVIEW

Merryl R. Goldberg
California State University, San Marcos

Music, in its many forms, has been a tool of literacy and a source for expression and communication throughout history, from disseminating information in the form of ballads, to the recounting of events and emotions of history through song. Musicologists have even posed the question, "Is there such a thing as autonomous music; a division between music and society?" (Leppert & McLary, 1987, p. 6). Music serves many functions in our lives. Merriam (1964, cited in Campbell & Scott-Kassnea, 1995) outlined these various functions of music as follows:

- Emotional expression: releasing of emotions and expression of feelings.
- Aesthetic enjoyment: using music for deep intellectual and emotional enjoyment for experiencing beauty deeply.
- Entertainment: using music for diversion and amusement.
- Communication: conveying of feelings and emotions understood by people within a particular culture.
- Symbolic representation: expression of symbols in the texts of songs and cultural meaning of the music.
- Physical response: using music for dancing and other physical activity.
- Enforcement of conformity to social norms: using music to provide instructions or warnings.
- Validation of social institutions and religious rituals: using music on state occasions and in religious services.
- Contribution to the continuity and stability of culture: using music to pass on cultural values.
- Contribution to the integration of society: using music to bring people together.

In addition to the extensive uses of music just listed, we might add healing to the list of uses of music, coupled with movement (Goldberg & Scott-Kassner, 2002). For example, music, dance, and other art forms are commonly used in therapeutic settings, such as hospitals, as a way to encourage patients to deal with their feelings concerning their physical illnesses, or in psychotherapy sessions to unlock hidden emotions and forgotten experiences.

Music and Movement as Disciplines and Tools for Expression

Since the 1700s music and movement have served many functions. We can categorize these functions into two primary purposes and categories: (a) music and movement as disciplines—something to study, and (b) music and movement as important tools for expression and communication. Both purposes have interesting implications for 21st-century conceptions of music and dance as literacies.

Music and Movement as a Discipline

Music and movement as disciplines, or sources of study, relate to literacy in Merriam's (1964) terms listed earlier as a means of expression, communication, and symbolic representation. By listening to, or making music, viewing dance, or creating a dance, individuals can communicate powerfully. In the 19th century, for example, **program music** was in vogue in the classical world. Program music, as persons in the 19th century used the term, was instrumental music associated with poetic, descriptive, or even narrative subject matter— "not by means of rhetorical musical figures or by imitation of natural sounds and movements, but by means of imaginative suggestion" (Grout, 1973, p. 541). In other words, instrumental music became a vehicle for narratives and the expression of thoughts, which were perhaps beyond the "power of words to express" (Grout, 1973, p. 541). Composers, including **Beethoven, Debussy, Mendelssohn, Schumann, Berlioz,**[1] and **Liszt,**[2] all composed pieces that told some story or narrative through music. In stark contrast to music that stands on its own, there is music that employs words (i.e., lyrics), such as popular songs, musical theater scores, or opera. In this case, music combined with words and often movements explicitly tells a story.

Communicating Through Dance

Choreographers (i.e., those who create dances) use the human body as a way to communicate feelings, ideas, information, and questions. More often than not, movement is blended with sound and music. Consider the stories that are told through ballet, modern dance, or African dance. History also unfolds through dance and the folk dances of people in all cultures. For example, in studying cultures of other countries, such as Mexico, dances from different Mexican states lend insight into the people of these states and give us a feeling for their culture, perhaps even more so than reading print-based information about that culture. Similarly, if students are studying the history of the United States, learning the Virginia reel enhances the story of a specific time period of U.S. history.

Music and Movement as Literacies

If we venture past Western practices and ways of communicating, we can tour the world as musicians and experience the use of music as a way to "read maps." In traditional Australian Aboriginal communities, rather than referring to printed or drawn maps (as most of us are accustomed to reading), maps are oral. Imagine singing directions using tones rather than see-

---

[1]Hector Berlioz wrote music that evokes drama, emotions, images, and shifting moods. Berlioz always thought in dual terms of music and literary works.

[2]For additional information on music and musicians, see Grout, D., & Palisca, C. (Eds.) (1998), *A History of Western Music* (4th ed.), New York: Norton; and Sadie, S., & Tyrell, J. (2000, January). *New Grove Dictionary of Music and Musicians* (2nd ed.). New York: Grove Dictionaries, Inc.

ing directions on a printed map. This is what you would do if you were living a traditional Aboriginal lifestyle in Australia.

Imagine living in Ghana. You would recount your poem through drumming and dancing. Various beats and rhythms on the drum as well as specific dance movements are equivalent to "words." Thus, an individual can "tell" a story through the engaging sounds of rhythmic beats and movements.

Music and Movement in Schools

An examination of the history of music in American schools highlights many of the functions of music as applied to education. It is interesting to note that when music was first introduced into the public schools, it was designed to create better singers in order to improve hymn singing in churches (Birge, 1928/1966). Now, we think of music and movement as important communication literacies that "should be an integral part of the lives of all [students]" (Cecil & Lauritzen, 1994, p. 82).

Certainly, the roles of music and dance have shifted along with expectations for what it means to be an educated person in the 21st century. The use of music and dance also has changed with alterations in beliefs about the nature of young children and modifications in understandings of the myriad ways young children learn. For example, engagements with music and dance provide young children with alternative ways to communicate. Music and dance activities also help to extend young children's oral language and understanding of the **syntax** of language (Cecil & Lauritzen, 1994). By participating in music and dance, young children learn body coordination and control, and practice group cooperation (e.g., through role playing to music, dancing in groups or with a partner, singing with body and hand movements, singing nursery songs and rhymes with sound effects; Cecil & Lauritzen, 1994; Goldberg & Scott-Kassner, 2002).

In the elementary and middle grades, students also benefit from music and dance endeavors. Using familiar melodies, students might compose original lyrics that connect to content areas of study. In conjunction with reading or computer technology activities, elementary and middle school students might create lyrics, dances, or melodies to accompany a story read or told or to demonstrate their understandings of social studies or science concepts. Music and dance have their own symbol system or system of notation. Therefore, students who compose music or dances and learn how to read music and dance notations have opportunities to learn and communicate through sign systems that use tools different from the tools used in print-based texts (Cecil & Lauritzen, 1994). In addition, students with special music and dance interests and aptitudes (i.e., multiple intelligences) (Gardner, 1993) have opportunities to participate in orchestra, band, glee club, chorus, and dance groups (Cecil & Lauritzen, 1994).

WHAT DO YOU NEED TO KNOW?
HOW CAN YOU BEGIN?

As a teacher, you need not have expertise in music and dance literacies to enable your students to use and enjoy these forms of communication. All students love making music and moving about in space and are not inhibited by lack of formal knowledge in the disciplines. What do you need to know? How can you begin? The following ideas may help you become more familiar with music and dance so that you feel comfortable integrating these two literacies with reading and writing lessons.

Begin by reading some good books on music and dance. For example, try Hoffer's (1990) chapter, "Artistic Intelligences and Music Education" in W. Moody's *Artistic Intelligence: Implications for Education.* Read Pappas, Kiefer, and Levstik's (1999) *An Integrated Language Perspective in the Elementary School: Theory Into Action,* and chapters 8, 10, and 12 in Cecil and Laritzen's (1994) *Literacy and the Arts for the Integrated Classroom: Alternative Ways of Knowing.* Other good resources are Merryl Goldberg's (2001) *Arts and Learning: An Integrated Approach to Teaching and Learning in Multicultural and Multilingual Settings* (2nd ed.) and Jalongo and Stamp's (1997) *The Arts in Children's Lives: Aesthetic Education in Early Childhood.*

Listen to many kinds of music. This can be accomplished while you drive to school, do the dishes, eat breakfast, read the newspaper, or socialize with friends. You also can listen to music with your students. Many teachers play soft, appropriate music throughout the school day. Discuss the instruments you and your students hear and the emotions the music evokes. For example, "The music sounds happy to me. What makes the music sound happy? Does it have a fast beat? Does it sound like circus music? What makes it sound like circus music versus an opera?"

The same activities apply to dance. Listen to music as you complete your household chores. Have fun and move in time to the music. Observe dance videos with your students and ask, "What makes this dance seem upbeat or sad? What do the movements suggest to you? Can you follow a story, or do you sense an emotion? What about the dance causes you to feel that way?"

Attend local music and dance concerts. Collect the performance programs and look for common themes, unusual lyrics, or dance descriptions and photographs of dancers. Live performances can be magical, and you might get ideas for adapting what you see to what you can do with the students in your classroom. If you live near a center for the arts, take your students to presentations. Most centers offer performances geared especially toward students. Equally important, become aware of music and dance events in your community—and go to performances! There is no better way to learn about music or dance than by going to live performances.

Visit local dance studios and learn how they work with their students. Interview the dance instructors. What theories of teaching do they hold? Do they believe in having their students practice long hours in order to showcase their talents in a culminating recital, or are they more interested in process? Do they accept all dance students or do they require students to audition?

Perhaps you will become so interested in music and dance that you might join a local dance troupe or take dancing lessons (e.g., ballroom dancing, African dancing, Irish step dancing, **Folklórico ballet,** tap dancing, square dancing). You might join a chorus or choir.

Start gathering recordings, videos, and instruments to keep in your classroom. Use them during class activities and encourage your students to experiment, investigate, and use the instruments on their own. In addition to collecting instruments, consider making instruments with your students. Percussion instruments, such as hand drums, tambourines, shakers, rain sticks, claves, or clappers, are very easy to make. The sounds created from varying what you put into a container to shake can be fascinating. Discussing these sounds engenders considerable student conversation and might be carried over to writing assignments and science or social studies units.

Don't be afraid to let your students go! Students love to move, especially younger students. Challenge them to choreograph stories and personal responses to literature. They can create or add narratives in sound, much like the **romantic composers** did when they created program music, or African musicians do when they relate poems through drumming, or Australian Aboriginal musicians do as they describe how to get from one place to another through song. Encourage students to "tell" their story in sound or movement, and then perhaps translate that story into visual texts.

If you are starting with "words," let your students invent new lyrics to familiar songs or create "**rants.**" A rant is a combination of rapping and chanting and can be done with any subject matter, from historical information, to biographies, to science processes. It is a unique way to engage your students in a musical literacy exercise often resulting in extremely imaginative and lively products. Students often add movements to their rants, making them even more interesting.

CASES AND COMMENTARIES

Case #5.1: "A Song That Never Was Finished" (by Deneen Vanaman)

Yesterday, I taught my eight first-grade students. I wanted to link our literacy lesson with music. I thought I had planned everything carefully, but I had not. When we finished reading the story *Mouse Party* (Durant, 1996), I told the students we were going to make up a song about the story. Well, the students started laughing. So, I modeled (like a good teacher is supposed to), and started the song. "Mouse Party, we're going to have a mouse party. We're going to . . . ," I sang. Then I stopped and asked the students one by one to add to the song.

I pointed to the first student and she did not respond. So, I added another phrase to the song.

"Mouse Party, we're going to have a mouse party. We're going to eat cake and ice cream."

Then, another student added a phrase to the song. Each time we added a new phrase or sentence, I started the song all over again. The students really enjoyed hearing me sing. They started singing with me and adding their own words. We all laughed at our funny song and we had great fun.

Well, just when I thought everything was going so well, the singing activity started to fall apart. Some students became a bit rowdy and I had to stop and ask them to settle down. Some of them continued talking. When I returned to the song, I realized I had forgotten some of the words and sentences. A few students tried to help me remember what we had created, but by then the majority of students were uninterested in singing. I just gave up on the song.

I know now that as we created our lyrics, I should have written them on a chart. I also could have tape recorded our song. In fact, there was a tape recorder in the classroom and I could have used it. As for the tune that we sang, I haven't a clue. I wonder how I can figure out what tunes to use the next time I link a print-based literacy lesson with music literacy. I know there is so much more to offering students music literacy opportunities than I have begun to know. I am just a beginner in the "music thing." I am surprised I even sang!

1. What do you think Deneen's students were thinking during this lesson?

_____

_____

2. When you offer a lesson similar to Deneen's, what might help to make the lesson go more smoothly?_____

_____

Commentary #5.1A: "A Song That Never Was Finished"
(by Alice Quiocho, Teacher Educator, California State
University, San Marcos)

Hello Deneen,

Language users can build on the power of words and the sounds and rhythm of words for generating ideas. Music is an aesthetic form that offers a different method of inquiry to the literacy learner, especially the **emergent literacy learner.** So, your decision to use music was a good one.

You can turn each aesthetic event into a literacy-enhancing event. Therefore, you are correct when you said you should have written down the lyrics of the song as you composed it with the students. The written lyrics then could be used as a shared reading experience with the whole group the next day, or in the afternoon as students do their free-choice reading or read with a friend.

My suggestion is to start with melodies with which students are familiar. There are many tapes that primary teachers use to teach students about the sounds of words and sounds of letters. The authors of these songs usually use melodies that young students know, melodies that have refrains that repeat the important theme or words or phrases you want students to learn. You will want to look for those kinds of songs and think about using refrains that repeat words or phrases. Young students love and learn from music because they love to move and sing (Piazza, 1999). It is thus important to use chants and repetition in our teaching. For example, a song that uses repetition could be based on "Here We Go 'Round the Mulberry Bush" (if your students already know this song) and the lyrics might be:

> We're going to have a mouse party, a mouse party, a mouse party,
> We're going to have a mouse party, so come along with me.
> We're going to eat ice cream, ice cream, ice cream,
> We're going to eat ice cream, so come along with me, etc.

As you think about selecting a melody, use one that is also culturally relevant and locally familiar to students, especially if you have English-language learners in your classroom. I would encourage you to write at least two verses of your song first, such as those just disccussed, and then ask students, "What else could we have or do at a party?" As students share their ideas, you write the next refrain with them. You might take this opportunity to do some shared writing with students where they come up to the chart paper and write the lyrics themselves.

I also encourage you to add rhythm instruments such as maracas, tambourines, chimes, or bells to your lesson. You might want to start with clapping to familiarize students with the beats of the song and show them how clapping helps them feel the rhythm of the song and enhances their ability to discern the number of syllables in words. Listen to the rhythm of the song you have selected and decide whether rhythm instruments or clapping as well as dancing might make the song come alive and keep students interested in the activity.

As for group management, you will need to set some ground rules that are positive and are intricately related to the activity, thus reducing the need to discipline in a negative manner when students get rowdy. For example, you might say, "Now, boys and girls, we are going to add some instruments to our song. I know this is a lot of fun, but let's all listen to how adding the instrument changes our music. Everyone will have to listen *very* hard. I will be listening, too. When we stop the music, we are all going to think quietly with our eyes closed about how the instruments changed our song. Then, we will share our ideas with a partner and with the entire group. Let's try this adding one instrument at a time. First, let's add the maracas. Everyone ready to listen?" In this way, you are being proactive rather than reactive.

As music becomes more a part of your students' literacy experiences, you can use music in other ways, such as having students draw what they see in their mind's eye as they listen to music. Creative-listening skills develop into critical-listening skills as students mature. That is, first students think about visions they see as they listen to music. They draw these visions. Next, they write about them, and finally, their visions and writing are published for others to read. Next, they listen and look for musical phrases in the materials they use during shared reading or guided reading. Finally, they use this understanding of music to talk about selecting the right kind of music that might be used in a dramatic enactment and are able to articulate why one musical score might be more appropriate than another.

Commentary #5.1B: "A Song That Never Was Finished" (by Carol Payne, Elementary Teacher, Gulfport, Mississippi)

Oh my goodness, Deneen—you learned an important lesson. You were not completely prepared because you were unsure about how to link print-based literacy with music literacy. Your students became confused because you were a bit confused. Therefore, their behavior deteriorated. That's okay. Please do not worry about the glitches in your lesson. Rather, learn from your mistakes. Actually, you tried very hard to offer a lesson that combined three literacies (or sign systems) (i.e., printed text, oral language, and music) so you are to be congratulated.

Now let's review your lesson. You are right to think that you should have written the lyrics on chart paper so you and your students could remember the words. If the lyrics were on chart paper, your students also could revisit their song throughout the school day. Thus, they could practice reading print-based text.

Your lesson might have been more successful if you had helped your students compose a poem and then had them link the poem with music. Or, they might have turned their poem into a chant, and after becoming familiar with the lyrics, students could have created music to accompany their chant.

I often use rhythm band instruments in the classroom. Students might chant their song accompanied by cymbals, tambourines, bells, drums, and triangles. I have found that my students sing more creatively and freely when they accompany themselves with instruments.

We have rules for using the instruments. Students are encouraged to play individual instruments for a few minutes before our lessons. That way they learn what sounds the instruments make, and they can investigate loudness, softness, and tones (rather like manipulating media in visual art) (see chap. 4, this volume). When we are ready to begin our structured lesson, students do not play their instrument unless it is appropriate to the music we are creating. If a student does not follow directions about using an instrument, I quietly take it away until our next music activity.

I urge you to continue connecting print text with music. What a wonderful opportunity for students to experience another literacy and another way to communicate as they participate in a joyful activity.

Case #5.2: "Big Bear Disaster" (by Christina Cumbest)

We had just completed the story, *We're Going on a Bear Hunt* (Rosen, 1946). My second-grade students enjoyed the lyrical, repetitious style of the book, and I thought they would enjoy singing a song that went along with that style. I was wrong! I had the words of the song printed on a poster board so the students could see the lyrics. I chose the tune of the song, "Row, Row, Row Your Boat." It was familiar to the students. I began by singing, "Big bear, hunting near the trees, feasting on honeycombs made by busy bees."

I lost the students after the first line. I could not get them to participate. We tried the song three different times, and each time they got quieter and quieter and would not participate. One student said, "I don't like to sing in front of others."

I knew then that this activity simply would not work.

As I reflected on the lesson, I first focused on my students. All of them are shy and quiet. They never give me any trouble with group management. I should have considered their personalities. By nature, they are unwilling to take risks. I can barely get them to speak, let alone sing in front of a group. In addition, I should have chosen a song they knew. The tune was familiar, but the words were not.

I spoke with the classroom teacher about the "Big Bear" disaster and she said, "We don't sing in the classroom."

She also said that these students are shy, and she has trouble drawing them out in discussions. She suggested that I try having them participate each week in choral reading. I think this is a great idea.

I know now that I should have read the words to the song aloud prior to having the students sing. Once they were familiar with the words, they might have been more agreeable to singing. In addition, the lyrics to the song were "wordy"; that is, there were too many words so that they didn't exactly match the beat and rhythm of the music. I wonder if I should ever sing with these students again?

1. What advice do you have for Christina? _____

_____

2. How will you weave music literacy with print-based literacy activities?___

_____

Commentary #5.2A: "Big Bear Disaster"
(by Peggy McCullough, Elementary Teacher,
Pass Christian, Mississippi)

Hello Christina,

Some of your comments in your teaching case make me think that you were a little bit too hasty making an interactive decision (i.e., within the context of teaching) regarding your students' inabilities to sing and take pleasure from music. For example, you say early on in the case, "I knew then that this activity simply would not work." Don't give up so easily.

Sure, the music connection to the story, *We're Going on a Bear Hunt,* would work. As a good teacher, you just have to figure out how it would work. Here are some ideas that have helped me when I have connected music to print-based literacy events.

You might have written the lyrics to the song on a chart and then helped your students do a choral-reading activity with the lyrics instead of requiring them to sing. You also might have taped the music ahead of time or located a tape of the music in the school library. Then you could have played the taped music a few times to familiarize your students with the tune. Then they could sing along with the taped version.

You might have formed cooperative groups and encouraged each group to create their own lyrics instead of predetermining what the lyrics would be. Another idea I have found helpful is to have students create movement to songs. Movement and dance keep students so active, they forget they are shy!

Let's talk next about the lyrics you used. They seem hard for me to sing to the tune of "Row Row Row Your Boat." Remember that students in second grade have difficulties enunciating words quickly. Use fewer words in your songs and make sure the words fit with the music.

I do want to tell you that I admire your willingness to provide opportunities for your students to link music literacy with print-based literacy activities—especially because the classroom teacher told you that she and her students never sing together. Keep up your momentum. Sing daily with your students. Make it fun, not something that is difficult and confusing. Try your lesson again. You will be surprised at how much enjoyment you and your students will have through music.

Commentary #5.2B: "Big Bear Disaster" (by Carol Lloyd, Teacher Educator, University of Nebraska)

Dear Christina,

My initial response as I read your description of your teaching experience was, "What a fun way to have students continue with the general idea of the story, and to connect print literacy to music literacy."

As I continued to read, my next response was about your insight into what happened. I was impressed! You were able to look beyond yourself and at your students. Your analysis of the students' unwillingness to participate in a music activity made a lot of sense. You described what seemed to be the salient characteristics of the students that explained what happened.

As I read your characterization of the students as "shy and quiet" and "unwilling to take risks," I wondered how these students came to develop this culture. How was it that *all* the students did not want to sing? What could you do as teacher if this were *your* classroom to encourage students to participate?

It seems as if there are at least a couple of things going on here. One, the song lyrics were too hard for the students to process. You noticed this. Two, these students seem unwilling to participate in general.

I agree with the classroom teacher's suggestion of choral reading. Students could chorally read a poem, for example, or the lyrics to a song. Have the words printed on the poster board as you did for the bear song. I would consider various ways to encourage singing as part of your concern for students working together. Also, music is part of our culture and certainly part of many students' experiences. You might think about focusing first on rhythm. For example, as students chorally read a poem or song lyrics, they can use their hands to drum on their desks or tables in time to the rhythm of their group reading. Bring in empty plastic milk cartons to use as drums. If you have access to percussion instruments, bring those in to use. Consider a call-and-response activity where you sing a line or two (call) and then students repeat it back (response).

I have two questions that I suggest you think about: Who are these students? What text (song or otherwise) relates to their lives, questions, or concerns? Answering these question may also increase the likelihood that they will interact.

Case #5.3: "An Egyptian Pyramid Music and Dance Disaster!" (by Brook Letort)

I work with eighth graders in a social studies class. As a culminating activity for our integrated study, we decided to do a musical presentation about ancient Egypt. I wanted to weave information gleaned from our textbooks with the literacies of music and dance. Things didn't go as I planned.

I decided that my students would represent some of the pyramids of ancient Egypt. I made two-sided pyramid costumes out of cardboard, and I spray painted both sides of the pyramids gold. Before we started practicing, I passed out the cardboard pyramids, and the students hung them with cords around their necks.

Chaz said, "This paint is getting all over my clothes."

I reassured him, "The paint is dry so it won't rub off."

"No," he replied. "This gold glitter is getting on my clothes."

Then, Alana started in, "It's getting all over my clothes, too."

This paint-and-glitter problem was only the beginning. I had planned for the students to create a little dance to go with the song, "Walk Like an Egyptian," recorded by The Bangles in their 1985 album, *Different Light*. Some of the lyrics are:

> All the old paintings on the tombs
> They do the sand dance don't you know
> If they move too quick (oh whey oh)
> They're falling down like dominoes
> All the school kids so sick of books
> They like the punk and the metal band
> When the buzzer rings (oh whey oh)
> They're walking like an Egyptian

I thought the students would love that song and would know how to dance to it. Well, when the students got on the stage, they just stood there, not knowing what to do. The music played on and on, and eventually I had to invent a little dance for them and had them follow my lead.

A half-broken cassette player caused further confusion. Because the cassette player was in bad shape, the music wasn't loud enough for us to hear it. Commotion is the right word to describe our musical endeavor. Thank goodness it was only a rehearsal.

As I drove home, I found myself wondering what I could have done better, or what I could have changed so that the music/dance activity was successful. I should have thought about the glitter getting on my students' clothing. I never thought they would complain. I know now never to assume anything when working with eighth-grade students. I also should have been better prepared. We should have talked things through as a group. We should have made a plan. As for the music, just because I liked the song and thought it would be so appropriate doesn't mean my students would enjoy dancing to it.

1. How might Brook have involved her students so that they were more successful? _____

_____

2. Could Brook have adjusted her lesson after she began teaching it? In what ways? _____

_____

Commentary #5.3A: "An Egyptian Pyramid Music and Dance Disaster" (by Renee Useforge, Elementary Teacher, Biloxi, Mississippi)

Dear Brook,

I would like to offer a number of suggestions to the dilemmas portrayed in your teaching case. I'll start with the pyramid costumes. I think you did too much work. You came to school with the pyramids all painted and glittered. Perhaps your students might have been more receptive to the pyramid costumes if you had given them the responsibility for designing their own, individual Egyptian pyramid costumes. Your students might collect data on different pyramids in Egypt according to dates of construction, purpose of the pyramid, location, contents, construction material, person (e.g., ruler, King, Queen) who authorized construction, and so on. Then, they could choose a "favorite" pyramid and design it.

Now about that song, "Walk Like an Egyptian." I sang that song when I was a teenager. Perhaps your students might have been happier with a song geared to their own generation. Another thought: They could have created their own Egyptian song after researching Egyptian musical (instruments, notes in the Egyptian music scale, etc.). That way, you get them more immersed in music literacy as opposed to just connecting music to a themed unit (although infusing music into a themed unit is wonderful).

You might have made several tape recordings of the song and structured your students into small groups so they could listen to the tape and create their own small-group dances. You could have helped them learn how to write dance notations that would involve representing meaning through a different sign system.

In the future, as a culminating activity to your Egyptian music and dance activity, you might make videos of each group performing their dance and have a "World Premiere Party" where students dress up in their personal ideas about Egyptian costumes. View all of the videos as a group. You could give music awards to each group for their various accomplishments. Don't worry. Your students are popular-culture smart (see chap. 10, this volume) and will know all about a "World Premiere Party."

I really admire your willingness and knowledge. You are just beginning your professional life and you are already attuned to multiple literacies and multiple sign and symbol systems. You will be a great 21st-century teacher!

Commentary #5.3B: "An Egyptian Pyramid Music and Dance Disaster!" (by George Hunt, Teacher Educator, University of Edinburgh, Scotland)

Dear Brook,

Your own evaluation of the lesson is so perceptive (almost cruelly so), that there is very little I feel I need to add. Interpreting information and facts about ancient Egypt through the literacies of music and dance is, of course, an excellent idea. However, the diversity of ways in which this might be achieved is so vast that the likelihood of your vision overlapping with that of your students is very small.

You yourself conclude that a more democratic approach based on prior discussion with the students would have been more likely to succeed. Indeed, throughout your teaching case it is you, the teacher, making and enacting the decisions. For example:

> "I decided that my students would represent . . ."
> "I made two-sided pyramid costumes . . ."
> "I had planned for the students to create a little dance . . ."

The cumulative impression is that your project construes the students as actors following your script, but at a crucial point, you demand that they make a creative and cooperative response to a stimulus chosen by you. This was surely confusing to them. If you expect student involvement, I think you should invite it at the earliest stage possible, rather than bolting it on at the end.

Ancient Egypt is presumably an item on a mandated curriculum. Your decision to link this content to the aesthetic curriculum is commendable, but it is at this point that student involvement should begin. Perhaps your students have ideas of their own as to what forms of representation or semiotic system (musical, visual, oral) they would prefer. If students select music, perhaps they have preferences about what music might be appropriate. What choices did you offer them? It is probable that by the eighth grade some students might prefer to create a composition of their own, or to interpret a piece selected from a broader cultural repertoire. For example, students might research the work of Giuseppe Verdi who composed *Aida* in 1869, when he was commissioned by the Khedive of Egypt to write an opera for the opening of a new opera house and the inauguration of the Suez Canal. In 1999, *Aida* was performed at the site of the Great Pyramids in Giza, Egypt. **Philip Glass'** work also is intriguing. He composed the opera *Akhnaten* to tell the story about an Egyptian pharaoh martyred for his religious beliefs (Grout & Palisca, 1988). In short, student involvement, choice, and discussion are the crucial ingredients that were missing from your original plan.

The only other thing to mention is that all audio visual "aids" were sent into the world to trip up dedicated teachers. That cassette player knew very well what it was doing. And, finally, don't be so hard on yourself. You are way ahead of many teachers with respect to multiple literacies.

Case #5.4: "An Under-the-Sea Dance Dilemma"
(by Amy Stokes)

I work in a sixth-grade science class. When I reported to the class, the teacher said they were starting a new unit of study about oceans. I wanted to introduce the unit using multiple literacies, so I decided that for an **advance organizer,** we would create a dance as an introduction to what we would be learning. I decided that we would have swimmers, fish, a girl holding a large papier-mâché sun, and students holding various shades of blue and green tissue paper cut like ocean waves (i.e., curvy, like waves).

I brought in all of my visual representations. As I started to explain what part each student would portray, I heard giggles. "See," I said, "this is how the swimmers will move through the ocean." (I then moved my arms and "swam" around the room.) The music is "Under the Sea" from the sound-track to *The Little Mermaid* (Walt Disney, 1990).

I put on the audiotape so the students could hear the music. Katie asked, "Do we have to do this?"

Kyra said, "This is silly."

But a few students thought it would be fun.

I began playing the music and we started our dance. The tissue-paper waves were making too much noise as the "wave" students moved their arms up and down to simulate wave motions. I had cut the waves too long so they stretched too far across the classroom. In addition, the swimmers and fish were getting tangled in the "waves."

"Why aren't you swimming?"' I asked Ryan. He was just standing there.

"I don't know how to swim," he replied.

I answered, "I'll show you," and I modeled some more.

The music went on and on and on. The paper waves began to rip. The students bumped into one another.

Overall, I think the lesson was successful, but my professor had some good suggestions. "You needed more room to dance," she said. "Also, the music went on far too long. If you had made shorter, sturdier waves from cardboard, they would not have ripped. Another thing: You should have planned your dance with your students and not told them what to do. I still liked your work. You really tried to offer an advance organizer that linked social studies content with the literacies of music and dance."

1. How might you restructure Amy's advance-organizer dance?_____
   _____
   _____

2. What were the good parts of Amy's lesson? _____
   _____

Commentary #5.4A: "An Under-the-Sea Dance Dilemma"
(by David Clarke, Middle School Teacher,
New Orleans, Louisiana)

Dear Amy,

According to some experts, using dance movement to provide students with an overview of concepts related to specific content (in your case, oceans), "may enhance the teaching of the lesson" (Drewe, 1996, p. 26). Therefore, in my opinion, your dance advance organizer was certainly appropriate and your reflections about the lesson were professional. In addition, you listened carefully to your professor's critique. Furthermore, I admire your courage offering a lesson in which your adolescent students danced (probably for the first time in science class). My eighth-grade students are great dancers, but they want to dance to their own music, using their own dance steps, so I understand what it's like to try to motivate students to dance in a way that is not "their style" (i.e., the latest popular-culture dance moves).

You seem to have figured out what went wrong with your advance organizer, and I am sure you will offer a similar type of lesson again, making certain that the dance is not too long, including your students in planning, and providing sturdy dance props.

Because you had the confidence and knowledge to link science concepts with the literacy of dance, I would like you to consider these questions as a way of assessing your lesson and moving your thinking forward about future lessons:

1. Were your students more knowledgeable about oceans and dance as literacy after they participated in the "ocean" dance?
2. Do you think the dance had artistic value?
3. Did the "ocean" dance provide your students with opportunities for personal, original, creative expression?
4. Did you ask your students to give their opinions about the dance after the activity was accomplished (e.g., through a quick-write?)
5. In the future, how will you give your students freedom to create their own original dances that are not just free expressions, but are your students' scholarly interpretations about content, such as science, social studies, and literature?

In closing, I applaud your efforts. Teachers who integrate the literacy of dance (and other literacies) with content/subject areas recognize that being able to learn and show what you know through multiple forms of communication (i.e., multiple sign systems) enhance students' conceptual learning and motivation for learning. You will be a fantastic teacher!

Commentary #5.4B: "An Under-the-Sea Dance Dilemma"
(by Alice Quiocho, Teacher Educator, University
of California, San Marcos)

I would like to add some suggestions to the comments made by Amy's professor. First of all, sixth graders (and some teachers and administrators) have to be convinced that dancing can relate to and enhance what is learned in school. It is sad that most students stop dancing in school after kindergarten because mandated curriculum objectives delete any sort of dance from the curriculum. Fortunately, newer ideas about multiple literacies may change these outdated curriculum objectives.

It might be helpful, Amy, if you offered a rationale up front to your adolescent students for using dance as a means to learn social studies. One way to do this is to record clips of all kinds of dances: ballet, rap songs, modern dance, and so on. There is an excellent videotape that depicts dances of the world (Collections of the Goodman Library, 2001). You might record short segments of different dances depicted on this tape. As you show students the recorded segments, you might pause after each dance and ask students what they think the dancers are conveying through their movements. You will need to guide this discussion because initially students probably will say that they see nothing at all. Model your thinking for them to scaffold the activity, and then pair students up as they review the dance tape.

Provide specific categories for them to look for as they watch the tape. For example, how are the dancers using movement? What is the rate/speed of the movement? Look for one explicit movement that the dancers use and ask students to demonstrate that movement for their peers.

In order to acquaint students with what to look for, you will want students to see that everyday movements such as walking, pointing at something, yawning, jumping, stretching, a runner's start-up position, or the act of running itself are incorporated into dance. Guide students to look for familiar movements as they view short video clips of some of the dances of the world.

Next, you may want students to become more specific and talk about the movements of ocean waves. Have them watch short video clips of ocean waves dashing up against rocks, surfers gliding over high waves, boats on the high seas as well as calm seas, swimmers in the ocean, and so on. Then play a tape of ocean music. Ask students to either draw or list everyday movements they make that seem to fit with the sounds of the ocean music being played. Remind them that they can get some ideas from the video of the ocean as well as the video clips of dances around the world.

Through these structured learning activities, you will be providing students with opportunities to build and activate their background knowledge (schemata). You also will be helping students give their own ideas and input for their advance-organizer dance. By the time you get to this part of the lesson, students will already have constructed considerable knowledge about oceans and dance movements. In addition, they will have become less intimidated about dancing in the classroom.

Each pair of students might develop one or two movements that could be incorporated into the ocean dance. The class could learn a few of these movements at a time. The teachers of the dance movements (i.e., peers) would be right there to remind the class of the movement(s).

I would encourage you to ask students what else they might need to make their dance come alive, such as wings or fins. Once students have created the dance themselves, they will be more willing to perform the dance, especially if each student has had a part in the creation of it and therefore feels a sense of ownership.

At the end of the dance, I think it is really important to ask students how the dance helped them learn critical concepts in social studies. For example, "How did the dance and the movements we developed to create our dance help us learn about the movements of oceans?" and "Describe oceans in a poem form. What could we say about these vast bodies of water?"

These kinds of reflective questions can facilitate students' abilities to write various kinds of poetry, such as **diamante, haiku, tanka, cinquain,** or whatever form of poetry you would like students to write (see Appendix at the end of this chapter for definitions and examples of these forms of poetry). Emphasize how dance is movement on the floor and poetry is movement on the page. Have available some poems students can read to "see" the movement on the page.

I like to connect aesthetic forms of learning directly to print-based literacy in order to convey to students that the creative parts of our brains help us learn so much more content because we are open and relaxed and allow ourselves to interact with information in a different way.

Amy, I urge you to try dance once again. Because an aesthetic learning activity does not completely work as we would like it to work the first time we try it, it is not the aesthetic activity that is at fault. As teachers, we just need to look at the activity itself and pay attention to how we can better support student learning and motivation. There will always be a need to support and connect students' literacy learning with aesthetic activities. Remember to always activate students' background knowledge (e.g., through the dance and ocean videos I described earlier). Remember to model your own ideas and thoughts. Remember also to engage your students in contributing their own suggestions and opinions.

REFLECTIONS AND EXPLORATIONS

1. What might you do to insure that your students achieve success when you weave music and dance literacy with print-based literacy?

2. When do you sing (e.g., in the shower, driving to school or work, at a party with a group of friends, in church)? Make a list of the songs you like to sing and share them with your teaching peers. What similarities and differences are evident in your lists?

3. Work with three of your teaching peers. Do some research and create a short, informal dance that depicts a specific historical time period. Use your critical-listening abilities and choose appropriate music for your dance. Present the dance to your peers. Explain how you chose the music (see chap. 3, "Music Literacy: Listening to Language" in Piazza's 1999 book, *Multiple Forms of Literacy: Teaching Literacy and the Arts*).

INTEGRATING THE LITERACIES OF MUSIC AND DANCE IN YOUR CLASSROOM: PRACTICAL APPLICATIONS

Planning your music and movement activities will help provide structure and continuity to ensure the success of your lessons regardless of your singing and dancing expertise. Here are a few questions to consider:

1. How will you find time to ensure that the equipment you plan to use in your lessons is in good working order (e.g., tape cassettes, CD players, video players, and **digital video disks** or **DVDs**)?

2. How will the music or movement activity enhance the literacy lesson?

3. How will connecting music or dance to the literacy lesson add to the length of the lesson?

4. What are your goals in terms of student outcome (e.g., further understanding of story characters' goals and actions, opportunities for students to portray their understandings through alternative communication forms, or transmediation; Leland & Harste, 1994)?

5. If you are going to have students listen to music or view a dance tape, did you review the music or dance to check for appropriateness?

6. If you plan to accomplish movement with your students, have you thought about the possibilities and limitations of your space? (Can you move around desks? Can you move desks aside? Are there spaces outside your classroom that might be conducive to the goals of your lesson?)

7. What signals have you and your students devised when the group needs to come to order? (Sounds of instruments and dancing feet are wonderful, but you also need time when the classroom is silent

so that you and your students can plan further or you can offer suggestions and instructions.)

8. How will you discover students in your classroom who have hidden music or dance talents?

9. How will you encourage students who are shy or reticent about singing and dancing in front of their peers?

10. Will you videotape your students as they participate in a dance activity?

11. What information will you provide to your school administrator and parents about adding music and dance to your literacy lessons?

12. What types of questions will you ask your students in order to develop their appreciation of music and dance (e.g., "What were you thinking as you listened to the music?" "What images came to your mind?" "What did you see in this dance video that reminded you of an experience you've had?"; see Cecil & Lauritzen, 1994)?

13. How can you extend your music or dance lesson to other forms of communication (e.g., dialogue journaling, choral reading, response journals, creative book making, mural constructions, computer technology activities)?

14. How can you extend your music and dance lesson to include study of composers, classical music, musical instruments, dances of particular cultures?

15. How will you provide opportunities for students from diverse cultures to share their special heritages through music and dance?

16. How will you assess your own and your students' efforts and their final music and dance products?

SUGGESTED READINGS

Cecil, N., & Lauritzen, P. (1994). *Literacy and the Arts for the Integrated Classroom: Alternative Ways of Knowing.* New York: Longman.

In chapter 8, the authors provide a rationale for music as an integral part of the classroom. Guidelines are offered for teachers who wish to become song leaders. Chapter 10 discusses dance, including ideas for classroom practice. Chapter 12 offers information about classical music, including ways to integrate music and literacy. Ideas encompass primary, elementary, and intermediate grades.

Piazza, C. (1999). *Multiple Forms of Literacy: Teaching Literacy and the Arts.* Upper Saddle River, NJ: Prentice-Hall, Inc.

Chapter 3 explains that music is a part of our history and our everyday lives. In addition, listening to music facilitates our creative listening, which in turn enhances our creativity in writing and other forms of literacy. Furthermore, creative listening develops critical listening, which involves evaluating and judging what we hear. The author supplies information about spirituals, chants, ballads, choral poems, raps, odes, folk songs, and opera. Chapter 4 raises awareness of dance expressions as interpretations of stories, dance improvisations, mime, sign language, dance, and games, turning dance movement into poetry, ballet, and choreography. Extensive professional references and resources are provided.

APPENDIX

Definitions and Examples of Poetry Forms

1. Diamante: a seven-line poem. The first line contains one word (a noun). The second line contains two words (adjectives). The third line contains three words (participles). The fourth line contains four words (nouns). The fifth line contains three words (participles). The sixth line contains two word (adjectives). The seventh line contains two words (nouns). For example:

> *comprehension*
> *wonderful, personal*
> *understanding, interpreting, thinking*
> *metacomprehension, prediction, background knowledge*
> *pondering, linking, reflecting*
> *exhilarating, powerful*
> *multiple literacies*

Haiku: a form of poetry developed in Japan over 400 years ago. Haiku is a short verse of 17 syllables divided into units of 5, 7, and 5 syllables. For example:

> *sparrows flutter down*
> *into bushes full of light*
> *without any leaves*

This haiku is from Strand, (1997)

3. Tanka: the name of an ancient form of Japanese poetry containing 31 syllables. In English, tanka is structured to contain five syllables in the first line, seven syllables in the second line, five syllables in the third line, and seven syllables in the fourth and fifth lines. For example:

> *communication*
> *expand to multiple forms*
> *tech applications*
> *visual art, music, dance*
> *all forms of literacy*

4. Cinquain: a five-line poem. The first line is a one-word description of a topic. The second line is a two-word description of the topic. Line 3 contains three words expressing action of the topic. The fourth line is a four-word phrase showing feeling for the topic. The last line is a one-word synonym that restates the essence of the topic (Steel, Meredith, & Temple, (1998). For example:

> *reading*
> *comprehension, thinking*
> *active, interpretation, understanding*
> *giving pleasure, knowledge, joy*
> *literacy*

6

Integrating Dramatic-Arts Literacy With Reading Lessons

> All drama, in the highest sense, can be a form of actual verbal and
> nonverbal language laboratory.
> —Cecil & Lauritzen (1994, p. 71)

> Reading, literature, and drama are inextricably related.
> —Heinig (1994, p. 437)

OVERVIEW

Janet C. Richards
University of Southern Mississippi

Merryl R. Goldberg
California State University, San Marcos

Beginning teachers may be surprised to learn that "the use of drama in education is certainly not new" (Heinig, 1994, p. 437). In fact, throughout history, drama has been used in many cultures as a venue for informing the public about news events, teaching about customs, religion, and traditions, promoting awareness about diversity, providing insights about historical events, and imparting moral lessons (Rosenberg & Prendergast, 1983).

In the 1920s progressive educators used drama as a process for promoting students' active learning (Cornett, 1999). New ideas about multiple literacies coupled with Howard Gardner's conceptions of multiple intelligences (1983, 1993) have helped to reintroduce drama activities in 21st-century classrooms. In addition, *Standards for the English Language Arts* (Farstrup & Meyers, 1996) and the 1994 *National Standards for Arts Education* adopted by 47 states (Music Educators National Conference, 1994, Reston,

VA; Web site: http://menc.org) provide an additional stimulus for the renewal of drama as an invaluable tool for learning. These standards, in part, indicate that students should be able to write scripts based on personal experiences, heritage, and literature; portray characters in improvised and scripted scenes; compare and incorporate art forms by analyzing methods of presentation and audience response; and analyze, evaluate, and construct meanings from theater, film, television, and electronic media (Piazza, 1999).

Studies show that drama activities unquestionably "support every aspect of students' literacy development" (McMaster, 1998, p. 575). Drama provides a way for students to comprehend and recall stories (Hamilton & Weiss, 1990). Engaging in various forms of drama, such as **Readers Theatre** (Buehl, 2001), puppet shows, choral reading, **improvisations,** role-playing, monologues, and mime, offers opportunities for students to experience literature and language in new ways. Drama also serves as a bridge to story writing (Jett-Simpson, 1989) and helps students understand story characters' thinking, conflicts, and goals, and characters' relationships to one another (Cornett, 1999). Drama is an effective medium for enhancing students' oral language and listening skills and "building decoding, vocabulary, **syntactic, discourse,** and **metacognitive** knowledge" (McMaster, 1998, p. 574). Engaging in drama enactments can pique **emergent readers'** and older students' motivation for reading, boost students' self-esteem and confidence, and provide opportunities for meaningful student collaborations and social interactions (McMaster, 1998).

Teachers who integrate drama with reading and writing lessons know that engaging in dramatic activities does not always mean staging elaborate productions, making intricate costumes, and participating in time-consuming preparation and rehearsals. Many drama projects take little effort or prior planning. For example, a spontaneous drama enactment might take place after students have read a particularly memorable story. Students informally take turns retelling the story for their own pleasure or play the part of favorite story characters for their peers' enjoyment. Readers Theatre experiences (Buehl, 2001) in which students choose favorite story paragraphs or pages to practice, and then read aloud in front of an audience, require more time. At the structured end of the continuum, students engage in script writing, rehearse the scripted play, create costumes and sets, and share their efforts in a formal setting.

WHAT DO YOU NEED TO KNOW?
HOW CAN YOU BEGIN?

Because drama nurtures every dimension of students' literacy development (McMaster, 1998), as a good teacher you will want to integrate reading and

writing lessons with dramatic improvisations, puppet shows, Readers Theatre, play writing, and occasionally, even more formal drama productions.[1,2] What do you need to know? How can you begin? You might read
chapter 7, "Drama: Bringing Ideas to Life," in Cecil and Lauritzen's book,
Literacy and the Arts for the Integrated Classroom: Alternative Ways of Knowing
(1994). This chapter discusses "drama's unique benefits as compared to
other arts forms" (p. 70). Another excellent source of information is chapter 10 in Constance Weaver's (1998) *Reading Process and Practice: From Soci-
olinguistics to Whole Language* (2nd ed.). Authored by Ruth Heinig, this
chapter describes the many forms and philosophies of classroom drama
and provides ideas for story dramatizations, play scripting, theater games,
choral speaking, radio drama, and improvisations. A good resource also
is Ruth Heinig's *Creative Drama for the Classroom Teacher* (4th ed.) (1993).
Read McCaslin's book, *Creative Drama in the Classroom and Beyond* (2000),
and J. Ball and Airs' book, *Taking Time to Act: A Guide to Cross-Curricula
Drama* (1995). Join a Little Theater group. If acting for an audience is not
your forte, volunteer to make costumes, collect admission fees, or write
publicity information. You could become a stagehand or a lighting specialist. View quality television theater productions and critique the performances. Attend local theater shows and become knowledgeable about the
various genres of theater, including comedies, musicals, and tragedies.
Read the Sunday *New York Times* theater reviews. Determine which Broad-
way shows have recently opened and which performances have been very
successful over time.

Join a theater games group. Become familiar with Spolin's (1983) method
of game playing, which gradually leads participants from simple to more
complex role playing. Learn about Heathcote's philosophy of role drama
(adapted by Morgan & Saxton, 1987; also see Wagner & Thorne, 1990).
Rather than using children's literature as a stimulus for drama work, Heathcote helped students find their own topics for drama (Heinig, 1987, 1994).
Observe a local drama coach. Note how this coach mentors and guides the
actors. Read biographies and memoirs of some popular actors, such as
Christopher Reeve, Alec Guiness, Drew Barrymore, Whoopi Goldberg,
Morgan Freeman, Ronald Reagan, and Rosie O'Donnell. Visit the circus
and observe the clowns and mimes. Recognize that both spontaneous
improvisations and formal drama productions should always be student
centered, enjoyable, interactive, and stimulating.

---

[1]Raines, S., & Isbell, R. (1994). "Stories, Storytelling, Creative Dramatics, and Puppetry." In
Stories: Children's Literature in Early Education (pp. 257–286) Albany, NY: Delmar Publishers.
[2]Schneider, J., & Jackson, S. (2000). Process drama: A special space and place for writing.
The Reading Teacher, 54(1), 38–51.

CASES AND COMMENTARIES

Case #6.1: "Drama Needs Democracy" (by Bill Reagan)

When I first told my kindergarten students that we would be performing a play, they immediately became disruptive and started yelling out what play they wanted to perform and what parts they wanted to take. Well, I got really upset over their behavior, so I said, "The next time we meet I will have our drama production typed and I will assign parts to everyone."

At our next session, I announced, "We are going to do a play about *Goldilocks and the Three Bears* (Brett, 1987). Jonah, you are the Papa Bear, Margie, you are the Momma Bear, and George, you are the Baby Bear. Salina is Goldilocks and Mercedes is the narrator."

I thought that my prior planning and concrete directions would solve everything, but was I wrong. Jonah said, "I want to be the narrator," and Salina said, "I want to be a bear." So, mass confusion reigned once more until finally we got the parts straightened out.

I knew George would make a great baby bear because I had seen him act in class. He really is quite a performer and he settled down and followed directions. For our practices I brought bears' noses for each of the bears and a blond wig for Goldilocks. This turned out to be a super idea because it helped the students imagine that they really were the characters. But, everyone in the group except George continued to be annoyed about their parts, and they argued about where they should stand on the stage. Their disruptive behavior continued throughout all of our play practices. We even had a few fights break out because they couldn't keep their hands to themselves. What a mess! When I told them that if they couldn't cooperate, we would all have to go back to the classroom, George shouted, "That's not fair to punish all of us because I didn't do anything!"

I finally went to the library and read *Start With a Story: Literature and Learning in Your Classroom* (Watson-Ellam, 1991). I learned that creating drama productions should bring about a sense of community among participants rather than chaos. I also found out that I shouldn't tell my students what play we will present or assign parts to them. Rather, I need to discuss drama possibilities with my students, serve as a resource as they create their drama productions, and then, give them choices about what characters they will play. All of this advice sounds great. But, what can a teacher really do to keep order when students are engaging in activities that are not part of their regular, daily routine and that require movement and lots of student talk and interaction?

1. What advice do you have for Bill? _____

_____

2. How might Bill take responsibility for his students' behavior? _____

_____

Commentary #6.1A: "Drama Needs Democracy"
(by Karen Parker Guillot, Elementary Teacher,
Baton Rouge, Louisiana)

Dear Bill,

I sympathize with your frustration about your students' rambunctious behavior during drama practice. As a classroom teacher for over 7 years, I have experienced the same dilemma myself. I always knew that participating in dramatic pursuits would strengthen my students' reading development and oral language. I also recognized that participating in dramatic enactments would increase my students' abilities to cooperate and follow directions as they interacted in social, interpersonal ways (see Gardner, 1983, 1993, for discussions of dramatic and interpersonal intelligence). I simply did not know how in the world I was going to stop my students from arguing about what drama enactment they would perform, who would play important characters, who was going to stand where, and all the other problems inherent in producing a formal play! It's a good thing I worked on my own abilities to organize students and extended my thinking about formal drama performances versus informal/improvisational activities. Now that newer ideas about literacy have moved far beyond reading and writing to include all of the visual and communicative arts, I want to provide many opportunities for my students to engage in dramatic explorations. And I will only consider drama as a worthwhile, beneficial, language-enriching, and satisfying classroom experience if my students' behaviors are appropriate.

Here is how I changed my views and my organizational scheme regarding drama in my classroom. The first item on my agenda was to change my thinking about the need for formal productions. I decided that having students practice lines until we were all fatigued and bored made little sense. Instead, we began to engage in improvisational exercises. For example, we pretended we were all lost in a giant rain forest after reading *The Great Kapok Tree: A Tale of the Amazon Rain Forest* (Cherry, 1990). We also participated in many short, informal dramatic scenes, using ideas from literature as motivation (e.g., "What do you think Blanche in *The Talking Eggs* [San Souci, 1989] was thinking when she had to go into the woods alone?"; "Why was *Gregory Cool* [Binch, 1994] so apprehensive about trying new food and experiences on the island of Tobago?"). Once we relaxed, students were more comfortable and their behavior improved considerably.

Occasionally, we still produce more formal plays. However, I encourage my students to vote on as many issues as possible. For example, I provide several scripted plays that reflect the age and abilities of my students and encourage them to vote for the play of their choice. I also encourage my students to create their own plays. I am still working on how characters will be chosen. Sometimes things work out just fine because students volunteer for parts and everyone is satisfied. However, just recently, I asked who would like to play the main part of the male character and five boys raised their hands. I knew I was in trouble. What we decided was to have each boy take turns playing the part of the main character. That way, each boy only had to learn a small part and five sets of parents could see their "star" perform!

Here are some more hints for formal drama productions. Practices can be complete chaos if you do not create a group management system. Know from the beginning how and where you will practice. I always move the desks in my classroom and perform many small practices in the classroom before I take my students to the auditorium stage. Then, when we are in the auditorium, I do not have to spend long amounts of time working with individual students, which causes group management difficulties. Students also should know to speak softly and sit quietly during practice.

Be sure someone videotapes a rehearsal. Your students can view the tape and determine what needs to be changed or strengthened. You'll be surprised at your students' acumen and awareness.

In closing, Bill, I applaud your willingness to provide activities that promote your students' dramatic arts literacy. As you work more with your students, you will discover that dramatic pursuits are definitely worthwhile. You also will learn how to structure drama exercises, improvisations, and scripted play productions so that your students know what is expected of them.

Commentary #6.1B: "Drama Needs Democracy" (by Susan Davis Lenski, Teacher Educator, Illinois State University)

Bill, as I read your case, I could just visualize the enthusiasm and energy that your students were bringing to your announcement that they would be able to act in a play. How exciting it is for young children to engage in a drama production. Any type of drama enactment, from spontaneous improvisations to a scripted play, is highly motivating and exciting for all students because drama is based on interpreting stories, personal experiences, hopes, and dreams through action. As you know, students like action!

Certainly, drama is a natural experience for young students, who frequently engage in sociodramatic play. Through such dramatic play, young children make sense of their world and enrich their oral language and ability to take turns and listen to others. Perhaps your students responded with such unbounded enthusiasm to the drama activity because they don't have many in-school experiences acting out stories. They may intuitively perceive that drama allows them to engage in needed social interactions as they choose roles, decide on lines, and play a character. The social interaction involved in developing even a short play allows students to actively express their thoughts and feelings while giving them an emotional outlet for their imaginations. Through drama, students can learn about themselves and others as they give expression to a role. Therefore, providing your kindergarten students with drama as a motivating experience should be a priority for you. However, having students engage in drama also helps them develop their reading and writing abilities. Drama provides a framework within which to teach reading and writing as active, social processes. Language has a central role in drama. Students use language to express their feelings and to present their visual interpretation of a story. They use verbal and non-verbal cues during the play itself. As students experience a play, they call on the multiple literacies of reading, writing, speaking, listening, imaging, and the dramatic arts—all at once!

From your story, then, I see a wonderful teaching opportunity. First, you are helping students develop their multiple literacies awareness and abilities as they engage in drama. Second, your students want to engage in the experience. Your only difficulty, as I see it, is in orchestrating the event so that you are able to maximize the learning of all your students.

You ask how you can keep order while students are experiencing drama. My first bit of advice is that you need to visualize a different kind of "order" for this experience. Think about experiences you have had with your own peer group trying to make choices and work in groups. I suspect that often you heard overlapping talk and maybe even quarrels. Think about the kinds of language events that are involved for accomplishing group goals and the routines and rules that are necessary. Then, try to mirror this type of positive social interaction with your students. As you work with them, remember that the heated interactions that your students are experiencing are an important part of learning.

Once you have raised your own tolerance for active group discussion, provide your students with reasonable boundaries and rules. For example, develop a way for students to choose a play and to choose their roles. Announce that you will be producing a drama enactment and that you are taking all types of suggestions for the activity. Then, have small groups of students develop lists of books or story characters that interest them. Kindergarten students don't need to write the lists. They can draw their ideas. Compile the lists together in class and have students vote for the play they want to produce at this time. Reassure students that the other ideas on the list could be used later in the year. Then, list the characters in the play and have students volunteer for the part they want. Because more than one student will most likely volunteer for many of the parts, you might have a main actor and a standby, or you might tell the students that as director you will make final decisions. If you don't have enough acting parts, give some students the important jobs of creating props and scenery. Explain to students that they will have more opportunities to act in plays and that they will have the chance to switch their roles in the future.

As students practice the play, keep a sense of humor and enjoy watching your students engage in complex social and group interactions. As they develop the play, watch for their growth in language-based literacies and dramatic-arts literacy. Be assured that all dramatic-arts-literacy events, from spontaneous role playing to more defined performances, enhance students' reading, writing, oral language, and collaborative social interactions.

Case #6.2: "Success at Last!" (by Janice Clark)

Poor Charles had problems with every language-arts activity I introduced this semester. He is a sixth grader who can hardly read and write. As the semester progressed, I could see Charles' spirit decreasing, and I felt as though I was letting him down. I teamed him up with a learning buddy, but it seemed like it was too late. Charles gave up trying, and he started to be a behavior problem. At the end of March we began working on our drama production. Well, who would have thought that the dramatic arts could have such a positive effect on a student?

First, we decided to practice and present a play for students in the nearby elementary school. Next, we voted to design and make invitations, create some costumes, and use the school stage and the microphone. Then, we chose names out of a hat to assign characters. When it was Charles' turn, he excitedly said, "I'm going to be the big, bad wolf!"

As the weeks went by, we practiced over and over, and created our invitations and costumes. Charles used our computer to design his invitations and it was the first time I noticed him being motivated about any kind of schoolwork. One day, Charles stopped me in the hall. He said, "Miss Clark, I've been thinking about my part as the wolf. Can I change some of my lines in the play so they will be easier for me to remember?"

"Sure," I replied.

The following Tuesday, I went to the elementary school auditorium to get my group ready to perform, and there was Charles in his wolf costume with the biggest grin I ever saw. I was not used to seeing him smile and it was a shock! Charles had "confidence" written all over his face. Well, we got up on the stage and he made me so proud! It was as if I were watching my own child perform. After our final bows, I gave him a big hug and then it hit me. Performing in a drama activity had provided Charles with the first school success he's had since I've known him. I bet Charles could learn to read and write by authoring, producing, and starring in plays.

Unfortunately, it may be too late for Charles. When he leaves this classroom at the end of the semester, I don't know if he will ever get another chance to perform in a drama presentation. In addition, he probably is going on to junior high school where he will be required to read and write considerable amounts of informational text. How can we help students like Charles?

1. Does this case discuss problems about helping a student use drama as a tool for thinking, or does this case portray the use of drama to help a struggling student? _____

2. What ideas in the case support your thinking about Question 1 posed above? _____

Commentary #6.2A: "Success at Last!" (by Patricia Smith, Teacher Educator, University of Melbourne, Australia)

Hello Janice,

It seems that you will always remember Charles. Your account of his excitement and participation in the drama was very engaging. He is the boy who helped you understand that there may be different ways to develop and support literacy and that there are different literacies—not just the literacies of reading and writing.

Charles, like all students, is unique. He is the living proof that a teacher need not give up on students just because they do not follow an expected continuum. There are many paths to literacy, just as there now are many literacies.

You are a truly caring teacher, bending over backwards to find a way to help Charles. You tried old strategies and a new strategy that reportedly had good results. You teamed him with a learning buddy and were disappointed that it didn't work. What went wrong with your efforts to help? It just wasn't the right strategy for Charles at that time. If you look at things from Charles' point of view, you could see that he wouldn't be too keen to show his inadequate reading strategies to someone he would want to admire him. The buddy system works well when it is carefully organized and all parties are prepared. It is not a miracle cure for someone who has the "shame" factor operating so strongly. A strategy must be matched very carefully to individual students.

You say, "Poor Charles," and in a way you are correct. He has been at school all those years and has not experienced success in reading. One reason may be that Charles has had teachers who didn't use literature, drama, music, and movement as integral parts of reading, writing, speaking, and listening instruction. These teachers haven't allowed Charles to explore ways of learning to be literate that would be enjoyable. It is only by accident in sixth grade that the possibility of different, rather than more of the same, instruction presented itself. Many teachers are learning that the division between reading and writing is an artificial one put in place by those with a very narrow view of what constitutes literacy learning. Drama is full of literacy! In fact, drama is a legitimate literacy!

In the last paragraph you also worry and state, "Unfortunately, it may be too late for Charles." That is possible, but on the other hand, at his new school he may be lucky enough to have teachers who are aware that they all must find alternative ways of teaching reading and writing. As educators, all of us must be prepared to think about reading and language arts and learn about how it may be in many genres or text forms. There can be drama enactments about science or math research, or poetry about biology or chemistry.

This case raises a question other than the one recognized by you, Janice. Yes, teachers should be caring and nurturing, but they also must be professionals. They must read widely, talk to their peers, and attend conferences so that they have a deep grab bag of strategies to scaffold their learners. In many educational professional journals, there are excellent articles about using drama for learning that would serve as an introduction for any teacher interested in this literacy. These articles often report the experiences of teachers anxious to find ways of engaging their students in purposeful classroom strategies and alternative literacies. I suggest that you read some of them (e.g., see McMaster, 1998, in *The Reading Teacher*). I am surprised that a student could be turned on to reading through drama only at the end of sixth grade. This avenue should have been explored years before.

In closing, may I say that I am impressed with your caring nature. I am equally impressed with your knowledge about dramatic-arts literacy and your recognition that engagements in drama can help all students and may especially benefit students who struggle with the language-based literacies of reading and writing.

Commentary #6.2B: "Success at Last!" (by Ann-Sofie Selin, Elementary Teacher, Turku/Abo, Finland)

Dear Janice,

You need to celebrate your good work. You recognize the importance of linking literacy lessons with drama enactments, and you offer different ways of learning and knowing to your students. Your use of dramatic-arts literacy helped Charles know what it feels like to be a successful learner. You are on your way to becoming an outstanding educator. Let's analyze what happened with Charles. Good teachers always sit down and reflect upon their work—lessons that were almost perfect and those that were not so successful. My professional portfolio includes many examples of what I did right and what I did wrong over the years—my ups and downs as a teacher.

First, let's examine your splendid emerging understanding of multiple literacies and how drama (one of many literacies) helped Charles experience learning, language, and literacy in new, exciting ways. At the moment, Charles is not a successful reader and writer. In fact, Charles, a sixth grader, apparently never achieved success as a literate person when being literate meant only the ability to read and write. Now, we know there are many literacies (e.g., computer literacy, music literacy, dramatic-arts literacy, visual-arts literacy, the ability to view and visually represent, and the like). As Tell stated, "We are expanding the definition of what literacy means" (1999, p. 7).

Charles experienced school success through the literacy of the dramatic arts. He then became a motivated learner. Research shows that when students have opportunities to work with communication forms in which they feel comfortable, they become more motivated, active learners (Westreich, 2000). My thinking is that Charles has an aptitude for the dramatic arts, and you provided the chance for him to discover one of his special aptitudes. The dramatic arts also gave Charles recognition from peers and teachers. Suppose Charles has other special gifts and aptitudes (see Gardner, 1993, 2000). Suppose he could easily master various aspects of computer technology? Suppose Charles could learn to compose using a word-processing program? Suppose Charles is musical or is a budding visual artist? That's the way teachers need to be thinking—the "what ifs" for students, not the "he can'ts."

You say you paired Charles with a learning buddy, but it didn't work. I have had the same experience. Now, I discuss with my students the reasons for learning buddies. I explain that we will all work with learning buddies for 6 weeks (good students and students who need some assistance). We all sign contracts. After the 6-week period, we gather together to discuss and assess what went on. We decide if the learning buddy arrangement should continue. Some students want to continue working with a partner and others do not. I respect whatever decisions my students make.

Finally, let's discuss where Charles is now. In Finland, it isn't easy to collaborate with middle or junior high school teachers if you are teaching at the elementary level. I imagine it is the same in the United States. Students move on to new school contexts, and there is no collaboration among K–6 teachers and those who teach older students. A good way to get around this dilemma is through student-owned **portfolios.** Students take their portfolios with them as they move through different grade levels and schools. The portfolios document students' learning achievements, milestones, interests, and needs.

Now, what advice can I offer you so that you become less anxious about Charles? Become the best teacher you can be. Do your very best for every student. Keep studying and learning. I am confident that you will be a great teacher of multiple literacies.

Case #6.3: "What Did We Do Wrong?" (by Patrice Sontag)

For our drama presentation we combined all three of our kindergarten groups together. The song we chose to include in our play had repetitive lyrics and a little dance that we thought would be easy for our kindergarten students to learn. We practiced that song and the dance day after day for 30 minutes at each session. We even did some **guided imagery** sessions (Buehl, 2001). But, each time we practiced, our management problems got worse. "I want to be in the front of the bus," Joyce would always yell.

Tyrone always complained, "He pushed me."

Other students ran up and down the stage and some even jumped off the edge of the stage to the floor below.

It went on and on like that until finally we decided that whoever spoke or acted out of turn would be put out of the group. We actually ended up with only 12 students by the last practice. Of course, when it was the day of our presentation, we relented and let all of the students participate. I know we didn't do a good job as preservice teachers and coproducers of a play. A dancing teacher told me that rehearsals should never be longer than 15 minutes or young students lose interest. Maybe that's one reason that we couldn't keep order. But, lurking in my mind is another reason for our dilemma. I think we didn't take charge of our large group. I am also wondering if young students should even have to practice such formal dramatic productions.

1. After reading this case, when you plan your dramatic-arts-literacy lessons, what will you avoid and why? _____

_____

2. How might Patrice and her peers have turned this traditional drama activity into an informal dramatic enactment where students improvise their feelings, ideas, and opinions about story characters? _____

_____

Commentary #6.3A: "What Did We Do Wrong?"
(by Terri Austin, Classroom Teacher, Fairbanks, Alaska)

Dear Patrice,

I smiled when I read your account of your kindergarten drama rehearsal. I have done some formal scripted drama presentations with students over the years and experienced some of the same dilemmas you mentioned. I believe there are some practical things you can do to help eliminate a few of the problems you encountered. Unless you forgo formal dramatic-literacy events and consider informal improvisations or you become more organized, you will not want to integrate literacy lessons with any of the dramatic arts. Wonderful, integrated teaching moments will be lost because you will not want to teach in a "chaotic" situation. Management considerations will stop you from helping your students engage in multiple forms of literacy.

If you are going to combine groups in a scripted production, I find it helpful to keep kindergarten students in their own classrooms during rehearsals until the last day or so before final presentations. Kindergartners are easily distracted and they like routine. When their routines are altered, they become anxious—no wonder they push, shove, and call out. Therefore, it makes sense for teachers and students to practice a production in familiar surroundings until students know what they are to do. You can bring all of the students together once they are fairly sure of their parts.

Having said all of that about formal drama productions, I would like you to consider a larger issue that you brought up in the last sentence of your case. Why are you having kindergarten students practice? What is the purpose of manipulating kindergartners so that they worry about forgetting their part or they are confused about where to stand on a stage? Is the performance staged to show your principal, classroom teacher, professor, or your students' parents what you can do as a teacher? Don't you think student performances should focus on students? What I am saying is that we all need to consider what is developmentally appropriate for young students. We and our young students need to forget formal dramatic experiences and learn to enjoy drama through informal improvisations and role playing. Relax! Encourage your students to use their imaginations and to invent their dialogue and realities as they go along. Presenting a published play occasionally has a place in the curriculum, but they are not for your very young students. I bet you knew that!

Commentary #6.3B: "What Did We Do Wrong?"
(by Paula Triche, Language Arts/Creative Arts
Supervisor, St. Tammany Parish Schools, Louisiana,
and Adjunct Professor, University of Southern Mississippi)

Hello Patrice,

You titled your teaching case, "What Did We Do Wrong?" but you need to be congratulated for what you did right! Incorporating the literacies of song and dance into a dramatic presentation reveals that you are on the leading edge of research regarding teaching literacy with and through the arts. After a long career as a teacher of kindergarten students and pre-service teachers, I would like to offer you a suggestion regarding concerns that arise when you weave artistic events with students' literacy learning as you teach for multiple literacies: Reflect upon how you may have contributed to the problem.

In most teaching catastrophes, teachers create their own problems. Knowing children's chronological ages, patterns of growth from birth, and profiles of behavior are essential to teaching/learning success. When my preservice teachers ask me what a classroom teacher should do first, my answer always is, "Investigate your students' interests, personalities, temperaments, needs, and backgrounds. Identify the expected behavior of the students your class based on their birth dates (i.e., chronological ages). Then, after intense reflection, make informed decisions regarding appropriate, manageable multiple literacy-teaching and -learning experiences."

Confounding our profession's efforts to provide appropriate learning experiences for young students is the obvious disinterest on the part of lawmakers in the principles of human growth and development. Traditionally, legislators levy grade expectations of students according to the day they were born. There is little or no attention allocated to whether a student is developmentally ready to participate in formal school tasks, such as learning to read and write, or sitting at a desk for long periods of time, practicing how to write the numbers from 1 to 10. However, regardless of legislative officers' sometimes inappropriate mandates, teachers working with young students are obligated to reflect their students' individual development when planning successful multiple-literacies-learning activities.

So, let's address the domains of child growth and development while we review your drama experience to determine why things went awry.

Social Development Domain.   Five-year-olds often are perfectionists. Because of their developmental levels and 5-minute attention spans (1 minute for every year of life), most of the children in your group could not rise to your expectations. When they could not participate any further, some children jumped off the stage, tattled, and spoke out of turn. By expecting behavior 5-year-olds are incapable of demonstrating, you and your fellow preservice teachers reinforced through punitive measures the behavior you wanted to eliminate. You removed the children from the group, which is exactly what they wanted. Remember, too, that 5-year-old children thrive in small rather than large groups. The egocentric nature of young children, coupled with short attention spans and the routines and rituals of school, is quite demanding. Home environments don't require children to raise their hands to speak, or to request permission to use the restroom. Children don't walk in straight lines in their homes either.

Physical Development Domain. The song-and-dance routine was most likely too difficult for the physical development of some of the children. During the early years, girls usually engage in activities that warrant small-muscle movement (e.g., arranging tea parties and playing with baby dolls). Therefore, girls are more capable of perfecting activities that require the use of small muscles. Boys, however, participate in running, climbing, and jumping activities and may not be capable of mastering tedious dance steps. Frustrations lead to deviant behavior.

Cognitive Domain. Charlesworth (1992) suggested that children learn through observation and imitation. If a child has not experienced sensory learning prior to coming to school, the lack of auditory and visual perception skills will have a significant effect on the child's level of cognition. Additionally, if a child has not imitated and practiced the emerging behaviors of following directions, identifying patterns, repeating a sequence, and listening for facts and details, the acquisition of these skills is more difficult. The song-and-dance routine was probably too difficult for some children in the class because they could not attend to your oral directions and therefore could not remember the patterns and sequence of your production.

Emotional Development Domain. The drama experience proved stressful for the children and the teachers. Most human beings respond positively to low levels of stress; however, high-stress events encourage negative responses. We all show our poorest "side" when we are stressed to the max! A teacher's ability to sense and feel what children are feeling is a powerful tool for success. Children's insecurity, discomfort, and anxiety were the driving forces behind disruptive behavior during rehearsals.

Creative Domain. Children are creative and spontaneous. Young children also are uniquely inquisitive and open-minded. Therefore, the wise teacher encourages problem solving and freedom of expression, which are two strengths of multiple-literacy activities.

In your drama production, the script was predetermined and there was no opportunity for creativity. No wonder the children displayed such "creative" disruptive behaviors. Stay away from scripted drama presentations (see the Overview to this chapter).

In closing, your hearts and minds were in the right place. Don't give up on drama enactments. Remember to have fun. Encourage your students to be spontaneous. Continue to teach for multiple literacies!

Case #6.4: "I Didn't Prepare" (by Mariela Meneses)

The day we did our drama presentation, I was a wreck. We chose to do *Alexander, Who's Not (Do You Hear Me? I Mean It!) Going to Move* (Viorst, 1998).

I knew that the book was on my fourth graders' reading level and because they move from neighborhood to neighborhood so often, I knew my students could relate to the topic of moving to a new house or community. There were two big problems, though. I did not practice my own part enough. Therefore, I did not sound or act decisive on the stage when I introduced the students and when I spoke about the book and the author. In addition, as always, I was very nervous because I detest public speaking.

For some reason, I had not paid much attention to the introductory part of our presentation. In fact, I was not sure of what I was supposed to do. First, I read the title of the book. Then, I read the author's name and I could not pronounce "Viorst." I also forgot to announce what grade the students were in and I never introduced each student. When we finished our presentation, I forgot to have the students take a bow, which they love to do. It just did not come to me, even though it is among the guidelines that specifically spell out what we preservice teachers are to do in our drama presentations. I really have no excuse for my forgetfulness. I just did not practice enough. But, as I stated earlier, I also was scared to death to get up in front of an audience. I usually am nervous when I speak in front of a group, especially a group of adults. This is not the first time this has happened to me. Some of my preservice teacher colleagues are just born hams. They love to sing, dance, and emote in front of an audience. But, I don't like to do things like that.

My professor had a long talk with me after our presentation, and she said things like, "Practice makes perfect," and "Always overprepare if you think you will be nervous."

I really need help or I will not be able to offer drama activities to my students when I have my own class. Do many teachers feel this way?

1. How might Mariela structure a dramatic-arts-literacy event rather than a dramatic-arts production? _____

_____

2. What is the real problem in this case? Consider the question above. ___

_____

Commentary #6.4A: "I Didn't Prepare" (by Barry Oreck, Arts Teacher Educator, University of Connecticut)

Dear Mariela,

More practice on your introduction couldn't hurt, and it is certainly allowed to carry some notes so that you don't forget anything. But, your willingness to get up in front of the audience when you were scared was the best model you could give to your students. Many teachers never even start a performing-arts project with their classes because they don't consider themselves artistic and don't feel that they can effectively model the skills involved in the art form. That's really not the point. You don't have to be the artist. You need to be willing to try, to have an artistic attitude, and enough understanding of the process to facilitate the creative and artistic expression of your students. They need a model of risk taking and a safe environment in which to try new things without the worry of being criticized. The initial risk that you took is a crucial step toward creating the environment they need to perform.

How is that environment created? By listening, supporting, and modeling risk taking, encouraging spontaneity and unique answers, repeating activities until they are comfortable, and providing a variety of structures and entry points for students. Some students will be willing to dive into anything right away. Others need more time to play with the material, practice on their own or with a friend, and try out a variety of roles. Unfortunately, unless you are a drama teacher there may be little time for that kind of exploration and development. As a classroom teacher, you may be informed that your students will perform for a school assembly next week, and you will be lucky to have two rehearsals with everyone there to get it together. That is one of the reasons why we need to introduce artistic processes, improvisations, role playing, movement, and music studies into the classroom on a regular basis. The qualities we appreciate so much in an excellent performance are also ones we strive for in the classroom: cooperation and teamwork, focus and concentration, confidence and stage presence, speaking clearly and loudly, moving with care and commitment, expressing feelings and emotions. We can't develop these attributes in the two rehearsals before the show.

Your awareness of your own insecurity can make you more sensitive and empathetic to the needs of all of your students as they approach performing, either on stage or just speaking in front of the class. One of the most damaging misconceptions about the performing arts is that only hams can act or dance or sing. Many performers are, in fact, quite shy by nature. They have found a way to express themselves on stage by concentrating on the imagined situation, the rules of the game, or their partners. The two rules of improvisation according to Keith Johnstone are "Always say 'Yes,'" and "Always make your partner look good" (Johnstone, 1979). When performers concentrate on making their partners look good rather than worrying about how they look, how clever they are, what their next line is, and so on, they can put themselves more fully into the moment and act with more commitment. They will be more successful and will have more fun.

This point of view can also help you in your own struggle with the rather formal, dry job of being an M.C. (master of ceremonies). Think about how your introduction can be part of the piece—setting the mood and segueing more easily into the next part. Also, you don't always have to be the one to make the introductions. Find a student or a few students to introduce the presentation, but have them work on it and practice in front of the class. This important part of the performance is often the last thing we think about and it shows. Introductions that are done in character with a bit of drama, surprise, or humor work much better. You may find that you will loosen up if you have something to play with rather than simply trying to remember to acknowledge everyone. Good luck.

Commentary #6.4B: "I Didn't Prepare" (by Terri Austin, Head Elementary Teacher, Fairbanks, Alaska)

Dear Mariela,

In answer to your question, yes! Many teachers are reluctant to speak in front of adults. It is part of our job as teachers, however, and most of us find ways to overcome our hesitations. There are three thoughts I would like to share with you concerning the incident you described.

First, learn from this particular experience. From what you say, I can tell you were not prepared. Being prepared encompasses much more than working with students on a stage in a dramatic-literacy event. Tell yourself right now that from now on you are always going to be prepared as a professional. The next time you find yourself in front of an audience, know what you are going to say. Write it out if necessary and practice saying it to your dog, parakeet, kitten, or the mirror. Visualize yourself speaking in front of an audience. I have done all of these activities to prepare myself to speak in front of a group. Remember, you are a model for your students. If they see you fumble and act nervous, they will pick that up and do likewise.

Second, this incident will help you to develop compassion and empathy for those students who are afraid to speak in front of groups. Just as you get nervous in front of adults, some students feel the same in front of their peers. Because you have experienced fear, you can help students overcome their fears by sharing the ways you have discovered to overcome your own anxieties.

Third, I believe as professional educators it is important that we move beyond our classroom and learn to be more public in our views. Though I imagine this seems very remote to you now as a beginning teacher focusing on the immediacy of the classroom, I think it is essential that we know how to speak effectively to wider audiences. Think about beginning small. Practice speaking up in a peer gathering of some sort. Then move to a larger gathering. Force yourself to talk. It will be hard, but you'll gain so much confidence. That confidence will shine through when working with students, colleagues, and parents.

REFLECTIONS AND EXPLORATIONS

1. Collaborate with two of your fellow educators and create a short, informal drama presentation that shows how dramatic-arts literacy can help solve problems that arise in the classroom. You might base your informal dramatic enactment on a case in this chapter. Do not write or memorize the characters' speaking parts. Rather, use your own informal language. Present the drama presentation to your peers. Involve your audience by soliciting their feelings and suggestions about the dilemmas in the case.

2. Create a **shape poem** and express your opinions and knowledge about how to work effectively with students in dramatic-arts literacy as opposed to presentations.

INTEGRATING DRAMATIC ARTS LITERACY
IN YOUR CLASSROOM:
PRACTICAL APPLICATIONS

You will want to plan your literacy/drama lessons carefully so that students enjoy themselves and at the same time are able to stretch their imaginations, creativity, confidence, oral language, and inventiveness in a calm, orderly environment. Reflecting upon the following questions may help you consider and offer effective lessons according to your students' needs and interests and your particular teaching situation:

1. How will you link drama activities to literacy lessons?
2. What expectations will you and your students have for students' behavior as they freely engage in drama enactments?
3. How will you ensure that students will adhere to the agreed-upon expectations for appropriate behavior?
4. Will your students have input regarding the type of drama enactment they will perform (e.g., informal improvisations, a puppet show, Readers Theatre, a formal play)?
5. If students play the parts of favorite story characters, how will they be selected for the parts? (Will you choose students to play the characters? Will students self-select character parts?)
6. Will you rely on a written script or will you encourage students to improvise and create their own dialogue?
7. How will you provide opportunities for students from diverse cultures to use their special heritages and experiences in creating plots and dialogue?

8. Will students work on a stage? If so, what are the guidelines for students? How close to the front of the stage do you want them to stand? Some teachers place a chalk line on the stage floor to situate student actors because students occasionally like to jump off the stage front, which can cause problems.

9. How will students enter and exit the stage? (Again, some students like to jump off the stage front, which can cause problems.)

10. Will students use a microphone or karaoke? Will they have sufficient time to practice speaking into a microphone?

11. Will students wear costumes? Who will create the costumes? Will you enlist help from parents?

12. Will you combine the drama enactment with music, popular culture, or the visual arts (e.g., videos, audiotape recordings, piano, flute, murals, painted scenery)?

13. How will you encourage introverted, shy students to give their own ideas about dialogue and actions?

14. How will you challenge students who are gifted in the dramatic arts?

15. What important responsibilities will be available for students who do not wish to perform for an audience? (They might serve as a lighting or scenery specialist, write letters of invitation, or design programs.)

16. How will you structure and time rehearsals so that students do not become bored, weary, or overstimulated?

17. How will you encourage students from diverse cultures and heritages to add their special customs and heritages to dramatic enactments?

18. How will you and your students assess the strengths and shortcomings of the drama event?

SUGGESTED READINGS

Cecil, N., & Lauritzen, P. (1994). *Literacy and the Arts for the Integrated Classroom: Alternative Ways of Knowing*. White Plains, NY: Longman.

In chapter 7, Cecil and Lauritzen show how drama brings ideas to life. Drama offers opportunities for students to reflect upon and explore life's issues and events and can help students conceptualize ideas. The authors supply improvisational exercises and offer examples of motivational play-writing prompts.

Cornett, C. (1999). *The Arts as Meaning Makers*. Upper Saddle River, NJ: Merrill/Prentice Hall.

Chapter 7 discusses why teachers should integrate creative drama throughout the curriculum and shows how teachers can use drama as an effective teaching tool. This chapter also provides a short review of the history of drama as it relates to human behavior and offers information about people who significantly shaped drama in the United States. Chapter 8 offers many ideas and strategies for connecting drama to curricular goals. Ideas include specific suggestions for warm-up activities, pantomime, verbal improvisations, role playing, and storytelling.

McMaster, J. (1998, April). "Doing" literature: Using drama to build literacy. *The Reading Teacher, 51*(7), 574–584.

This article begins with a vignette that demonstrates the power of drama throughout the curriculum. McMaster states that drama is also one of the few vehicles of instruction that can support every aspect of students' literacy development while boosting students' self-concept and motivation for learning.

7

Integrating the Literacies of Reading and Writing

> Within the area of literacy, writing is a young area of study and indeed has been the forgotten one of the three Rs.
> —Freedman, Flower, Hull, and Hayes (1997, p. 735)

OVERVIEW

Sharon Miller

Southern Arizona Writing Project, University of Arizona, Tucson

Terri Austin

Head Elementary Teacher, Fairbanks, Alaska

Good teachers at all levels connect reading and writing instruction (Routman, 1991). Primary teachers know that young students' awareness and understanding of the processes of reading and writing develop concurrently (Chomsky, 1972; Clay, 1975, 1993; Morrow, 1993; Ross & Roe, 1990). "Writing, like reading, speaking, and listening, is a process that emerges naturally as children explore the various ways people express themselves" (Raines & Isbell, 1994, p. 97) (also see Y. Goodman, 1986).

At the elementary level, teachers observe that when students are encouraged to read and write, they employ ideas, vocabulary, and syntax in their writing that are present in stories they hear or read. In classrooms where reading and writing workshops are employed, students learn to view reading from the "inside," from a writer's point of view, and they learn to view their own texts from the "outside," from the reader's point of view (Atwell, 1987, 1998) (also see Newkirk, 1982, 1985, 1989). In addition, students frequently borrow and build upon the ideas found in books and stories written by friends.

Middle school students also benefit when reading and writing activities are merged. Often, they transpose ideas from many areas of reading into their writing. For example, a student who is familiar with the literary concept of point of view might use this concept in social studies when creating a journal about early American pioneer life. Middle school students who consider themselves as writers[1,2] are "less likely to be intimidated by written language" (Newkirk, 1982, p. 457), and studies show that in classrooms where reading and writing merge, reading scores go up (Graves & Murray, 1980). There is "no doubt that daily writing promotes and enhances reading" (Dionisio, 1989, p. 747).

The interconnectedness of reading and writing is not coincidental; they are flip sides of the same coin. As processes, they are stimulated by experiences; they support each other; they require many of the same proficiencies; they enhance higher level thinking skills; they function together to make meaning. And finally, they share an identical goal: communication (Emory, 1986).

Reading and Writing as Similar Processes

Reading and writing are similar processes. For example, in prewriting tasks, students engage in activities designed to, among other things, explore their ideas and understandings, consider topics for writing, generate prior knowledge, organize their thinking, and plan for drafting. In prereading tasks, students engage in activities designed to motivate interest in the subject of the reading, explore related ideas, and generate prior knowledge and understandings about the subject. Just as we do not rush students into writing without adequate mental and physical preparation, we should not rush them to read passages without adequate preparation. This is true when students are reading for information or for pleasure.

During the drafting stage of writing, students experiment with sequencing and expression of the ideas about which they are writing. They try to organize their writing so that a reader will understand their purpose and the message they wish to convey. Content of the writing is paramount at this stage; judgment of correctness of mechanics is withheld. In the reading process, the initial act of reading parallels drafting. The reader engages with the text, trying to construct personal meaning from the organizational structure and the ideas expressed. In a first-time reading, the student tries to understand the content and the message the writer intends to convey. In this part of the reading process, the student may seek clarification and raise questions in an effort to make meaning.

---

[1]Cohle, D., & Towle, W. (2001). *Connecting Reading and Writing in the Intermediate Grades: A Workshop Approach.* Newark, DE: International Reading Association.

[2]Baines, I., & Kunkel, A. (Eds.). (2000). *Going Bohemian: Activities That Engage Adolescents in the Act of Writing Well.* Newark, DE: International Reading Association.

In writing, writers have opportunities to revise the text, adding content where necessary, reorganizing the ideas, and making an active and purposeful effort to address the needs of the reader. In reading, students have opportunities to revisit the text, rereading and revising understandings and meaning. In both reading and writing, this may be done individually or in collaboration with other students. Talk is important in the process of making and clarifying meaning.

The writer prepares, after revision, to publish his or her work by proofreading and editing so that issues of correctness and spelling do not interfere with readers' understanding of the text.[3] The reader reflects on and synthesizes his or her understandings and considers how to express this new knowledge in his or her own language or in some creative demonstration.

Finally, the writer publishes the work, formally sharing it in the author's chair, posting it in the classroom, sharing informally with peers and in print-based or online student publications. As teachers of reading and writing, we offer our students options in the books they read, for the topics about which they write, and for the manner in which they demonstrate their knowledge.

Although the stages of the reading and writing processes have been described here in a step-by-step fashion, it is important to understand that neither process is linear. Each process should be considered recursive, allowing for individuals to move back and forth within the stages. We might move from revision to an entirely new draft, or we may return to particularly difficult or dense text to read and reread in order to arrive at an initial understanding.

Teachers must be attentive to the various stages of each process and provide students with learning activities that integrate reading and writing and maintain the awareness of the obvious: What we write is to be read, and what we read has been written. We can't have one without the other.

Two Broad Categories of Writing

There are two broad categories of writing activities that teachers use in the classroom. These are (a) nonstructured, nonprocess writing and (b) structured, process writing. Both categories provide multiple opportunities to integrate reading and writing.

The purposes of nonstructured, nonprocess writing are to provide students with a nonthreatening, nonevaluative framework for writing and to promote experimentation and exploration of ideas and understandings. One of the most popular forms of this kind of writing is the journal. A journal may be used for multiple purposes; in fact, students may keep more than

---

[3]Gentry, J. (2000, November). A retrospective on invented spelling and a look forward. *The Reading Teacher, 54*(3), 318–332.

one kind of journal. For writing workshop, students may have a process log or "day-book" in which they record ideas and observations that may be used for structured writing (Murray, 1982, 1984). For reading workshop, or for literature study, they may have a reading response journal, or literature log, in which they record personal response to their reading, raise questions, or examine the author's craft, among other things (see Routman, 1991). Reading response journals may be used as **dialogue journals,** where students write back and forth to one another in written conversation, exploring the meaning of the texts. The teacher may participate in the dialogue journals as a means of supporting understanding and participating in the conversation, but she or he must never evaluate, correct, or criticize student ideas or the writing in these informal journals. She or he may, however, raise questions that push students to deeper understandings.

Learning logs are another type of journal that students may keep. The learning log, however, does not always take the form of a bound book in which students write on a regular basis. Learning logs often are used for **metacognition** (i.e., monitoring and thinking about one's thinking) and ongoing self-assessment. At the end of a lesson, the teacher may request a reflection on learning from students, such as:

- "What was the easiest part of today's lesson?"
- "What was the most difficult?"
- "Tell me two things you learned today."
- "Tell me what you didn't understand."

Learning logs benefit not only students, who make their learning visible through writing, but also teachers, who are able to evaluate the effectiveness of their lessons based on students' comments and questions.

These types of writing activities are very effective when used with literature and reading assignments. Because they are often written spontaneously, there should be no expectation of correct conventions of writing. Students need to feel free to write their questions and express their understandings without fear of judgment, otherwise they will be reluctant to engage in thoughtful response to reading and a risky exploration of their own learning.

Structured, process writing assignments generally come about in the classroom as a result of curriculum requirements. When students are writing something that will be graded, they must be given every opportunity to do their best work. This involves creating a classroom environment that promotes writing and an instructional program that provides time for students to engage in all of the stages of the writing process. Frequently, such structured writing assignments can be associated with the literature being read in the classroom. Students, for a literature lesson on point of view, may read

The True Story of the Three Little Pigs by A. Wolf (Scieszka, 1989) and follow it by writing their own versions of well-known fairy tales and stories presenting an alternative point of view.

Sometimes, writing assignments might involve reports or research papers for content area classes. *Journey to Topaz* (Uchida, 1971) and *Number the Stars* (Lowry, 1989) offer students the opportunity to explore historical and political issues and generate interest in the plight of Japanese Americans and Jews during World War II. Reading and discussing these books can provide the background that precedes further content area study and research on historical events. Whether reading and writing for language arts or content areas, students need time to use the reading and writing processes effectively.

Throughout the two processes, students should be offered multiple opportunities for collaboration. When prewriting, small groups can meet to generate ideas for writing. During the revision stage, they might bring drafts to peer-response groups for feedback. After revision, students may work in pairs or small groups to peer-evaluate according to a rubric established for the assignment. Conferences with the teacher throughout the process would include content conferences during the drafting and revision stages and editing conferences prior to publication (Stires, 1983, 1991a). For example, during prereading, students may pair-share ideas, or work in small groups completing **K-W-L** charts (Ogle, 1986), for example. Following reading, they may pair-share again, generate questions in small groups, and, finally, they may even work in groups to write assigned compositions, create and perform dramatizations or other creative demonstrations of learning. When students work in collaboration to compose something original, be it a traditional piece of writing or a dramatic performance, process should be followed.

During the writing and reading processes, teachers also must attend to the issues of language conventions and the author's craft. This is done effectively through a series of minilessons. Minilessons generally are very short lessons that involve sharing models and guiding the students through initial efforts to imitate the models. With their collected minilesson activities, students will have a thorough library of resources for creative and expository writing (see Calkins, 1986; Routman, 1991). These are teacher-guided writing lessons that are devised to help students concentrate on discrete aspects of written language, such as spelling, punctuation, capitalization, and paragraphing. They also are teacher-guided reading lessons devised to help students understand an author's use of specific literary elements, such as characterization, dialogue, mood, and setting. These are purposefully presented in an effort to support students' experimentation with these literary elements in their own writing.

WHAT DO YOU NEED TO KNOW?
HOW CAN YOU BEGIN?

As you begin to plan how you will weave reading and writing in your classroom, what do you need to know? How can you begin? Practical information that helps teachers understand how to structure and offer an effective reading/writing program is offered in the *Guided Reading* series by Fountas and Pinnell (1996, 2000), and *Framing Literacy* by Mallow and Patterson (1999). These authors help teachers of both primary and intermediate grades see the interconnectedness of writing and reading. They touch on such topics as classroom routines, emergent readers and writers, room arrangements, assessments, reluctant writers and readers, and instructional options. Additionally, *Invitations* by Regie Routman (1991) and *Seeking Diversity* by Linda Rief (1992) are extremely rich resources for teaching reading and writing to students of all grades and all ability levels.

Remember to read about the processes of reading and writing (Avery, 1993; Rief, 1992; Routman, 1991). Look for articles and books that view reading and writing as a blended action rather than two separate subjects. Look to writers such as Peter Elbow (2000), Donald Graves (1984), and Donald Murray (1985, 1989, 2000). Read what they have to say about the relationship between living events and writing. Listen to their voices as they help us discover how they write. Read popular writers on their craft as well. Stephen King's book *On Writing* (2000) reveals much about his processes and experiences as a writer finding his voice.

KEEPING CURRENT

Teachers need to be aware of all the local and national threads of conversations and positions about literacy instruction in order to make sound instructional decisions and also to have up-to-date information they might call upon to effect positive changes in local reading/writing positions and instruction. Therefore, it is important for teachers to look at their state's standards in reading and writing. State standards provide good summaries of the reading/writing skills and issues valued by individual communities. For example, in Alaska, some of the reading/writing standards include the following: (a) being a competent and thoughtful reader, (b) being able to use information, both oral and written, and literature of many types and cultures to understand the self and others, and (c) being able to apply elements of effective writing and speaking that include ideas, organization, vocabulary, sentence structure, and personal style. Most states have standards for learning, and literacy teachers must be knowledgeable regarding these standards and how they are being addressed in their classrooms. The

National Council of Teachers of English and the International Reading Association have jointly established a broad range of learning standards for all students of English and language arts (Farstrup & Myers, 1996). Awareness of these standards can provide teachers with the knowledge needed to participate in local discussions when the issue of standards arises.

Moreover, teachers must understand that all literacy issues are embedded within a public political context (Routman, 1996) and as such can bring about widely polarized viewpoints that are argued in the media and in public forums. For example, the debate about the merits of whole language and phonics has continued for decades after Chall's call for phonics instruction (Chall, 1967; Dahl, Scharer, Lawson, & Grogan, 1999; K. Goodman, 1986; Price, 1998). In addition, journals, such as *Educational Leadership* ("Redefining Literacy," 1999) have dedicated specific issues to controversies surrounding writing and reading instruction. Some popular media magazines, such as *Newsweek* (November 22, 1999), also have also reviewed questions surrounding the teaching of reading and writing. Some good sources that supply information about dilemmas surrounding current reading/writing instruction are *Phonic Phacts* (K. Goodman, 1993), *What's Whole in Whole Language* (K. Goodman, 1986), and Regie Routman's (1996) *Literacy at the Crossroads.*

Sooner or later you will have to explain your philosophy, along with your current instructional approaches to reading and writing, to parents and administrators. Therefore, you will want to be familiar with the processes of reading and writing, your state's standards, and the controversies surrounding literacy issues so that you can make informed decisions and explain your position in a thoughtful, knowledgeable manner.

APPLYING WHAT YOU KNOW

In addition to being fully informed about reading and writing, think about your own reading and writing processes, and remember those teachers who honored your processes and those who placed obstacles in your way. Think about how you can support your students as they struggle to develop their own processes. How do you merge reading and writing in your private and professional life? Do you scribble margin notes in texts, documenting your ideas? Do you underline important points in books you read? How can you make these strategies available to students when they cannot write in their textbooks? Do you draw maps and carefully refer to them to help you get to where you want to go? How can you support students who are visual learners and need "road maps" for their writing?

Learn about the developmental stages of young students' writing. Recognize that emerging development of spelling skills may be marked by a progression from constructed spellings, scribbling, pretend writing using letterlike forms, random use of actual letters, single consonants representing beginning sounds of words, the addition of ending sounds and then vowels, and finally to standard spelling (Bear, Invernizzi, Templeton, & Johnston, 2000; Heller, 1991; Temple, Nathan, Burris, & Temple, 1988). Know where your students are in their development, and be prepared to build on their developing understandings of writing.

Assume that all students, including those who are learning disabled and those identified as having other special needs, can learn to read and write through process instruction. According to Graves (1991), students with learning disabilities who work on writing skills in isolation are disconnected from themselves as persons. He pointed out that "skills work merely supplies additional evidence for the misconception that they are less intelligent than other children (p. 115). Graves made a similar point regarding an overemphasis on reading skills for the student he called the "reader in trouble" (p. 127). When getting the words right is more important than understanding and making meaning, "each unconquered word is a symbol of defeat" (p. 129). This attitude is counterproductive to learning and progress. Kenneth Goodman (1991) stressed the need for teachers to help these students to revalue themselves as learners and readers, which involves providing meaningful, real texts through which students learn to appreciate their meaning-making abilities, and the elimination of nonproductive strategies generally associated with traditional remediation programs.

Understand that even though students have advanced through the grades, it doesn't mean that their individual reading and writing issues have been resolved favorably. The reading and writing of middle school students deserve serious attention because a number of older students "continue to struggle with the basic processes of reading and writing beyond the third grade" (Moje, Young, Readence, & Moore, 2000, p. 400). Offering a literature-rich classroom with multiple opportunities to write can make a great difference in student achievement in reading and writing.

Recognize the value of the varied literacies students bring into your classroom; encourage their exploration of and development of these literacies by integrating them into the reading and writing processes and permitting students to demonstrate their learning in a variety of ways.

GROWING AS A PROFESSIONAL

As a teacher, you have an obligation to continue learning about both reading and writing in order to improve your skills and refine your theory. One way to do this is to locate your state affiliate(s) of the National Writing Project (NWP; http:/www.writingproject.org) and attend their conferences, programs and institutes. The mission of the NWP is to improve the teaching of writing and improve learning in the nation's schools. In recognition of teacher knowledge, expertise, and leadership, its professional development model involves "teachers teaching teachers." NWP summer institutes provide settings where teachers come together to examine their own classroom practices, to share best practices with one another, to examine and develop professional theories of writing and learning, and to develop their own writing skills. After completion of the summer institute these teachers provide professional development workshops for other teachers in their schools and communities. Local sites also design programs that address the needs of teachers and learners in their local communities. Through participation in a local NWP affiliate, you not only become part of a local network of educators who share your concerns about teaching writing, but you also become part of a national community with a shared vision for learning. The resources available through NWP and its local affiliates are endless. There are affiliates in all 50 states, as well as Puerto Rico and the District of Columbia. For more information, as well as the location of your nearest affiliate, visit their Web site (www.writingproject.org).

Through local NWP activities, you may be able to join a literacy support group, or you might establish a small group in your own school. With this group, you can explore your knowledge about the reading/writing connection by discussing your thoughts and ideas with fellow teachers. Your purpose might be to discuss writing in many forms. Challenge your group to look beyond the obvious and routine in reading and writing. Consider every author as a long-distance mentor.

Join the International Reading Association and the National Council of Teachers of English, as well as their local affiliates. Through membership in these professional organizations, you will have access to journals, publications, and professional development opportunities. Visit their Web sites for further information (www.reading.org and www.ncte.org).

Look for online courses that support literacy development. The book publisher Heinemann, for example, frequently offers such courses for reasonable enrollment fees. Check their Web site for upcoming classes (www.Heinemann.com). Universities and colleges around the nation also offer online courses that might provide you with important skills and understandings regarding teaching reading and writing.

GROWING PERSONALLY
AS A READER AND WRITER

Most important, to be an exemplary teacher of reading and writing, you should read and write daily. You cannot teach something you do not do yourself. Keep a journal. Write for publication. Read good fiction and use e-mail to share your reactions with friends. Don't forget that there is wonderful nonfiction available. There are many talented authors who make nonfiction texts sing. Barry Lopez's (1986) skillfully crafted *Arctic Dreams* will radically change your views of nonfiction writing. Start a book club with teaching peers and keep reading logs that describe your opinions about the books you have read.[4] Explore Oprah Winfrey's online book club as a means of joining conversations about books (www.oprah.com/obc/obc_landing. html). Read the books Oprah recommends and participate in the discussions through her live, online book club chats; see the Web site for current days and times. If cyber-chatting about books does not appeal to you, locate reading groups available at local bookstores.[5,6]

Model your habits as a reader/writer for your students. Talk about what you are reading. Share your writing and ask their advice. When they read, you read; when they write, you write. Do this regularly with writing, before you begin to circulate the room to answer questions and support their engagement. A 5-minute delay is often the right amount of time for students to get moving in their writing. Circulate too soon and they will bombard you with questions they might answer for themselves as they begin their own writing (Graves, 1984).

Your "own literacy behaviors have enormous influence on [your students]" (Hubbard, 1989, p. 150). Your organization of materials for instruction, your structure of lessons, and your classroom environment convey clear messages to students regarding your identity as a reader and writer and exactly what you value about reading and writing. Your beliefs about teaching and learning—that is, your personal theory—drive your instructional decisions; those decisions, in turn, make your theory visible. Students will know what you believe about them and their learning either implicitly or explicitly by your actions. Consequently, what you can do to improve your own understanding of teaching and learning, of reading and writing, of multiple literacies, of yourself as a reader and writer, as well as what you bring into the classroom from these new understandings, will reap significant rewards for your students.

---

[4]Raphael, T., Pardo, L., Highfield, K., & McMahon, S. (1997). *Book Club: A Literature-Based Curriculum*. Newark, DE: International Reading Association.

[5]Gambrell, L., & Almasi, J. (Eds.). (1996). *Lively Discussions! Fostering Engaged Reading*. Newark, DE: International Reading Association.

[6]Evans, K. (2001). *Literature Discussion Groups in the Intermediate Grades*. Newark, DE: International Reading Association.

CASES AND COMMENTARIES

Case #7.1: "What You See Is What You Talk About and What You Dream at Night" (by Eli Jacobs)

First, we read a great book: *Who Lost a Shoe?* (Hazen, 1992). Then we talked about the important parts of stories. The kindergartners really grasped the concept of **story features** (i.e., characters, story settings, problems, and solutions) so I decided they were ready to dictate their stories to me. Roger was first. He said, "Somebody stold my shoes and I asked my momma for new ones and she said, 'No,' so I went to steal some shoes."

Next was Tyrone. He said, "My sister peed in my momma's bed and my momma whooped her until she cried and fell asleep and didn't wake up for a long time."

Devonte told his story by saying, "They crashed in the windows of my grandmaw's truck and scart me in the middle of the night. My brother was running out and yelling. Then, they stold the truck."

I sat very still for a minute. I did not want to continue with these stories. I was distraught. I didn't know what to do, so I said, "We'll finish these stories, type them on the computer, and illustrate them the next time we meet."

None of my fellow preservice teachers knew what to do about what these sad students dictated to me, so I went to the library and skimmed two books: *Abuse in the Family: An Introduction* (Kemp, 1997), and *Violence—Our Fastest Growing Public Health Problem* (Langone, 1984). Both of these books share the opinion that what you see and experience in your environment is what you talk about during the day and what you dream about at night. When the children told me stories about violence, they were really telling me about their everyday realities. How can I help these children?

1. Do the issues in this case shock you? Why or why not? _____

_____

2. How would you handle Eli's dilemma? _____

_____

Commentary #7.1A: "What You See Is What You Talk About and What You Dream at Night" (by Patricia Bloem, Teacher Educator, Grand Valley State University, Allendale, Michigan)

Dear Eli,

Your worry about the violence that your students encounter daily is one I share, too. I think it should nag and bother us because ours is a violent culture where young students have to deal with far too many issues that demand maturity. My preservice teachers often tell me stories like yours. They are amazed about what they hear and learn from some urban children. My preservice teachers tell me that Mondays are the worst days for students to act out because many of them have tough weekends and haven't been in that safe and nurturing environment of their classroom for two whole days. The students have to readjust emotionally and try to let go of whatever it was they experienced over the weekend.[7,8,9]

Please don't label your students as "sad." Let me tell you a story that might help put this in perspective. I have a student right now who is a master teacher in one of the toughest neighborhoods in Cleveland. Mary has been designated "Teacher in Charge" in her building, which means that whenever the principal leaves, Mary accepts responsibilities for making school decisions. I have always been impressed with Mary's "level head," deep love for her students, and ability to reflect thoughtfully on teaching situations. So, when she came to class one evening, shaken, we spent time talking about what had happened to her. She was "Teacher in Charge" and had rounded up the kids from the playground and had just gotten the last child into the building when shots rang out on the sidewalk next to where kids had been playing moments before. "I got them in just in time," she said, "before a neighborhood thug took out his anger on another neighborhood thug."

She talked about what could have happened if the students had been outside when the shooting occurred and how she hated having the enormous responsibility of being in charge. I asked how she handled it with the kids. "I let them talk," she said, "and I didn't let them see how rattled I was. The students shared other close calls they had with violence. They were very matter of fact about, handling it with more aplomb than I'd been doing. They said, 'The bathtub is the safest place to go if you hear gunfire.'"

As Mary talked to us, she noticed some of the sympathetic expressions on the faces of her graduate student classmates. "Oh," she said, "don't ever feel sorry for my students. These are not some poor kids who need pity. They are strong and street-smart. These are survivors."

I think that's the right attitude to have, Eli. Don't waste time feeling sorry for them and don't think of them as poor kids. The other thing I would do

---

[7] *Keeping Schools and Communities Safe: What Is the Department of Education Doing to Help Americans Keep Schools and Communities Safe?* Retrieved, April 1997. (http://www.edgov/offices/OESE/SDFS)

[8] Brownlie, F., & King, J. (2000). *Learning in Safe Schools: Creating Classrooms Where All Students Belong.* Portland, ME: Stenhouse.

[9] Barone, D. (1999). *Resilient Children: Stories of Poverty, Drug Exposure, and Literacy Development.* Newark, DE: International Reading Association.

for yourself and your own understanding of their lives is read deeply into the fiction of kids with violent lives. Read *Make Lemonade* by Virginia Euwer Wolf (1993), *What Jamie Saw* by Caroline Coman (1995), and *Like Sisters on the Home Front* by Rita Garcia-Williams (1995)—all books where kids pull through violent times and survive, not without wounds, but with courage.

Now, what to do with your students? I would accept the writing they give you and try again. Give them more models, give them lots of encouragement for the kind of writing you want, and try until you get some writing that you are excited about and can share with the rest of the school community—their parents, their families, other students.

I also would find some good stories about kids who are acquainted with stealing and other disturbing issues. Read these stories to your students and encourage discussion. I just discovered the picture book *A Handful of Seeds* by Monica Hughes (1996), the story of a girl who tries to get other kids to find another way to live besides stealing. It may be a bit of a stretch for some kindergartners, but you read it and decide.

And don't dwell on the violence. Yes, it's part of your students' lives, but their lives are so much fuller and bigger than brutality and destructiveness—full of favorite foods and love, and hope, and crazy toys, and all the parts of childhood. Let them write poetry, paint, create songs, dance, and participate in impromptu drama presentations. The arts can help them express all the good parts of their lives.

Commentary #7.1B: "What You See Is What You Talk About and What You Dream at Night" (by Sharon Miller, Retired Language Arts Supervisor, Bel Aire, Maryland, and Co-Director for Teacher Research, Southern Arizona Writing Project Tucson, Arizona)

Dear Eli,

Your experience with your students clearly illustrates a dilemma faced by many teachers in schools where violence in the community is a fact of life (see http://www.ncsu.edu/cpsv/statistics.html for a listing of statistics related to school violence). I think you're on the right track by looking for the literature to read about the problem, but I would suggest you look more specifically for the literature as it relates to teaching and dealing with such problems in the classroom. The two readings you mention are no doubt excellent treatises on the problems, but I suspect they offered you very little practical advice for helping your students. They told you that "What you see and experience in your environment is what you talk about during the day and what you dream about at night." That is depressing and not very helpful.

Look at it another way. How can you give your students something to see and experience in the school environment that will change the nature of what they talk about and dream about? You must come to terms with the realities that exist outside your school and classroom. These are realities over which you have very little control. You cannot change what these students face each evening when they leave the school setting. What you can control is the reality of the school and classroom. You must create a community in the classroom where students feel safe, a community in which they can trust their teacher to love them unconditionally, in which learning is not only empowering, but clearly expected of all, in which they believe that the teacher, who honors them as human beings with the potential for greatness, is telling them the truth, and in which they can trust each other to be kind, generous, and supportive.

If all of this sounds very idealistic and unachievable, then I refer you to the book, *Possible Lives: The Promise of Public Education in America,* by Mike Rose (1995). In it is a chapter entitled, "Baltimore, Maryland," which tells about an African American teacher in the inner city of Baltimore, who has created the very classroom I have just described. Rose described her as follows:

> Stephanie Terry taught, by paradoxical logic, at the intersection of hope and despair. There were a host of probabilities that could lead one to believe that the academic future of her students would not be bright: the danger and seduction of the streets, the limited resources her students' families have for education, the over restrictions and hidden injuries of class bias and racism. Yet, Stephanie knew how profound was the desire in some of those row houses for achievement. She knew in her bones the brilliance of her people and believed, in the deepest way, in the promise of their children . . . [she] assumed therefore, that her students could "do better than many people expect them to," that "if you put good stuff in front of them, wonderful things will happen." (p. 107)

Read that chapter, Eli. Read it and know that if you bring just a little bit of Stephanie's courage and faith into your classroom with you, a difference will be made. Your students' stories of violence and abuse will surface again and again, but you must offer them alternative stories through the experience of reading and discussing other realities in the world. Immerse them in folklore, literature, and their cultural heritage through stories, legends, music, and mythology. Teach them to honor their own ethnic backgrounds in order to develop their own sense of self-respect. Use these experiences as springboards for discussion, story creation, drawing, singing, dramatic enactments. Help them write new dreams. Plaster the classroom with posters and photographs of those who have accomplished greatness against overwhelming odds. Give them all of the experiences possible in the classroom so that their lives become enriched rather than mired in both economic and cultural poverty. The safe harbor of the classroom, although it will not resolve their out-of-school issues, will teach them that there are other realities to talk about and dream about. Don't feel sorry for them; advocate for them!

Although I am not familiar with the book you read to your students, *Who Lost a Shoe?*, I am sure it is a fine book. However, its focus on something lost or missing generated in the students thinking about something they have lost or seen go missing. Give them stories about achievement and gain. For example, *Amazing Grace* by Mary Hoffman (1991) is a wonderful story about an African American girl who loved to act out stories and believed she could do anything she wanted to do. Grace is a wonderful role model for students.

Additionally, I want to refer you to the May 2000 issue of *English Journal.* Even though this journal is aimed at secondary teachers, the theme of the issue is "A Curriculum of Peace." It is rich with real stories from real teachers who are trying to create safe environments for their students. Best of all, each of the articles is followed by a bibliography, thereby offering you a virtual library of resources.

Finally, regarding your concern about abuse, I have no doubt that it will come up again. For Tyrone's sister, your hands are tied. You can't charge child abuse based on hearsay. But you must be vigilant for Tyrone's and his sister's well-being, and report any suspected abuse according to the law. At the very least, report what you have heard to the school principal. In the meantime, teach and believe in your kids. And believe in yourself.

Case #7.2: "Confusion about Little Jack" (by Joni Spiers)

It all started when my five kindergarten students and I finished reading *A Big Day for Little Jack* (I. Moore, 1994). I thought it was a perfect opportunity to have my students write a poem about the story events as a postreading strategy. The students got very excited when I said we were going to be authors of a poem. I should have realized they didn't know what a poem was. I started off by explaining that a poem is speech or writing that may or may not rhyme.

Well, the students couldn't agree on the title for our poem. Samantha said, "Let it be 'Little Jack.' " Vicky wanted, "The Presents."

I finally said, "It is going to be titled, 'The Birthday Party.' "

I started off the poem by saying, "Little Jack went to a birthday party."

Then Vicky said, "Opened his presents and he is so excited."

That did not make sense so we all started over by saying, "Little Jack went to a birthday party."

Next, Dorrie said, "Little Jack rode a bicycle." That event had never taken place in the story. Little Jack had never ridden a bicycle.

Vicky started yelling, "Little Jack did not do that!"

She wanted to take charge and not let any of the other students participate. Naturally, the students became angry.

The students continued creating the poem, putting all sorts of ideas into their work, and not following the story. For example, Donnie said, "Little Jack rode a bike when he had delivered Little Jack's invitation to the party."

In the book, Little Jack didn't ride a bike. The mailman did. The students were getting the story characters' roles and actions all mixed up.

The lesson was a disaster. I should have done many things to prepare myself and to help my students participate in a successful postreading activity that linked two types of narrative text: fiction and poetry. I did not help my students become familiar with different types of poetry. I never read any poems to them. Evidently, the classroom teacher doesn't read poems to the students either. I should have started off by talking about group collaboration. In other words, all ideas are important and good. I should have helped the students brainstorm ideas for their poem by creating a semantic map and filling in the map with their ideas. I could have had the students work in pairs, creating as many poems as they liked. I should have written their ideas on large sheets of paper. Do you have any other suggestions for me?

1. Do you have any suggestions for Joni? _____

_____

2. How might Joni have helped her students become familiar with poetry?

_____

**Commentary #7.2A: "Confusion About Little Jack"
(by Kathleen McKenna, Middle School Teacher,
Evanston, Illinois)**

Dear Joni,

What a really impressive list of reflections you wrote for yourself about this lesson! You delved into so many possibilities for how this might have worked more effectively, including ideas about having children work cooperatively. You are a very thoughtful teacher. I offer here a couple of additional ideas for you to consider.

I always start with my objectives. What were you hoping the students would understand or be able to do when the lesson was over? Do the state, school, or national standards call for 5-year-olds to be able to discern different genres of writing? Were you hoping the students could point out the major ideas, or the important details, in the story through the postreading activity? I find that when I start from my goals and objectives I am able to plan the activities in such a way that they will work together toward the ends I have in sight.

The librarian at my school was able to get me a copy of *A Big Day for Little Jack* so I could get a sense of the story's purpose. Like all good stories for young students, this one repeats the main idea and the same line (i.e., no big person can go with Jack to the party, Mommies aren't invited, big brothers aren't invited, etc.). If your objective was to connect poetry with narrative, you might have started the group poem with a line like, "Big people aren't invited," as a way of both reinforcing one of the main ideas, eliciting a discussion about how difficult it is to go to some places alone, and trying to find words that end in *ed* for the purposes of rhyming. That way you get three goals in one: different genres, social and emotional growth, and word endings.

I'm wondering if you scaffolded the idea of poetry before reading the story. It seems to me that the students need to understand something about that form of composition (i.e., poetic "voice") before you attempt to create it. If the teacher in the classroom doesn't read poetry to her students, you might talk about some of the songs they sing. Songs are generally structured around rhymes, repetition, feet and meters, and other poetic devices. In fact, the students might have done better creating a song with words about the story to some tune they already know (e.g.,"Jack is taking Bunnikins with him, *HOOray!*").

Finally, if your objective was to employ a good postreading strategy to get at main ideas and to help your students engage in transmediation (i.e., movement between and among sign systems, such as taking something we know and reconstructing it into an art form; Leland & Harste, 1994), I have some other possibilities. The students could have planned and performed a play about the story, planned a party of their own, making birthday cards or invitations inviting stuffed animals, or written a letter to Jack to tell about a party they've attended telling whether they brought their own stuffed animal. Drawing pictures for story strips that you or they create is a time-tested device that young students love, too.

I hope you'll be reading and creating a lot more poetry with your students. It's a wonderful thing for people of all ages to do! As long as you continue to reflect so well on your own work, and plan around your goals and objectives, you'll have great fun and be an effective teacher. Good luck!

Commentary #7.2B: "Confusion about Little Jack" (by Patricia Bloem, Teacher Educator, Grand Valley State University, Allendale, Michigan)

Dear Joni,

Oh, dear. It sounds as though you had the tough experience of a lesson that flopped. But, you are doing exactly the right thing now. You are reflecting on what happened, you are figuring out why it flopped, and you are thinking through what you could have done differently. Here is an action you can take right now. Resolve how to fix the situation, and put the flop behind you. Too many preservice teachers brood about their mistakes and let them eat away at their confidence. Don't let that happen to you.

But, oh, how fun to start poetry with kindergartners! You are absolutely right to fill their ears with poetry before you ask them to write poems. Recite to them funny poems, sad poems, silly poems, any poems that you love. Say a pretty phrase aloud with a good clear image when you are doing the calendar, or helping them on with their coats and say to them, "Doesn't that sound like a poem?"

Make up a rhyming ditty about someone's shoes, so they hear that poems can rhyme, too. Tell them about a song that you heard on the radio and ask them if they know the words. Tell them that it's a poem. See how many of them can say Mother Goose poems. Read them a poem and tell them to draw a picture of what the poem makes them think of.

And then, after their ears are filled with good language, and they've caught on that poems are all around us, I would pull out a good, easy poem to use as a model. Do you know Eloise Greenfield's poems? (She's the African American poet who wrote *Honey, I Love* [1978] a wonderful poem, just right for choral reading by young children.) Greenfield and Little's poem *I Can Do It by Myself* (1987) celebrates imagination and all the things a child can imagine he or she could be (e.g., a twin, a dimple in a chin). Read it to them several times. Then start a class poem with Greenfield's first two lines followed by your students' words. I would begin the collaborative writing by asking each child to imagine something and creating one line for a group poem. Make sure that every contribution is valued.

I've just discovered the magic of Douglas Florian's poems and paintings. How about reading poems from his *A Winter Day* (1987) and his *Winter Eyes* (1999) and using them as models for class poems? After that, I'd guess that your students would be ready for more difficult tasks, perhaps poetry writing in pairs or perhaps a whole-class collaboration working from a story. You may want to model for the students how you yourself would create a poem from a picture book story, thinking aloud so that they can see your process of choosing the right words and the right images.

Have fun with it, Joni, and make sure to celebrate your students' creativity.

Case #7.3: "She Can Write About the Books We Read" (by Kristy Park)

I teach four second graders. Every week we write in journals. I write individual entries to each student based on their interests and writing instructional needs. Each student writes back to me. I noticed early in the semester that Kim did not respond to the questions I asked her in my journal entries. For example, I wrote, "Who reads to you at home?"

Kim's reply was, "I have a computer at my howse it is fun to play Becausw i have a <u>Birdy docter</u> c.d and it is fun to play this is a list of c.d's that I play <u>Dram Doll Howse</u>, <u>Birdy Dictater</u>, <u>Bridey rideing club</u>."

I noticed that Kim underlined certain words, so I asked the classroom teacher about it. She replied, "I teach students in this class to underline words they think might not be spelled in standard form. This is a good step in writing because students are responsible for monitoring their spelling and determining if they need help with certain words."

I also told the teacher, "I notice that Kim does not answer the questions I ask her in my journal entries."

The teacher said, "When students write in this class, they write what they want to write. There are no writing restrictions."

During the next few weeks we did many lessons where we connected reading and writing. My professor suggested that I write questions in my students' journals, asking them about the books we have read.

The next week I wrote to Kim, "Do you like the book <u>Elbert's bad word</u>? What book do you like better, <u>Elbert's bad word</u>,[10] or <u>The napping house</u>[11]?"

Well, Kim responded appropriately. She wrote, "I liked the book <u>Elbert's bad word.</u> I liked <u>Elbert's bad word</u> better than <u>The napping house</u>."

Kim's reply shocked me. She appropriately answered my question about two books, and she followed my modeling and underlined the book titles.

Of course, in my next entry to Kim, I asked her another question about a book we had just read. I wrote, "What was your favorite part in the book <u>Rude giants</u>?" Kim responded, "I liked the hole book and I liked the giant in <u>Rude giants</u>."[12]

My question is where do I go from here? Kim is responding to my questions about books, so I imagine I should continue asking her these types of questions. I wonder what other types of questions I should ask to promote a reading/writing connection.

1. What types of questions should Kristy ask her students to promote a reading/writing connection? _____

2. Do you agree with the classroom teacher in this case when she says, "There are no writing restrictions"?_____

Commentary #7.3A: "She Can Write About the Books We Read" (by Jane Osterman, Elementary Teacher, Oldham County, Kentucky)

Dear Kristy,

I love how you individualize literacy instruction by responding to your students in their journals. It's also a great way to strengthen the relationship

---

[10]Wood, A. (1988). *Elbert's Bad Word*. San Diego, CA: Harcourt Brace Jovanovich.

[11]Wood, A. (1984). *The Napping House*. San Diego, CA: Harcourt Brace Jovanovich.

[12]Wood, A. (1993). *Rude Giants*. San Diego, CA: Harcourt Brace Jovanovich.

you are building with each student. One thing that I noticed is that the questions you asked Kim in her journal changed over time. Initially, you asked a literal type question about reading that wasn't really related to anything you knew about Kim's background experiences (i.e., "Who reads to you at home?"). When you started to write questions about books you and Kim had read together (i.e., a shared book experience), you also asked literal questions (e.g., "Do you like the book <u>Elbert's bad word</u>? Which book do you like better <u>The napping house</u> or <u>Elbert's bad word</u>?"). But when you asked, "What was your favorite part in the book <u>Rude giants</u>?, you asked a different type of question. Not only was it open-ended, it also provided an opportunity for Kim to use higher level thinking skills because you asked her to evaluate a text. Evaluation is the highest category or level of thinking according to **Bloom's Taxonomy**[13] (1956). The move from asking Kim literal questions that require brief answers to those that require more thought and elaboration is an important one, and you've made it.

You asked where you should go from here? What do you truly want to know about each student? Personally, I wonder why Kim liked the giant in *Rude Giants* best so I would write to her in her journal, "Why did you like the giant so much?"

I also would add my own comments about what I liked about the book or what I thought about the giant. It is always worthwhile to participate in an authentic written conversation with your students rather than worrying so much about asking just the right question. This provides a great opportunity to model various conventions of print that students have yet to master, like what you did with underlining the titles of the books.

A question to consider as you think about the types of questions you are asking in their journals is "What is the purpose of the journals?" If it is to build the reading/writing connection through responding to books in writing, then you are on the right track. If it is to communicate back and forth in a meaningful way with another person, you are also headed in the right direction. However, if the purpose is much broader, like encouraging students to write for pleasure or write to express interests, thoughts, and ideas that are important, you may want to expand the topics that you ask. Remember that even though asking Kim about books seems to get her to answer your questions, you don't want her to limit her journal entries to reading responses unless this is a reading response journal specifically dedicated to that type of writing. If this is also her free-choice writing space, then you should welcome and encourage her ability to choose her own writing topic independently.

---

[13]Bloom, B. (1956). *Taxonomy of Educational Objectives: The Classification of Educational Goals: Handbook 1, Cognitive Domain*. New York: Longmans Green.

Think carefully about what was problematic for you about Kim's not answering your questions. Were the objectives of the assignment not being met when she was choosing her own topics?

Commentary #7.3B: "She Can Write About the Books We Read" (by Anita McClain, Teacher Educator, Pacific University, Oregon)

Dear Kristy,

I appreciate and admire your taking the time to respond to each of your students in individual journals! What a wonderful way to scaffold for students and individualize instruction (Vygotsky, 1986).

I agree with Jane Osterman (see Commentary #7.3A) that your teaching objectives should be clear. I assume your objective for this lesson might be to provide opportunities for students to expand their informal writing abilities and understandings about quality children's literature by responding to questions you ask in their dialogue journals. Therefore, I suggest that you try to concentrate on dialogue between you and your students and also the types or levels of questions you ask them. In addition, it might prove beneficial to put more emphasis on your part as a mentor of writing, rather than just adding comments in response to your students' writing. Encourage your students to write questions to you and answer their questions in ways that model good writing. You might help your students learn about three levels of questions. For example, consider the **Question-Answer-Relationship (QAR) strategy** devised by Raphael (1986). Raphael offered a scheme to help students learn to recognize four types of questions in accordance to where they might find the answers to the questions. The answers to right there questions are found "right there" in the text. The answers to my own questions require a response based on the reader's background knowledge, personal experiences, thinking, and ideas. The answers to think-and-search questions and author and me questions require readers to combine ideas in the text with previously acquired background knowledge (i.e., to make inferences). I caution you, however, to keep your journaling from becoming a grilling experience of questions from you and questions from students.

I have another suggestion. Before you journal with your students about the books they read and hear, why don't you structure a shared reading experience with your students followed by journal writing? Prior to having your students write in their journals, meet as a group and discuss interesting, hard to understand, and unusual aspects of the book. In this way, students will have activated their schemata for the book read or heard, and interacted with their classmates, sharing ideas prior to writing.

Here's another thought. Students might compose in their journals using a combination of print and drawings. In this way they can utilize multiple literacies. Many times students can express themselves more fully through the visual arts.

To address the words that Kim underlined in her journal entry, you might ask her why she did so. If she underlined words and book titles for spelling clarification, make sure you use these words again in your next entry to Kim. She will then see those words spelled in standard form.

When you do ask questions to students in their journals, try to encourage them to relate their personal experiences to ideas expressed in the book. For example, try open-ended, personalized questions such as "Have you ever been lonely like Gregory Cool?" (Binch, 1994), or "What would you have done if you were Gregory Cool and you were served very salty fish for breakfast?"

Remember as you plan all of your lessons to ask yourself what your objectives are and to make sure your objectives are clear to your students. Good luck! You have made a great start as a 21st-century teacher who recognizes the reading/writing connection.

REFLECTIONS AND EXPLORATIONS

1. Conduct an ERIC Document search or use a CD-ROM encyclopedia to find some definitive statistics about the number of children in the United States who live in unstable homes or harsh neighborhood conditions. Share these statistics with your teaching peers. How might participating in the visual and communicative arts help these children achieve academic success?

2. Do you read poetry? What types of poetry do you read (e.g., **cinquains, haiku,** Walt Whitman,[14] Shel Silverstein)? What are some of your favorite poems? Why do you enjoy these poems?

3. Reflect on Joni's lesson (Case #7.2). Use combinations of multiple literacies (i.e., multiple semiotic systems) to respond to Joni. For example, you might express yourself by authoring a poem, and accompanying the poem with music, or you might sketch your response.

INTEGRATING THE LITERACIES OF READING AND WRITING IN YOUR CLASSROOM: PRACTICAL APPLICATIONS

There are a number of considerations to attend to when you plan your integrated reading and writing lessons. Responding to the following questions

---

[14]The Poetry of Walt Whitman (http://www.liglobal.com/walt/waltbio.html).

will help you recognize and take into account the multitude of aspects involved as you design and organize your instruction:

1. What do you wish to accomplish with this lesson?
2. How are reading and writing used to support each other within the lesson?
3. Have you accomplished this lesson yourself? (I.e., Have you personally completed the reading and writing you will assign the students?)
4. How will you model this lesson for your students?
5. How will you motivate reluctant readers and writers?
6. How will you modify the reading and writing tasks to individualize instruction for students who need additional help and for students who are gifted readers and talented writers?
7. Will students be involved in the development of assessment instruments? If not, will they know in advance the standards by which they will be assessed?
8. How will you help your students revise and edit their writing?
9. How will you structure your time to allow for effective use of the reading and writing processes, including reading and writing?
10. If your students will be moving about the room to engage in collaborative writing or to share their work with peers, how will you efficiently move them in and out of groups?
11. What time constraints will you and your students have? (e.g., Do your students have opportunities to write continuously until they are satisfied with their work, or do you teach in an upper-grade context where students change classes every 55 minutes?)
12. Will you engage in individual writing conferences with each of your students?
13. How will you structure your time to allow for individual student/ teacher writing conferences? In Cunningham's Four Block model (P. M. Cunningham, Hall, & Defee, 1991), she recommends conducting conferences during self-selected reading time. Would her system work for you?

SUGGESTED READINGS

Graves, D. (1991). *Build a Literate Classroom.* Portsmouth, NH: Heinemann.
In this book, part of a series called "The Reading/Writing Teacher's Companion," Graves provides specific strategies for building a literate environment in classrooms. He suggests a series of actions, followed by reflection that encourages teachers to rethink learning and change their use of time so students can become lifelong readers

and writers and learners. Included are ideas about how to organize the classroom, shorten conferences, keep records, work with skills, conduct minilessons, and systematically evaluate students' progress.

Solley, B. (2000). *Writers' Workshop: Reflections of Elementary and Middle School Teachers.* Boston: Allyn & Bacon.
Written by teachers for teachers, this book offers honest, practical, firsthand perspectives of seven teachers who use the writing workshop approach. This text provides guidance, support, and encouragement for teachers in Grades 1–8.

Routman, R. (1996). *Literacy at the Crossroads: Crucial Talk About Reading, Writing, and Other Teaching Dilemmas.* Portsmouth, NH: Heinemann.
So much of what is said about education today is said by those who have never experienced the classroom from the teacher's side of the desk. In this book, Routman provides the voice of reason in what is often an unreasonable discussion. Written for teachers who need to understand the issues confronting education and the teaching of reading and writing, she clarifies the arguments and provides the background and research related to each issue. All teachers must, at some time, confront the political nature of education; this book offers suggestions for entering the conversation armed with facts and reasoned support.

Stires, S. (1991b). *With Promise: Redefining Reading and Writing for "Special" Students.* Portsmouth, NH: Heinemann.
With inclusion programs and expectations of the "least restrictive environment" for special-education students throughout the nation, teachers need good resources to help them provide students who are "at risk" with effective reading and writing instruction. Stires' book is a collection of articles about special students written by very special teachers. These teacher researchers tell their stories of building positive learning environments, confronting such issues as labeling, testing, and skills-based approaches. They bring their students to life while illuminating the learning processes of special students. You will see your own students in these pages, and you will discover the possibilities and the promise of expanding the boundaries for these students.

Wood, K. & Dickinson, T. (2000). *Promoting Literacy in Grades 4–9: A Handbook for Teachers and Administrators.* Boston: Allyn & Bacon.
This reader-friendly text is a practical reference source for teachers who want to develop the literacy abilities of students in Grades 4–9. Topics include what makes an effective literacy program, strategies for enhancing students' literacy, and the role of school principals in maintaining an effective literacy-learning environment.

Integrating the Literacies of Reading and Writing With Computer Technology

Teachers concerned with literacy instruction and achievement cannot afford to slink around the edges of . . . new ideas and practices, uncertain of their roles. They must acknowledge that encounters with technology are pervasive and, consequently, technology of all varieties is becoming commonplace.
—Blanchard (1999, p. 2)

[W]hen Y3K pundits look back on our time, they'll remember it as the Last Century of the Book. Why? As a common item of communication, artistic expression and celebrity anecdote, the physical object consisting of bound dead trees in shiny wrapper is headed for the antique heap. Its replacement will be a lightning-quick injection of digital bits into a handheld device with an ultra sharp display.
—Levy (2000, p. 96)

Information technology . . . particularly the Internet . . . can help you gain knowledge. But first you need to know how to use it. And even if you know the basics, if you're not using the Internet to its full potential, you're likely missing out.
—Goldsborough (2000, p. 14)

OVERVIEW

Michael C. McKenna
Georgia Southern University

You may think of computers as existing apart from books and literacy, as tools for learning, to be sure, but tools that do not alter our basic ideas about what literacy is. But, computers have done much more than provide a new and improved means to an age-old goal. They have changed the very nature of literacy and literate behavior.

What exactly does it mean, then, to be computer literate?[1] Some writers in the field of literacy and technology are uncomfortable with this phrase because it connotes mere knowledgeability about computers—knowing your way around hardware and software. That's part of computer literacy, certainly, but there's another dimension that we must recognize, for it profoundly influences the very nature of reading and writing and challenges a number of our traditional notions about how to foster literacy growth in our students.[2]

When a student encounters text in an electronic environment, there are fundamental differences from the print version of the same text. These differences define a new literacy, one with important implications for instruction. Reinking (1994) indicated a number of these distinctions:

1. First, electronic text is fluid and can easily move and change. Think about a letter you might compose using a word processor. When you print the letter, the text becomes fixed and unchanging. Before you print it, however, the content can be edited, new ideas can be included, old ones discarded. Even the font (i.e., shape and style of print) and size of the type can be altered. The digital signals that define your letter can be directed along wires to a recipient or onto a disk or hard drive for storage. These differences, and knowing how to take advantage of them, constitute aspects of literacy that simply did not exist a few years ago.

2. Electronic text can incorporate other media. A quick visit to the Internet and its graphic support system, the World Wide Web, will reveal that text in electronic settings usually is accompanied by flashing art, animation, audio options, and hot links to other Web sites. Such an experience is far removed from reading traditional print. It also suggests that students, in order to be literate, must develop the skills needed to act purposefully in electronic environments that offer complex choices. Students must be prepared to use the features they wish, and they must also learn to discriminate within an array of options that are potentially confusing and distracting.

3. Electronic text permits the reader to interact with it in novel ways. At one level, of course, any reading experience is interactive. Good readers, after all, employ strategies that suit their purposes. They decide what is important and what to attend to and they reflect about ideas as they read, but such interaction with text is decidedly one-sided. The text does not

[1]LeBaron, J., & Collier, C. (Eds.). (2001). *Technology in its Place: Successful Technology Infusion in Schools*. San Francisco: Jossey-Bass.

[2]Baker, E. (2001). Approaches used to integrate literacy and technology. *Reading Online*, 1–14. (http://www.readingonline.org/articles/baker/index.html)

change at all in the process. In the case of electronic text, however, the reader may take interaction a giant step further. Portions of the text might be boldfaced, deleted, amended, glossed, copied and pasted, or equipped with multimedia features.

We can respond to an everyday e-mail by interjecting our own reply at key points within the original message to us. We can prepare a report by patching together material from other sources. We can change the size of the print to accommodate our failing vision or access online pronunciations or glossary entries to help us through difficult new material. This sort of interaction can make reading a far more active process than the one students customarily use with print materials. It is up to teachers to find ways of capitalizing on this potential so that their students become more fully engaged in what they read, engaged in new and exciting ways that are redefining the notion of literacy.

4. Electronic text is often nonlinear. It allows a reader the flexibility to navigate among sources by taking nonlinear routes. This can be done, slowly, in print environments as well. Pick up a magazine, for example, and you will immediately find yourself confronted with ads, sidebars, and alternative feature articles that invite browsing and exploration. Electronic text facilitates such exploration, almost to a fault, by multiplying, sometimes exponentially, the number of choices networked together. We call these networks of linked sources **hypertexts** (see M. McKenna, in press), and the most elaborate example is the Internet. Smaller hypertexts can be created, however, such as documents equipped with online glossaries, sidebars, and other branching resources available on demand. A CD-ROM encyclopedia is a good example of a closed hypertext environment. The development of hypertext poses one of the important challenges to literacy educators, for it necessitates new reading and writing strategies. Will you be ready to help your students read and write hypertextually?

If you are inclined to believe that conventional literacy instruction based on paper, pencils, chalk, and markers is adequate, consider the wired world for which you are presumably preparing your students. In that world, computers have become indispensable. Whether or not we feel comfortable with computer technology in our classrooms, there is no denying that the world of work is increasingly computer oriented. This trend is reason enough to ask whether traditional, print-based instruction is adequate. Still another reason to embrace technology is the fact that it can simply do some things more effectively and a few things that would be downright impossible without it. Incorporating animation and audio, for example, has no counterpart in conventional writing. In short, technology can make your life easier and make you a better literacy instructor into the bargain.

WHAT DO YOU NEED TO KNOW?
HOW CAN YOU BEGIN?

As a 21st-century teacher you will want to know how technology can best be applied to foster your students' literacy growth. What do you need to know? How can you begin? If you are a novice about computer applications with respect to your own literacy, here are some suggestions for painlessly improving your expertise:

1. Choose a mentor. Nearly every school has faculty who are "into" computers. These teachers have examined software and how to apply it in classrooms. Seek them out and learn from their successes (and their mistakes).

2. Join a technology listserv. Several good ones exist and all are free. Once you've subscribed, you can pose questions or just "lurk," learning from the public conversation that you will become privy to as a subscriber. The EdTech list brings together teachers with considerable expertise in classroom technology applications (visit http://www2.h-net.msu.edu/~edweb/list.html). Another fine, less high-powered technology listserv is the Connected Teacher (http://www.classroom.com/community/email/archives/jhtml?A0=CRC). You can also locate listservs on any topic by visiting Tile Net, a powerful search tool (http://www.tile.net). You can subscribe to most listservs in digest form, meaning that you receive only one message a day, containing all of the individual postings. Many teachers prefer this arrangement. Don't be fearful about subscribing to a listserv. It's easy to unsubscribe if you find it's not for you.

3. Do some reading about computer technology. Many nontechnical books are available for teachers, and their authors tend to assume only a modest level of knowledgeability. It's easier reading than you might imagine! Here are two excellent titles to get you started:

- Leu, D., Jr., & Leu, D. (2000). *Teaching With the Internet: Lessons From the Classroom* (3rd ed.). Norwood, MA: Christopher-Gordon.
- Wepner, S., Valmont, W., & Thurlow, R. (2000). *Linking Literacy and Technology: A Guide for K–8 Classrooms*. Newark, DE: International Reading Association.

4. Explore your server. Spend some time exploring the many programs housed within your school's file server. Chances are your classroom is part of a local area network (LAN), making a wide range of software available from a central location.

5. Create a center. Establish a center containing one or more computers and encourage students to rotate through it during center time or at some

other designated period. Experiment with different applications. Keep a journal with notes to yourself about what works and what doesn't.

6. Take a class. Sign up for a graduate class in computer applications, preferably one that is oriented toward literacy instruction. Most universities now offer such courses, and many school districts and regional agencies offer the staff-development equivalent of a credit-bearing course.

Once you acquire some expertise in operating and understanding computers, you are ready to move forward to considering how you can link print-based literacy lessons with computer applications and software. Teachers today face a variety of software applications that can be difficult to select among and to integrate effectively into day-to-day instruction. An important first step is to acquaint yourself with some of the major applications. They can help you effectively integrate computer technology into your daily literacy instruction. For example, consider the following:

• **Word Processors.** These programs allow students to produce their best work in ways that make the steps of revising and editing much easier than with conventional pencil-and-paper instruction. In addition, word-processing software for students now routinely provides the option of incorporating other media into compositions. Still photos, other types of graphics, videos, and audio bring new dimensions to what it means to "write."

• **Tutorials and Drill-and-Practice.** A variety of sophisticated programs for improving reading skills is now available to teachers. Knowing about the best of these and how to make the most productive use of them is increasingly important. Tutorials are designed to introduce new skills, drill-and-practice software to reinforce those introduced by the teacher.

• **Integrated Learning Systems.** When tutorials and drill-and-practice software are combined in a comprehensive system together with an assessment component, the result is called an integrated learning system, or ILS. The learning experiences are structured so that students enter a progressive sequence at their own level. The software then prescribes further activities based on how well the student performs. The ILS is therefore a self-contained system and its use raises questions about the teacher's role and how to coordinate what students experience through the ILS with the kind of classroom instruction they receive.

• **Teacher Utilities.** These programs allow teachers to more easily do the things they must do in order to deliver high-quality instruction. With the aid of utilities, for example, teachers can create materials, keep student records, and locate useful resources.

- **The Internet.** The ever-expanding electronic network among computers, called the Internet, already serves many teachers and students with a means of contacting others, acquiring information, and interacting with online software. Originally, the term Internet referred to the textual side of this network. When we add graphics and sound, we think of the result as the **World Wide Web** (Bolter, 1998). The distinction has blurred, however, and the words *web* and *Internet* seem to have become interchangeable in common usage.

Becoming familiar with all of these applications is vital, and previewing software available in your school or college lab is an important first step. A related action involves turning the Internet into a teacher utility by locating Web sites that can enhance your teaching. An excellent annotated list of literacy-related sites was compiled by M. McKenna, Stratton, B. McKenna, and Hanak (2000) and can be found at http://www.readingonline.org. (Click on the Index to locate the article.) This listing organizes nearly 200 sites into 16 categories, including Links to Teachers and Kids, Children's Literature and Teacher Resources, Children's Book Awards, Hands-on Sites for Kids, Author Sites, Exceptional Students, Literacy-Related Organizations, Online Journals, Government Sites, and many others.

A second way of harnessing the Internet is to join *the* Reading Teacher (RT) listserv, which puts you in contact with hundreds of reading educators across the country. The RT list was the brainchild of Don Leu, but has "migrated" to IRA (International Reading Association) headquarters. Use these directions to subscribe:

1. Send an e-mail message to listserv@bookmark.reading.org.
2. In the message window, type SUBSCRIBE RTEACHER (plus your full name).
3. Be certain your message does not contain any other information. Disable your signature option if you have one so that this is not included at the end of your message.
4. Send your message.
5. You will soon receive a confirmation message. Within 48 hours, follow the directions given to confirm your subscription.

Instructions for subscribing also can be found at this site: http://www.reading.org/publications/rt/rteacherdirections.html. On the listserv you can pose questions about materials, methods, and even specific students. Or you can just "lurk," reading the messages posted by others. Remember that you can subscribe to a digest form of the RT listserv if you find that receiving 10 to 15 messages per day (the average) is too much. It's also easy to unsubscribe if you decide that the RT list is not for you.

CASES AND COMMENTARIES

Case #8.1: "Having Computers in Classrooms Isn't Always the Answer" (by Victoria Cooper)

I work with seven fourth graders every week, helping them comprehend content text material. We always link reading lessons with writing, and connect our lessons to the arts and technology. Two weeks ago, after completing a chapter about the state of Mississippi, I decided to have my students create an imaginary brochure, describing the interesting sights and activities in the state. First, I had the students create their brochures on paper. Then, all eight of us (seven students and me) sat around the three computers in the room. As three students typed their brochures, the other four watched. Can you already figure out that I had problems? Here is what happened. First, the four students who were watching their peers type got bored and began to disturb the other students in the room. Then my professor came in to observe, and she looked at my students transferring their writing to the computer. "Why did you have them compose first on paper?" she asked.

I had to reply, "I don't know. I never thought of having the students compose directly at the computer."

Then, my professor looked carefully at the students' writing. Here is how Mary's brochure looked on the computer screen:

1) We can go swimming.
2) We have beaches.
3) It is warm here.

"Why is Mary typing a list, rather than a complete descriptive paragraph?" asked my professor.

Again, I had no clever answer.

"Next week, I'll do a demonstration lesson about the processes of prewriting, writing, and postwriting," my professor said. "I'll use a strategy titled 'Steps to Independent Writing.' It helps writers figure out what they know about a writing topic and it helps writers structure cohesive paragraphs" (Richards, 2002).

The following week, after learning the steps in the strategy, I presented it to my students. They loved it! First, they created a semantic map of their ideas and then they transformed the ideas in their semantic maps into category columns (e.g., ideas that were related to one another were grouped together, such as all of the interesting places to visit in Mississippi).

Well, we were ready now to get to the computers. I left four of my students sitting in a semicircle. Their task was to read the next chapter in their book.

I took the remaining three students with me to the computers. I expected them to really *zoom* along with their writing. *Wrong!!* Each student typed in a laborious, slow way. They used only one hand and rested their other hand in their laps. Two just used their index fingers to type. "Come on," I said. "Let's get going. We need to move along so the others can type, too."

"We can't type," said Jennie.

"Why can't you type?" I asked. "You all go to the computer lab and get 45 minutes of computer instruction every day."

"Yeah, but we don't learn how to type," replied Carey.

Well, these incidents have let me know that there is more to linking literacy lessons with computers than just sitting kids down in front of computer monitors. Using the computers actually slowed up my students' efforts at composing brochures. How do other teachers handle this?

1. How might Vicki accomplish her goals for her students' computer-literacy development? _____

_____

2. After reading this case, what steps will you take to ensure that computer-technology-literacy activities in your classroom go smoothly? _____

_____

Commentary #8.1A: "Having Computers in Classrooms Isn't Always the Answer" (by Terri Austin, Elementary Head Teacher, Fairbanks, Alaska)

Dear Victoria,

For the past 2 years, I've used a well-known typing program with my fifth- and sixth-grade students that claims guaranteed results. However, I have only seen a small bit of improvement in my students' keyboarding abilities. I think there are many reasons for this dilemma. Students in the middle grades are so used to using computers in their own way, it's hard to get them to convert to efficient typing methods. For example, many of my students here in Alaska are connected to the rest of the world through e-mail. The "hunt-and-peck" typing method works for them because their e-mail messages are so short. Most of the games they play on the computer don't call for typing ability either. Therefore, I think many students do not see the need to learn keyboarding other than for school-based writing. Consider, too, that everything young people do in this, the 21st century, has to be fast, fun, and immediately gratifying. Learning to type is laborious, time-consuming, and let's face it, somewhat dull compared to playing those marvelous computer games.

James Lerman, a teacher in New York City, noted that the students he works with need to become proficient in keyboarding by the fourth grade because it is "an important skill that one needs in order to take maximum advantage of technology" (in Westreich, 2000, p. 23). Donald and Debbie Leu (1997) concurred and stated that "students need to learn keyboarding at a young age to prevent the development of bad habits" (p. 61). However, Leu and Leu asked the following questions that teachers need to consider: (a) Is keyboarding beyond the fine motor control of young typists? (b) How should keyboarding be taught? (c) Is teaching keyboarding worth the time or will students lose interest? (d) What is the school district policy for teaching keyboarding? (p. 61).

Currently, I am still using the "guaranteed results" typing program in my classroom and my students still compose using a pencil. The majority of my students also use just one or two fingers to type. Other than standing over them to make them use proper finger positions or scheduling a daily typing class, I am leaning toward scheduling daily keyboarding sessions, but I am at a loss as to how to make this change in my daily schedule. Although keyboarding lessons are a means to an end (like learning multiplication tables), this type of instruction is time-consuming, and it is not linked to any sort of authentic study. However, I believe that keyboarding practice will enhance the quality of students' narrative and expository writing by facilitating their revisions (Leu & Leu, 2000).

The other issue attached to your question is the issue of computer use as a tool for a writing lesson. When I incorporate the computer into our composing lessons, I make myself think about every bit of knowledge a student needs to know to accomplish the task. Using the computer requires a tremendous amount of information. I have found that some of my students didn't know how to space punctuation. They also didn't know how to indent the beginnings of paragraphs. I now delineate every step my students need to know before they begin to compose on the computer.

Another concern with computers that you haven't addressed involves technical knowledge of computers. Sooner or later, if you work with computers in your classroom, something technical in nature will go awry. Students can do the most interesting things on computers, and it takes me a long time to undo them. This is the biggest problem for me. Do I know enough to troubleshoot the problems that arise? And, if I can't fix the problem, do I have a back-up plan for those students who are on the crashed computer? What will the other students do while I'm working on the computer? Is it worth my time to try to fix the problem now, or would it be better to move in another direction?

In closing, I want to say that I have not fully answered your concerns. What I have tried to do, though, is to help you recognize that technology can be fantastic, but without trained teachers, explicit school board policies regarding keyboarding instruction, and an ever-ready support system to "fix" computers that have become damaged or are out of order, there will be frustrations. You are lucky that you are receiving up-to-date instruction now so that you know how to incorporate computer literacy as part of your students' overall multiple-literacy development.

Commentary #8.1B: "Having Computers in Classrooms Isn't Always the Answer" (by George Hunt, Teacher Educator, University of Edinburgh, Scotland)

Dear Victoria,

First of all, congratulations on your enthusiasm, perseverance, and willingness to adapt your teaching in light of what we now know about multiple literacies. Secondly, you are not alone when you have problems with computers in the classroom. Many teachers will recognize the disappointment you felt at the slow progress and pitfalls involved in helping your students make a transfer from print to electronic literacy.

Your objective appears to have been an appropriate one: creating a sense of pride, excitement, and authorship in your fourth graders by helping them to produce a professional-looking word-processed product. However, you came across two big problems encountered by many of us in introducing computers to elementary classrooms. First, there just aren't enough computers to go round, so students who were waiting their turn to type naturally become restless. "Classrooms in the United States rarely have more than five computers available for students' use" (Colburn, 2000b, p. 8). Second, word processing requires secretarial keyboard skills that do not, and maybe should not, have a dedicated slot on most elementary school timetables (see Leu & Leu, 1997, p. 61). Now it would be easy to say that we should keep our hopes high and our funding campaigns active until the day when there is a computer at every student's desk, loaded with the kind of high-quality and reliable speech recognition software that will make keyboard skills redundant. However, we all have a lot of teaching time ahead of us before that day arrives.

In suggesting ways forward, I would invite you to consider the distinctive contribution that electronic communication can make to literacy. We have all felt the excitement of seeing our work in print for the first time, and it has clearly been your intention to bestow some of that excitement on your fourth graders, but perhaps your lesson had more creative potential than simply offering word processing as an equally laborious alternative to handwriting.

I would propose that the essence of electronic composition is in the opportunities it affords for showing students how their imaginative oral language can be rapidly transformed into print, then subjected to creative restructuring. Word-processing and desktop-publishing programs give the writer unprecedented power of text mobility through cutting and pasting, dragging and dropping, ease of deletion and expansion, instant access to thesauri, and formatting of fonts, layout, and illustrations (i.e., multiple ways of showing what one knows). It can offer novice writers like your students a visible interactive model of the composing process itself, but only if they are liberated from the secretarial demands of typing. In my opinion, the best way to introduce students to composing on the computer is through the traditional whole-language method of shared writing.

Imagine a session employing your professor's recommended "Steps to Independent Writing" strategy (Richards, 2002b). Students' semantic maps and category columns are created orally and simultaneously translated into large bold print by you working at a keyboard while a teaching monitor displays the emerging text in exactly the same way as a flip chart or chalkboard would in a conventional writing lesson. Teacher-led discussion can then guide the composition of complete descriptive paragraphs if descriptive paragraphs are what you and your students think a brochure about Mississippi should contain. You also could consider alternate types of presentations. For example, Mary's rather dry fact list could be transformed before her eyes and at her prompted dictation, into punchy, bulleted invitations to: * swim in Mississippi's historical river; * bask on its beautiful beaches; and * soak up wonderful warmth. You could then present Mary with a font menu from which she could select the style, size, and color in which to present these invitational brochures, and a clip-art folder or graphics kit to provide illustrations.

The point I am making is that computer technology is new for your fourth graders and is one in which they need the same type of scaffolded instruction they have received in print literacy. They need you to model all of these technology processes for them, just as you model new reading comprehension and writing strategies for them. Perhaps you need to learn a bit more about how to make the best use of computer technology. That's OK. Most of us need to learn more about how best to promote our own and our students' computer literacy.

Case #8.2: "I Didn't Expect This!" (by Karen Breland)

First, my fifth graders and I completed the text chapter on the heritage and culture of the Mississippi Natchez Trace. We read about the Choctaw Indians and viewed photographs of Native-American artifacts, like tomahawks and flint arrow points. The text also discussed how wagons were pulled by mules 100 years ago. We used the **SQ3R strategy** (Robinson, 1961[3]), and the students really did well turning the subtitles and first sentence of every paragraph into questions. Surprisingly, they didn't think that the strategy was

[3]Robinson, F. (1961). *Effective Study*. New York: Harper & Row.

too tedious or boring. I had heard that this strategy is effective because it helps readers remember what they have read. But, some students don't like SQ3R because it requires them to carefully read and reread informational text. Consequently, it slows down their reading time.

After we completed the chapter, I assembled my group of eight students around the only computer in the classroom. I had brought in what I thought was a wonderful interactive CD-ROM video. It depicted horses native to the American West. The video is designed so that viewers can manipulate the horses' tails, hooves, movements, and so on, and the scenery, such as barns, trees, mountains, pastures, and fences. The students loved it and we stayed at the computer for about 25 minutes. Only later did I find out that there were concerns about my linking the content of the text with a computer activity.

When the lesson was over, the classroom teacher asked me, "Didn't you realize that the other students in the room were angry because they didn't get to use the computer?"

She also said, "You were on the computer too long. Your students needed to be reading." Then she told me, "I think that the *game* you brought in had nothing to do with the text chapter."

Well, I have to rethink everything about the lesson. I know that my students absolutely loved the computer venture. It was the very first time I ever linked a reading lesson with technology and I thought the connection helped to reinforce what my students read in the chapter. It also helped my students visualize horses and their surroundings. And, I noticed that the students who had some difficulties reading the text especially were enthralled with manipulating the pictures on the computer screen. What went wrong?

1. What went wrong with Karen's lesson?_____

_____

2. What do you think Karen did right? Why?_____

_____

Commentary #8.2.A: "I Didn't Expect This!"
(by Camille Blachowicz, Teacher Educator,
National-Louis University, Illinois)

Dear Karen,

Congratulations for trying to help your students become strategic readers by teaching them the SQ3R strategy (Robinson, 1961). You also worked hard to integrate computer technology into your literacy lesson. First, let me comment on the reading strategy part of your lesson. You've hit on a big issue with strategy instruction. Some students (usually good readers) already have a good repertoire of strategies for approaching content text.

Going through the motions as if they were learning a new approach slows them down and makes them angry. I've even had students say, "Dr. B, can't we just *go* ahead and read? We know what to do." And, these students do know what to do.

Other students just want to whiz through a text and get it done without thinking much about being strategic. One way to approach this is to differentiate instruction. If you think all your students don't need to learn a reading comprehension strategy, you may want to structure small learning groups so that you can individualize reading instruction according to students' instructional needs.

As for the computer issue, you have encountered an educational "biggie." Isn't it interesting to note that as we learn how to teach for multiple literacies in the 21st century, we also must solve new teaching problems? In this case, when you didn't have enough computers for all students in the group, it was almost like having one pencil for all of them!

You might try this teaching idea. I have found that I can place three students at one computer. One student deals with the keyboard and mouse; one student keeps the group on task (I find a task sheet can be helpful); a third student is the secretary and records what facts and information the group discovers. Time limits also help (e.g., 20 minutes on the computer), as do differentiated assignments: One group of students works at the computer; a second group uses the encyclopedia; a third group goes to the library to find more information using multiple texts, formats, and genres; a fourth group employs their visual aptitudes to represent what they know through sketching and drawing. Following these group activities, I engage students in a cooperative jigsaw activity (Buehl, 2001; Johnson, Johnson, & Holubec, 1990) where each small group investigates a particular topic and then shares what they have discovered. I alternate group activities the following day.

One significant final issue you need to think about is your selectivity of computer activities and use of time. Is moving the tails on horses really what is going to help your kids become better readers? Of course, sometimes it is just good to do something fun in the classroom, but spending a lot of time on an activity like this is questionable, as your mentor teacher pointed out. Maybe having a bunch of resources on the Choctaw Indians, some books and maps of the Mississippi, and having students complete an inquiry **I-Chart** (i.e., a large chart where students record and compare ideas presented in their core text and ideas from other sources) (J. Hoffman, 1992) would be both fun and a better learning experience. Brainstorm some categories related to the questions of your SQ3R and see which group can find information to fill in the chart.

Successful strategy instruction, use of time, selection of meaningful learning activities, and working within the limits of your technology resources are critical issues in today's classrooms. You have made a good first step in teaching multiple literacies and reflecting about what parts of the lesson went well and what components you might like to change. The fact that you are interested in making technology a part of this process is great. Technology is the "big child" of education these days. But, like the old Polish proverb, "Little children, little problems; big children, big problems." Just remember, plan each of your lessons carefully. Responding to the questions at the end of chapters 4–12 in this text will help you predetermine how to structure your multiple-literacy lessons. Keep the open and reflective attitude you have now and you will continue to grow as a teacher.

Commentary #8.2.B: "I Didn't Expect This!" (by Kathleen McKenna, Middle School Teacher, Evanston, Illinois)

Dear Karen,

Bravo for using the important SQ3R (Robinson, 1961) strategy to build your students' expository reading skills. When I want my students to learn a new strategy, I always call it by a big, sophisticated name and explain to them that they are going to engage in metacognition (i.e., thinking about their thinking to learn about how they learn). Imagine how thrilled they are to know that they'll be working at the high end of Bloom's Taxonomy (Anderson & Sosniak, 1994; Bloom, 1956), doing things that only older people are supposed to know and do! I do not mince words with my students or try to bring down thinking to their level. I tell them that to be good thinkers and learners they have to have multiple strategies for decoding and translating everything they read and for connecting to what they already know to create their own new knowledge. This technique really empowers my students to take responsibility for their own learning.[4]

One of my professors taught me to expand the SQ3R strategy to S(PH)Q3R. Skim everything, especially the pictures and headings (i.e., the PH), then do the questioning, reading, reviewing and rereading. He has students walk through every possible resource in the chapter of a textbook so they use every opportunity to activate prior knowledge, connect to what they're reading, and understand it thoroughly. From that standpoint, I think the use of the CD-ROM was a good idea. In other words, you were trying to help your students approach what they were learning from as many angles as possible to make sense of it.

What if you had given them 10 minutes on the computer with the interactive horses *before* the reading? Then, the video could have served as an anticipatory set that helped your students relate to the topic by connecting new ideas to their own life experiences (see Hunter, 1994). That might have

---

[4]Hunter, M. (1994). *Mastery Teaching.* Thousand Oaks, CA: Corwin Press.

whetted their appetites for information on the Choctaws, expanded their knowledge base prior to reading, given your use of the computer a more objective base, and satisfied your mentor teacher's desire for you to use less time and give other students a chance at the computer. Furthermore, if your students had then done very well with the SQ3R, you might have rewarded them with extra time at the computer with the horses' tails later in the day.

When I am working with student teachers, I always ask them to hold their overriding objective(s) for lessons or units in mind when they plan or engage in any activities with the students. You might ask yourself, "What was my objective in teaching this lesson from the chapter?" If the answer is, "To understand the social systems of the Choctaws and interrelations of the Native Americans with their surroundings," then using the CD-ROM on horses has an important historical and geographical purpose. However, unless you or the students make that connection explicit, your mentor teacher is correct; the use of the CD-ROM does not seem completely worthwhile.

There seems to me to be another issue here as well. It appears that your mentor teacher did not see your lesson plan beforehand or did not understand its objectives completely. Thus, after class was over, she had two objections: other students being disappointed at the amount of time your group used the computers and the appropriateness of the CD-ROM with your lesson. You need to make sure that you clear all your plans ahead of time with your classroom teacher and your university supervisor so you all agree about what will happen, and why and how it will happen. And, most important, you should be writing your lesson plans with objectives clearly stated. That way you can continue to be reflective about whether or not your lessons, with all their attached activities, are working to help students connect to the important goals of the learning.

Case #8.3: "Blank Screens" (by Melinda Brown)

When I met my second-grade students' classroom teacher, one of my first questions was, "Do you use the computers in your room and access the Internet very often?" To my surprise she answered, "Not very often."

Of course, I decided to link my print-based literacy lessons with computer-technology-literacy activities as often as I could. Therefore, as a postreading activity last week, I planned to help my students find information on the Internet about the author of our story. From day one, two fully-equipped computers were in the classroom, and I wanted to make good use of them.

As I was setting up my supplies for the lesson, I told the teacher that we would be using the Internet. She said matter-of-factly, "The computers are out, but I have a set of encyclopedias."

I asked, "Why aren't the computers working?"

She answered, "I don't know. I only complete a form and turn it into the office. They handle it from there. It's not just me either. Three or four other teachers can't use their computers either. They've been out for a week or longer."

I went to the office to inquire about the problem, and the secretary said, "I'm not familiar with that particular concern, but a man comes to the school once every other week and works on computer difficulties. It sounds like a wiring problem if four computers are out."

I was really upset because I did not have a back-up for a postreading strategy. I did not know what to tell the students. Should I have tried to look up the author in the encyclopedia? I doubt if I could have found the information. I was in a panic, but I did not want my students to know that I was upset. Should I have tried to "plug in" another postreading strategy?

Reflecting on my dilemma, I could have asked the classroom teacher if we could go to another teacher's room and use the computers. I could have gone to the school library. I bet they have computers there. A little prior planning on my part would have saved the end of the lesson and kept me from a panic attack.

1. What would you have done in Melinda's situation? _____

_____

2. Who are the people involved in this case and what roles do they play?

_____

_____

Commentary #8.3A: "Blank Screens"
(by Jane Percival, Head Elementary Teacher,
Haydenville, Massachusetts)

Hello Melinda,

As a longtime K–8 classroom teacher, I, too, have been in situations when the materials or physical space on which my lesson plans relied have not been there. Just like you, during those teaching moments, panic was usually the first feeling I experienced. I have found it helpful to breathe deeply a few times, focus on what I have available, and make a "midflight correction." For example, in your computer technology glitch, I might have asked the students to gather in a circle. I might hold up the book that we just read together and review its contents. Then, I might ask my students what they could guess about the author of the book from its contents. I would write their responses on an easel or board in a column headed "Best Guesses." In a second column, labeled "Clues," I would list their reasons for their responses. In a third column, titled "Questions," I would write what questions they have about the author and for the author. Depending on the time available and the children's interests, I might do any of the following:

- Reread the book to focus more on what we are learning about the author from what the author has written.
- Read a second book by the author and see if we can find more clues about him or her.
- Determine what type of resources might help us find answers to our questions (e.g., encyclopedia, Internet, letter to author, interview of the school librarian).

As you can see, this "midflight correction," among other things, provides me with time to gather my composure and adapt my plan, builds on prior instruction, and helps me assess what the children know about researching using a variety of multiple semiotic systems.

At the end of the teaching day, my next step is always to reflect upon my instruction and its effectiveness. I then decide what I might keep and what I might change if reteaching the same lesson. For example, in a situation in which I didn't have the computer on which my lesson relied, I would ask myself questions, such as the following:

1. Did I communicate with all school personnel who use the computer and are responsible for its use and working effectiveness?
2. Did I plan for a "worst-case scenario" (i.e., What will I do as a postreading activity if the computer does not work?)?
3. Did I ascertain ahead of time if the computer was working?

In spite of all of my years of K–12 teaching, I still find myself in situations like yours, Melinda, especially when I rely on new technologies. I have found that integrating any technology into the classroom always requires a back-up plan, just in case. For example, what might I do if an overhead projector's bulb burns out in the middle of instruction or the VCR rejects the taped interview with noted children's author Eric Carle that students are excited to see and hear, or the camcorder cannot be used for an animation project because its electrical plug doesn't fit the classroom outlets, and so forth.

Now, what might you do if you were a classroom teacher in a school where there is technology support personnel available to you and your colleagues only every other week? For example, would you work with other teachers to apply for a grant to fund increased technical support? Could you contact the local high school to find students with technical expertise to do some community service in your school? Could you contact a local computer repair company to ask if they might loan technicians to the school once a week to support students' computer literacy?

What might you do when you are a full-time teacher with just two computers in your classroom for 20 or more students? For instance, would you contact local industries about their donating old computers when they update their system? Might parents have computers that they are no longer using but that would be excellent for word processing? What approaches have other teachers in your school taken to make a few computers benefit the learning of all the children? What have teachers in other schools accomplished in similar circumstances?

Remember that although utilizing instructional technology in the classroom is challenging, it is also rewarding. You apparently have experienced those rewards because you chose to build students' use of the Internet into your literacy plan. In addition, you tried to use technology as a tool to do that which would be difficult to do in any other way.

I hope you continue to be enthusiastic about integrating technology into your instruction. Perhaps your classroom teacher has had many experiences that did not result in positive learning experiences for her students. Maybe that is why she did not seem more enthusiastic about integrating technology into her everyday instruction.

Commentary #8.3B: "Blank Screens" (by Katherine Perez, Teacher Educator, St. Mary's College, California)

Dear Melinda,

The dilemma you face in your second-grade classroom is a concern that many teachers now experience. Sometimes in our zeal to infuse technology into the literacy curriculum, it becomes glaringly apparent that sufficient resources are not available. In your case, it seems that the classroom teacher does not utilize technology often, and may even lack interest or expertise in this area. Considering this classroom teacher factor, it is important to check out the viability of technology resources before you invest time in planning a lesson that may not be successful. This entails checking out the hardware and software prior to teaching the lesson and discussing the use of technology with your classroom teacher.

One of the most important factors to consider is your students. How familiar are they with these two unused or underused computers in the class? This may need to be the first lesson you offer to your students—how to use the computers and what information can be gleaned, given the software in your classroom. You need to investigate these areas first before you integrate literacy lessons with computer activities. Here are some tips for implementation:

1. Find out about the computers in your classroom (i.e., Do they work? What software is available?).

2. Investigate the computers in the school library (e.g., Can you operate them? Will the librarian be in the library? How long is the travel time from your classroom to the library?).

3. What classroom management and grouping plans have you shared and practiced with your students?

4. What plans have you made so that all of your students will have access to the computers during the lesson?

5. What will the rest of your students be doing when they are not working on the computers?

6. What prior experiences do your students have in using computers?

7. What software is available to you and your students?

8. Are you familiar with the software installed in the computers?

In this era of multiple literacies, consider differentiating your lesson, so that you would have an array of optional activities to extend the comprehension of your students. It is problematic to rely exclusively on the use of computers for any lesson.

Remember, you want *all* of your students actively engaged in the literacy process. Therefore, I would definitely plan other postreading activities. I would not depend on the encyclopedia. Oftentimes they are outdated and probably would not list meaningful information about individual authors. Why not find the author's address (available through the publisher) and have students write a letter to the author, questioning them about the characters, settings, problems, themes, and so on. Another option that you mentioned was to go to another teacher's classroom to see if their computers work. This would be disruptive to both classes, and should be avoided.

The essence of my advice to you is this: Get to know the resources available to you thoroughly in advance of the lesson, plan optional activities for students to choose from after the reading has occurred to foster more interaction, and support your classroom teacher to feel more comfortable in the use of computers in the classroom.

Case #8.4: "Cannot Reconnect—Server Failure" (by Patti Alexander)

I teach a multiage group of kindergarten students. We were reading the story *If the Dinosaurs Came Back* (Most, 1995) and a word in the story was *skyscrapers*. Instead of using the word *skyscrapers* in a sentence, I asked the students if they knew what a skyscraper was (first mistake—I should have continued to use the word in meaningful sentences until my students understood). Clayton said, "I know, it's a big machine that scrapes clouds from the sky."

Because these students live in south Mississippi, they had never seen a skyscraper. I tried to explain. "Skyscrapers are tall, tall buildings in large cities."

"You mean like a casino?" Haley asked. (We have casinos in South Mississippi so Haley knew about them.)

I laughed and explained, "Skyscrapers are located in big cities, like New York, Dallas, and Houston."

The students just stared at me. They didn't have any idea about what I was saying. I suddenly thought, "We'll go find skyscraper pictures on the Internet."

I was unfamiliar with the class's computer set-up, so it took me a few minutes to familiarize myself with the system. As I worked, the students climbed into their cubbies and wrestled.

I finally got the Internet browser up, typed in "New York City," and hit the search button. I found a Web site that was a photo gallery of New York City. I also discovered that this computer was *slow!* While I was waiting for the photos to download, I completely lost my students' attention. They were messing with the other computers and drifting around the room. At last, the photos came up. "Come see what I've got," I said.

All of the students came running over only to see thumbnail-sized pictures that were hard to distinguish. I finally found a photograph of the Empire State Building, and the students were impressed by its size. "Is that the biggest building in the whole world?" asked Trevor.

"No," I replied, "There is a bigger one in Chicago. It's the Sears Tower."

Of course, the students wanted to see it, so I typed in "Chicago" and hit the search button. Two seconds later the screen went blank. I panicked, wondering what I'd done to the computer. Haley started yelling, "Miss Patti broke the computer."

The other students picked up the chant. I was frantic! I shut down the computer and started it right back up again. When it came "alive," I tried to get the Internet again, but a box saying, "cannot reconnect—server failure," kept coming up on the screen.

What I should have done was familiarize myself with the computer before the lesson. I am used to a Windows operating system and this was a Macintosh. After this incident, the classroom teacher told me that the computer we were using is notoriously slow and frequently crashed. If I had told her about my lesson, she would have forewarned me. I also should have anticipated that the students would not know what a skyscraper was. I should have been prepared with photographs and books about large cities and skyscrapers.

1. Do you think Patti is too hard on herself? Why or why not? _____

_____

2. How might Patti have "saved" the lesson? _____

_____

Commentary #8.4A: "Cannot Reconnect—Server Failure"
(by Ann-Sofie Selin, Elementary Teacher,
Abu/Turku, Finland)

Dear Patti,

Thank you for giving us the opportunity to "live" your lesson with you. I think it is most important to put oneself at risk to promote professional understanding and growth. Your lesson offers all of us a "real life" experience for us to reflect upon and consider. In my professional portfolio I have similar stories turned into successes by the thinking that came out of them. You have commented on crucial points of the lesson where you could have changed the outcome by choosing another path, an important insight, Patti. I do hope you continue keeping a journal—maybe in dialogue with a colleague.

Obviously the computer got both you and the students off track. I don't think you will face the same problem again. You now know the importance of checking out the technology in advance.

In your story, Patti, there are so many comments made by the students that I want to talk about. I'm picturing you with a multiage group around you reading the dinosaur book. You get into a discussion about skyscrapers and your students have no mental images of a skyscraper. You work on finding them a picture to help them, but lose quite a few students during the process.

I would turn the students' questions back to them. Donald Graves (1983) taught me to catch students where their realities are and help them build from there. For example, Clayton explained a skyscraper by saying, "I know, it's a big machine that scrapes clouds from the sky."

You might have responded, "Clayton, you have figured out that a skyscraper reaches out to the sky. Good for you, but it's not a machine but a very tall . . ." and someone will probably say "building."

"You mean like a casino?" Haley asked.

"Yes, like a casino, Haley," I would respond. (As you say, Patti, there are casinos in South Mississippi, so your students had a good deal of schemata for them.) In fact, when I traveled from Finland to the United States to study, I saw tall casino buildings in Atlantic City and they looked like skyscrapers to me. So, Haley's answer is not that far off the mark. Your next response might have been, "Yes, Haley, there are many big buildings and casinos are big. What's special about a skyscraper is that it goes up so high. It is so tall that when you stand beside it and look up, it seems to be continuing all the way to the sky."

Now, about your third situation, Patti. You say that your students climbed into their cubbies and wrestled. Do you have group management rules that you talk about daily with your students? Do you follow the rules? Are you fair, firm, and consistent? Are there consequences for your students when they act inappropriately? You needed to call your students back to order so you could go on with the lesson. Once you had your students' attention, you might have asked them, "How can we learn about what a skyscraper is?"

I always get fantastic ideas from my students when I turn the problem over to them. For example, the next time your computer crashes in front of your students ask them, "What should I do now?" and I'll bet someone will come up with a good solution like, "Draw us a skyscraper, Miss Patti," or "Let's go use the computer in the library."

In closing, let me summarize: (a) Build on your students' responses; (b) check out your technology equipment prior to a lesson; (c) always use your classroom management scheme; (d) rely on your students for innovative and practical suggestions.

Commentary #8.4B: "Cannot Reconnect—Server Failure" (by Timothy Rasinski, Teacher Educator, Kent State University, Ohio)

Hello Patti,

Your compelling story helps us see the importance of being prepared for teaching and the importance of both vocabulary and technology in students' learning. Today's teachers have more to learn and consider than ever before. In addition, today's teachers have to be more prepared and have more to prepare than in previous centuries.

Looking back at my own teaching in elementary and middle school, as well as at the university level, my greatest teaching difficulties came when I was not as prepared as I should have been. And, students' learning was often hampered by unresolved misconceptions about key ideas that were presented in text.

I think you understand now just how important it is to be as prepared as possible for teaching. To your credit, you had anticipated that *skyscraper* might be a difficult word. What you didn't realize at the time was just how difficult the concept would be for your students. This certainly was a teachable moment, but being unfamiliar with the resources at your disposal in the classroom, and the problem with your computer, you may have wanted to defer your presentation to the following day. Then, you would have time to think through the problem and mustered sufficient resources to help the students fully understand the concept.

One key to learning is to have as many students as possible engaged in the learning, not just one or two. This could have been accomplished by asking students to ask their parents what they know about skyscrapers and to report back to school on the next day. You also might have asked if your students had personal computers at home so they could investigate the concept of skyscrapers. This would have given you the time you needed to think through the problem, gotten every student involved in the problem, and gotten parents involved in their child's learning.

The skyscraper concept itself is a challenging one because of its metaphorical nature. **Metaphors** can be difficult to understand as people often interpret them literally as your student, Clayton, did. Thus, in addition to speaking directly to the meaning of skyscraper and sharing responses gleaned from home, I think it may have been worthwhile to discuss with your students why and how the term *skyscraper* may have been coined. Certainly skyscrapers do not literally scrape or touch the sky. However, viewed from a historical context, a little over a century ago no building was taller than a few stories. Yet, during the 20th century, buildings of immense height began to be built. Therefore, it is not difficult to see how a person looking up at these buildings and comparing them with the buildings that had preceded them might want to comment that they almost seemed to scrape the clouds and sky.

Perhaps the most important lesson we can all take from your teaching case is that good teachers learn from experience. Teaching is a complex act with many interrelated variables. What works with one group of students may not work with another. I think the best we can do is reflect on what we have done in the past that worked well and what didn't, try to figure out the nature of the success or difficulty, and respond in our future teaching enlightened by our understanding of the experience. In the future, I am certain you will make sure that the computer you want to use is in good working order. Judging from your case, I am equally certain that you are on your way to becoming a reflective and effective teacher.

REFLECTIONS AND EXPLORATIONS

1. What are your biggest worries when you use a computer? Share your concerns with your teaching peers.

2. Interview three teachers. Ask them what difficulties they have encountered when they use computers with their students. Record their responses and share them with your teaching peers.

3. Learn how to do one new application on the computer. For example, you might learn how to create your own Web site, or **listserv,** or construct a database. Share your new knowledge with your teaching peers.

4. Interview some middle school students about their abilities to type on a computer keyboard. Are they proficient typists or do they need instruction?

INTEGRATING COMPUTER TECHNOLOGY
LITERACY IN YOUR CLASSROOM:
PRACTICAL APPLICATIONS

Because of the wide variety of computer applications, there is no single format for making these applications in your classroom. If you are using an ILS, the considerations are far different, for example, than if your students are using word-processing software to write and publish. Instead of prescribing a single approach to best practice, consider the following questions:

1. How can you make the most of limited computer hardware in a classroom setting?
2. How can you coordinate the instruction you provide in the classroom with the experiences your students have when they visit the computer lab?
3. How can you find out about effective literacy-related software, and how can you arrive at critical judgments about the software you may already have?
4. How can you harness the Internet to best serve your students?
5. How can you receive the additional training you may need in order to utilize the technology available to you?
6. How can you take advantage of what your students may already know about computers?
7. What is the best way to use computers in your classroom to foster literacy growth?
8. What contingency plans do you have if the computers suddenly become inoperable?
9. How will you assure that all students have access to computers (not just those who finish their assignments first)?
10. How can you best introduce students to the idea of writing in an electronic environment?
11. How can you help students improve some of the prerequisite skills they will need for computer literacy, such as keyboarding?
12. How can you accommodate the diverse needs of students whose past experiences range from nightly use at home to no computer accessibility whatsoever?
13. In what ways do the technology-literacy lessons you envision capitalize on the differences and advantages of electronic text and print?

SUGGESTED READINGS

Calvert, S. (1999). *Children's Journeys Through the Information Age*. Boston: McGraw-Hill College.
This text spells out the nature and scope of the effects of information technology on students' thinking and perceptions and discusses implications for parents, teachers, and policymakers.

CNET Help.com (http://www.help.com)
This Web site supplies tips and tutorials about the Internet, hardware, software, games, and consumer electronics. The site also includes relevant discussion from Usenet news groups and lets you post your own questions.

Typing Tutor—Grades 2–5 and Grades 5 and up (for Mac/PC computers; available from Apple Corp.).
These tutorials are designed to teach students how to type and enhance students' typing speed, accuracy, and confidence by offering exciting games combined with music and sound effects.

9

Integrating a Semiotic View
of Literacy

Literacy in a semiotic system is facility in the process of creating or
interpreting the signs of one or more semiotic systems used in
agreed upon ways in a social collective.
—Albers and Murphy (2000, p. 3)

Sign systems are significant because they form the basis for creative
and critical thought processes.
—Short, Kauffman, and Kahn (2000, p. 169)

Each sign system is unique and best suited to a particular perspective
of the world . . . it is difficult to express horror in mathematical symbols, and love is expressed quite differently in art than in language.
Moving from sign system to sign system is like turning an artifact
so that we can suddenly see a new facet that was previously hidden
from our view.
—Harste (2000, p. 3)

OVERVIEW

Peggy Albers
Georgia State University

For the past few years, many reading researchers and teachers have come to
understand that literacy does not mean ability to read, write, and think only
in print-based texts. Rather, an expanded notion of literacy now suggests
that readers construct meaning drawing from multiple systems of communication, or what is known as semiotics.

The semiotic theory of American pragmatist Charles Sanders Peirce
(Thayer, 1981, 1982) embodies several components central to understanding a semiotic construction of meaning. First, signs are always in a triadic

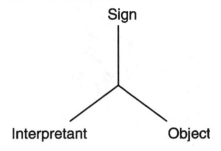

Sign

Interpretant **Object**

FIG. 9.1.   Peirce's Triadic Relationship of Signs.

relationship (see Fig. 9.1). The sign, the object, and the interpretant can be understood only in relation to each other.

A sign (i.e., the word *chair*) is meaningful only when considered in *relationship* with the object (physical chair) and interpretant (interpretation of chair) (Siegel, 1984). Second, our experience with signs is always in *connection* with some context and, as such, our understanding is partially inferential and always incomplete (D. Cunningham, 1992). Meaning, therefore, is not inherent in signs but derives from the way humans interpret those signs as they have experienced them directly or vicariously. And, third, sign systems offer alternative perspectives; that is to say, through the multiplicity of signs available and the multiple relationships among the signs and interpretants, alternative perspectives to our world are offered (Harste, 2000).

The sign system theory adhered to by socio-semiotic scholars deals with meaning in the following ways: (a) Meaning makers situate their meaning within their own experiences; (b) sign systems enable meaning makers to be reflective about the constructed meaning; (c) sign systems allow for multiple interpretations of nonprint and print texts; and (d) legitimate expressions are derived from the communication systems of music, math, movement, art, and drama (Harste, 1994). This semiotic perspective recognizes the importance of the "whole of knowing" (Berghoff, 1995, p. 23).

The whole of knowing for many literacy educators, though, often lies within a single perspective articulated through talk, writing, or signed language. These means of expressions limit meaning making because of their linearity (Langer, 1942; Siegel, 1995). Gardner (1991) argued that the absence of multiple entry points in learning leads to "misconceptions, biases, and stereotypes" and "a single perspective or tack on a concept or problem" will enable the student to understand the concept in "only the most limited and rigid fashion" (p. 246).

Many scholars (Albers & Murphy, 2000; Berghoff, 1995; Eisner, 1978, 1991, 1992; Greene, 1995; Grumet, 1991, 1995; Harste, 1994, 2000) claim that to ignore other systems of communication, sign systems, that lie within

FIG. 9.2.   A model of the rotating world.

the meaning-making expressions, is to stifle the imagination of students and to disregard the culture from which these expressions arise (Albers, 1997). Sign systems are "communication systems" and are "used to construct and represent meaning" (Berghoff et al., 2000, p. x) and have their own "grammar" (Burke, personal communication, 2002). That is, each of these systems has its own form of representation and conventions (Berghoff et al., 2000). For example, a model of the rotating world shown in Fig. 9.2 illustrates the concept of meaning making, and as readers construct meaning, they do so drawing upon more than one system of communication.[1]

Moving this explanation of semiotics into a larger social understanding of how sign systems work in meaning construction, Albers and Murphy (2000) argued that when readers represent meaning, they do so through "semiotic systems," or "collections of elements [signs] used in relation to other elements to represent meaning" (p. 8). In their book, *Telling Pieces: Art as Literacy in Middle School Classes,* they outlined five principles that guide our understanding of literacy through a semiotic perspective:

- Semiotic systems are collections of elements used in relation to other elements to represent meaning.
- Semiotic systems can be of different types: visual, social, cultural, and so on.
- In any particular text that is created, semiotic systems may overlap, co-occur, and work with or against the meanings of other systems.
- Literacy is the ease in which we can create and interpret the signs of one or more semiotic systems through shared meanings with others.
- Texts are ideological.

First, semiotic systems are collections of elements used in relation to other elements to represent meaning.[1] A traffic light is one example of a semiotic system. Together, in a specific context, the red, amber, and green colors of the traffic light create the system. The meaning of the system does

[1]Helfman, E. (2000). *Signs and Symbols Around the World.* Available from Backinprint.com.

not reside in any one of the lights, but in how the lights are interpreted in relation to each other.

Second, semiotic systems can be of different types: visual, social, cultural, and so on. It is possible to imagine many types of semiotic systems. Visual semiotic systems, for example, can include representations as diverse as oil canvas paintings, films, magazine advertisements, or modes of dress. Each of these examples comprises multiple signs that operate together to create a semiotic system. For example, in oil paintings, the collective signs of the oil paint, canvas, image, colors, and so on, all work together to create this single semiotic representation.

Third, in any particular text that is created, semiotic systems may overlap, co-occur, and work with or against the meanings of other systems. Texts may use multiple resources to represent meaning. For example, the mode of a telephone conversation is verbal. The text is understood through intonation, pitch, silence, and sound along with unseen gestures (interpreted by the listener). However, if this conversation is written down, it changes: Even though the word choice is the same, ambiguity or even opposite meanings may result because print does not fully capture the intonation of oral conversation, even when we use typographic elements like punctuation, font size, or font style. Let's say you are talking to a friend about an event at school and say, "I can't believe the principal did that!" (emphasis on "believe") or, if you write your friend an e-mail and say, "I can't believe the principal did that." Even though the words are identical, the meaning of the sentence is different. Written language must use typographic elements to reduce ambiguity (principal) whereas oral language can reduce some ambiguity through intonation ("believe").

Fourth, literacy is the ease with which we can create, interpret, and/or invent the signs of one or more semiotic systems. Each of the elements in a semiotic system is a sign. In pottery, among the signs that the potter works with are composition, color, shape, line, and form. In a written text, the signs the writer works with are graphic letters and characters and language, their presentation on the page, and the words of language. Sometimes, we may not even be aware of the conventions that guide our use of signs. For example, we know that the ball illustrated in Fig. 9.2 is in motion because we use lines to represent that movement. However, some non-Western cultures do not interpret the curving lines as indicative of motion. Yet, to members of Western culture, the meaning of this convention is so obvious that they may not even recognize it as a convention.

And, fifth, texts are ideological and are often shaped by the social collective to which we most align ourselves and our thinking. That is, texts that we create come from our set of beliefs and assumptions about the world. In written texts, and language in general, the historical use of the male pronoun in referring to all of humanity (he = humanity) illustrates a male-centered value system (Simpson, 1993). This usage virtually rendered the female invisible. Ideology, or our beliefs about the world, permeates every representation that we create. Furthermore, we can only understand a sign when the social collective(s) to which we belong have enabled us to know what these signs mean. For example, it is possible that a white pointed cap with two cutouts for the eyes may signify (e.g., in the social collective of the Ku Klux Klan), strength, power, and leadership. Another group belonging to a different social collective might interpret this hat as a sign for hatred, intolerance, and bigotry. So, it's important to note that signs do not transmit meaning; meaning lies in the mind of the human based on her or his beliefs within social collectives to which they belong. Thus, interpreted and created meanings are always ideological and never innocently free of assumptions and beliefs.

When considering semiotics as a way of working with literacy in reading/language arts classes, it is important to note that like print-based literacy, educators must understand that facility in creating semiotic systems also implies the need to teach students the literacies of various sign systems. Often, students are asked to represent meanings in semiotic ways (visual arts, drama, music, etc.) through projects assigned by teachers; however, students may find this difficult because they have not learned what it means to represent meaning through art, drama, and/or music. Unlike in written and oral language in which they are given instruction on how to write narratives and nonfiction pieces, students are left to their own limited knowledge of the forms of representation and/or conventions of a particular sign system, like art. As young children, representing meaning in systems outside of written language isn't as problematic because they may be less concerned about how others view their interpretations. In addition, at an early age, children are less apt to place judgment on their peers' representation in terms of their literacy in that sign system. But, as students grow older, they are often dissatisfied with their non-print-based representations and become less and less confident of representing meaning except through written language. Therefore, it is important, if we want students to think and express meaning in more complex and expanded ways through semiotic systems, that we must offer them tools and the language to express meaning in this way. An expanded definition of literacy in semiotic terms, then, means that students must have continual and constructive instruction in systems of communication that lie outside written and oral language.

Teaching from a semiotic perspective involves more than providing students with a series of arts-based activities that merely and conveniently attach themselves to what is considered the most important representation, the written work. It requires that teachers understand how literacies operate within each of these sign systems. I'm not suggesting that teachers become experts in each of these systems of communication. Rather, they should, like they did with written and oral language, begin to learn basic literacies of various sign systems (Albers, 1997, 1998). Because cutbacks in the arts in schools provide less instruction from art, drama, and music educators, teachers are more responsible for working with these sign systems in their classes. By learning the basic literacies within these systems, teachers will be able to more easily assist students in their own growing understanding of literacy and representations. When students know literacies in various sign systems, they will more easily be able to represent their meaning in more semiotic ways.[2]

In this chapter on preservice teachers' work with texts in multiple and semiotic ways, one of their assumptions is that students can and will be able to represent meaning in semiotic ways and with facility. Wouldn't it be nice if we could learn the language and conventions of various sign systems through osmosis?! However, when novice educators, and "seasoned" educators alike, work with multiple sign systems in their classes, they must realize that along with this work comes instruction in the languages of the various sign systems. Larisa Shaw's teaching case (the first case in this chapter) shows us that when working with multiple texts, students must have some instruction in reading both images and words. Furthermore, educators must realize that semiotic systems are also cultural. Common tales like Cinderella told from a non-White perspective may not be evident to young students who are asked to make connections to their own cultural community and literature. In the second teaching case in this chapter, Joni Spiers assumed that students would be able to construct a song about a children's story that they had read. Even when given familiar music, her students were unable to do what Joni asked because they had not had instruction in writing lyrics, noting rhythm, rhyme, and so on, important tools in creating songs. This teaching case allows us to more clearly understand the need for teachers to work with the literacies of music that would then enable these students to more easily represent their interpretation of this picture book through music.

The importance of the arts as literacy has been articulated by the 1996 Standards for English Language Arts developed by a steering committee from the National Council of Teachers of English (NCTE) and the International Reading Association (IRA). This committee understands and promotes among educators who work with the English-language arts that "visual literacy plays a growing role in education and learning" (NCTE Elementary Section Steering Committee, 1996, p. 12) (see chap. 11, this volume). Educators who desire to build language arts classes that understand semiotics as a complex way to create and interpret representations also must recognize the work that a semiotic perspective in teaching entails.

In sum, an educator's use of multiple ways of knowing[2] in a classroom in and of themselves may not enable a student to become more literate; rather,

---

[2]Leland, C., & Harste, J. (1994, September). Multiple ways of knowing: Curriculum in a new key. *Language Arts, 71,* 337–345.

it is the study of the literacies of the art form and the student's ability to use, interpret, and invent within and across sign systems that will help the learner become more literate. When this is understood at a basic level, we know that literacy lies not in the project/product or in the arts-based activities of the lesson, but rather in our ability to *use* and *interpret* elements in a sign system and in our ability to *invent* elements in the sign system.

WHAT DO YOU NEED TO KNOW?
HOW CAN YOU BEGIN?

As a teacher, in order to begin working meaningfully, thoughtfully, and in literate ways with students in artistic semiotic systems it is important for you to seek out resources that enable you to study the various tools that are pertinent to each system. Teachers must understand that meaning is created semiotically and that literacies in art forms can be studied and taught. A good starting point is to read Albers and Murphy (2000), *Telling Pieces: Art as Literacy in Sixth Grade Classes*. This book offers a comprehensible explanation of semiotics as a theory of meaning making. Although this book addresses students in the middle grades, the processes through which learners construct art cut across age levels. This book outlines how students use the various tools, elements, and principles of art and design to become more literate in the visual arts. Also read the overviews to chapters 4–12 in this text. Semiotic dimensions of the visual arts, drama, dance, music, and technology are offered in easy-to-understand terms.

You need to become literate in the visual, dramatic, dance, and musical arts without having to spend a great deal of money on classes. What I suggest is quite simple. First, I would draw upon the resources in your own school, and talk with the arts teachers to get a sense of what they consider to be basic literacies in their own art form. Ask them to explain, through demonstration, how one creates meaning in this art form, and how best to teach some of the basic literacies to learners. Another way to become more knowledgeable about various art forms is to study informally how artists, dramatists, dancers, and musicians work and learn their art. I often look at the "how-to" books in art forms to get a sense of what literacy means in the various art forms, and how to construct meaning using the tools of the art form. In other words, I'm always looking at how I can become more literate in an art form.

One way to become more literate in the visual arts is to use color as a starting point. For example, you might consider how color represents various emotions. How does yellow make you feel? How does red make you feel? When you see blue, what emotions are evoked? You can also bring in the concept of metaphor with color. Red makes me feel like. . . . Blue is a ____.

(Be careful not to make this a worksheet assignment in metaphor and **simile.**) After a general study of color study some artists' prints (e.g., van Gogh's *Sunflowers,* which can be easily accessed through the Internet). Determine how various artists use color to represent meaning. Reflect upon how various colors represent meaning to you. Think about your favorite colors. What makes these colors so attractive to you?

Next, work with tempera paint, and learn how all colors are created from primary colors. Learn the vocabulary of color (e.g., hue, bright, somber).

When you've become fairly knowledgeable about color, ponder how you might represent story characters or events through color. This is what I call "thinking meaningfully through the arts." This activity in color pushes you and your students to think about what color represents and, with the introduction of the elements of narrative, students more easily see how to include visual imagery in their narratives to shape characterization.

To study the mixing of color, construct makeshift palettes (you can use styrofoam packing sheets, plastic plates, etc.) and begin to explore color by mixing the various colors of tempera paints on the palette. After you get a sense of how color works, make a symmetrical print. Take a piece of white paper, and fold the paper in half. Open the paper pour/dot paint on one side of the paper. Fold the paper carefully, pressing down to mix the colors. Then open up the paper and study the imagery you have created. What do you see in the images? What characters do you see? What emotions does this image evoke? As a culmination to this activity, create a story using the symmetrical image as the focal point.

Above all, never assume that your students have knowledge of a specific semiotic system. Just as you might learn about color through direct experiences (observing, reflecting, mixing colors), so do your students need direct experiences in specific semiotic systems before they can skillfully begin to represent meaning through the visual arts, dance, music, or drama.

CASES AND COMMENTARIES

Case #9.1: "Who Is Cinderella, Really?" (by Larisa Shaw)

I teach four second graders and last week I decided to jump right in and combine sign systems in order to enhance my students' literacy development. Of course, I was apprehensive. I had only just heard about multiple sign systems, and multiple literacies this semester. I think I understand the concepts: Sign systems, such as art, music, drama, and math, are communication systems that are all uniquely different languages (Berghoff et al., 2000).

Because our theme for the semester is "Overcoming Difficulties," I decided that I would cautiously enter the murky waters of multiple sign systems by reading the book, *The Rough-Face Girl* (Martin, 1992), to my students. Like all Cinderella stories (there are over 1,500 versions), in this wonderful Algonquin Indian Cinderella tale, good is rewarded and evil is not. *The Rough-Face Girl* tells the truth and gets a husband who is called, "The Invisible Being," whereas her two sisters tell lies and don't get a husband.

I tried hard to plan what sign systems I would assemble and offer in the lesson. I did not do a very good job. First, I read *The Rough-Face Girl* aloud to my students. I knew I was going to link that story with the traditional story of Cinderella (retold by Elrich, 1985). After our reading, I asked the students, "What other story does *The Rough-Face Girl* remind you of?"

One girl raised her hand and said, "It reminds me of when my sisters are mean to me."

I was taken aback by her response, so I said, "That isn't very nice of them."

Then I said, "Can anyone tell us what other story you know that is like *The Rough-Face Girl?*"

The students just sat there. So, I brought out the book *Cinderella* and showed the front cover to my students. Then, I made the outline of a Venn diagram (Taylor, 1999). I printed *The Rough-Faced Girl* on top of the the circle on the left and *Cinderella* on top of the circle on the right. "Let's compare these two stories," I said. (These were multiple texts, even if I only had two texts and they were both print-based texts.)

I tried to show similarities and differences between the two stories, but I had to do most of the work myself. So, I showed them the illustrations in *Cinderella* to jog their memories. Finally, Robert said, "Both girls had two mean sisters, but Cinderella's sisters were stepsisters, and The Rough-Face Girl's sisters were her completely real sisters."

At last we had something to put into each of the Venn diagram's big circles (see Taylor, 1999). Then, Sara said, "Cinderella's husband was a prince, but the Rough-Face Girl's husband was an Invisible Being." Thank goodness, we now had something else to place on the chart.

Of course, I was disappointed in the lesson. One of my preservice teacher friends said, "Maybe you should have read *Cinderella* to your students first."

I recognize that I have more problems with my lesson than just reading *Cinderella* to my students before I read *The Rough-Face Girl* to them. There is far more to sign systems than what I offered in my lesson. I could have brought in costumes and had one student dress like Cinderella and another student dress like The Rough-Face Girl. One of the students could have played the part of the Prince and another The Invisible Being. I could have supplied videos of the two stories. I could have played tapes of music that were appropriate to both stories. I could have brought in visuals that included wigwams and a "glass" slipper. We could have used the Internet to discover what information is available about fairy tales and Cinderella fairy tales in particular. We could have viewed a Cinderella video (e.g., *Walt Disney Studio's Masterpiece Cinderella*). We could have created maps that depicted Cinderella's and the Rough-Face Girl's actions. We could have studied how the story characters communicate in each of the stories (e.g., in *The Rough-Face Girl*, the Invisible Being's sister acts as a gatekeeper and asks the three sisters many questions to determine their truthfulness). After our readings, we could have created songs and chants about the stories. We even could have danced as people might have danced at the Prince's ball in *Cinderella* and around the campfire in *The Rough-Face Girl*. We could have painted scenes from both books. Most important, we could have discussed the fundamental elements in a Cinderella story: a kind-hearted, but mistreated central character, an evil stepfamily, a magical guardian, a handsome nobleman or prestigious lady who come to the rescue, and the true beauty and love of nature.

As you can tell, I learned a lot from reflecting about this lesson. I learned that I did not use multiple sign systems. My next step is to repeat this type of lesson and do it right!

1. What was Larisa's first teaching problem and how might she have solved the problem during the context of instruction? _____

_____

2. What does Larisa mean when she says, "I learned that I did not use multiple sign systems"? _____

_____

Commentary 9.1A: "Who is Cinderella, Really?"
(by Sharon Miller, Retired Language Arts Supervisor,
Bel Aire, Maryland, and Co-Director for Teacher Research,
Southern Arizona Writing Project, Tucson)

Hello, Larisa,

Wow! I have to say, first of all, that I am really impressed with your reflections of the lesson. It is so very important for a teacher not only to recognize that a lesson was not what she had hoped, but also to consider options for improving it the next time. You seem to have some ideas about where the lesson might have gone had you done some things differently, but I suggest you think a little more deeply about the next presentation before jumping in with too many of your ideas.

You say you had only just heard about multiple literacies and sign systems this semester. I applaud your bravery for taking the risk and jumping in, but I would like to remind you that whatever you choose to do with multiple semiotic systems, keep in mind the overriding purpose of your lesson(s). Your goal is not just to to use multiple signs, but rather to promote your students' understandings of your unit theme: "Overcoming Difficulties." The use of multiple signs must be in service of your desired learning outcomes. That said, let's look at how your lesson went.

First, you selected a wonderful Native-American tale that linked well to the theme of the unit. As a Cinderella story, it fits. The problem was not with the text, but rather with what you expected of your students after hearing the tale. You assumed the students had sufficient prior knowledge of the traditional Cinderella tale to make the connections you expected. Either this was not the case, or you needed to include a more detailed effort at activating their prior knowledge. You ended up playing what I call "Guess What the Teacher Is Thinking." You had answers in mind and you wanted students to come up with them. It is very important to guide the students through recall of prior knowledge or, when it is lacking, to provide it during the lesson. Your preservice teacher friend gave you good advice about reading Cinderella first. Or, in the interest of multiple sign systems you might have shown a film of Cinderella.

You missed a chance to link the theme of the inquiry with real life when you dismissed the response of the student who was reminded of her sisters being mean to her. I think students must first be encouraged to express personal responses to a text before being asked to make critical or interpretive connections. Students' personal experiences can yield many opportunities for them to produce multiple texts, formats, and genres by telling their own stories.

Second, you chose the format through which students might make the connection to Cinderella—a Venn diagram (Taylor, 1999). Perhaps, after helping students generate the information needed to make comparisons, you might have presented them with choices for comparisons and let them choose. This assumes that you have given them experiences, not only with Venn diagrams, but with other visual structures for thinking, such as an I-Chart (J. Hoffman, 1992).

In your reflection, you lament that you did not provide students with a greater variety of signs through the use of costumes for acting out roles, films, mapping the characters' journeys, creating songs and chants, dancing, and painting scenes. Although these ideas would, indeed, have made the lesson more fun and changed the way students could think and learn about a concept, I urge you to think very carefully about how those ideas might be used to promote understanding of the unit theme. Furthermore, I suspect that your lesson was only one of many associated with the inquiry and that within the inquiry there are specific learning objectives that you hope to accomplish with the lessons. For example, will students understand that a narrative has a beginning, middle, and end? Will you be asking them to demonstrate their ability to retell a story? How can the use of multiple signs support the specific learning objectives while encouraging understanding of the themed concepts? And remember, you don't have to do it all in one lesson. Be selective about your choices (based on what you need to achieve) and be prepared to offer students some choices in how they may take advantage of multiple signs for demonstrating their learning and understandings.

I wish you the best as you continue your efforts to take advantage of multiple signs in your instructional program. And, I encourage you to continue reflecting on all of your lessons—even the ones that go well!

Commentary #9.1B: "Who is Cinderella, Really?" (by Deborah Begoray, Teacher Educator, University of Victoria, Canada)

Dear Larisa,

I think there comes a time in every beginning teacher's experience when she feels like Cinderella—sitting alone in the ashes while others get to dress up for glorious and exciting teaching events. Alas, most of us do not have fairy godmothers, and cannot (maybe should not) wait for a prince or "Invisible Being" to save us. Rather, we have to save ourselves. This notion reminds me that you might want to include Robert Munsch's children's book, *The Paperbag Princess* (1980), in your unit on Overcoming Difficulties. It features a princess who defeats a dragon with her wits and saves the prince, only to discover that he wasn't such a great guy after all. She ventures off on her own and lives happily ever after. A lesson for modern women and Grade 2 girls everywhere, don't you think? And you've made a great start at picking yourself up from the ashes of your first attempt at including multiple texts, dusting yourself off and working on your party dress for what will undoubtedly be a much more successful next effort.

First of all, you are obviously a risk taker. You jumped right in and tried a new idea. I hope you continue to try lessons that have been suggested to you in your methods class. Too many beginning teachers try to do only safe lessons. Today's 7- and 8-year-olds need the best teaching we can offer, even if you sometimes feel as though you are traveling in a converted pumpkin that might revert back to its gourdlike origins at the most inopportune time. Venture out boldly.

Try taking your cues from your students. They clearly identified with poor Cinderella's problems, but you let their feelings slip by you. We've probably all had a family member who made us feel badly. What might your students have done at this point to allow them to think more deeply about how to overcome this difficulty? Dramatic enactments would be one way to start. Students could pair up and show each other what their sad faces and happy faces look like. They could move like people who are sad and then like people who are happy. (How would they do this? Ask them for ideas!)

They could share their ideas about what to say to someone who is "mean" to them so that everyone will feel happier (e.g., "You can't play with my Barbie!" "Okay, I'll play with my own toys.") Then, they could role-play their problems and solutions. They could also use puppets.

If you want to include technology (another communication or sign system), take photographs of your students during the dramatic literacy events, enter the photos into the computer, and let the students compose different captions for the same picture using presentation software such as Power-Point or class web pages. Another alternative is for the students to draw their responses. Their artwork could be presented in cartoon strips, accompanied by writing in "balloons" above the characters' heads. This way you will also integrate writing into your language arts lesson, and when they share each other's work, they will be encouraged to read as well.

You clearly have much background in the literary elements of Cinderella, and it is always tempting to use our own knowledge about stories, often studied in adult literature classes. Consider, however, that your main job with young students is to help them to discover more about themselves in developmentally appropriate ways. The arts, for example, are wonderful ways to experience the world and to express our understanding of life. However, a Grade 2 student's personal development is at a very different stage than, for example, a woman in her 20s! While we probably don't remember what it is like to be 7 or 8, close "kid watching" tells us as teachers what a student needs to investigate next. So, try to let them take the lead. Have your materials ready—boxes of costumes, puppets, paints, paper, brushes, sound makers, audio- and videotapes, cameras—and let them take you to the ball. Remember that it's their lives you want to enrich, but once you set off on this journey, you'll feel like you have a party dress on too. Relax, and remember, using sign systems (multiple literacies) is the mark of an outstanding teacher. But, you don't have to use *all* sign systems in one lesson.

Case #9.2: "Well, This Didn't Work!" (by Joni Spiers)

It all started when I read the book, *The Talking Eggs* (San Souci, 1989), to my second-grade students. I thought it was a perfect opportunity for me to extend the ideas in the book using multiple semiotic systems. My idea was to have my students compose a poem as a postreading strategy (I will tell you right now that I had the wrong idea about semiotic systems and forms of representations). My students were very excited about the idea of writing a poem, but they did not really know what a poem was. I knew that, but I just kept on going with the lesson. I tried to explain to them that a poem can rhyme or it does not have to rhyme. I was getting nowhere, so I asked the students if they would rather compose a song instead. You can tell that I was floundering in the lesson simply because I was determined to link the story with some sort of multiple communications system. My professor modeled a lesson for us where she connected literature with the literacies (i.e., semiotic systems) of the visual and dramatic arts and I wanted to do something similar.

My students all agreed they would rather compose a song than a poem. More problems occurred when they could not agree on a title. Samantha wanted the title to be *Rose and Blanche* and Vicky wanted it to be *The Eggs*. I finally said that the title of our song would be *The Talking Eggs*.

I started off by singing, "There once lived a mean mother and her two daughters."

I had no idea about the music. I just made it up as I went along.

Then, Vicky sang, "Blanche and Rose were sisters."

Next, Donnie said, "Eggs don't talk."

This made our song inaccurate so Vicky started yelling, "Do it right!!"

She wanted to take charge and not let the others contribute. Consequently, the other students began to get angry.

I became worried because the students were not composing a song that reflected the story. It wasn't anything like the story.

Then Donnie sang, "Rose was mean and Blanche was nice."

The students were getting all of the characters mixed.

Well, we finished the activity, but it was a disaster. Samantha held her ears and Donnie played with his pencil. Other students paid no attention.

Reflecting on this disaster, I came to the conclusion that I lost sight of my original objective, which was to somehow link multiple communication or sign systems. The literature was appropriate, but I was just grasping at anything to extend the lesson. What are multiple sign systems and how many different signs do teachers have to use in one lesson? I need help.

1. In her case, Joni says, "I need help." What advice do you have for her?

_____

_____

2. Why might Joni want to link multiple communication systems in her lesson? _____

_____

Commentary #9.2A: "Well, This Didn't Work!" (by George Hunt, Teacher Educator, University of Edinburgh, Scotland)

Dear Joni,

Ten out of ten for your choice of text. *The Talking Eggs* (San Souci, 1989) is a fascinating folk story featuring the motif of virtue rewarded. Children of the age you teach, being social animals with a strong sense of right and wrong, relate to this theme very easily, especially when it's conveyed through the sort of vivid and eerie imagery featured in this particular tale (see Buehl, 2001, for a description of **guided imagery**). After your reading of the story, it's hardly surprising that the children were eager to do some kind of follow-up.

This is where we encounter the first problem. You state that your objective was to explore communication systems. Did this objective emanate from your own convictions about the best way to explore this story further, or was it imposed by your professor or the school district's curriculum?

Stories have long been recognized as fertile sources for language exploration (for some fascinating examples, see Garvie, 1990). *The Talking Eggs* offers opportunities for discussing a range of texts (e.g., other stories featuring the same motif), formats (e.g., creating a map, informal dramatic enactment, or picture book of the story), and genres (e.g., retelling the story as autobiography or newspaper copy). But preceding all such elaborations, and acting as a prerequisite for them, is the simple practice of *talking about the story. Talking is an oral text.*

Young students need to be convinced that open-ended conversations about their reading are an integral part of school life (Chambers, 1990). Furthermore, such conversation is likely to be richer and less inhibited if it is not immediately tied to specific curricular objectives (Hunt, 2001). That is to say, students need opportunities simply to share personal responses to the story and to make links between the text and their own lives *before* the teacher introduces any other follow-up tasks. This is not to say that your idea of responding in poetic form is necessarily inappropriate, but the decision as to what form of response is most effective should arise from the talk that the students share in the immediate aftermath of their reading or listening. Perhaps they will want to recount personal experiences related to the theme; perhaps they will want to draw pictures or diagrams of a talking egg's anatomy; in many cases, it might be best to accept that the very process of talk is a sufficient product of this particular literary experience.

However, this will not satisfy curriculum managers who demand that students cover a particular range of texts, genres, and formats within each term. If this is the situation you are in, the first step is to decide what semiotic systems are most appropriate for your class in terms of age and interest level and to make very tentative links between particular stimulus texts and texts, formats, and genres well in advance of the lessons that you teach. It is, I think, important to see such links as provisional. If you decide, for example, that you will read "They went to sea in a Sieve, they did, In a Sieve they went to sea; In spite of all their friends could say, In a Sieve they went to sea" from *The Jumblies*[3] (Lear, 1968) and use it to stimulate writing within the

---

[3]Lear, E. (1968). *The Jumblies*. London: Chatto and Windus (http://www.engr.mun.ca/~john/jumblies.html).

travelogue genre, you are likely to end up as you did with *The Talking Eggs*. To reiterate, choice of a particular route for extending reading should be contingent on the children's interactive responses to the text.

This is not to say that you shouldn't make suggestions, but you need to do so from a position of confidence based on your own knowledge of text and genre conventions. It sounds as if the strife among Vickie, Donnie, and Samantha arose partly from your own uncertainties as to how to progress with the lesson. There are plenty of books on the market that would familiarize you with genre conventions (see, e.g., Buss and Karnowski, 2000). My own favorite sources for ideas on how both rhyming and nonrhyming poems work and on how they can inspire classroom writing are Gerard Benson's *This Poem Doesn't Rhyme* (1991) and *Does W Trouble You?* (1994).

To answer the questions with which you end your case ("What are multiple semiotic systems and how many different texts, etc., do teachers have to use in one lesson?"), multiple sign systems refer to the infinite number of ways in which meaning can be represented. You don't have to employ all of them at once or require use of multiple signs that are developmentally beyond your students to enhance their appreciation of literature.

Commentary #9.2B: "Well, This Didn't Work!" (by David Clarke, Middle School Teacher, New Orleans, Louisiana)

Oh dear, Joni. You tried so hard and your intentions were admirable, but you were a bit off base with your lesson. That's okay. Just do some reading, talk to your professor, and try a lesson again where you offer students opportunities to learn through multiple communication systems. First, you need to get a solid understanding about the concept of multiple texts, formats, and genres, and multiple literacies or semiotic systems. Then, you need to include your students' ideas and "voices" in the lesson. Finally, you need to determine what your students know and need to know about poetry, music, time lines, charts, graphs, and the like, before you integrate any of these communication systems within your lesson.

Your question at the end of your case is very revealing. You need to construct some knowledge about what multiple texts, formats, and genres are in order to ensure the future success of your lessons. In your *Talking Eggs* lesson, multiple texts might mean providing other stories with the same encompassing theme (i.e., good overcoming evil; good deeds being rewarded) (see Commentary #9.2A) or other texts dealing with sisters, mean stepmothers, and so on. However, also consider that in keeping with newer ideas about multiple literacies, other forms of communication besides print are considered a text (e.g., an oral text, or a CD-ROM of *The Talking Eggs*).

Now consider the term, *formats*. Information and communication can be accomplished through many different forms or formats. For example, in your *Talking Eggs* lesson, your students might have shared their impressions of Blanche, Rose, or the mean mother through dance, poetry, drawings, typing their ideas on a computer, singing, talking to a partner, and the like (i.e., multiple sign systems). Just remember that in order to be successful, your students need to know how to accomplish a dance, type on a computer, draw time lines, and so on. Finally, let's think about genres. Do you like mystery novels? That's a genre. Do you like action-packed films? That's a genre. A genre refers to any particular type of class or category, like fairy tales, folk songs, ballads, or even "hip hop" music.

In closing may I say that I am impressed that you are aware of multiple communication systems. You are well on your way toward success as a 21st-century teacher.

Case: #9.3: "Too Many Sign Systems" (by Patti Alexander)

I work with five first graders, and my students really enjoy learning about different places in the world. In my last lesson I read *Gregory Cool* (Binch, 1994) to them. This story takes place on the island of Tobago. To enhance my students' learning, I brought the entire island of Tobago into the classroom. Well, not really, but almost, and that is how my lesson went awry.

I had fiction books, a globe, photographs, a CD of calypso and reggae music, a fresh coconut, and a listing of Web sites about islands and Tobago for us to call up. After we read the story (print-based text), listened to calypso and reggae (music text), ate the coconut (experiential text), discussed the book (oral text), and utilized the Internet (electronic text), I planned for us to create a mural about the story (visual text), and participate in an informal drama presentation (oral text). That's a lot of semiotic systems!

The first thing I did was pass around the coconut. As the students examined it, I turned on the music and began to read *Gregory Cool*. No one paid any attention to me or the story.

"When can we eat this coconut?' Reese asked.

"In a little while," I replied.

"Is it time for the coconut yet?" asked Gavin.

"Not yet," I said, "Just a few more minutes."

We were going nowhere with *Gregory Cool* and all of my multiple sign system planning seemed futile. Was my lesson doomed?

Turning off the music, out we went into the school courtyard to open up the coconut, forgetting the reason why we had the coconut in the first place. After we opened it, the students did not want to eat it anyway because it smelled funny. It took so long to open the coconut that we had no time to finish the book, create a mural, collaborate in a drama enactment, or go on the Internet. I understand the concept of multiple semiotic systems, but I cannot seem to plan and offer a cohesive lesson in which the connections among signs are seamless and smooth. I need help.

1. Patti is a reflective practitioner. In what ways does she reflect about her lesson? _____

_____

2. Why did Patti title her case, "Too Many Sign Systems"? _____

_____

Commentary #9.3A: "Too Many Sign Systems"
(by Timothy Morse, Teacher Educator,
University of Southern Mississippi)

Dear Patti,

I think you did a great job in trying to plan and offer a lesson that incorporated multiple sign systems. You certainly considered your students' interests (i.e., learning about different places in the world). However, the irony is that your extensive planning ended up being your worst enemy. That is, after you planned every detail, you then felt compelled to use your plan as you originally designed it, irrespective of what transpired with your students. In the future, it might prove beneficial if you think about your planning activities as an opportunity for you to get a sense of the big picture, and then use this big picture to guide you during the implementation of your lessons.

Think for a second about what happens if, on your way home from work, you notice that traffic is coming to a standstill in front of you. Because you do not want to sit idly on the road for an indefinite period of time, you use your knowledge of the big picture—alternative roads in the area—to take a detour to reach your final destination—your home. Understanding the big picture allowed you to adjust to the circumstances that arose at that particular moment.

How does this relate to the teaching experience you just described? You stated that you wanted your students to learn about the island of Tobago, and you created a plan, or path, for them to follow (i.e., read the story *Gregory Cool*, listen to calypso and reggae, eat a coconut, discuss the book, utilize the Internet, create a mural about the story, and participate in an informal drama presentation). In creating this plan, you personally developed a strong sense of the big picture. However, as you set out down the path you had planned to take, an unforeseen circumstance arose. Your students expressed more interest in the coconut than the story. Instead of using your knowledge of the big picture and deciding upon an alternative path that would lead to the same end, you insisted that your students follow along the original course you had charted. I think your insistence on using one course is captured in your description of what happened when you went outside to open the coconut. You said that after the music was turned off, "We went to open up the coconut, forgetting the reason why we had the coconut in the first place."

Actually, there was a reason why you as the teacher had selected the coconut, but this did not necessarily coincide with anything the students had in mind. When the students expressed an interest in the coconut at the outset of the lesson, you could have followed their lead and gradually incorporated your other activities into the lesson. For example, you could have let the students open up the coconut right away, as an advanced organizer (Ausubel, 1960[4]). When they determined that it was distasteful, you could have used the Internet to research where coconuts are grown and how they are harvested and prepared for consumption. These activities could have led to your reading of *Gregory Cool* and your informal drama presentation and music-literacy activity (e.g., perhaps the students might have listened to the music while they learned how to harvest coconuts).

Think of how the "six *p*'s"—"proper prior planning prevents poor performance"—enable you to develop a sense of the big picture when you plan for your lessons. Then, trust that these planning experiences will enable you to make smooth and seamless connections among multiple texts, formats, and genres. In the lesson you describe, I think that you may not have realized how easily you could have adjusted what you had planned to do. If you think of your lesson plan as one road among many that can lead to your final destination (i.e., enabling your students to learn about the island of Tobago), I think you will find that you will easily achieve your aim in the future. One more bit of advice. Extend that single lesson into three lessons. The best teacher in the world could not offer all of those learning activities in one session.

Commentary #9.3B: "Too Many Sign Systems" (by Jane Percival, Head Elementary Teacher, Haydenville, Massachusetts)

Patti, it is evident that prior to your lesson with first graders you thoroughly prepared to make the distant island of Tobago a real place for them. This was a very important goal to have as a planner of instruction and required a huge commitment of time and energy. It had to be very frustrating to have your dream for your students—to have a wonder-filled, cultural experience thwarted by a mere coconut. I cannot count how many times something similar has happened to me during my many years as a teacher. Each time,

---

[4]Ausubel, D. (1960). The use of advanced organizers in the learning and retention of meaningful verbal material. *Journal of Educational Psychology, 51,* 267–272.

I feel thoroughly discouraged at the end of the experience. As I reflect further upon the lesson, I usually discover that I have tried to bring "too many sign systems" into one learning experience for my students. Then, I remember helpful advice that a mentor gave me several years ago. He said to think of a lesson plan as a story with a beginning, middle, and end. Be sure that you and the students can tell the story in the time that you have. He added that it's all right to continue the story at a later time.

Let's apply that advice to your plan and see what emerges. We might begin our trip and our story by sitting with the students and asking them if anyone has been to Tobago Island. In this way we could discover that someone has traveled there in reality, through a book, or by viewing a TV show. Your globe could be brought into the group and each student could take the trip from where they are in the classroom to where Tobago is located. This would require a wonderful discussion of land masses, oceans, and cardinal directions. Predictions could be made about the weather in Tobago, given its latitude and longitude position and the latitude and longitude of the classroom. Discussion could continue around what a first grader there might see, hear, taste, touch, and smell. The beginning of the story is now complete.

The globe is then replaced by the book *Gregory Cool* (Binch, 1994). Much of the preparation for the students entering this story has been accomplished. At this point, you might ask your students to listen carefully to the story to discover what life is like for Gregory who lives on Tobago Island. Tell them that at the end of the story, the group will be creating a mural that shows others what they have learned about life on Tobago Island. At points in the story, you might stop and ask students what they have already discovered about the island. As the teacher you have now come to the end of the middle of your lesson (i.e., your story).

Perhaps an intermission can be planned at this time during which you can set up what is needed for the mural construction. Students also will have the opportunity to move their bodies; they've been sitting for quite a long time at this point. Another "ending" for your story might be to have students do creative movement to music that is often played on Tobago Island —the calypso and reggae music that you had ready to play for them in your original planning. You might even play just one of the types of music and end the lesson with the promise of doing creative movement to another kind of music from Tobago the next time you are together. In this way, you have created a seam between lessons and built on the interest that has developed throughout this learning experience. Though your story has ended on this day, it will be continued on another.

By approaching planning in this way, I have found that I can be more relaxed and open to student responses. I know the story that I have planned to tell, feel confident that it can be told in the time provided, and can create stories within that story that are meaningful additions for students. Because the plan is like a story, it flows so that the seams hardly show. Yet, if you revisit your lesson retold in this way, you will also find that there are multiple texts, formats, and genres evident. Although the coconut did not find a place in this day's story, it certainly will in future ones, or will it? That decision is yours; you are the guide on this and future adventures with your first graders. You are the weaver of your plans—a storyteller.

REFLECTIONS AND EXPLORATIONS

1. Think for a moment about your understanding of sign systems. Jot down your ideas. Share your conceptions of multiple sign systems with three of your teaching colleagues. Do their ideas agree or disagree with yours?

2. Now, read pp. x and xi and 78–80 in *Beyond Reading and Writing: Inquiry, Curriculum, and Multiple Ways of Knowing* by Berghoff et al. (2000) and chapter 2, "The representation of meaning," in Alber and Murphy's book, *Telling Pieces: Art as Literacy in Middle School Classes*. How do the ideas you wrote for Item 1 Reflection and Exploration compare/contrast with your ideas now?

INTEGRATING MULTIPLE SIGN SYSTEMS IN YOUR CLASSROOM: PRACTICAL APPLICATIONS

The first few times you offer lessons that include multiple semiotic systems in your classroom will most likely require additional planning efforts on your part. Therefore, considering and responding to the following questions may help you offer cohesive, successful instruction:

1. How can you as a teacher become literate in the visual and dramatic arts?
2. What literacies do your students bring to their representations of meaning?
3. How can the study of literacy in various art forms help your students think through the arts in more complex ways?
4. How can you find ways to talk with arts teachers across your school?
5. What other ways, like the illustrations with color in this chapter, can you scaffold students' learning through the arts?
6. How can various pieces of literature invite students to see art in the text?
7. What resources, both print and nonprint, will help you and your students study art, drama, dance, music, and mathematics?

8. How might you and your students make art forms a part of your everyday life?

9. How can you help your students begin to notice, learn, and appreciate artists' techniques to represent meaning?

10. How will the integration of sign systems enhance your lesson (e.g., primary or elementary reading lesson, middle or junior high school history, science, or literature lesson)? (Dana Grisham, personal communication, November 2001)?

SUGGESTED READINGS

Albers, P., & Murphy, S. (2000). *Telling Pieces: Art as Literacy in Middle School Classes.* Mahwah, NJ: Lawrence Erlbaum Associates.
The authors of this text present a comprehensible understanding of social semiotics and how people represent meaning through semiotic systems.

Berghoff, B., Egawa, K., Harste, J., & Hoonan, B. (2000). *Beyond Reading and Writing: Inquiry, Curriculum, and Multiple Ways of Knowing.* Urbana, IL: National Council of Teachers of English.
The authors explain classroom learning based on inquiry and multiple ways of knowing and offer a new perspective that places students rather than standards at the center of curriculum.

Cowan, K. (2001). The arts and emergent literacy. *Primary Voices K–6, 9*(4), 11–17.
In this article, the author describes how the visual arts have provided her kindergarten students with another language system that allows them to create a story that more fully represents their meaning.

Koshewa, A. (2001). Multiple cultures, multiple literacies. *Primary Voices K–6, 9*(4), 27–33.
In this article, the author invites readers into his fifth-grade class as he helps students understand the importance that culture plays in their representation of meaning. Students' representations cannot and do not rest within print-based language alone.

Short, K., Kauffman, G., & Kahn, L. (2000, October). "I just *need* to draw": Responding to literature across multiple sign systems. *The Reading Teacher, 54*(2), 160–171.
The authors offer theory and practical applications in the form of stories that help to make multiple semiotic systems easy to understand. By sign systems, the authors mean "multiple ways of knowing . . . the ways in which humans share and make meaning" (p. 160).

10

Integrating Media and Popular-Culture Literacy With Content Reading

What does it mean to be media literate? There are two components
. . . teaching people to be critical consumers of entertainment and
advertising fare, and teaching them to gain more insight and information about what they watch.
—Desmond (1997, p. 23)

Pop culture *is* American culture.

—Statement articulated by the producers of the CBS "Survivor"
television show on "The Today Show" (August 14, 2000;
see http://tvtalkshows.com/todayshow)

Film and television shape the way we dress, how we think, and how
we talk.

—Statement articulated by Spike Lee, noted Hollywood film
director and producer, on "The Today Show"
(October 12, 2000; see http://tvtalkshows.com/todayshow)

OVERVIEW

Ann Watts Pailliotet

Whitman College, Washington

Teaching media literacy and using **popular culture texts** (e.g., television
programs, magazines, videos, films, newspaper advertisements) to enhance
students' language and literacy development has proven successful in Australian and Canadian classrooms (Desmond, 1997; Quin & McMahon, 1992).
In the United States, there is a slowly growing movement toward implementing similar instruction. Advocates of employing media literacy and
popular-culture texts to enhance students' understandings in U.S. schools
are highly diverse. They include educators across all subjects and levels:

community, health, political, and parent organizations; psychologists, counselors, and social workers; cultural critics and media producers. Their aims are also mixed. Some assume "protectionist" or "inoculationist" stances that seek to protect children from objectionable content and values in mass media (e.g., in television, films, or music videos), or to "inoculate" them through education against the dangers of popular culture through education. Others employ media literacy education to further goals (presented earlier in this book) of connecting literacy proficiencies, and using varied print, electronic, and experiential sources; stress critical thinking and prepare democratic citizens (Considine, 1987; Considine, Haley, & Lacy, 1994); and promote self-empowerment or social action through analysis and production of multiple texts (Semali & Watts Pailliotet, 1999).

Although their agendas and methods differ widely, most media educators define media-literate individuals as being able to "access, analyze, evaluate, or create media texts" (Hobbs, 1998, p. 16). Furthermore, those who teach media literacy and add popular-culture texts to their curricula are likely guided by the following principles (Ferrington & Anderson-Iman, 1996; Hobbs, 1998; Thoman, 1999):

1. Media messages are constructed.
2. Media messages are produced within economic, social, political, historical, and aesthetic contexts.
3. Each form of media is constructed with unique creative language. Understanding the characteristics of each form—genres, grammar, syntax, symbols, devices, and metaphor systems of media languages —increases our appreciation and lessens our susceptibility to manipulation.
4. Audiences actively negotiate meaning—different people experience the same media message differently; the interpretative meaning-making processes involved consist of interactions among readers, texts, and cultures.
5. Media are primarily driven by a profit motive.
6. Media representations play a role in an individual's understanding of social reality.
7. Media have embedded values and points of view.

There are many compelling reasons to include media literacy and popular-culture instruction in primary, elementary, and middle school classrooms. Engaging with mass media is the largest leisure activity in the United States (Buckingham, 1993). American students spend 5.5 hours per day engaged with varied mass media outside of classrooms and are exposed to over 400 commercial images every day (Adult Learning Service Associates, 1999). Mass media and popular culture are "powerful source[s] of social learning that shape attitudes, social and consumer behaviors and people's world views." Popular culture therefore impacts literate behaviors in home and school (Dyson, 1997) and can promote pleasure, motivation, and academic interest in diverse students (Alvermann et al., 1999). Additionally, literacy competencies in one medium support and extend those in others (Neuman, 1991; Watts Pailliotet, 1998, 2000).

Media-literacy instruction has the capacity to extend and complement numerous instructional frameworks and approaches, including promoting students' critical thinking (Considine & Haley, 1999) and inquiry learning (Hobbs, 1997; Macaul, Giles, & Rodenberg, 1999); expanding whole-language activities (Fehlman, 1996); enhancing multicultural curricula (Kincheloe & Steinberg, 1997); augmenting cooperative learning initiatives (Watts Pailliotet, 1998); optimizing content area reading assignments (Watts Pailliotet, 1997); promoting students' active construction of knowledge (Alvermann et al., 1999; Vygotsky, 1986); supporting values programs (Considine & Haley, 1999); maximizing interdisciplinary (Leveranz & Tyner, 1996) or thematic teaching (Considine, 1987); extending literature appreciation and study (Considine et al., 1994); and contributing to skills-based literacy programs (Moline, 1995; Thoman, 1999).

Recognizing the extensive instructional benefits of media education, 48 states now have media-literacy standards (Kubey & Baker, 1999). In addition, the NCTE/IRA English Language Arts Standards (Farstrup & Myers, 1996) reflect a broad range of instructional goals for teaching media and popular culture. For example:

> Students read a wide range of print and nonprint texts to build an understanding of texts, of themselves, and of the cultures of the United States and the world . . . Apply a wide range of strategies to comprehend, interpret, evaluate and appreciate texts . . . adjust their use of spoken, written and visual language . . . to communicate effectively with a variety of audiences and for different purposes . . . Gather, evaluate and synthesize data . . . Use a variety of technological and informational resources (libraries, databases, computer networks, video) . . . Use spoken, written, and visual language to accomplish their own purposes. . . . (p. 3)

WHAT DO YOU NEED TO KNOW?
HOW DO YOU BEGIN?

As an effective teacher, you already know that teaching media literacy and using popular-culture texts to enhance students' literacy proficiencies does not mean simply popping a handy video into the VCR at the end of a class period or school day. You also recognize that it is vital for teachers to gain some explicit information in order to successfully link media and popular-culture texts and activities with literacy lessons. What do you need to know? How can you begin? You may want to begin by reading some excellent resources. Sue Lockwood Summers' *Media Alert! 200 Activities to Create Media-Savvy Kids* (1997) is a fabulous place to start. There are 50 pages of teaching ideas categorized into age-appropriate levels: preschool/first grade, elementary, middle, and high school. Many of the activities offered employ easily accessed media texts like newspapers, advertisements, radio, newscasts, and magazines. Students can cut out or highlight describing words and discriminate between fact and opinion, write new stories about comics and story board plots, identify common elements in music and poetry, identify missing items in news stories, or analyze picture books and illustrations. Lockwood Summers also coauthored *Changing the World Through Media Education* (1998) with Rosen and Quesada. This text offers units that further curricula in social studies and health, as well as ready-to-go lesson plans, forms, materials, media organization resources, and a useful glossary.

Considine and Haley's *Visual Messages: Integrating Imagery Into Instruction* (2nd ed.) (1999) is perhaps the classic in media education. It begins with clearly written explanations and rationales and includes a range of activities for varied media texts (e.g., news, advertising, television, movies), thematic teaching (stereotypes, race, gender, violence, and the culture of slimness), ready-to-teach materials, and up-to-date reference lists for organizations, readings, related films, and additional resources.

I highly recommend two other texts by Chris Worsnop. *Screening Images: Ideas for Media Education* (2nd ed.) (1999b) provides extensive lists of lesson ideas. *Assessing Media Work: Authentic Assessment in Media Education* (1999a) is an essential text with multiple examples of media project assessments like rubrics, narrative criteria, and process grading procedures.

For teachers interested in video production, a best bet is William J. Valmont's *Creating Videos for School Use* (1995). This text is packed with "how to" information, diagrams, and lesson materials, ranging from the simplest to most sophisticated projects.

It also is important for you to research the many recent articles in *Journal of Adolescent and Adult Literacy, The Reading Teacher,* and the International Reading Association's free electronic *Reading Online* (http://www.reading online.org), which is devoted in part to media literacy and popular texts. Do an ERIC Documents or Internet search. Great places to start are the Center for Media Literacy (http://www.medialit.org) and Ferrington's extensive site at (http://interact.uoregon.edu/MediaLit/HomePage).

After reading some of these excellent sources, try some media/popular-culture/critical-thinking activities with your students. Research accuracy in media texts; compare information from varied sources; evaluate relevant and irrelevant information in advertisements; determine points of view and target audience in advertisements; compare genres in multiple texts like film and print; or compare and contrast "hard" and "soft" news.

Promote students' awareness of media and print texts by using graphic organizers (Buehl, 2001) in which students list electronic-media elements and circle the ones shared with print. Foster awareness of advertising strategies by having students keep viewing logs. Arrange group media scavenger hunts and ask students to record their responses to newspaper headlines about given topics. Help them analyze toy packaging. Encourage students to consider the rewards they achieve through playing video games and listening to language in music. Students also can design bumper stickers, T-shirts, or advertising slogans for a favorite book.

Ask students to examine tobacco and alcohol marketing for persuasive tactics. Invite a social worker, police official, medical professional, judge, or lawyer to discuss community or health consequences attributed to these addictive habits. Develop advertisements or bulletin boards that depict the real consequences of substance abuse. Investigate tobacco- or alcohol-related Web sites and critically read them for bias and fact. Explore and discuss the accuracy and impact of media depictions about violence, racism, or sexism. Ask students to examine values and behaviors of media characters and their heroes and then compare them to their own values through narratives. Research diverse historic figures through the Internet, newspapers, and print, or interview community leaders and create a video about them.

You and your students also can track news stories each day and record how many days the stories are reported and through which media. Compare and contrast the views presented. Begin your class or after-recess activity with a current-events report or a media watch session. Use markers or crayons to highlight sections on a world map that show which parts of the world are featured with respect to current news and which nations are overlooked in network newscasts, newspapers, or news magazines. Discuss the possible reasons for this dichotomy.

Begin a media and popular-culture lending library for parents and colleagues. Use videos, articles, and Web sites. Join a listserv to exchange teaching ideas. Compile a classroom resource of students' written or video reviews of music, videos, games, or other popular texts. Construct a print or electronic **zine** (i.e., low-budget magazine) with a theme related to some aspect of your curriculum. Contact your local "Newspapers in Education" coordinators. They have a multitude of resources and teaching ideas, and they often offer reduced subscription rates for classrooms. Finally, at the end of each week or as a culminating activity for a thematic unit, foster student collaboration and community by creating a class scrapbook, public service announcement, or video that illustrates and synthesizes students' learning, thinking, and opinions.

CASES AND COMMENTARIES

Case #10.1: "'Hip-Hop' and All That Rock"
(by Michael Harden)

"Dr. Love, Rapper Chuck D, Flavor Flav, and Puff Daddy are COOOL," David shouted when we were talking about putting on a play about our science inquiry.

"Yeah," Anthony responded. "Let's do a play about Dr. Love, Rapper Chuck D., Flavor Flav, and Puff Daddy and their wicked ways."

"I don't know who they are," I answered. The idea of putting on a play with sixth-grade boys about hip-hop stars named Dr. Love, Rapper Chuck D, Flavor Flav, and Puff Daddy was not on my science-teaching agenda.

The same thing happened when we painted. The boys created terrible-looking creatures that they had seen on TV. They also tried to paint really provocative women that looked like the Spice Girls to me and they got frustrated when they couldn't create animated cars, trains, and animals like they see in high-tech films and videos. Well, I finally had to make some rules. "No more TV and rap stuff in our work," I announced. "We need to use our own imaginations and ideas."

I wonder if I am fooling myself? These sixth-grade students are significantly influenced by television, high-tech films, and "hip hop" and rock music as Alvermann et al. state in their text *Popular Culture in the Classroom: Teaching and Researching Critical Media Literacy* (1999). How can I counteract what they see and hear daily and consider "cool"? How can I bring out their own creativity? Should I even try to counteract the influences of media that surround them? I don't feel comfortable allowing my students to write about people like Dr. Love and Puff Daddy.

1. Do you think Michael should try to counteract the influences of media that surround his students?_____

_____

2. Would you allow your students to write about Dr. Love and Puff Daddy? Why or why not? _____

_____

Commentary #10.1A: "'Hip-Hop' and All That Rock"
(by Jay Stetzer, Elementary and Middle School
Arts Teacher, Rochester, New York)

Dear Michael,

Congratulations! You ask profound questions in your teaching case, which suggests to me that you are deeply engaged in your work with your students. All artists create from their surroundings—from what they experience, see, hear, and perceive in their world. Your students are no different from other artists. They create what they know to be truth and reality. You think that this is a problem. Perhaps the problem is that you are working with a limited definition of the word *art*. I immediately think of the themes in Hollywood director Spike Lee's exceptionally popular films (see Spike Lee's comments at the beginning of this chapter). His work arises from his own life experiences. And, though I agree that some aspects of pop culture are profoundly disturbing, they are still "fodder for the creative mill" in my opinion.

So what kind of art do you want your students to make? You mention that you want to bring out their own creativity. How about bringing in some model artwork for them to look at—**Edvard Munch's** "The Scream" (one of his best-known works and used in *Scary Movie,* which most of your students will have seen), or perhaps **Pablo Picasso's** "Guernica" (a condemnation of the bombing of the Spanish town, Guernica). Check out any book on 20th-century art and you'll probably find more material than you'll ever need. Then, get your students reading and writing, and after that, drawing (or vice versa—drawing first, then reading and writing). Find writings that reflect your students' particular experiences. There are plenty of urban writers and poets, for instance, who have actually transformed their mundane experience into something of a mystical nature, and they are very inspiring for students who are trying to make sense of their world.

If you want to influence your students' creative thinking, you need to become the agent of change relative to their surroundings. In other words, do not expect your students to turn out exceptionally creative and thoughtful work unless you become a significant part of their lessons by introducing them to various artists' work and the media they utilize to express themselves. This type of teaching takes planning, extra time, and commitment to good pedagogy, but these additional efforts are well worth your time and energy. Your students will surprise you.

Commentary #10.1B: " 'Hip-Hop' and All That Rock"
(by Bruce Fischman, Middle School Teacher,
Hereford, Pennsylvania)

Hello Michael,

In the text *Scaffolding Emergent Literacy: A Child-Centered Approach for Pre-school Through Grade 5* (Soderman, Gregory, & O'Neill, 1999), the concept of literacy is discussed as a very complex process that intertwines the components of oral-language development, writing development, and reading development (p. 41). The framework for this integrated process includes reading, writing, speaking, listening, and viewing. This comparatively new idea about the importance of the dimension of **critical viewing** is the essence for creating and offering literacy-based arts instruction. Using the arts as ways of learning literacy motivates students and serves to bridge the gap in meaning-making activities (also see Fisherkeller, 2000).

So, my response to you is "yes," begin with what your students know and admire (i.e., Dr. Love, Rapper Chuck D, Flavor Flav, and Puff Daddy), but then engage them in understanding just how these artists' life experiences and perceptions have influenced their creative work.

I have always integrated the arts (as literacy) with my students' literacy learning. For example, at the beginning of each school year, I spend time teaching my students about **Leonardo da Vinci.** His life story and struggles open the way for all of us to use our imaginations. We learn that daVinci kept a journal where he sketched his ideas and made up a code to describe his inventions (writing upside down and backwards—which your students would love to learn to do). We learn about the **Renaissance** and how daVinci coped with the patron system and with contemporary artists of his time. We learn how daVinci influenced new ideas and conceptions about art and what risks he took to advance his theories. And, after we read about daVinci's life, we make our own sketch journals, just like daVinci.

For the remainder of the school year, our sketch journals are our connecting force to what we read as we picture story characters and events. We even sketch alternative solutions to story problems. Thus, we use our journals to think about and personally respond to what we've read.

In addition to using our sketch journals for reading, we use them to complete graphic organizers (http://www.graphic.org) and story maps (Buehl, 2001) for plotting our writing. Sketching and creating visual organizers help us picture, contemplate, and rethink our ideas for writing stories and informative material. Our sketch journals also serve as an authentic assessment tool because they detail the developmental history of our thinking related to what we've read and what we have seen or dreamed—our visualizations. It's a place we can return to again and again to find more details and ask more questions. Throughout the day, my students often hear me say, "Get out your sketch journals," when we're working. In fact, the journals are a place to which my students turn when they need to think or sort out their ideas . . . just like daVinci! So, Michael, you might try using sketch journals (see Harste et al., 1988; Rasinski & Padak, 2000; Scott & Villagrana, 1999). One final word—don't be anxious about your students' experiences with pop culture. Pop culture permeates our world. Recognize and use Dr. Love and Puff Daddy to build upon and enhance what your students know.

Case #10.2: "Pokemon Problems" (by Beth LeBlanc)

Brandon, one of my fifth graders, is obsessed with Pokemon, a popular Gameboy series of characters. When he authored his book about the rain forest, he wrote about Pokemon. Anytime we do a visual-arts activity, he draws characters from Pokemon. His obsession interferes with the lessons I plan and offer the students. For example, I started off this spring semester with a journal entry that said, "What was the best part about your Christmas holiday?"

Brandon, who has difficulty writing, wrote, "My best thing I have for Christmas is Pokemon Yellow. Tomorrow I'm suppose to get a Gameboy Color."

Then, when I asked the students to decorate their journals, Brandon covered the front and back of his journal with sketches of Pokemon characters and their names.

In last week's session we read folktales about animals. The readings complemented our study of mammals and reptiles. Following our reading, each student wrote a short folktale about an animal and illustrated it for our mural. I was encouraged when I read Brandon's story because it was about an eagle and his previous stories had all been about Pokemon. "At last!" I thought. "I have found a topic that Brandon is interested in besides Pokemon."

As the students were looking for models of animals to copy for their story, Brandon got a book on Pokemon characters and began to copy the character that looked like an eagle. His work was very detailed, but he changed the focus of his writing and visual art to match his fascination with Pokemon. This prompted the other students to stop working. They began looking at Brandon's Pokemon artwork and commenting about it because many of them also are preoccupied with Pokemon. They gave Brandon considerable positive reinforcement and attention, and this made it even more difficult for me to divert Brandon's obsession to our goal—creating drawings of animal characters in our stories.

Brandon's teacher also agrees that he is obsessed with Pokemon. She says that whenever he must create visual art other than Pokemon, he says, "I can't draw."

For our next lesson, I plan to bring in some accurate pictures of eagles for Brandon to use as a model. I guess I should have done that in the first place. I continue to wonder how to wean Brandon from his obsession with Pokemon. I am not sure if I can—or if I should. What do other teachers do about students' fascination with popular-culture computer games, videos, and music?

1. Why is Beth so firm in her beliefs that Brandon should not think, draw, or write about Pokemon? _____

_____

2. Why do you think Brandon is preoccupied with Pokemon? _____

_____

Commentary #10.2A: "Pokemon Problems" (by Dana Grisham, Teacher Educator, San Diego State University)

It seems to me that teachers are always trying to decide when to acknowledge students' outside interests and when to intervene and limit students' choices so that new-content learning occurs. I consider Beth's dilemma a difficult one to solve because today's popular-culture artifacts, such as rap or "hip-hop" music, cartoons, or video game characters most definitely are here to stay and significantly influence students' thinking and perceptions. For example, in a recent survey, college-bound seniors were asked if they had to give up either their computer or their television which would they choose? All responded that they would give away their computer because they were addicted to sitcoms and MTV.

If I were Beth, I would use a problem-solving stance to consider and brainstorm solutions to her Pokemon problem. For example, Beth might ban Pokemon from the classroom. But, that's probably too simplistic (not to mention heavy-handed). A teacher can ban Pokemon or any other popular-culture fad, but it most likely will just go underground. Not only that, I believe that we should make school more responsive to students' lives, including their interests. Also, banning Pokemon might provoke a power struggle that would most likely result in a negative classroom atmosphere, which is harmful for students' learning.

I suggest that rather than banning Pokemon Beth could use Pokemon productively. She might encourage projects where Pokemon responses are appropriate and use Pokemon as a springboard for learning. For instance, students might write stories that portray Pokemon characters. They might author and present a drama production that contains Pokemon characters. Pokemon characters could decorate their notebooks, journals, and murals. Beth also could teach points of view by presenting a story in which two Pokemon characters have opposing convictions. Additionally, Beth could offer Pokemon character stickers or cards to reward students for their behavior and motivation to work.

Another idea might be to limit Pokemon in the classroom and only encourage these cute, exotic creatures to emerge at previously agreed-upon times. That is, Brandon and his classmates could use the Pokemon characters in some writing and content lessons. However, at other times, there are "non-Pokemon" lesson. In these lessons, students must play by the teacher's rules. A good example is the animal research mural Beth describes. Beth could have told the class that only real animals could be drawn. At other times, a lesson might contrast mythical animals (including Gameboy characters) with real animals and could include a compare-and-contrast essay suitable for fifth-grade students. (Then Brandon could use his Pokemon characters.)

What happens if Brandon balks at not getting to do something involved with Pokemon? Well, then I think Beth has a classroom management problem as well as a curriculum problem. I think I would try to solve this by sitting down with Brandon individually to explain why he may not continue to use Pokemon in an unlimited fashion. Beth might have to enlist parent support and/or provide rewards and sanctions. I do believe that a compromise may allow Brandon to save face and provide a solution to Beth's problem.

In closing, I want to tell Beth that she shouldn't get too upset over her students' popular-culture obsessions. We all succumb to popular fads. I was (and still am) wild over the Beatles. My niece is crazy about the Backstreet Boys. I know a literacy teacher educator who wears a silver toe ring and paints her toenails greenish-gold. I've taught some excellent preservice teachers who wore studs in their tongues. The important thing to remember is that teachers can help students become informed consumers by recognizing how popular-culture fads can (and do) influence their reasoning and have the capacity to consume their time, energy, and money. For example, teachers and students could plan a popular-culture thematic unit. Students could interview all of the students in the school to determine what specific fads are prevalent at each grade level. They also can interview their parents and grandparents to determine what popular-culture music, films, and so on, they remember and consider influential to their lives as adolescents. Students also could research how much money is spent on popular-culture fads, such as Gameboy Pokemon characters, music videos, and the like.

Commentary 10.2B: "Pokemon Problems"
(by Sharon Miller, Retired Language Arts Supervisor,
Bel Aire, Maryland, and Co-Director for Teacher
Research, Southern Arizona Writing Project, Tucson)

Hello Beth,

I think there is absolutely nothing wrong with Brandon's passionate interest in Pokemon. Why can't he believe that getting Pokemon Yellow was his best Christmas holiday experience? Who are we, as adults, to judge how a fifth grader should respond to his Christmas? Brandon is simply giving an honest answer to what he thought was an honest question.

I suggest that you think carefully about your strong reactions to Brandon's infatuation with Pokemon. For example, why don't you want Brandon to decorate his journal with Pokemon characters? Students' journals should reflect their individual thoughts, opinions, likes, dislikes, and feelings. Right now Brandon likes Pokemon so that's why he draws Pokemon figures on his journal. His interest in Pokemon is genuine and should be respected. Now, if he wanted to draw and write about gory, dismembered figures, I wouldn't support that.

I can even understand Brandon's perception that each Pokemon is a folk character. The Pokemon phenomenon has become significant to the popular culture of youngsters everywhere. To Brandon, Pokemon characters are folk heroes. I admire Brandon's persistence and his ability to make a connection between the eagle and his interest in Pokemon. Why must a folk eagle be physically and anatomically equivalent to a real eagle? In many folktales, animals talk and are otherwise anthropomorphic; Brandon made his eagle "pokemorphic." So what? And, why assume that he changed his eagle? Maybe that was how he saw him when he was writing the story.

Now, let's examine your distress about the other students in your group getting distracted by Brandon's refusal to abandon his personal interests in favor of your well-prepared lessons. I agree with you that Brandon's preoccupations with Pokemon have the potential to interfere with the lessons you planned. I have a suspicion that the school has banned all Pokemon card activity as distracting and disruptive, which is well within their rights. If this is true, prohibiting students from thinking, talking, drawing, and writing about Pokemon (or anything they have a passionate interest in) has only served to heighten students' interests and fascination with the banned topic.

Let's think more positively about Pokemon. Though I don't profess to know a great deal about the Pokemon phenomenon, I do know that even very young children understand and can articulate and draw incredibly complex relationships between and among the various Pokemon characters. Older students engage in sophisticated and complex negotiations when buying, selling, or trading cards that require using various combinations of multiple literacies. For example, students are well aware of the worth of individual Pokemon cards. They use their verbal, social, and cognitive abilities to barter a successful exchange of cards. They even keep track of what cards they have traded and acquired, sometimes using a sophisticated, computer-generated recording system. They go online to gather up-to-date information about which Pokemon characters are "hot." They read to discover what new characters will soon be available and they plan carefully to acquire new Pokemon cards at the cheapest price. Is there a discrepancy between these behaviors and what is expected of students in 21st-century classrooms? Are students asked to think and act using such sophisticated multiple literacy tasks as part of a lesson? I wonder. I think teachers should take a long, analytical look at the developmental processes involved in this popular-culture phenomenon and apply it to classroom activities designed to help students further develop these complex critical-thinking and communication skills.

One last thought about your classroom Pokemon problems, Beth. Some good, healthy, respectful conversation between you and your students about what interests them will go a lot further in restoring order to a lesson than acting as the thought police. Come on, Beth. Lighten up. I remember when my generation was thoroughly "obsessed" with Elvis and rock and roll. We turned out okay.

Case #10.3: "Too Much Popular Culture for Me" (by Marci Andrews)

My five eighth-grade language arts students (all girls) think of nothing except media stars like the Spice Girls; Eminem, the controversial rap star; and Jennifer Lopez. Every time I observe my students they are creating and practicing dance routines and dialogue they see on TV and in videos. They slink and slide all over the floor and sing the latest songs.

I really do have to admire the way they can imitate the Spice Girls' British accent. They carry on impromptu conversations that are very clever, like "Oh, Baby Spice, where are you going tonight?"

"Oh, Posh Spice, I am going out to dinner with a new boyfriend and then we are going to a new British Dance Club in Soho. Where are you going, Ginger Spice?"

They even know the Spice Girls' old Web site: http://www.spicegirls.org.

My dilemma is that my ideas differ from my students about how we should engage in informal drama enactments that are part of our language arts postreading strategies. I think the characters in our drama initiatives should resemble the characters in our literature books. Instead, my students insist on mimicking their pop heroes and heroines. For example, after we finished reading excerpts from *Little Women* (Alcott, adapted by Gerver, 1868/1999) they played the parts of Jo, Amy, Meg, the mother, and Beth using Spice Girl British accents. I have to admit they were humorous and clever.

I don't want to ignore my students' ideas and interests. Yet, the only drama they want to engage in is taking on the identities of popular-culture stars. In fact, they overly exaggerate the way Jennifer Lopez and the Spice Girls talk, sing, and act. I know they are being creative and imaginative, but where are my students' own identities and ideas? Should I put limits on their creativity?

1. How might Marci solve her problem? _____

_____

2. Do you think Marci should try to redirect her students' creativity and use of popular-culture icons? _____

_____

Commentary #10.3A: "Too Much Popular Culture for Me"
(by Timothy Morse, Teacher Educator, University
of Southern Mississippi)

Dear Marci,

I applaud you for considering your students' ideas and strong fascinations with popular culture when you plan your lessons. That is responsive teaching (Moje et al., 2000,). You obviously recognize that your lessons will be more meaningful to your students when you capitalize on their interests and adoration of popular-culture stars (i.e., *fandom*) (Alvermann & Hagood, 2000). Therefore, you are addressing one of the principles recently adopted by the International Reading Association: "Adolescents deserve access to a wide variety of materials that they can and want to read" (D. Moore, Beane, Birdyshaw, & Rycil, 1999, p. 101).

I suspect that as you struggle to resolve your dilemma about including or not including your students' infatuation with popular-culture stars in your literacy lessons, inwardly you are looking for a compromise. I say this because you acknowledged that your ideas differ from your students. Yet, you also acknowledge the validity of your students' personal adolescent literacies (Alvermann et al., 1999). You think their drama initiatives should resemble the characters in their literature books, but at the same time you admit that your students' informal drama enactments are humorous and clever. You never fully concede that your students should be encouraged to take on the identities of Eminem, Jennifer Lopez, and the Spice Girls. In fact, you even state that you want more of their own identities and ideas to emerge. Yet you continue to go along with your students' affinity for celebrities. I think that your situation may readily lend itself to becoming one in which both sides' interests can be accommodated.

What will the compromise be? Your compromise might consist of informal drama enactments in which you create a drama initiative that resembles the characters in your literature books whereas your students create one that is based on how the characters in your literature books might be recast as your students' heroes and heroines. Think for a moment about how the recent movie *The Family Man*, with Nicholas Cage (Ratner, 2000), recast the main character from the film *It's a Wonderful Life*, who was played by Jimmy Stewart (Capra, 1946). Your students might do something similar in their drama initiatives. You may even want to begin this process by showing your students both movies and having them discuss how the main characters were recast to reflect changes that have occurred in society over time.

As you work to make your compromise happen, you must be mindful of the fact that someone must take charge so that a compromise can be reached. When business management and labor unions negotiate, a mediator takes the lead. Because classrooms are run by teachers and not mediators, you will have to take the lead. This should not present a problem once your students see that they will be given a fair shake. In fact, adolescents tell us they want their parents and teachers to be authority figures and not their friends, so you should not be afraid to take the lead (Steinberg, 1997). Rather, in the long run you will earn your students' respect as they come to see you as an adult who directs them in some ways but respects their emerging independence as young adults in other ways.

When both you and your students create different drama initiatives, you will discover ideas from each other's creativity. This will enable your students to learn from your modeling (Maag, 1999), and both of you to learn from examining multiple viewpoints. Also, when students create their drama, they will bring their own identities and ideas to the fore as they determine how the characters in the story would be recast to reflect today's pop culture, which, in fact, is their pop culture (Alvermann & Hagood, 2000). These activities can also serve as a springboard for discussions about the numerous changes that have occurred in society over the years, such as changes in dress, language, and values. The list of topics you can explore will be endless.

Let me close by saying that I, too, have questions concerning whether we should limit or welcome adolescents' personal literacies into the classroom. What do we do when our students' pop-culture interests do not match stated curriculum guidelines? How can we tap students' interests to extend their knowledge and motivations for reading? How can we teach so that we provide students with opportunities to consider multiple perspectives and texts other than their own? How can we use popular-culture texts and students' self-expression and passions to ensure that we teach responsively?

Commentary #10.3B: "Too Much Popular Culture for Me" (by Jane Percival, Head Elementary Teacher, Haydenville, Massachusetts)

Well, Marci, your students certainly seem to be enjoying acting in your class. You are providing these adolescents with a developmentally appropriate means of trying out a variety of ways of being in this world. Also, they are working cooperatively to produce the informal dramatic enactments while individually being creative. What a combination! As your observations indicate, their obsession with media stars has stimulated them to learn much about drama (e.g., improvisation, choreography, speaking with an accent).

At the same time, your question is an important one that needs to be addressed: How can teachers build on students' ideas and interests, support their being creative and imaginative, and simultaneously expand the roles and genres they are willing to dramatize? Though at first, it seems that your students need to have limits set on the characters that they can bring to life, I believe that opening more channels through which their creativity can flow might be more productive.

Let's see how this might look in a given situation: dramatizing excerpts from *Little Women* (Alcott, adapted by Graves, 1868/1999). For instance, you might begin by having each student assume the role of one of the characters from the book. Ask each student to answer the following questions the way she knows the character would answer the questions, given the information in the excerpts read:

1. What did you have for breakfast this morning? What kinds of sounds did you hear as you got dressed?
2. By the way, how did you select what you were going to wear?
3. Did you have to do anything you didn't want to do recently? How do you feel about that?
4. Was there anyone today who made you feel very happy? How did they accomplish that?
5. How are you feeling about my asking you these questions? Why?
6. If you could ask any question of the rest of your family what would it be?

By asking these questions, and similar ones, you are focusing your students' attention on *who the characters are* prior to the improvisation. When answering the questions, students should speak in the dialect as written by the author, Louisa May Alcott. Once the students have a clear idea of who they are when in a scene, then they can truly act and react like those individuals. Because your students also seem to enjoy creating humorous enactments, a next step might be to work with the same scenes from the book but this time introduce a time-traveling pop star like Eminem or a Spice Girl. You, as the teacher, might even act as the pop star. Your students could then become the director and help you develop your character by using a method similar to the one that you used with them. Everyone might enjoy seeing what happens, for example, when Jo, Meg, and Beth try to have afternoon tea with Ginger Spice.

Building on your students' interests in singing and dancing, you might have the students write songs that each character could sing and still remain true to who they are. Dance movements would be planned similarly—always guided by who the characters actually are as discovered in the texts read. From your description of your students, it seems that this approach is similar to the one that has worked for these young actors in the past. For example, their viewing of videos and reading of other texts has guided their enactment of their favorite pop stars. They have "checked out" the accents and movements they are using with those in the media "texts" just as you now would be asking them to do with Jo, Meg, and Beth in Alcott's *Little Women*. Eventually, your class might decide to take their enactments to a larger audience, perhaps another class that is reading or is about to read *Little Women*. Therefore, Marci, I recommend that you choose the pop star that you would really like be for a while and, also, definitely continue giving your students many opportunities to reenter literary works through drama.

REFLECTIONS AND EXPLORATIONS

1. When you were in seventh or eighth grade which pop stars did you admire? How did you express your admiration? What connections, if any, could you make to these pop stars and the texts you were reading then?
2. Survey 10 seventh or eighth graders. Ask them to name their favorite music, film, and television stars. Discover why they admire these stars. What attributes do the seventh and eighth graders admire in pop stars?
3. Why do you think so many young people enjoy popular-culture characters like Pokemon?
4. As a teacher, would you link all types of popular culture with your literacy lessons? What criteria would you use for your decisions?

INTEGRATING POPULAR-MEDIA-CULTURE LITERACY IN YOUR CLASSROOM: PRACTICAL APPLICATIONS

You will want to plan and construct classroom media/popular-culture activities carefully to make sure that each endeavor is educational and extends your students' literacy learning and critical-thinking abilities. Responding to the following questions will help you consider your students' instructional needs and your teaching context as you organize and offer effective lessons:

1. How does the media-literacy lesson or the inclusion of popular-culture texts relate to your teaching objectives?
2. Can you articulate a clear and sound rationale about the lesson to your students, administrator, parents, and colleagues?
3. What curriculum standards does your lesson support in reading, writing, communication, content areas, and/or technology?
4. How long will your activity or unit take?

5. What means and criteria will you use to assess student processes, products, and learning?

6. Does your school or district have any guidelines or restrictions for the content of media and popular-culture texts?

7. Are there any problems with the content of media or popular-culture texts you plan to use (e.g., music videos or zines)?

8. If needed, how will you get parental permission for using a media or popular-culture text or activity, and what will you plan for alternative activities for students who do not have parental permission?

9. How will you establish and convey rules for student use of equipment, such as video cameras?

10. What criteria will you use to establish guidelines for the types of texts students may select or generate?

11. What suitable equipment and texts do you already have?

12. What equipment and texts do you need?

13. How can you acquire needed texts and equipment? Are there ways to collaborate with other teachers, use parent or community resources, or obtain grant funds?

SUGGESTED READINGS

Epstein, S. (Ed.). (1999). *Adolescents and Their Music: If It's Too Loud, You're Too Old*. London: Falmer Press.

Many teachers have been reluctant to consider the messages portrayed in music that adolescents admire. This book provides cultural and developmental insights about adolescents and their music.

McBrien, J. L. (Ed.). (1999). *Media Matters: Critical Thinking in the Information Age*. Cincinnati, OH: South-Western Educational Publishing.

The authors believe that teachers should teach media literacy to empower students to take control of their actions and to recognize the effects that popular culture and media messages have on their emotions, desires, and beliefs.

Simmons, J., & Baines, J. (Eds.). (1998). *Language Study in Middle School, High School, and Beyond: Views on Enhancing the Study of Language*. Newark, DE: International Reading Association.

Chapters 8 and 9 discuss language education in the 21st century and reading and writing in the shadow of film and television.

11

Integrating the Literacies of Viewing and Visually Representing With Content Reading

> Some U.S. states specifically list viewing as one of the communication skills and include it in curriculum guidelines. Others use the terms media or visual literacy, and still others promote an integrated approach in which the processes of listening, speaking, reading, writing, and viewing lead to higher order thinking and problem solving.
> —Flood, Lapp, & D. Wood (1998, p. 300)

> I always do my pictures first because then I can get looks at my pictures to help me with my describing words. If I wrote my words first,
> I wouldn't be able to see my describing words in my pictures.
> —Hannah (a third grader quoted in Olshansky, 1995, p. 45)

OVERVIEW

Deborah Begoray

University of Victoria, Canada

A listing of the traditional language arts includes reading, writing, listening, and speaking. Viewing and representing as language arts processes recently have been added to the list because we now recognize how important viewing and representing are to students' learning (see Flood & Lapp, 1997–1998).

In the 21st century, we have moved beyond thinking of text as just words and concepts printed on a page (i.e., *print text*). Now, we think of a picture as an *image text,* and we think of a formal speech or an informal conversation as an *oral text.* Did you know that sign language and **Bliss symbol boards** are oral texts, too? Bliss boards have over 500 symbols that enable individuals with oral-language difficulties to express complex abstract thoughts.

Perhaps you know some elementary students who struggle with mathematics because they cannot read well enough to understand word problems. Or perhaps you know a few middle or junior high school students who have problems with history because they have difficulty paying attention to their teachers' lectures. In all probability, offering these students opportunities to read *print* text, hear *oral* text, and view *image* text within the same lesson would help these students become effective learners.

Why should we include viewing and representing (i.e., image texts) in all of our students' literacy lessons? Well, we know that people learn in a variety of ways. You already are familiar with Gardner's (1993) theory of multiple intelligences (MI theory). Gardner (2000) stated that we all "can learn through many ways: through exploration with our hands, the use of several senses . . . and the development of many different kinds of symbols, ranging from paintings or graphs to **semaphore** and dance" (p. 32). Following Gardner's MI theory, many teachers address a variety of ways for their students to learn and depict what they know to ensure that their students will achieve as much academic success as possible.

In the 1990s, some researchers began to suggest that including viewing and visually representing as equal partners with reading and writing would be beneficial for all students "not so much as talents that some may have and others may not have [but] as potentials by which all humans might mean [i.e., the possibilities available to gain and give meaning]" (Leland & Harste, 1994, p. 339). So, it makes sense that you and your students should read, write, listen, and speak, and also view and represent to learn in every content area.

Integrating Viewing and Representing in a Social Studies Lesson

Lessons accompanied by visuals, such as illustrated trade books, pictures, films, props, costumes, drama presentations, drawings, technical diagrams, and charts, can be played back in students' "eyes" as they try to recall important facts and details in content instruction. For example, consider the following lesson about the desert.

You might begin the lesson by asking students to visualize what a desert looks like (i.e., create a picture in their minds). Then, they might do a quick sketch that depicts their ideas about desert scenes (see Rasinski & Padak, 2000).

During the lesson, students might listen while you read them a description of a desert. Then, they might create a second drawing based on their new knowledge about deserts. After the reading, students might work in small groups, comparing their two drawings. Finally, students might use multiple communication systems as research sources (e.g., finding descriptions, maps, charts, and photographs of deserts on computer Web sites and CD-ROM applications). Then, they might collaborate in a larger group to develop a drama enactment where they create puppets and scenery, compose dialogue, and offer a presentation to peers that focuses on desert foxes. In this type of lesson, students have viewed their own drawings, studied computer technology resources, and enjoyed a puppet show. They have represented by drawing and building puppets and scenery for their play. Listening and speaking were included as well. Other language arts could be integrated into the lesson by having students write a **transactional voice** composition about the desert to accompany their drawings.

WHAT DO YOU NEED TO KNOW?
HOW CAN YOU BEGIN?

As a teacher who wants to help all students recognize their literacy potential by integrating viewing and representing literacy with content and fiction-reading instruction, you will need to become a good viewer and representer yourself. Your students see you as a model for what is valuable in the classroom. What do you need to know? How can you begin?

At first, you may think that developing your viewing and representing aptitudes is a bit unusual. You may think that being a good teacher is mostly about being an effective speaker. Being a good teacher requires effective oral-language skills, of course, but it also includes being skillful in the visual domain.

Your knowledge of the reading process will help you get started. Remember the lessons you learned in elementary school about slowing down and rereading when comprehension is challenging. The same applies to viewing and representing. For example, you might begin to hone your viewing abilities by examining a tiny ant. Take time to observe the ant carefully. Inspect the legs. Notice the thorax and abdomen. Determine the exact color of the ant. Close your eyes and try to visualize every dimension of the ant. If you have difficulty remembering every facet of the ant, look carefully again. Then, write a detailed description of your observations. In addition to writing, draw (i.e., represent) the ant, including the smallest details. Then, think about how your drawings helped you recognize what you did and did not remember about the ant's eyes, legs, and other body parts. Consider how your representations helped you to visualize small details of the ant's anatomy.

The next step in your viewing and representing journey might be for you to think about your own talents and interests. For example, if you travel, you might collect photographs and souvenirs that you can use to introduce a historical text to your students. If you sew, you might create a box of simple costumes to facilitate skits during the reading of a play or novel. If you play the guitar, use it in the classroom to accompany your students as they sing a song they have created that contains new vocabulary terms pertinent to a science unit. Once you have shared your own talents with your students, involve them and their talents—seek out the dancers, painters, builders, musicians, and video game creators in your classroom. Learn from them and ask them to teach each other. Model risk taking for your more timid students by sharing your own fledgling skills.

Of course, you will also need to develop contacts with knowledgeable adults. For instance, seek colleagues and parents who will teach you and your students how to hone your observation skills so that you can create scientific drawings, such as the developing root systems of plants or the life cycle of a butterfly. Find other teachers who are film enthusiasts and ask them to recommend clips from videos to introduce concepts. For example, to facilitate a better understanding of slavery, students might view the 1977 miniseries, *Roots,* in which the author, Alex Haley, traces his African ancestors (see Schellaci, 1977). Students might also view *Fantasia* (Walt Disney Home Video, 2000, originally produced in 1940), a film that blends animation and classical music. Short films can be rented at a reasonable cost and used as a viewing center to support themed content units. Cable companies frequently offer programming that can be videotaped free of charge and without copyright infringement.

Of course, there are many reference books in the library that will help you learn new ideas about viewing and representing. I recommend *Video Camcorder School: A Practical Guide to Making Great Home Videos* (Squires, 1992), *Masks* (McNiven & McNiven, 1994), and *Activities for Creating Pictures and Poetry* (Bunchman & Briggs, 1994). Children's bookstores and gift shops at art galleries and museums contain high-quality books on the art and craft of creating visuals. *Watercolor for the Artistically Undiscovered* (Hurd & Cassidy, 1992) includes inspiring ideas, paints, and a brush, and authentic watercolor paper to encourage any beginner.

The children's section of the library also is a good place to start. Writers and illustrators of children's books understand beautifully how to visually represent story characters and story events. I suggest that you start with your library's recent acquisitions in the children's nonfiction section. For example, *Firefly Guide to Space: A Photographic Journey Through the Universe* (Bond, 1999) has photographs that were taken using the Hubble telescope to show the wonders of planets, nebula, and other astronomical phenomena. *Penguins* (Gibbons, 1998) displays colorful, labeled drawings to show Antarctic habitats. *Pyramid* (Macaulay, 1975) contains detailed black-and-white illustrations and architectural diagrams.

Another source of help and information is your school library media specialist, who often has the technical expertise to show you and your students how to use camcorders to create video documentaries. The media specialist also can help you use search engines (e.g. Yahoo, Lycos, Google, and Excite) to navigate your way through the Internet.

Read the other chapters in this book for ideas, too. Think, for example, about how drama, discussed in chapter 5, might apply to learning in a content area. In science, your students could become parts of a cell and move about the room imitating their various functions. In mathematics, they might become the pieces of patterns illustrated in *Anno's Three Little Pigs* (Anno & Mori, 1985), moving to create different sequences. For history content, your students might use ideas discussed in chapter 4 (visual art). For example, after viewing the paintings in *A Medieval Feast* (Aliki, 1983), they might create murals of elaborate meals consumed by nobility in the Middle Ages. They might use digital cameras (see chap. 9) to take photos of themselves in historical costumes or they might create crafts depicted in the book *Pioneer Projects* (Kalman, 1997) and post their work on a class Web site.

Also, look to the real world (we call this looking for authentic ideas). What viewing and representing activities are important in your school's community? Schools in Greenwich Village, New York, might consider inviting a local artist, such as a weaver, to introduce a lesson on how some birds construct their nests. Silicon Valley, California, schools might seek a computer expert on presentation software to help students build charts and tables that represent their findings on population growth in the Third World. Elders in Australian and New Zealand Aboriginal communities and Native Americans in the southwest United States might be invited to demonstrate how to visually "read" the land.

Of course you don't have to live in a specialized community to take advantage of local experts. Most towns and cities offer guest experts in a variety of viewing and representing areas during the year. Volunteer at the local museum and you might receive a free pass so that you can listen to speakers throughout the year. Go to the zoo and observe demonstrations by animal experts. Ask to observe a television program in production at a local station. Take a class in model building or talk to salespeople at the local hobby store.

Universities and colleges usually publish lists of experts who would be pleased to help you learn more about viewing and representing. Call upon these experts to speak at professional development days at your school.

Finally, remember that you are not alone in seeking more understanding about how to integrate viewing and representing into your content area lessons. Many highly educated and experienced teachers are just beginning to learn about visual literacy themselves. Everyone is looking for ideas, and an experienced and enthusiastic teacher determined to expand the viewing and representing in his or her classroom is usually happy to have a newcomer join in the quest. Ask your principal to recommend someone you can approach.

CASES AND COMMENTARIES

Case #11.1: "What Visuals Can Do" (by Alison Sconyers)

I teach language arts/English to a group of four eighth graders—two boys and two girls. One of the boys, Thomas, thinks he is not bright and he lacks self-confidence. He refuses to do anything and always says, "I can't."

He shocked me when he said, "I can't read or write."

This went on for a couple of weeks, and I believed that he had minimal literacy abilities. What I should have done was go to the classroom teacher and ask him about Thomas' reading and writing skills. When I finally did talk to the classroom teacher, he said, "Thomas is a student who needs lots of reassurance. He can read and write. He also only does his work when he is particularly interested in a topic."

Last Monday, Thomas suddenly got turned on to reading. I had the book *The Dragon and the Unicorn* (Cherry, 1995) with me. I used this book to complement our content study of reptiles. For a visual I had a metal dragon with stone eyes. All of the students were amazed, especially Thomas. Along with the metal dragon, I also had multiple texts of *The Dragon and the Unicorn.* This made it possible for all of the students to observe the illustrations very closely as we read the text. We used the reading comprehension strategies, "What Do You See" (Richards, 2001), and "Find the Features and Connect Them" (Richards, Gipe, & Necaise, 1994).

I noted immediately that the beautiful visual representations of the dragons in the text coupled with the visual of the metal dragon and the reading comprehension strategies lured Thomas into a positive, motivated attitude. He even decided that he could read and write. He became so stimulated that he kept raising his hand to join in the discussion and answer questions. In the story there is a part where the dragon and the unicorn are talking about how old the forest is. Thomas raised his hand and said, "Oooh, I know how old the forest is. Look at this picture. You can tell how old a tree is by counting its rings. That will tell us how old the forest might be."

This was an observation that none of the other students or even I noticed, and it showed me that Thomas is most likely a visual learner. This incident also revealed to me how important and beneficial visuals are for students' motivation and learning. Despite the fact that it is time-consuming to collect appropriate visuals to complement ideas offered in literature and topics presented in content text, I will certainly continue using visuals with my students. My concern is that I will not have sufficient time to discover and collect all of the visuals I will need.

1. How might Alison acquire the visuals she and her students need? _____

2. In your opinion, what are the benefits of using visuals to complement content text? _____

_____

Commentary #11.1A: "What Visuals Can Do" (by Timothy Rasinski, Teacher Educator, Kent State University, Ohio)

Alison's case illustrates the importance of knowing students' interests as well as providing students with engaging and motivating reading activities. Thomas neither believes in himself as a reader, nor does he find reading an enjoyable and satisfying activity. Yet, when he was presented with a topic he found interesting (i.e. dragons), he jumped right into the reading and appeared to comprehend well.

All of us have our own particular and peculiar reading interests. It is essential that teachers find out each student's interests so that they might help connect each student to those texts that he or she will most likely find interesting. Whether it is through interest surveys administered at the beginning of each year, periodically interviewing children about their interests, or closely observing students in order to determine their interests, it is incumbent on us as teachers to determine our students' interests so that we can recommend books and other reading materials that they will most likely read and enjoy. We learn to read by reading, and we most readily read those materials that we find internally satisfying. Therefore, teachers need to be aware of students' interests and the reading materials that are most likely to match those interests.

Alison also mentions that Thomas responds well to activities that allow him to visualize the materials he reads. This is an important point as we know that visualization or imagery is a form of comprehension (see Buehl, 2001). Indeed, back in the 1980s, Linda Gambrell and her colleagues' work on imagery and reading helped us understand that students who experience difficulty in comprehending what they read often have difficulty in creating mental images during reading. They demonstrated that training students in creating images, first on paper, then later in their heads, could significantly improve students' comprehension (Gambrell & Bates, 1984; Gambrell, Kapinus, & Wilson, 1987).

Engaging Thomas in visualization activities should pay off in better comprehension as well as more satisfying reading experiences for Thomas. I would advise Alison to have Thomas put his images on paper to share with classmates and the teacher, and then to generally and gently move to more internalized images. One visualization activity that often works well with unmotivated readers is called A Sketch-to-Stretch (Rasinski & Padak, 2000) (also see Short, Harste, & Burke, 1996). In this activity, students draw images of significant events in response to their reading. They share their sketches with fellow readers without telling their peers about their sketch. The job of the other readers is to try to figure out (or infer) what is being portrayed and interpreted in each sketch. Sketch-to-Stretch is a double-inference activity as each reader needs to create inferences in making his or her original sketch. Then, as each sketch is shared, groups of students create inferences as they attempt to explain the sketches. Through such engaging inferencing activities, students are involved in comprehension discussions and thoroughly enjoy trying to interpret each student's personal interpretation (sketch) of the text.

Commentary #11.1B: "What Visuals Can Do" (by Deborah Schussler, High School English Teacher, Williamson County Public Schools, Tennessee)

This case describes a very good example of how one lesson can lead to an amazing breakthrough with a student. The more a teacher can learn about a student, the more likely it is that this breakthrough will occur. Building rapport and developing a relationship with a student is vital for a teacher to get to know the different aspects of a student's learning, including his or her cognitive and affective needs. Creating a variety of activities at the beginning of the year that appeal to different learning styles also facilitates the kind of breakthroughs that Alison experienced with Thomas.

Now that Alison has figured out that the use of visuals facilitates Thomas' reading comprehension and motivation to read, the logistics of incorporating this into her lessons is not a trivial concern. Teachers often know which strategies will work with different students, but they lack the time or resources to implement these strategies. Alison expresses this concern; however, she is not as restricted as she may think. She seems to be under the assumption that she must "discover and collect" all of the visuals for each individual reading assignment. This is only one option. Alison can incorporate visuals into her daily instruction with Thomas without having to collect every visual herself. Visuals can take many forms, many of which are student generated. When students generate or devise their own visuals, they are more likely to be involved in active learning. Student-generated visuals can be created prior to reading as well as during and after reading. For example, prior to reading Alison might tell Thomas that the following day they will read a story about dragons. She can ask him if he has anything at home that resembles a dragon. If not, Alison can help Thomas get on the Internet and find a picture of a dragon. If Thomas is into drawing, he can create his own dragon. For a during- or postreading activity, Thomas might draw what he thinks will happen next in the story and then describe his drawing to Alison. If Thomas is not very artistic, he can use magazines and computer icons to create a collage. In addition to objects or pictures of objects, visual learners often do well with story maps (Buehl, 2001) and character webs that aid their comprehension of a text. Pictures, drawings, and magazine cutouts can be added to these depending on how detailed you want them.

If visuals are the key to getting Thomas involved in literacy activities, then a combination of teacher-generated visuals and student-generated visuals is a good way to manage the concern for lack of time and resources when the visuals are collected solely by the teacher.

Case #11.2: "Where Is My Flashlight? and Stop Playing With the Bear! You Are Fifth Graders" (by Cassandra Lane)

I teach six fifth graders who have learning difficulties. We are studying problem-solving skills. To support our content text and to enhance my students' understanding, I always bring in fiction and visuals that relate to the topic we are focusing on.

This is my first experience with reinforcing students' reading development with visuals. My students seem more interested in the visuals than the texts we read. For example, yesterday, after we read a text chapter that discussed feelings of insecurities, I read the story *Ira Sleeps Over* (Waber, 1972) to the group. The story is about a young boy who wonders how he will manage without his teddy bear at a sleep-over party. I brought a flashlight as a visual representation of one of the important ideas in the story. I had the flashlight sitting in front of me on the table. Of course, the students kept picking it up and turning it on and off. I stopped the story, took the flashlight, and placed it beside me on the table. Before I knew it, the flashlight was gone. I stopped the story and asked, "Who took the flashlight?"

The students just sat there and stared at me. I got up and walked around the group until I found the flashlight in a student's lap. I took the flashlight and put it in my own lap.

The following week, because we needed to complete the story, I brought a stuffed bear as the visual and I experienced another problem after placing the bear on the table. This time, Dylan asked, "Can I hold the bear?"

I did not think it would be a problem, so I gave him the bear and kept on reading. I did think Dylan was rather old to want to hold a toy teddy bear. Yet, before I knew it, the other students began petting and pulling on the bear, and no one was listening to the story. Everyone wanted to hold the bear. I said, "If you cannot stop playing with the bear, I will put it away."

I began reading again, but in 1 minute the students went back to playing with the bear. This time, I placed the bear under my chair.

The visuals had become a distraction rather than an enhancement. I spoke to several people about my dilemma and got these two suggestions:

1. Let one student hold the visual. As I read and turned to the next page of the book, the student holding the visual must pass it to the next student, and so on.

2. Place the visual out of the students' reach if they continue to try to play with it.

I know this sounds negative. Students remember stories better (and content material) if they can see or hold a visual that enhances text ideas and information. Why are visuals hindering my students' attention to reading?

1. Do you think Cassandra's students were too old to listen to the story, *Ira Sleeps Over,* and to want to hold a teddy bear? _____

_____

2. Why do you think it is important to link content text with fiction? _____

_____

Commentary #11.2A: "Where Is My Flashlight? and Stop Playing With the Bear! You Are Fifth Graders" (by Jane Osterman, Elementary Teacher, Oldham County, Kentucky)

Hi, Cassandra!

I want to congratulate you on taking the first step to improve your teaching practice: identifying a problem to solve. As I understand it, the visuals you have been using during read-alouds are distracting your students from paying attention to the books. I am glad to know that you already took the initiative to ask some other teachers for ideas. Many times teachers don't want to admit they don't know what to do, so they just continue to do what they have been doing and get increasingly frustrated. Developing cooperative working relationships with other teachers is key to a successful teaching career.

First, I have some questions about the purpose of the visuals you have been using. Are you using them to help students comprehend the stories and informational text? To build their background knowledge? To retell the story? To connect the story to their previous experiences? To enhance your storytelling? Just for fun? I'm confused about exactly how you've been using the visuals. Do you use them before, during, or after reading? What do you or the students do with them? Become clear on your objectives for using visuals.

Second, though it is important to think about why and how you are using visuals, it is equally important to establish a system for using them that maintains the flow of your lessons. Set clear expectations for how your students should interact with the visuals and communicate them clearly. Then, be consistent in enforcing them. Make sure that when you say things like, "If you cannot stop playing with the bear, I will put it away," that you are going to follow through with what you said. In some cases that may mean altering your lesson so that it does not include a visual.

There are many possible routines you could develop for use of visuals. They range from providing students a certain time before school or at the beginning, or end of the lesson where they can pass visuals around and satisfy their curiosity, to keeping them out of reach until you use them, and placing them back out of reach when you finish. You'll need to think through the possibilities and decide what will work for you and for the group of students you teach.

I think that I would consider creating a special box that is not to be opened until the story or informational text is being read. Only the person reading the text is allowed to remove items from the box. This creates a special class-reading ritual and adds suspense to keep students' attention. Then, when students read to the class (e.g., in a Readers Theatre format, Buehl, 2001) or retell a story, they can use the visual box too.

It is my opinion that you need to choose visuals carefully so that they have a meaningful part to play in meeting the objectives for your lesson and in enhancing students' comprehension and recall of a story or content text.

It's always good to vary the way you use visuals. Think about other visual ways that students can respond to text. They can use puppets to help retell stories. They can choose visuals that represent the main ideas in a story, and illustrate different parts of a story or content text through a Sketch-to-Stretch activity (Scott & Villagrana, 1999) (also see Harste et al., 1988, and Rasinski & Padak, 2000). You can present graphic organizers like Venn diagrams (Taylor, 1999), story maps (Buehl, 2001), and K-W-L charts (Ogle, 1986) (also see Buehl, 2001, for a description of **K-W-L Plus**). Semantic webs/concept maps (Buehl, 2001) are other visual ways to aid students' understanding.

Have fun trying out new ways of using visuals—and remember, once you decide what rules you need to establish for "read aloud time," be firm in enforcing them. Above all, continue to evaluate your own teaching and to think about how you can improve the instruction that you provide. Reflection is the key to effective teaching.

Commentary #11.2B: "Where Is My Flashlight? and Stop Playing With the Bear! You Are Fifth Graders" (by Mary Ellen Cosgrove, Teacher Educator, Armstrong Atlantic State University, Savannah, Georgia)

Hi, Cassandra.

I am so glad you are supporting your students' literacy development using visuals, even if this has caused you some concern. I applaud your using visuals for several reasons. As I am sure you know, the term *literacy* was previously defined as knowing how to read and write, but our ideas about literacy have now expanded to encompass all of the visual and communicative arts. We have identified literacies that include computer literacy, dramatic-arts literacy, music literacy, and visual literacy (i.e., semiotic systems). By creating and using visual images in your print-based literacy lessons, you are addressing and enhancing your students' visual literacy, which is the ability to gain meaning from visual images. Using visuals in conjunction with print-based literacy lessons also offers opportunities for your students to become more involved with story events and story characters' goals and actions, thereby enhancing their involvement with text and their reading comprehension.

Because your students are all unique individuals with different strengths, preferences, and modalities, it is also important that you present text to them in a variety of ways that gives them opportunities to experience success as readers. This support connects to Howard Gardner's multiple intelligence (MI) theory (1993). As you know, Gardner includes **spatial intelligence** in his scheme, that is, the ability to think three-dimensionally, to form mental images, and to perceive the visual world more accurately. So, by providing visuals to accompany your print-based literacy lessons, you are helping them gain a deeper understanding of the text.

Reading is also a social process. Your visuals create a topic for discussion as the students view and touch them. There is considerable evidence that discussion and dialogue about books relates to improved reading comprehension (Daniels, 1994). By examining and sharing visuals before or during your oral reading, you are affording your students opportunities to socialize about a common topic related to the book.

I would like to offer a few suggestions so that your next lesson will proceed more smoothly: It is important to set some ground rules for students' behavior as they view or hold visuals. Therefore, before passing around a particular visual, participate in a group discussion with your students where you review rules about visuals and you discuss the visuals' importance to the story. For example, prior to reading the story *Ira Sleeps Over* (Waber, 1972), provide a big teddy bear as a visual. Direct students' attention to the cover of the story and ask them to predict why Ira is holding a teddy bear. After students share their predictions, you might say to them, "I am going to pass around the teddy bear. Remember our rules for visuals. You may hold the teddy bear for a few seconds and whisper in its ear why you think Ira is holding the bear."

Or, you might tell your students, "All good listeners will be able to hug the teddy bear when we finish reading the story."

At the completion of your oral reading, revisit your students' predictions about why Ira was holding the teddy bear so that students will further understand why the visual was an important element of the story.

Use the visual as a catalyst for retelling and rereading the story, too. Leave both the book and visual out for your students to reread and hold at their convenience. This idea also will inform your students that they can examine the visual further. Therefore, they do not have to become overly involved with trying to touch visuals during story time because they will have the opportunity later in the day. In closing, I have some questions for you to consider. Do you think your students are too old to hold a teddy bear? Might another visual have been more appropriate for students studying life skills? Do you think the story *Ira Sleeps Over* was not developmentally mature enough for your students?

Case #11.3: "Musical Chairs: Visual Representations That Went Awry" (by Cecil Gregory)

I teach eight seventh graders in a science class. Before we read about the destruction of the rain forest, I planned an advance organizer (Ausubel, 1960) that was a modified version of the party game, "Musical Chairs." Instead of chairs, I taped cards in a big circle on the floor. Most of the cards had the names and pictures of rain forest animals, birds, or reptiles on them, such as python, bamboo viper, jaguar, parrot, macaw, tapir, sloth, frogs, toads, insects, and so on. A few cards had photographs of people and the term *human* printed on them. My idea was to use the "Musical Chair" concept as a visual representation that showed what would happen if we continue to desecrate and destroy the rain forests in our world. I planned to play "rain forest" music as the students moved around the circle. I would take away one animal or reptile card at a time, stopping the music at an appropriate place. Any student who did not have a card to stand on would be eliminated from the activity. There would always be more students than cards. My idea was not to have a competition. Rather, my idea was to show that all the animals and reptiles in the rain forest would be eliminated if we keep on with our desecration of their habitat. After the activity, I hoped to lead a stimulating student discussion about what the students had observed during the **simulation.**

Here is how the advanced organizer went awry. The activity went on way too long. My professor came in and noted that we were engaging in the advanced organizer for over 15 minutes. The students did not move around the circle quickly enough because they did not want to be eliminated from the activity when the music stopped. They were worried that they would not be near a card to stand on. In addition, when the music did stop, the students ran so fast to stand on cards that they slipped and looked like they were going to fall. Then, the tape started coming off the floor and the cards were trampled and crushed.

"Have your students walk inside the circle so they will stay off the cards," my professor said. She also said, "This is taking too long."

Despite these problems, the students loved the advance organizer. They remembered every single one of the animals, birds, and reptiles, and wanted to keep all of the cards. I know the visual representations of the animals and reptiles paved the way for our text reading. I also know though that my advance organizer was too noisy and confusing.

1. What benefits do advance organizers provide for students reading content text? _____

_____

2. Do you think Cecil's advance organizer was appropriate? too long? worth the trouble she went to when she collected the visuals and taped them to the floor? _____

_____

Commentary #11.3A: "Musical Chairs: Visual Representations That Went Awry (by Deborah Schussler, High School English Teacher, Williamson County Public Schools, Tennessee)

Dear Cecil,

I see a number of very positive things with your visual representation activity. You chose an advance organizer that helped your students become interested in the content of the lesson. The motivational hook is often overlooked as teachers attempt to squeeze too much information from their overloaded curricula into each lesson. Good for you for not succumbing to this tendency! Before diving into the content material, you planned a high-interest activity to prepare students for the lesson's goals. Your activity promoted active student involvement. I am glad you value the importance of student involvement, especially at the middle school level. By the time students reach middle school, unfortunately, learning often ceases to be fun and instead becomes drudgery (although it doesn't have to be). Keeping students actively involved is one way to alleviate this predicament.

The problem you ran into with the musical chairs activity was one that you stated you wanted to avoid: not to have a competition. The behavior you described in your students as the activity progressed indicates that they did see it as a competition, and they were intent on winning. This is not a negative, unless it detracts from the learning that the activity is intended to promote. (I will return to the issue of student learning in a moment.) Because your lively, visual representation took so long, students engaged in potentially dangerous behaviors in their efforts to win. Therefore, I suggest conducting an abbreviated visual representation activity that does not conclude with a winner. For example, rather than having all the cards taken up at the end of the activity, go through only three or four rounds and then initiate a discussion. You stated that you wanted this activity to instigate a "stimulating discussion," so you could begin your discussion by asking, "What would happen if the activity continued?"

Regarding student learning, you stated that despite problems with your advance organizer, students remembered the animals and reptiles from the cards placed on the floor. This is a good sign and substantiates the value of visual representations. However, I am curious to know what they did with this information. Was your goal just for them to remember certain animals and reptiles, or was the goal for them to do something with this information? A really good advance organizer not only gets students interested in the content to be studied, it also tightly links to instructional goals. I think you met the first criterion, but I am not sure about the second as I do not know your overall instructional goals for this unit on rain forests.

I see a number of ways you could use this activity as a step to meeting various instructional goals. For example, if you wanted students to know how various species were affected by rain forest desecration, each student might be assigned one of the cards and be in charge of that animal, bird, or reptile represented on the card. You might then have students find information about their particular animal, bird, or reptile, and how it is affected by the desecration of the rain forests. If one of your goals was to help students understand the interconnectedness of the animals, you might place them into **Jigsaw** groups (Buehl, 2001) based on the species on the cards so that students had opportunities to teach one another about certain animals, birds, or reptiles. You might present the mixed groups of students with different scenarios (e.g., hunters poached too many elephants in one year; humans destroyed watering holes or chopped down trees) and ask students to determine the outcome and provide justification based on what they know about their animals. The possibilities are numerous.

Despite the problems you encountered with musical chairs, I hope you continue to use advance organizers and visual representations as motivational hooks for your lessons, techniques to assist student learning, and as a method for meeting your instructional goals.

Commentary #11.3B: "Musical Chairs: Visual Representations That Went Awry" (by Victoria J. Risko, Teacher Educator, Peabody College of Vanderbilt University, Tennessee)

Hi, Cecil.

I read with much interest your plan for using the musical chair activity to help your students visualize and remember information about rain forests. I agree with you that advance organizers can be extremely useful for helping students comprehend new information. Sometimes textbooks are not "reader friendly" for middle school students. Often, there are too many concepts embedded on every page, and main ideas are not clearly identified. Thus, your plan to bridge new text concepts with an advance organizer was a good teaching decision.

Here are a couple of my ideas about advance organizers and their use with content textbooks. First, I believe advance organizers are most useful when they help students understand the major concepts of a text passage or unit of materials. Several years ago, a colleague and I conducted a series of experimental studies to analyze how advance organizers may influence reading comprehension (Alvarez & Risko, 1989; Risko & Alvarez, 1986). We talked with fifth-grade students about their social studies textbooks and asked them what they remembered about the section they had just read. This section in the book focused on the Depression era and reformers who were trying to change working conditions for workers, some of whom were young children. We learned that the fifth graders remembered quite easily some of the details from the passage (e.g., how much the workers earned an hour) and information that related most directly to them (e.g., that young children had to work long days). They had great difficulty, though, understanding the main idea of the material—that a group of people, called reformers, were trying to change the horrible working conditions that existed in factories and farms.

Having learned this about our fifth graders, we designed an advance organize called a thematic organizer that told them a story about unfair working conditions and invited the students to respond to questions and actual quotes from the book. These responses required the students to activate their prior knowledge about unfair situations and think about their own reactions to these horrible working conditions. Use of these thematic organizers helped our students understand the "big picture" (the main idea of the material) and connect their own experiences and knowledge to this main idea.

Second, we learned that once the fifth graders understood the main idea, they were able to connect it to the lower order details in the text (e.g., workers' wages, children working in factories). Instead of just remembering lists of facts that were not connected to each other or a main concept, our students were now able to explain why these details were important to know within the context of considering unfair working conditions.

I share this story to ask you to consider the goals and content of your visual organizer. It seems that the main concept you wanted to teach was the destruction of the rain forest. You chose the musical chair idea to illustrate how forest animals, birds, and reptiles are disappearing from the rain forest, but I wonder if the students were more attuned to playing the game than they were to understanding the relationship between this activity and the loss of rain forest animals, birds, and reptiles. You indicate that they remembered the names of these animals and reptiles long after the game was over, but did they understand the significance of this information? Did they understand why they played this game? Thus, if you decide to play such a game again (and I know you will establish some ground rules about behavior and the length of time you will play), I suggest you think about how you can maximize the use of an advanced organizer. As we learned in our two studies, students often are able to recall facts and details (e.g., names of the animals and reptiles), but they have a much harder time understanding more abstract themes and concepts. Therefore, I recommend you think about introducing the theme, such as rain forest destruction, in a way that helps students understand why it is important to notice that animals and reptiles are disappearing in the forests just as they did during the playing of the game. Helping them think about the theme early on provides a reason for learning about the animals while they play the game and helps them know how to use this newly acquired information as they continue to think about losses that result from rain forest destruction.

Keep up your good work with visuals. You understand the importance of providing students with pictures and visual representations (i.e., an image text) to enhance students' understandings so they will achieve as much academic success as possible (see the Overview to this chapter).

REFLECTIONS AND EXPLORATIONS

1. Read *The Great Kapok Tree* (Cherry, 1990). Create a visual representation of the ideas in the text. Share your work with your teaching peers.

2. Read a short content text to a group of students. Prepare pertinent visuals that enhance the text. How did the visuals enhance students' understanding of the information presented? What guidelines did you and your students follow about holding or moving the visuals? How do you think the use of visuals optimized your students' interest in the story? How did the use of visuals optimize your students' comprehension of the text?

3. Enhancing students' comprehension of text with visuals is just one small part of viewing and representing activities. Jot down other important viewing and representing activities that have the potential for enhancing students' literacy development.

4. Skim through chapter 11 again. Then, choose a way to represent the concepts discussed in the chapter (e.g., a semantic or concept map, a diorama, a graph or chart, photographs, computer-generated icons, drawings). Share your visual representations with your teaching colleagues.

INTEGRATING VIEWING AND REPRESENTING LESSONS IN YOUR CLASSROOM: PRACTICAL APPLICATIONS

Careful planning will help you successfully integrate viewing and visually representing activities into your content lessons. The following questions may help guide your thinking and reflections:

1. How will involvement in viewing and representing activities help your students learn subject content?

2. How might viewing and representing activities help your students prepare for a content-area lesson by accessing or building prior knowledge and providing motivation?

3. How might viewing and representing activities help your students during a content area lesson to process new information more readily?

4. Following a content lesson, how might viewing and representing activities help your students to apply and extend their knowledge?

5. How might viewing and representing activities be integrated with the other language arts (reading and writing, listening and speaking) to ensure that all students can learn and demonstrate content-area understanding in a variety of ways?

6. How can the arts (drama, music, movement/dance, art) contribute to content-area literacy? For example, how can they contribute to factual understanding in language arts, mathematics, or science and still maintain their aesthetic purpose?

7. How can technical visuals, such as maps, graphs, charts, tables, and diagrams, contribute to content-area literacy?

8. How can multimedia, such as television, newspapers, Web sites, and PowerPoint presentations that integrate visual text with print and oral text, contribute to content-area literacy? What media resources are particularly valuable in helping your students become involved in content-area knowledge?

9. How will you find time and expertise to prepare materials needed to include viewing and representing in your content-area lessons? (Most teachers find that building a set of useful pictures, props, and ideas is a gradual process.)

10. What resources exist in your school and community to build your own viewing and representing abilities? How might you discover your abilities?

11. How can you discover what viewing and representing talents your students already possess? How can you help them teach each other so that everyone benefits? (Sometimes the ablest students intimidate those with less ability, or they become so busy helping others that their own talents are not nurtured.)

12. How can critical thinking best be applied to visuals represented in popular media to ensure that we appreciate good models and know when we are being manipulated? (Visuals have an immediacy that is very powerful. How can we help students become aware of their emotional response?)

13. How can you provide additional, prime opportunities for students who have special aptitudes for viewing and representing to develop their talents and also expand their reading, writing, listening, and speaking abilities?

SUGGESTED READINGS

Bunchman, L., & Briggs, S. (1994). *Activities for Creating Pictures and Poetry.* Worcester, MA: Davis Publications.

A fine reference for teachers on how to teach art and poetry together. Using biographical summaries and illustrations, artists and poets, such as Georgia O'Keeffe and Chief Dan George, are paired together. The illustrations and ideas in this book could be used to support lessons about science, language arts, and social studies, including environmental issues.

Gibbons, G. (1998). *Penguins.* New York: Holiday House.

Gibbons explores the many species of penguins and their life in Antarctica through print, drawings, and technical sketches. Appropriate for introductions to Antarctica and all animal life, this book is a must for classroom libraries because of its beautiful illustrations.

Hurd, R., & Cassidy, J. (1992). *Watercolor for the Artistically Undiscovered.* Palo Alto, CA: Klutz.

This book offers a gentle and humorous introduction to painting for anyone. Using the paints, paper, and brush supplied, you will soon be creating watercolor washes, and learning about all sorts of visual-arts techniques (also see chap. 5, this volume).

Macaulay, D. (1975). *Pyramid.* New York: Houghton Mifflin.

All of Macaulay's books are classics in expository writing and illustrations. Pyramid offers detailed, technical drawings that are combined with narrative. Information about the people involved in construction of pyramids also is included.

Stilley, L., & Wolf, D. (1999). The art of observation: The place of visual thinking in science. In D. Wolf & D Balick, (Eds.). *Art works! Interdisciplinary Learning Powered by the Arts.* (pp. 78–97). Portsmouth, NH: Heinemann.

This chapter describes the journey of a secondary teacher and her students as they practice and learn how to observe natural phenomena in an archeology project. Students soon acquired aptitudes for visual thinking. The teacher determined that students who are academically challenged benefit from viewing charts and graphs.

12

Integrating Multiple Literacies With Curriculum as Inquiry

Sign systems allow learners to explore and create new ideas and to share what they are learning as they examine a topic through their own personal experiences and different knowledge systems.
—Short, Schroeder, Laird, Kauffman, Ferguson, and Crawford (1996, p. 11)

The shift from thematic units to curriculum as inquiry is a . . . subtle shift because the classroom does not look different on the surface— the same materials and activities are there. But many of these materials are now gathered up by the entire classroom community, not just the teacher; and students set up and create their own sites for exploration instead of only engaging in . . . preplanned activities.
—Short, Schroeder, Laird, Kauffman, Ferguson, and Crawford (1996, p. 12)

OVERVIEW

Kathryn Chapman Carr

Central Missouri State University

We can trace the historical, philosophical, and pedagogical roots of the integrated curriculum model to John Dewey in the early part of the 20th century (see Dewey, 1913). Dewey noted the contrast between the practice of teaching separate subjects (i.e., a fragmented curriculum), and the holistic, effective manner in which students integrated their learning outside of school (Dworkin, 1952).

In this chapter you will learn why integrating the arts with social studies, science, and language arts enhances learning and critical thinking and also builds a classroom atmosphere of cooperation through a focus on inquiry. The chapter also presents some ideas to help you organize for instruction.

As we expand the definition of literacy for the 21st century to include semiotic systems, we recognize that multiple literacies fit nicely with integrated curricula because multiple forms of representations are all vehicles for communication of ideas—historical ideas, scientific and mathematical ideas, literary ideas, and the range of human thoughts and emotions through the arts (Moffett & Wagner, 1992).

Long-term learning occurs when students are engaged in investigation of real problems, inquiring into topics of vital interest to them, and challenged to think critically. Such a curriculum goes well beyond basic skills to include integration of the whole person—the physical, social, aesthetic, or thinking and feeling, as well as the intellectual being.

For example, think back to your own elementary school days. Chances are the types of learning you recall are not facts, such as the circumference of the earth or the number of moons circling Saturn, nor times when you were learning about something. Rather, you are more likely to remember times when you were actively experiencing and problem solving to create a castle from a cardboard box, churn butter during Pioneer Days, learn old railroad songs, and conduct a scientific experiment of the Doppler Effect (changes in sound waves noticed in the pitch of the whistle when a train passes by).

The integrated curriculum fosters critical inquiry by creating an environment conducive to small-group and individual investigation of real problems. Furthermore, it fosters critical thinking by helping students make connections across subjects.

An inquiry-based, integrated curriculum supports the constructivist theory that knowledge is socially constructed and leads to higher academic achievement (Guthrie & McCann, 1997). The class that learns to collaborate in the investigation of real issues, discussion of literature, and creation of artistic works "shares a body of knowledge and understanding that has been jointly created" (Pappas et al., 1999, p. 49), and thus becomes a community of learners.

What Are the Roles of the Teacher in an Inquiry-Based Classroom?

The teacher in an inquiry-based classroom becomes a facilitator and coinvestigator, planning with students and making resources and field trips available. Managing this type of study, while incorporating state or district learning objectives or standards, may present a challenge for the beginning teacher. Scheduling blocks of time for student inquiry may prove to be the biggest challenge, however. The trend toward block scheduling recognizes that students need more time than 30- to 50-minute periods to investigate and read, discuss and write, and share their learning creatively.

Because classroom management is often a concern, teachers for whom this is a new teaching style may be advised to begin with a more structured approach and more advance planning until students have learned to work independently and cooperatively in small groups. One option is to begin with a **thematic unit.** Teachers also benefit from collaborating with other teachers to plan units of study based on broad concepts that foster a variety of student interests.[1]

Change is an example of a broad concept that occurs in nature throughout the plant and animal world, the physical world, and even in astronomy. Likewise, change is an element of people's lives, in their growth stages, ways of living, social and political relationships, and cultural and intellectual pursuits. Desire for harmony and balance is another broad concept that can be explored through music, art, literature, science, and social studies.

It might be easier to begin integrating the curriculum slowly by relating just two areas; for example, the arts to social studies, and later adding literature and other subjects. Teachers seldom integrate the entire curriculum all the time. As they continually evaluate their teaching and students' learning, they may decide that a particular subject needs concentrated work for a time. The important thing is to be flexible and to adapt to students' changing needs, while pointing out how the subject or skill relates to broad concepts.[2]

How Will You Arrange for Resources?

An essential role of teachers and students is to gather resources together for inquiry, such as books, both nonfiction and literature, photos, recordings, videos, Internet resources, and primary sources and artifacts. Budget permitting, field trips to art galleries, concerts, and theatrical performances are important ways to learn through the arts. The school librarian may prove to be an invaluable resource in locating materials, but also consider the availability of community resources and members of various professions who will share their expertise with students.[3] For example, one teacher located a marine biologist to assist a young student in his study of ocean fish, whereas the local historical society helped other students discover early-day settlers in the county. During a study of the Renaissance, students compared romanesque and Gothic architecture on a field trip to city cathedrals. The collection of resources has a two-fold purpose: first, to capture students'

---

[1] Biondo, S., Raphael, T., & Gavelek, J. (2000). *Mapping the Possibilities of Integrated Literacy Instruction* (http://www.readingonline.org/research/biondo/biondo.html)

[2] Matthews, M., & Rainer, J. (2001). The quandaries of teachers and teacher educators in integrating literacy and mathematics. *Language Arts, 78*(4), 357–364.

[3] Warner, M. (2001, March). Interdisciplinary team training for prospective middle school grade teachers. *Middle School Journal 31*(4), 30–39.

interests as they explore a general topic, and second, to assist students in locating information on their chosen topics.

How Will Students Begin Their Inquiry?

Another job of the facilitator/teacher is to help students select a topic and design appropriate questions for inquiry. Students will vary in their ability to work independently versus the amount of teacher guidance they need. Many will need help in narrowing their topic to something achievable. For example, a fifth-grade student chose to study World War II. After brainstorming various subtopics in conference with his teacher, for example, aircraft and air raids, naval engagements and submarines, famous battles and leaders of ground troops, hardships and patriotism at home, he was able to narrow the topic to "Famous Air Engagements of WWII."

How Will Students Learn Skills in an Inquiry-Based Classroom?

Teachers are accountable for helping students achieve certain learning objectives. Although skills learning (e.g., using reference materials, taking notes and summarizing information, or estimating, weighing, and measuring) is more meaningful when students are investigating real problems, it should be neither incidental nor haphazard. You will want to review the standards to see which skills can be demonstrated, applied, or practiced during independent or group investigation and list them in your plan book. Skill needs for students will vary based on individual differences.

How Will Students Express and Share Their Learning?

In one class discussion students and teacher developed a poster titled "Ways to Share Your Learning." Students were encouraged to try new means of expression on the list, but not limited to the list (e.g., create a poster, skit, poem, written report, oral demonstration talk, video, TV commercial, musical composition; design a web page; write an editorial; or express their learning through fabric, clay, or other media).

An important skill for students who are engaged in inquiry is time management. A planning map or contract can provide structure or guideposts for students to help them complete projects in a timely manner. A typical planning map will list the following:

My/our topic is _____:
My/our questions are: (three to five questions)
Some resources for learning are _____.
I/we will have information gathered by (reasonable date).

I/we will develop the following product (see list of Ways to Share Learning).

I/will share the product by (date of presentation).

I/we will use the following teacher and student self-evaluation guide:

- Kept to the topic.
- Answered my questions.
- Demonstrated organization skill.
- Demonstrated appropriate skills learning.
- Completed the project on time.
- Made an effective presentation (content, poise, eye contact, voice, etc.).
- I/we enjoyed the study.
- Ways to improve next time.

In summary, an inquiry-based, integrated curriculum is worth the effort in benefits for student learning, critical and creative thinking, motivation, and collaboration.

WHAT DO YOU NEED TO KNOW?
HOW CAN YOU BEGIN?

Students' learning is optimized when teachers organize and integrate multiple communication forms into an integrated curriculum (Guthrie, 1996; Short et al., 1996). Therefore, you will want to coordinate students' central interests and questions about interdisciplinary units of study that incorporate multiple forms of representation. What do you need to know? How can you begin? As a starting point, read John Westreich's chapter entitled, "High-Tech Kids: Trailblazers or Guinea Pigs" in *The Digital Classroom: How Technology Is Changing the Way We Teach and Learn* (Gordon, 2000). The chapter discusses a highly successful themed inquiry offered in New York's Dalton School that was developed by Dalton's resident archeologist as a "network-based multimedia alternative to the textbook-bound sixth grade curriculum in the Ancient World" (Westreich, 2000, p. 19). Another good resource is Timothy Shanahan's article, "Reading–Writing Relationships, Thematic Units, Inquiry Learning. In Pursuit of Effective Literacy Instruction." Published in *The Reading Teacher* (1997, September), the article reviews research and offers guidelines for integrated instruction. Teachers of young children will find the text, *Critical Thinking Handbook: K–3rd Grades. A Guide for Remodeling Lesson Plans in Language Arts, Social Studies and Science* (Paul, Binker, Jensen, & Krecklau, 1990a) helpful as they remodel and rethink their lesson plans to demonstrate that it is possible and practical to integrate instruction for critical thinking into the teaching of all subjects.

These authors also have published a similar text for Grades 4–6 (Paul et al., 1990b). *Learning Together Through Inquiry: From Columbus to Integrated Curriculum* (Short et al., 1996) explores curriculum where students and teachers have a voice. A very useful chapter on integrated literacy instruction appears in Volume 3 of the *Handbook of Reading Research* (Kamil, Mosenthal, Pearson, & Barr, 2000). Chapter authors Gavelek, Raphael, Biondo, and Wang spent a good deal of time defining terms associated with thematic teaching, and they examined the existing research base on integrated literacy instruction (Dana Grisham, personal communication, December 2000). Three additional sources for practical help in thematic teaching are: Altwerger and Flores' (1994) article "Theme cycles: Creating communities of learners" in *Primary Voices K–6;* Volume 2, Issue 1 of *Primary Voices K–6* (1994; the entire issue is devoted to themes); and Pappas et al. (1999) *An Integrated Language Perspective in the Elementary School* (3rd ed.).

You also might want to try some inquiry-oriented activities yourself. For example, keep a Connections Log in which you record "new" or innovative ideas you encounter through reading, engaging in conversations with a friend or colleague, watching a television show or film, traveling to a faraway city, and the like. Next, jot down how this "new" or innovative idea connects to other ideas you have encountered, or leads to new discoveries.

Another idea is to take a few moments to reflect about a topic of study you have been considering for a long time. Make a decision to explore this topic in depth. Formulate some questions that might help you thoughtfully explore your topic, and then investigate the answers to your questions. For example, have you ever speculated about our universe? Have you pondered about the concept of infinity? Do you worry that eventually our universe as we know it might vanish? Have you wondered if another universe exists? Consider how you might research issues such as these. What types of literacies (i.e., sign systems) might you use to conduct your inquiry? What multiple communication forms might prove most helpful to your inquiry?

When you have completed your inquiry, consider how concentrating thoughtfully on central concepts and issues related to a theme differs considerably from problematic activity-based learning where teachers try to include all subject areas and students engage in shallow, superficial activities.

CASES AND COMMENTARIES

Case #12.1: "I Need the Time!" (by Angelique Bathhurst)

As a preservice teacher in a sixth-grade social studies class, I am using a themed inquiry approach for the first time. When using themed instruction, teachers are supposed to incorporate all subject areas into a cohesive theme, aren't they?

Our theme is "Adventures in Time and Place." The particular social studies subthemes are Canada and Latin America. I know this sounds odd—having a country and a region in the same unit—but that is the way our text is structured and that is what our classroom teacher wants us to do because it is on her curriculum goals and objectives.

It has been very difficult to achieve total integration of subjects because of time constraints. The actual teaching time we have is 50 minutes. This is not sufficient time to include science or mathematics with social studies. Actually, time limitations make us basically just teach social studies. As the classroom teacher stated, "As soon as you get started, it's time to clean up. There just isn't enough time in 50-minute class periods."

We have tried to do our best, however. We have integrated music, literature, and the visual and dramatic arts into our unit. For example, for our advance organizer (Ausubel, 1960) on Latin America we played the song "Vamos" (Walt Disney Records, 2000). Our students listened to the music and tried to guess what region we would be studying.

We also have used many quality children's literature books to complement the information in our social studies text. In addition, when we were studying Canada, we invited our local professional hockey team to speak to our students. Most of the players are Canadian. We also incorporated technology into our work by researching Canadian and Latin American topics on the Internet. I even think we got a little math into our lessons by using Venn diagrams (Taylor, 1999) to compare and contrast the United States and Canada. We integrated music and art when we created a drama enactment and scenery for our Latin American topic. We presented our version of *The Great Kapok Tree* (Cherry, 1994).

I do think that we could have done more if we had had the time. I spoke with my professor and after she thought for a while, she said, "One solution would be to change the school schedule to block scheduling, which would provide double class periods."

Another professor suggested **team teaching.** She said, "The entire team could choose a theme that could meet curriculum guidelines and also connect each discipline."

What do other schools and school districts do about themed teaching? Time constraints are really a barrier to me.

1. Is Angelique correct when she says, "Teachers are supposed to incorporate all subject areas into a cohesive theme, aren't they?" _____

_____

2. What advice do you have for Angelique? _____

_____

Commentary #12.1A: "I Need the Time!" (by David Clarke, Middle School Teacher, New Orleans, Louisiana)

Hello, Angelique.

I teach social studies to eighth-grade students so I can relate to your dilemma regarding time constraints and themed teaching. We know that teaching through an integrated curriculum does not have to incorporate all subject matter, although this type of teaching does provide opportunities for students to make connections within and across disciplines. For example, students might study about New York City in a social studies class. At the same time, in mathematics class they might investigate the span of the George Washington Bridge and study engineers' equations that determined how wide the bridge should be and how strong the bridge cables must be to hold the bridge up. Other mathematics inquiry might include the following: (a) How far in each direction does the bridge sway? (b) How heavy is the bridge? and (c) How old is the George Washington Bridge?

History and music also might be coordinated, but only if these disciplines help students find answers to their own personal questions. For example, students might ask, "Who were the early settlers in New York City?" "What is the history of Ellis Island?" "What types of music and musical scores describe New York City?"

In a culminating activity, students might read *Tar Beach* (Ringgold, 1991) and discover a different perspective about New York and the George Washington Bridge. The visual arts might include a group mural based on the book *Tar Beach*. Ideas for an integrated curriculum are limitless.

Unfortunately, some of our school district policies impede this type of teaching—not because school administrators do not appreciate the considerable student learning that occurs through interdisciplinary teaching, but because administrators schedule classes that are only 50 minutes in length in order to expedite student movement, lunch, and so on—like the class you describe. Solutions to this problem, as your professors said, are to provide block scheduling (i.e., double time periods), or to include all of your students' teachers and your students in planning and constructing a unit. Imagine what excitement this type of school environment would generate!

I wish I could offer you some more ideas, but I can't. In my opinion, scheduling is one important key to the success of teaching through thematic units. You are to be commended for your efforts. You got a considerable amount of interdisciplinary teaching into your 50 minutes, but in the future, focus on central concepts and issues rather than trying frantically to include all subjects. Perhaps, when you have your own classroom, you will become a proactive school leader and be instrumental in determining some school policies. As a leader you could provide suggestions about scheduling for themed teaching and lobby for what you believe is best for students' learning.

Commentary #12.1B: "I Need the Time!"
(by Kathryn Chapman Carr, Teacher Educator
and Professor Emerita, Central Missouri State University)

Dear Angelique,

I want to congratulate you on your efforts to help students integrate learning. Inquiry-oriented instruction can be challenging at first, but the rewards for students are many. It sounds as if you have made a good beginning by selecting a broad theme and by integrating music, literature, and the visual and dramatic arts.

Of course, it is not possible to also include science, math, and language arts with social studies within one 50-minute period. Perhaps you are trying to infuse too many separate subjects into your theme. The way teachers manage integrated instruction is to use (i.e., borrow) the time allotted for other subjects for theme-based instruction. If you are in a self-contained classroom, you probably can change the daily schedule to gain a block of time.

I would recommend a half day, or a 2-hour block of time as a minimum. That would leave some time in the day to work on a separate subject, such as math, if you decide that your students need additional instruction. At the same time, you always seek ways for students to apply math principles and skills within the theme in order to make connections among disciplines.

I am aware that even in a self-contained classroom the schedule may be riddled with periods when students leave the room to work with other teachers. That problem can sometimes be alleviated through scheduling by the principal or block scheduling, as one of your professors suggested. I assume by the fact that you mention trying to integrate science, math, and social studies that you are not teaching in a departmentalized school. If you do teach in a departmentalized school, I would recommend forming a planning team with other teachers who come in contact with your students. Doing so will be helpful in several ways. First, students will benefit when teachers are aware of and coordinate the instruction with topics offered in other classes. Also, unit planning is easier and richer when several teachers and their students brainstorm ideas together. For example, music teachers would likely think of ways to incorporate music within the theme and would know musical selections that might not be familiar or available to you. The library media specialist is another faculty member who can be extremely helpful. I think that when approached as a team player most teachers would be pleased to share their expertise. Some on the planning team might volunteer to team teach with you for several days or longer. But even if they continue to see students at other periods outside your classroom, they will likely find ways to coordinate with your theme. Another benefit of team planning is the communication that will occur and the coordination of efforts with regard to meeting individual students' needs.

Finally, remember that flexibility is important. A team-teaching arrangement doesn't have to last all year. Likewise, it doesn't have to always be math that rates an additional class period. When you determine that some subject or skill area needs additional work, as a good teacher you stop and attend to it. You are probably familiar with the district or state curriculum goals or performance standards for your grade. Consult this document during unit planning and select several objectives that can be developed or reinforced during the unit. It is good practice to state performance objectives clearly in your unit plan. Then it will be relatively easy to evaluate learning and provide for individual needs through performance assessment during unit activities.

Case #12.2: "How Do You Incorporate All Subjects?" (by Kelly Daniels)

I teach content reading to seven sixth graders in a science class. When we began our themed inquiry on "Astronomy and Ancient Astronomers," I used the K-W-L strategy (Ogle, 1986) for my first lesson. I wanted to know how much my students knew about astronomy. I also wanted to determine what my students wanted to learn about astronomy because that topic is so broad. After a discussion with my students, I recorded what they knew about astronomy. I also asked for ideas about what they wanted to learn. George responded, "I would like to learn about constellations."

Ashley said, "Yeah, constellations are cool."

The other students agreed and I set to work finding resources for constellations, astronomy in general, and ancient astronomers.

I got the **Caldecott Medal**–winning book, *Starry Messenger: Galileo Galilei* (Sis, 1996). It depicts the life of Galileo Galilei, a famous ancient astronomer who experienced terrible hardships because of his innovative views. This book is captivating because of the beautiful illustrations. I also browsed the Internet and found a text titled *People in the History of Astronomy* (www. geocities.com/CapeCanaveral/Launchpad/4515/History.html). After we read these two texts, my students could fill in some information in the "L" section of the K-W-L chart.

At our next session, we read *Her Seven Brothers* (Goble, 1998). It is a fictional tale based on a Cheyenne Indian myth about the creation of the Big Dipper. I linked the ideas in *Her Seven Brothers* with the content text, *The Big Dipper and You* (Krupp, 1989). Then we all created our own constellations in a visual-arts activity, which really motivated my students.

During the following meeting, we read *The Glow in the Dark Night Sky Book* (Hatchett, 1988), which contains full-color photographs and 34 maps of constellations arranged by seasons. We also read *Star Gazers* (Gibbons, 1992) and I brought in a star chart so my students could see how constellations are mapped out. Then we used the Web site http://www.astro.wisc.edu/~dolan/constellations to accomplish more research on constellations. The research helped us with our constellation mural. For example, we learned that an asterism is a group of stars that form a shape within a constellation.

At our next session, it was time to plan our drama enactment. We based our drama on the ideas in the book *Her Seven Brothers*. We made props and costumes and the students were so excited and motivated. We created a teepee and used our mural and paintings of constellations for our scenery. We played songs from a collection of Native-American music.

My concern is that because of time constraints, we never fully incorporated all subjects, like math and social studies. How do other teachers handle problems like this? Do they incorporate all subjects in a themed unit or only those that particularly seem to fit with the theme?

1. Do teachers have to incorporate all subjects into a themed unit of instruction? _____

_____

2. As a teacher, how would you help your students plan this themed inquiry? _____

_____

Commentary #12.2A: "How Do You Incorporate All Subjects?" (by Kathleen McKenna, Middle School Teacher, Evanston, Illinois)

Dear Kelly,

You have what the French call "un embarrasse de richesse," literally an embarrassment of riches! What an extraordinarily rich and comprehensive unit you have created for your students. I can't wait to share it with our science teacher here.

As to your question about incorporating all subjects, you have done so already. The only piece I can see from your description that you missed was to help your students see those connections, explicitly. (Although I rush to say that given what a creative teacher you are, you probably did incorporate some discussions along the way!) Here's what I mean. When you read about Galileo and Native-American myths, and study star charts, you are doing social studies. You can embellish Galileo with a brief time line and discussion of the Renaissance and Enlightenment, according to what you think your students can take in cognitively. You can talk about how there are myths all around the world, all through history to explain constellations. You can connect the idea of reading star charts to reading maps and other charts. All these are just icing on your kids' social studies cake. On the other hand, if all you do is mention social studies as you use those resources and ask your students to make the connections explicitly, you've invited them to actively work to see and use those opportunities for synthesis. I generally do a combination with my students, the first for modeling, the second to get them thinking. After a few months with me, many of my students rush into my class saying, "Mrs. McKenna, guess what? I just made a connection to something that happened in Latin class!" Those moments convince me I'm doing my job.

Everyone worries about math: parents, teachers, administrators, folks poring over test scores. Never enough. How do we cover it all? What's the best way to teach math? How can we incorporate more across the curriculum? Math is very often "the tail that wags the middle school dog." Here again, I believe you can create opportunities for the children to discover the math in what you are doing. And, all the research indicates that students who do well in math do so because they see practical applications for it in all they do, *not* because they have memorized multiplication facts or algorithms. Additionally, the purpose of math is to become more logical thinkers, to realize there are a number of ways to approach problem solving and to be open to more than one, and to become good problem solvers. How do astronomers study the sky? Don't they have to know a lot about calculus? Isn't the sky divided into discernible portions for the purposes of finding one's way around it? How do we measure the distances between us and heavenly bodies and between them out there? If your students are not actively calculating those kinds of things, they can at least be pondering them during your study. And, you'll come up with some student who wants to learn how to do those kinds of calculations. Again, you need only supply the opportunity, the role modeling, and the sense that learning is an exciting pursuit, all interconnected.

Stop worrying about coverage. Coverage is the enemy of students' understanding. I live by that motto, and you and your kids can too. Just help them to see the connections, applaud them when they make them themselves, and you will all be working toward making the learning deeper and richer. Keep up the great work!

Commentary #12.2B: "How Do You Incorporate All Subjects?" (by Deborah Begoray, Teacher Educator, University of Victoria, Canada)

Hi, Kelly!

You certainly sound like a creative and student-centered teacher. You also are making great use of music, drama, art, and technology in your unit, and your students are actively and enthusiastically involved. You don't need coaching from anyone on how to integrate the arts or capture student interest. What you might need, however, are a few ideas on planning to make sure that your students are studying all the curricula outcomes for Grade 6.

Though you don't say specifically, your decision to study astronomy and ancient astronomers must have been based on more than just your own interest. I'll presume either that astronomy is a topic in your science curriculum or that you thought you could address other science concepts through an astronomy unit (such as observation or hypothesis making, perhaps). If you plan in advance, however, you can include ideas from a number of curricula.

Curriculum design is not terribly difficult if you think of it as lesson planning "enlarged." You must, for example, help your students plan what they will do on a given day. A unit is an organized series of lesson plans. Planning for an entire unit can begin by looking at all of the curricula you would like to include. Such inclusion does *not* have to include language arts, science, social studies, and math every time. Because you do have to address all of these areas by the end of the year (now we're talking about year planning as a series of units), you'll have to think about how to address all the curricula eventually. Sometimes teachers avoid those subjects that they feel less comfortable planning, and then they may end up doing a rush job on them (a situation you want to avoid).

So, we're back to planning again. Now that you've got a science and language arts unit you are happy with, prepare to teach it again by looking for social studies and mathematics ideas that would fit in. For example, mathematics integration can be accomplished by looking for authentic connections of interest to middle years students *and* called for by your mathematics curriculum. You could look at ratios by comparing the distances between Earth and the other planets with the distances between Earth and the stars. Take your students out on the playground and use balls to show the relative distances to scale and then do the ratios in class (the differences are enormous and astounding even to adults!). You could apply knowledge of ratios to the magnification of telescopes next. Your students will quickly understand why historically we knew so much more about the planets, as they are relatively easy to see even with low-powered instruments, than we did about the stars. This might lead to a discussion of the Hubble telescope and an examination of the wonderful photographs available now. Social studies integration, once again, has to be planned. What does your curriculum want you to accomplish during the year? Which ideas would fit into an astronomy unit?

Try mapping your target outcomes for each unit and from each curriculum, on large pieces of paper. Some teachers I know have laminated their curriculum outcomes. Then they check off the ones they have used in an inquiry according to a system of color coding (you decide that green is for Astronomy unit, red is for Mysteries unit, and so on). As you plan units, you check off outcomes. So, you will realize which ones you are addressing frequently and which ones you are leaving out. You can then redress the situation. You don't say if your school does any planning in teams. Group meetings to map out units, where different teachers bring different areas of subject expertise to the table, are tremendously helpful.

Share your plans with your students and their parents. Everyone likes to see what they are accomplishing. Your principal will also be impressed by how organized you are. And, you can relax and get back to great teaching, secure in the knowledge that your Grade 6 students are doing Grade 6 curricula and will be ready to move to Grade 7.

Case #12.3: "Less Is Probably More" (by Brook Letort)

I work with seven eighth graders, helping them learn about ancient Egypt. The title of our thematic unit is "Exploring Ancient Egypt." When our unit of study started, I just didn't know where to begin. I discovered that there is so much information on ancient Egypt and I didn't want to present material that my students already know. So, I tried to offer a little bit of everything and that is why the unit of study backfired.

I started off by reading a book to my students titled *Cat Mummies* (Trumble, 1999), but the book was very confusing and boring for them. They enjoyed the first chapter, but after that they said things like, "BORING!" and "Ho Hum!"

I tried getting my students interested in the book by asking them questions. They just replied, "We don't know."

Why did I choose that book? Why didn't the students like it? Equally important, why did I continue reading the book if the students didn't like it?

Here is the rest of the story. Because I tried to put everything I could think of in the unit, I ended up confusing myself. At each lesson, I would introduce new subtopics about ancient Egypt, such as important rulers, mummy masks, temples, sculpture, Tutankhamen, trade, customs, modes of dress, pyramids, and money. Then my students would ask all sorts of questions about all of these topics and I couldn't answer them. I tried to cover myself by saying, "What do you think?" or "That is something for us to research."

It wasn't that I did not know anything about ancient Egypt. We explored too many topics at the same time. As a result, our discussions were too broad and superficial, and I could not keep up with all of the information pertaining to each subtopic. I know now that I should have focused on certain aspects of ancient Egypt—not everything there is to know. I will never forget this experience. Less is better than more. My question is: How do teachers determine what aspects of study or what specific subtopics to incorporate into a themed unit?

1. How would you respond to Brook's last question? _____

_____

2. Do you think that curriculum should be determined through collaboration among students and teachers? Why or why not? _____

_____

Commentary #12.3A: "Less Is Probably More"
(by Carol Lloyd, Teacher Educator, University of Nebraska)

Dear Brook,

You end your case by asking: "How do teachers determine what aspects of study or what specific subtopics to incorporate into a themed unit?" I'd prefer to answer how I think teachers *should* consider what to incorporate into a themed unit. But first, let me react to what happened in your lesson. You didn't do anything awful or unusual. In fact, most of the secondary teachers I see include too much information. It's too much because students don't have a chance to *think* about the ideas and concepts presented. As a result, at best, they can only memorize large quantities of isolated information. Why do teachers do this? Lots of reasons. Often it's because of the textbook, especially in a social studies class like the one you describe. Teachers often feel compelled to teach or "cover" all of the content in the chapter. (Take a minute to think about the difference between "covering content" and student learning.) Covering all of this content doesn't occur because teachers are thoughtless. It's the context of schools. When teachers are issued textbooks, when schools often expect teachers teaching different sections of the same course to be on the same chapter at the same time, and when most teachers assess students using objective tests (multiple choice, fill in the blanks, etc.), then you see instruction that merely covers lots of facts.

Now here's my response about an alternative, what I think you could consider in your planning. First, I'd ask you to think about what a thematic unit is. People have different descriptions, but here's mine. To me, a thematic unit revolves around a theme, not a topic. The theme is the central idea (concept) that teachers and students come up with together. What is it about ancient Egypt that would be important and interesting to students and meets the school district's curriculum requirements related to this general topic? I'd have to research it a little myself. You don't need to (ever) know everything about a topic or theme. That's not only impossible, but puts you in the position of being the source of all knowledge, a power position that will not encourage the conversation you seem to be seeking. (You described your discomfort at putting yourself in this position.) A theme that comes to mind might be "The ancient Egyptians developed advanced scientific and mathematical knowledge." Now your unit has a focus. Students may not learn about all those subtopics you listed, but they are more likely to learn related ideas, those that revolve around a major concept. And, they are likely to also learn how to learn. A theme such as this, by the way, positions the ancient Egyptians as a knowledgeable people, rather than as objects to study. There's more to developing a thematic unit than this, of course, but it's a beginning.

Following this type of theme would influence the ways in which you structured your daily lessons. For example, you might assemble various books or magazine articles (i.e., a text set or genre). Students choose a text to read. Then you help students devise questions for further study. In this way, you develop a classroom that focuses on inquiry. Students develop important questions based on the theme and research the answers to their questions.

By the way, through their national organizations, educators across all disciplines (i.e., social sciences, mathematics, science, etc.) have come to the same conclusion as you, that "less is better than more." They have encouraged textbook writers and teachers to stop trying to include vast quantities of content. Instead, they encourage the teaching of fewer, but more general concepts so that students can learn how to think within a discipline.

Commentary #12.3B: "Less Is Probably More"
(by Mary Gobert, Elementary Teacher, Hancock
County Schools, Mississippi, and Instructor,
University of Southern Mississippi)

Hello, Brook.

Don't be so hard on yourself. You understand the benefits of teaching with themed units. You tried hard to incorporate all disciplines within your theme, and you know how to reflect about your work as a teacher. You also ask good questions that apply to the problems portrayed in your case: "Why did I choose that book?" "Why didn't the students like it?" "Why did I continue to read the book if the students didn't like it?" and "How do teachers determine what aspects of study or what specific subtopics to incorporate into a themed unit?"

For a beginning teacher, those are excellent questions. Let me try to give you some answers. And remember, there are no "just right" answers in teaching. As all good teachers know, there are many ways to solve teaching problems. Good teachers may have to try a number of alternative solutions before their lessons really "click."

I would have initiated the unit by preparing a dynamite advance organizer (Ausubel, 1960) that replicated a pyramid. Inside the pyramid, I would insert questions geared toward determining students' particular interests about Egypt. The questions also would awaken students' curiosities about our new unit. Questions might include: "Have you ever heard about cat mummies? "Why do you think some ancient cultures in Egypt engaged in mummifying cats?" "Who do you think Tutankhamen was?" "How could you find out facts about this person?" "Why do you think the Egyptians constructed pyramids?" "Do all pyramids look the same?" "What type of money did the ancient Egyptians use?" After our advance-organizer activity, I would help my students decide which particular subtopics of ancient Egypt they would research in order to become experts. Students could work alone or in pairs. We would learn from one another in a true spirit of inquiry. Thus, students would be taking responsibility for some of their learning, and you wouldn't feel so anxious and confused, and responsible for doing all the work. Students would, of course, use multiple sign and symbol systems to discover facts and information. They would use multiple literacies (i.e., multiple sign systems) to show what they know (e.g., computer technology, music, dance, print-based and electronic text, videos). And, you would use multiple literacies to assess your students' understandings of concepts and facts.

Now to the easy part. Your book problem would not have occurred if you had provided opportunities for a group of students to take responsibility for choosing the texts used in the unit. So, in summary, place more responsibility on your students. You will love the results.

Case #12.4: "Searching Everywhere for Nothing?" (by Trudy Fore)

I work with nine third-grade students. When we were starting our unit on the wetlands, which is part of the third-grade curriculum, I had a great deal of trouble finding information that was not too difficult for my students to read and understand.

First, I visited the library to locate books on the wetlands. Sure enough, all of the content books were just too far beyond my students' reading abilities. I also surfed the Internet.

Next, I looked at videos. This took an awful amount of time because I had to read the books, view the videos, and carefully preview the Web sites on the wetlands.

The next thing I did was purchase some maps showing wetlands in North America. I also contacted the Marine Resource Department, asking them for information on coastal wetlands. In addition, I requested that the Marine Resource Department send us a guest speaker.

At our next session, I came to the school armed with books, Web sites, maps, and videos. I started my lesson using a K-W-L chart (Ogle, 1986). I asked my students to tell me what they knew about the wetlands. I know I should not have been surprised, but I was—my students knew practically nothing about our topic. "What are wetlands?" asked Joseph.

When we got to the "W" category of the K-W-L chart, my students were very bored. They did not want to know about the wetlands. Thinking that I could pique their interest, I read the book *Wetlands* (Stone, 1989) to them. This book describes the importance of the wetlands and the plant and animal life wetlands support. Following our reading, we played a wetlands hopscotch game I devised. The students enjoyed the game, but I could tell they still were not interested in the topic of wetlands.

Here are my questions: How could I have helped my students become interested in our topic of study? What do teachers do when they must offer a particular themed unit because of curriculum guidelines, but students are not interested in the topic? Where do teachers get the time to find and assemble all of the realia, books, and multiple texts, formats, and genres pertinent to the study of a particular topic?

1. Can you answer all of Trudy's questions in the last paragraph of her case?

_____

_____

2. How might Trudy have motivated her students to be inquirers? _____

_____

Commentary #12.4A: "Searching Everywhere for Nothing?"
(by Katherine Schlick Noe, Teacher Educator,
Seattle University, Seattle, Washington)

Dear Trudy,

You've run head-on into a common problem in teaching—how to entice students into a subject for which they have no expressed need to know. If your students have little experience with wetlands, this crucial environmental concept may seem very abstract and uninteresting to them. Third graders whose experience may lead them to equate wetlands with puddles may have a hard time getting excited. If wetlands are part of your third-grade curriculum, you may be able to plant that need to know by providing some experiences that engage students as learners. As Stephanie Harvey (1998) wrote, you need a launch pad for investigation: "Inquiry starts with one condition, and it simply will not lift off without it: wonder" (p. 208).

You may need to help your students generate motivation for learning by finding a personal connection with the topic. Personal connections often stem from questions: Is there concern in your own community about saving wetlands? Are there wetlands in students' own neighborhoods that are threatened? Can you find newspaper articles dealing with wetlands or old photographs of local sites where wetlands have been paved over? Regie Routman called this "developing a questioning stance toward learning" (2000, p. 465).

Next, provide direct experience, if possible, to develop students' schemata for wetlands. For example, can you visit a wetlands area together to find out what animals depend on it for habitat? Third graders often are fascinated by animals and care a great deal about how we humans treat animals. As you learn about animals and their habitats, you also can consider the role that wetlands play in the environment. If it's not possible to visit a wetland area directly, then you might provide vicarious experiences through photographs, videos, and simulations (i.e., multiple texts, formats, and genres and experiences that mimic real-life happenings). You also might start with something your students do know and care about, such as their own neighborhoods. Explore the neighborhood around your school to build students' concepts of that particular ecosystem. Guide students to consider the components of their own environment—things like houses or apartments, streets, telephones, cars, running water, and stores. Ask students what might happen if any of these elements were removed. This experience should help them as you move into material on wetlands. In addition, it should help you to focus your efforts to gather useful resources as you consider the components of the wetlands environment and how this environment fits into the larger ecosystem.

Next, focus students specifically on wetlands through open-ended questions such as, "We know that people depend on each other in our neighborhood. How do you think animals depend on one another in wetlands?" Furthermore, you may be able to model an excitement for learning about this topic through your own concern. You might generate some open-ended questions that you have about this topic, then invite students to add theirs. I highly recommend Stephanie Harvey's book *Nonfiction Matters* (1998) as an excellent resource for guiding students to build research projects around learners' deeply felt, important questions. Additionally, Regie Routman has an excellent chapter on curriculum inquiry in her book, *Conversations: Strategies for Teaching, Learning, and Evaluating* (2000).

Finally, provide a way for students to share what they learn with the real world. Students may make a greater investment in an investigation when they know that their results serve some authentic purpose. For example, could they develop a brochure on ways to protect the environment, make posters to educate the community about the hazards of waste water on wetland habitats, or write letters to the newspaper?

The time factor is a key challenge when you're trying to gather materials for any topic of study. But first, give yourself a lot of credit for the strategies you tried: gathering a wide array of materials, inviting guest speakers, using a combination of print, Internet, and video resources, and exploring students' background knowledge of wetlands. All of these can be good routes to intrigue students into learning. You now have an impressive array of resources to use if and when you study wetlands again! You can certainly share these with colleagues who may be interested in a similar topic. One way to cut down on the time it takes to gather materials is to find out from peers what topics they've studied with their classes and to share materials among your staff. I think that building up a strong collection of resources (i.e., **realia,** books, Internet sources, guest speakers, etc.) must be something that occurs over time. Each time you delve into a topic, you can add new resources and delete those that didn't work as well to meet your learning targets. For other science-related explorations, I recommend two Internet resources as jumping-off places: (a) National Science Teachers Association: Recommended Web Sites (http://www.nsta.org/onlineresources/site/), and (b) Discovery Channel: Planet Earth (http://www.discovery.com/guides/earth/earth.html).

Commentary #12.4B: "Searching Everywhere for Nothing?" (by Jane Percival, Head Elementary Teacher, Haydenville, Massachusetts)

Trudy, as I read your description of your approach to developing a curriculum unit for your third-grade students, I was extremely impressed. You began by developing your own knowledge base on wetlands. Then you found a variety of print and nonprint materials that were not only readable by your students but also likely to stimulate their interest in the topic. You also searched for members of the community who could share their expertise on the topic. Once you had many resources at your fingertips, you began the unit by assessing the students' current knowledge and interests. Although the information that you gained from the K-W-L (Ogle, 1986) and from your observations of the students was not what you had anticipated, you did what an excellent planner of instruction does: You began to search for ways to develop the unit so that students would be actively engaged and enthusiastic learners. You wanted to do more than "cover the required content."

In response to your question, "How could I have helped my students become interested in our topic of study?" I suggest elements of an approach that I have personally used and have also seen used in circumstances similar to yours. They are based on a philosophy of preschool education in Emilia, Italy, called The Reggio Emilia Approach,[4,5] where students explore

[4]Katz, L., & Cesarone, B. (Eds.). *Reflections on the Reggio Emelia Approach.* Urbana, IL: ERIC Clearinghouse on Elementary and Early Childhood Education (ED 375 986).

[5]Hendrick, J. (Ed.). (1997). *First Steps toward the Reggio Emelia Way.* Upper Saddle River, NJ: Merrill/Prentice Hall.

a wide range of semiotic systems (Albers & Murphy, 2000). As you may already know, that set of beliefs about learning and teaching is now guiding instruction in several elementary schools in the United States as well as in numerous preschools. To develop students' interest in a curriculum topic, you could do the following: Begin with a "provocation." That is, immerse students in a concrete, hands-on experience with the topic. For instance, in this case, take them on a field trip to a wetlands. Explore the area together. Listen to the students' conversations with one another to find out what aspects of the wetlands are intriguing to them.

Once back in the classroom, do a follow-up activity that deepens the experience in the wetlands (e.g., murals to share with an audience, illustrated stories about the experience, dioramas depicting the wetland). Involve parents in the planning of the curriculum unit. Your students, for example, might write a letter in which they ask their family members for suggestions regarding this unit of study. Perhaps a parent has expertise in the area and would share it with the class or knows someone who could. Families may have materials from trips that they've taken to wetland areas or may be members of conservation groups protecting wetlands.

Next, the K-W-L (Ogle, 1986), or a variation, can become a way to involve the students in the planning of the unit, but after they already are invested in it.

The success of the aforementioned approach, or any unit-planning endeavor, rests on excellent preparation by the teacher—all that you did prior to meeting with your third graders to begin the wetlands unit. Therefore, in response to your second question, "Where do teachers get the time to find and assemble all of the realia, books, and multiple texts, formats, and genres pertinent to the study of a particular topic?" I have to say that they must find the time. In my experience, it is rare that teachers have time built into their daily schedule to work on unit development. Sometimes, school districts provide half days for grade-level teams of teachers to develop a unit together. More often, teachers meet during the summer to work together on required curriculum units. Sometimes grants are available so that they are paid for their efforts. Generally, however, teachers do not receive monetary reimbursement, but gain much from being with their colleagues, sharing ideas, and leaving with a quality product that they can adapt to their students' needs and interests in the coming year. (Also, there's usually at least one excellent baker who brings delectable delicacies to make the experience even more pleasurable.)

As a beginning teacher, a teacher new to a grade level, or one receiving a brand-new curriculum framework in September, you would not have the opportunities that I just described. In these cases, you might want to network with grade-level colleagues not only in your district, but also across districts. In many areas there are collaboratives or teachers' centers where advice and materials can be gathered. Membership in professional organizations also entitles you to journals filled with excellent ideas and introductions to outstanding teaching resources. Attending their conferences also helps teachers expand their networks of colleagues to contact when they have questions like yours. Continue your outstanding behind-the-scenes preparation and commitment to providing environments in which students want to learn.

REFLECTIONS AND EXPLORATIONS

1. What is wrong with focusing on all subject areas in a themed inquiry?
2. What do you think Brook means in Case #12.3 when she reflects about her unit and says, "Less is more"?
3. Read pages 128–129 in *Telling Pieces: Art as Literacy in Middle School Classes* (Albers & Murphy, 2000). Then jot down your understanding of the Reggio Emelia Approach and its explorations of sign systems.
4. Devise three advance organizers for three different integrated units of study and present them to your teaching peers. Remember, advance organizers are offered to activate students' motivation, background knowledge, and enthusiasm for a particular unit of study. Advance organizers are especially beneficial when they provide opportunities for student movement and interactions.

INTEGRATING CURRICULUM INQUIRY IN YOUR CLASSROOM: PRACTICAL APPLICATIONS

Planning is the key to successful curriculum integration. For ease of management your first unit should be fairly simple. Later, when you become more familiar with teaching through inquiry, you and your students will plan themes for the year, all related to a broad or global concept, such as Change or Interdependence in Nature. In some schools the entire faculty plans themes for a 3-year period to avoid duplication as students progress through the grades. Schoolwide planning and collaboration maximizes faculty strengths and leads to curriculum coherence and organization (Guthrie & McCann, 1997; Short & Burke, 1991). Responding to the following questions may help you plan your first thematic unit in an orderly, successful fashion:

1. How will you and your students select a topic of study?

2. How will you help your students focus on central concepts and issues related to a particular area of study?

3. How will the topic of study relate to your grade-level curriculum guidelines and objectives?

4. Integrated units usually run from 2 to 5 weeks, or even longer, depending on the subject and maturity of the students. They also require large blocks of time. How will you manage time constraints?

5. What will determine the resources or collections you and your students need to gather? Such a collection is called a **jackdaw** and also is known as realia. Jackdaws consist of artifacts (e.g., maps, photos, models, souvenirs, postcards, clothing, or anything that students may handle and that leads to understanding).

6. What combinations of multiple communication forms will be particularly useful with this unit of study?

7. What will your students learn about science or social studies?

8. What literature will your students read?

9. How will students apply math concepts or skills?

10. How will your students apply written communication skills?

11. How will you and your students integrate technology into the unit of study?

12. How will you incorporate music, art, creative dramatics, and body movement to enhance students' learning?

13. Where can you and your students locate 20 or more trade books on the topic of study, including fiction and nonfiction on varying levels of readability?

14. Are there guest speakers, field trips, and other community resources available for this particular themed unit of inquiry?

15. How can you develop a bibliography of media resources, including books, videos, computer software, art prints, songs, poems, and other reference materials that relate to the unit?

16. What exploratory activity might as an introduction to the unit build students' motivations, and facilitate teacher–pupil planning (e.g., a bulletin board or a video that would stimulate student discussion)?

17. What choices of learning activities will you offer to students daily, weekly, or as a home task?

18. How will you plan for individual students' interests and learning capabilities (e.g., gifted students and those with special learning requirements)?

19. What opportunities will there be for cooperative learning and discussion?

20. What products will students develop and what combinations of forms of communication will students use to demonstrate their learning (e.g., booklets, posters, plays, murals, maps, demonstrations, music, dance, charts, graphs,videos, or computer presentations)?

21. What culminating experiences will you plan that include opportunities for your students to share their learning with authentic audiences (e.g., parents or students and teachers from other classes)?

22. What assessments, including student self-evaluation, will enable you and your students to determine growth in students' learning?

23. How will you evaluate the success of the unit in terms of your students' use of multiple forms of communication?

24. How will you make sure that your students have opportunities to use their life experiences and interests to help plan the unit of study and discover the answers to their questions?

SUGGESTED READINGS

Caney, S. (1980). *Steven Caney's Kids America*. New York: Workman Publishing.
This older book may be the elementary teachers' best investment. Its 400-plus pages are full of hands-on learning activities for the integrated curriculum. There are directions, along with diagrams and photographs, for such diverse activities as churning butter, creating musical instruments, making hygrometers, designing your personal coat of arms, and writing poetry.

Guthrie, J., & Wigfield, A. (Eds.). (1997). *Reading Engagement: Motivating Readers Through Integrated Instruction*. Newark, DE: International Reading Association.
In Section I of the text, Motivations, Beliefs, and Self-Efficacy in Literacy Development, several authors share differing perspectives on motivating students to read. Section II, Classroom Contexts That Promote Literacy Engagement, describes classroom settings and the rationale for integrating curricular areas.

Pappas, C., Kiefer, B., & Levstik, L. (1999). *An Integrated Language Perspective in the Elementary School: An Action Approach*. (3rd ed.). New York: Longman.
This is a highly practical guide to planning and teaching interdisciplinary thematic units. The authors include suggestions and examples for each stage in the process.

Glossary

advance organizer. A summary of written material, provided to students before they read in order to improve comprehension; developed by psychologist David Ausubel.

aesthetic reading. Louise Rosenblatt's term for reading done primarily for edification or entertainment; cf. efferent reading.

Aida. Opera by Verdi, featuring a tragic love story set in ancient Egypt.

Akhnaten. Opera by Philip Glass based on the Egyptian pharoah who believed in a single god, the sun.

auding. To receive and interpret information through hearing; thus, the term extends beyond the mere act of hearing and refers to how the information heard is interpreted.

Beethoven, Ludwig van. (1770–1827) German composer credited with founding the Romantic Movement.

Berlioz, (Louise) Hector. (1803–1869) French composer of music characterized by evoking dreams, emotions, images, and rapidly shifting moods.

Bliss symbol board. A board divided into squares, with each square containing a symbol that crosses all language barriers; people without understandable language can point to the symbols to communicate ideas; developed in the 1940s by Charles Bliss.

Bloom's Taxonomy. Devised by Benjamin Bloom as a way of categorizing the level of abstraction of questions: knowledge, comprehension, application, analysis, synthesis, evaluation.

Caldecott Medal. A prestigious award for outstanding book illustrations. The first Caldecott Medal was awarded in 1938.

case method. An educational system in which important concepts and principles are learned by studying specific examples (cases) rather than by relying on textbooks; the study of law, for example, has long depended on the case method.

Chagall, Marc. (1887–1985) Russian-born French painter whose paintings were colorful fantasies that anticipated surrealism; also known for his stained-glass windows.

choreographer. A person who plans the movements made by dancers during a piece of music, such as ballet.

cinquain. A five-line poem in which the following formula is used: The first line is a one-word description of a topic, the second line is a two-word description of the topic, the third line contains three words expressing action related to the topic, the fourth line is a four-word phrase showing feeling for the topic, and the last line is a one-word synonym that restates the essence of the topic.

cognitive tools. Any strategies individuals apply to accomplish mental tasks.

collage. A picture created by gluing other, smaller pictures and sometimes objects onto a flat surface; the overall effect is characterized by the simultaneous blending of many images.

communicative literacy. A broad concept that encompasses the entire range of new and conventional literacies.

conditional knowledge. Knowledge that is only true if a particular condition or set of conditions are true; e.g., our knowledge of what Socrates believed is conditioned by our assumption that his student, Plato, accurately recorded his words; in a sense, of course, all knowledge is conditional.

content-reading lesson. A lesson that involves a nonfiction reading selection associated with a content subject, such as math, social studies, or science; appropriate instructional methods facilitate students' reading of the selection by giving them background and focus.

critical literacy. A perspective on literacy that focuses on the purposes (and in particular the political and social goals) for which literate actions are undertaken.

critical viewing. The counterpart of critical reading applied to viewing television and movies.

daVinci, Leonardo. (1452–1519) Italian painter, sculptor, and inventor; among his best-known paintings are the *Mona Lisa* and *The Last Supper.*

Debussy, Claude. (1862–1918) French composer whose style is termed *impressionism,* a word first applied to a school of French painters (see chap. 5).

Degas, (Hillaire Germaine) Edgar. (1834–1917) French painter and sculptor, a master of drawing the human form in motion; Degas preferred to work in pastels and is known for his paintings of ballerinas.

deixis. (adjective is deictic) The use of a word that depends on context for its full meaning; *now, he, there,* and *you* are deictic words.

dialogue journals. Journals in which regular (e.g., daily or weekly), interactive writing occurs between two partners (e.g., a teacher and a student).

diamante. A seven-line poem in which the following formula is used: The first line contains one word (a noun), the second line contains two words (adjectives), the third line contains three words (participles), the fourth line contains four words (nouns), the fifth line contains three words (participles), the sixth line contains two words (adjectives), and the seventh line contains two words (nouns).

Diebenkorn, Richard. (b. 1922) An American painter from California, noted for his "Ocean Park" series of abstract paintings featuring vertical, geometric abstractions.

digital literacy. Literacy based on the ability to use text and multimedia that have been electronically coded so that they can be transmitted, stored, and displayed by electronic means.

digital video disk. A type of high-capacity optical compact disk; abbreviated DVD.

diorama. A three-dimensional depiction of a scene, usually, but not always, in miniature; a student diorama might be created in a shoebox with a small hole through which the viewer peers, whereas a professional diorama might be life-size and exhibited in a museum.

discourse. Any language unit longer than a sentence.

docent. A museum guide, often a volunteer.

drill-and-practice. Software designed to reinforce previously introduced material, by affording guided practice opportunities.

DVD. See digital video disk.

efferent reading. Louise Rosenblatt's term for reading done primarily to learn; opposite cf. aesthetic reading.

electronic symbol making. The use of digital technologies to convey meaning in ways not limited to alphabetic representation (e.g., graphic interfaces, icons).

electronic text. Any digitized written material presented on a computer screen; its fluidity, lack of permanence, and the opportunity for the reader to flexibly interact with it are among the features that distinguish it from printed text.

emergent literacy learner. One who is acquiring the skills and knowledge needed to commence the process of learning to read (e.g., appreciation of the directionality of print, oral language development, understanding that print represents speech, phonological awareness, alphabet recognition, book-handling knowledge, etc.).

emergent readers. Children in the earliest phases of becoming literate; term used to indicate that the process of learning to read and write has no precise beginning but emerges gradually.

fandom. The collective admirers (fans) of a given celebrity.

feminist perspective. A manner of interpreting events, documents, and art with those issues in mind that are especially relevant to care and concern.

Folklórico Ballet. Mexican ballet company established in 1979 by Jose Tena to preserve the rich heritage of traditional, original Mexican dances.

fresco. See mural.

Glass, Philip. (b. 1937) American composer, known for minimalist compositions.

guided imagery. A comprehension strategy in which students create mental images of story characters and text settings, emotions, and events.

haiku. A form of poetry developed in Japan over 400 years ago; consists of 17 syllables, divided into lines of 5, 7, and 5 syllables.

hypertext. A digitized form of text characterized by a branching arrangement allowing the reader choices as to how it is read; its nonlinear nature makes it possible for a reader to enter a hypertext document at any point and move through internal or external links in any order.

I-Chart. A chart shpaed like a capital *I* and used to categorize and compare ideas that students research.

image text. Any representation involving visual components; a film, a painting, or a video are examples.

impressionism. A style of painting originating and developed in France during the 1870s and characterized by the use of unmixed primary colors and small brush strokes to simulate actual reflected light; impressionist artists include Monet, Manet, Pissaro, Degas, Morisot, and Renoir.

improvisation. Role playing in a nonstructured, imaginative way.

information and communication technologies (ICT). All computer-related technology uses, including but not limited to the Internet.

integrated learning system (ILS). A complex software system organized into a sequenced curriculum and including a diagnostic-prescriptive component that places students at appropriate points in the sequence, monitors their success, and makes adjustments when necessary.

Internet. A worldwide electronic network linking computers and their users; originally, the term *Internet* was associated with text representations, such as e-mail and other documents, while the phrase *World Wide Web* denoted the graphic side of the system; this distinction has blurred in recent years and the term *Internet* is often used to refer to the entire system.

Internet technologies. All technological applications involved with Internet use (computers, servers, files, e-mail systems, Web sites, etc.).

jackdaw. See realia.

jigsaw groups. A way of grouping students for collaborative interactions in which each member of the group is responsible for teaching portions of a text to peers.

Kandinsky, Wassily. (1866–1944) A painter of the postimpresssionist era noted for abstractness and exciting use of color.

khedive. Title of any of the Turkish viceroys who governed Egypt from 1867 to 1914, a period when Egypt was controlled by Turkey.

Klee, Paul. (1879–1940) Swiss painter who influenced cubism and surrealism; his style was inspired by children's drawings.

K-W-L. An instructional technique developed by Donna Ogle for improving reading comprehension; its three phases are as follows: (a) students brainstorm concerning what they already **K**now about the topic of a nonfiction selection; (b) they decide on what they **W**ant to learn; and (c) after reading, they discuss what they have **L**earned.

K-W-L Plus. A variation of K-W-L, differing chiefly by the addition of graphic organizers.

listserv. An e-mail arrangement linking a group of people sharing a common interest; when one member addresses the list, all members receive the message.

Liszt, Franz. (1811–1886) Hungarian composer and pianist.

Manet, Édouard. (1832–1883) French impressionist who reasoned that art should reflect modern-day life.

Mendelssohn, Felix. (1809–1847) German romantic composer.

metacognition. Knowledge concerning one's own cognitive processes, or "thinking about one's thinking"; it is used to ensure that an individual's thinking is proceeding in a meaningful way; when applied to reading, metacognition is often called "comprehension monitoring" because proficient readers continually check their own understanding.

metacognitive. Pertaining to the process of monitoring one's thinking in order to accomplish one's purposes.

metaphor. A figure of speech in which one thing is equated with another in order to make a comparison (e.g., "Your hair is spun gold"); somewhat stronger than a simile, in which one thing is merely likened to another (e.g., "Your hair is like spun gold").

minimalism. A school of music in which simple themes are repeated over and over with minor variations.

mobile. A type of sculpture originated by Alexander Calder (1898–1976) and consisting of moving parts. (Web site: http://kidsartscrafts.about. com. Type "mobile" in the Search field.)

Monet, Claude. (1840–1926) French impressionist noted for his studies of the effects of light on objects and nature scenes; one of Monet's paintings, "Impression Sunrise," gave the impressionist arts their name.

mp3. A system for compressing standard audio tracks into much smaller sizes for transmission over the Internet; the names of the mp3 files that result always end in .mp3; the term originated from its sponsorship by the Moving Picture Experts Group (MPEG); the abbreviation is often used to refer to the files themselves (e.g., "I downloaded an mp3").

multiple intelligences. a theory devised by Howard Gardner in 1983. Gardner believes that the traditional notion of intelligence based on I.Q. testing is too limited. He proposed eight different intelligences to account for a wide range of human potential.

multiple literacies. A broadening of the conventional idea that literacy be defined solely in terms of reading and writing, to include other sign systems, such as those associated with the visual arts.

Munch, Edvard. (1863–1944) Norwegian painter, an expressionist who focused on death and love; known for his bright colors and constantly curving images.

mural. Originally, a large painting created on a wall after the plaster has dried (compare with a fresco, which is painted while the plaster is still wet); today, murals may appear on walls made of other materials.

new literacies. Communication that transcends the conventional definition of literacy, which is limited to written language (e.g., visual literacy, computer literacy).

papier-mâché. A type of sculpture created from torn paper mixed with flour and water; this mixture is molded into the desired form and then allowed to harden. (Web site: http://familycrafts.about.com/parenting/ familycrafts/library/weekly/aa051500a.htm)

oral text. The product of attempting to convey meaning through oral language; could be informal (e.g., a conversation) or formal (e.g., a speech); entails language elements, such as pitch and stress that are not easily conveyed through print.

PDA. Abbr. of *personal digital assistant,* a handheld electronic device for storing information such as phone numbers and appointments, and in some cases for accessing the Internet.

pdf. Abbr. of *portable document format,* a type of computer file used mainly for the storage and transfer of graphics.

Picasso, Pablo. (1881–1973) Spanish painter and sculptor; influenced cubism and became the central figure in modern abstract art.

pointillism. A painting technique in which tiny dots of paint are combined to create familiar patterns; Georges Seurat (1859–1891) originated the pointillist style.

popular-culture texts. Any information source, such as television, magazines, newspapers, films, videos, and the like, that reflects the interests of large numbers of people; as opposed to "high culture," which appeals to far fewer people.

postimpressionism. A French art movement immediately following impressionism that showed a greater concern for expression, structure, and form; postimpressionist artists include Vincent van Gogh (1853–1890), Paul Cézanne (1839–1906), and Paul Gaugin (1948–1903).

Question-Answer Relationships (QARs). An instructional technique in which students are directly taught four key types of reading comprehension questions in terms of how their answers are derived; developed by Taffy Raphael.

rant. A song in rap format with invented lyrics linked to a particular theme or topic; this blend word was created from *rap* and *chant*.

readers theatre. A theatrical form in which actors (or students) read dialogue but do not engage in physical actions associated with the script; they are often seated while reading.

realia. a collection of resources useful in teaching a unit, particularly artifacts and other real-life sources; also called a jackdaw.

Renaissance. Literally, rebirth; a period extending roughly from the mid-15th century to the end of the 16th century and made possible by the successful translation of Ancient Greek; England and Italy were the two countries chiefly affected.

Renoir, Pierre Auguste. (1841–1919) French painter and sculptor; a leading impressionist, he worked closely with Monet.

romantic composers. A group of composers who wrote during the late 18th and early 19th centuries and whose work stressed the emotions and altered or abandoned many of the restrictions placed on musical composition during the classical period; romantic composers include Ludwig van Beethoven (1770–1827), Franz Schubert (1797–1828), Hector Berlioz (1803–1869), Felix Mendelssohn (1809–1847), Robert Schumann (1810–1856), and Frédéric Chopin (1810–1849).

Rothko, Mark. (1903–70) Russian-born U.S. painter; his work is recognized as abstract expressionism.

Schumann, Robert. (1810–1856) German romantic composer whose work is emotionally charged.

search engine. An automated system for searching the information available through the Internet; some search engines automatically search other systems whereas others contain only material manually approved for inclusion in a database.

semaphore. A signal system using flags, lights, or a moving apparatus (e.g., to signal trains).

semiotic systems. Complex systems of communications that include language but go beyond it, encompassing such varied avenues as facial expressions, gestures, and seating arrangements.

semiotics. The study of how signs of all kinds represent meaning and relate to the meaning they symbolize.

shape poem. A poem written in such a way that its shape suggests or reinforces its meaning (e.g., in George Herbert's poem, *The Church Altar,* the lines are actually shaped like an altar).

sign system. Any set of symbols used to express and interpret meaning; the symbols may include conventional symbols like letters and numerals but may also include other visual symbols (e.g., computer icons, dance movements, graphics, expressions conveyed through painting, sculpture, and music, and others).

simile. See metaphor.

simulation. An activity that mimics an authentic happening (e.g., in a social studies class, students might play the part of Civil War soldiers); also, computer software that approximates a real-life situation or process (e.g., a flight simulator, used to train pilots).

social psychology. A branch of psychology that focuses on an individual's role within groups and on how groups behave.

sociocultural perspective. A manner of interpreting events by examining their relationship to social situations and cultural forces; for example, poor test performance by members of a particular minority group might be analyzed by studying group beliefs about testing and shared perceptions about schooling.

spatial intelligence. One of Howard Gardner's multiple intelligences; characterized by an appreciation for and sense of spatial relationships; often applied in the visual arts, architecture, and so on.

SQ3R. A study strategy designed to bolster comprehension of nonfiction material that must be read independently; its steps are: **S**urvey the selection, noting its organizational pattern, graphics, and so on; form a **Q**uestion for each subheading, jotting it in the book; **R**ead each subsection; try to **R**ecite the answer to the question; **R**eview the entire selection after finishing.

story features. Key components of a story, including its settings, characters, problems, and solutions.

streaming. Playing sound or video in real time, as it is downloaded over the Internet, as opposed to storing it in a file first.

syntactic. Pertaining to the syntax, or grammatical structure, of sentences and to the rules governing how sentences may be structured.

sytax. Rules governing word order and sentence structure in a language.

Ta'i Chi. A method of slow, flowing body movements practiced since ancient times in China; it incorporates principles for health, body, mind, and spirit as well as harmony in human interactions. (Web Site: http://www.taichihealth.com/health.html)

tanka. An ancient form of Japanese poetry containing 31 syllables; in English, a tanka is structured to contain 5 syllables in the first line, 7 syllables in the second line, 5 syllables in the third line, and 7 syllables in the fourth and fifth lines.

teacher utilities. Software useful to teachers outside the classroom (e.g., word processors, electronic grade books, graphics programs, puzzle makers, etc.).

team teaching. A cooperative approach to instruction through which two or more teachers plan and conduct a lesson to the same group of students through flexible grouping or some other division of responsibilities.

thematic unit. A unit of instruction that approaches a topic from several disciplinary perspectives.

time line. A graphic organizer in which events are arranged in chronological order, usually from left to right on a straight line.

transactional voice. The orientation of writing that explains, informs, or describes.

transmediation. Moving among sign systems; in particular, the process of responding in one medium to a work created in another (e.g., writing an essay about a painting or drawing a picture inspired by a song).

tutorials. Software designed to supplant the need for a teacher by introducing new material in a supportive, systematic manner.

van Gogh, Vincent (Willem). (1853–1890) Dutch painter whose art was produced entirely within a 10-year span; influenced expressionism; his work is characterized by bright colors and bold brushstrokes.

viewing. A form of literate activity in which an individual constructs meaning by interpreting information conveyed through a nonprint medium, such as painting, television, film, and so on; the reciprocal process of visually representing.

ways of knowing. The multiple means by which individuals arrive at knowledge by accepting some evidence and rejecting other evidence.

Williams, William Carlos. (1883–1963) American poet and physician; much of his poetry, such as his epic poem *Patterson* (after Patterson, New Jersey), celebrated everyday American life.

word processor. Software enabling a user to compose electronic documents in various formats.

World Wide Web. Technically, this term refers to the Internet plus its graphic component, but it is now often used interchangeably with the term.

zine. An independent Internet or paper publication, usually with a low budget; sometimes an underground paper or teen magazine; the term is a shortening of the word *magazine* and is therefore pronounced "zeen."

References

Adult Learning Service Associates. (1999). *Scanning television* [Video]. Alexandria, VA: Face to Face Media Ltd/PBS Adult Learning Service.

Albers, P. (1997). Art as literacy. *Language Arts, 74*(5), 338–350.

Albers, P. (1988, April). *Transmediation and transformation: Six preservice teachers explore their beliefs about pedagogy and practice.* Paper presented at the annual meeting of the American Educational Research Association, Montreal, Canada.

Albers, P., & Murphy, S. (2000). *Telling pieces: Art as literacy in middle school classes.* Mahwah, NJ: Lawrence Erlbaum Associates.

Alcott, L. (1999). *Little Women* (adapted by Jane Gerver). New York: D. K. Publications. (Original work published 1868)

Aliki. (1983). *A medieval feast.* New York: Thomas Crowell.

Altwerger, B., & Flores, B. (1994, January). Theme cycles: "Creating communities of learners." *Primary Voices K–6, 2*(1), 2–6.

Alvarez, M., & Risko, V. (1989). Using a thematic organizer to facilitate transfer learning with college developmental reading students. *Reading Research and Instruction, 28,* 1–15.

Alvermann, D., & Hagood, M. (2000, February). Fandom and critical media literacy. *Journal of Adolescent & Adult Literacy, 43*(5), 436–446.

Alvermann, D. E., Moon, J. S., & Hagood, M. C. (1999). *Popular culture in the classroom: Teaching and researching critical media literacy.* Newark, DE: International Reading Association.

Anderson, L., & Sosniack, L. (Eds.). (1994). *Bloom's taxonomy: A forty-year retrospective.* Chicago: University of Chicago Press.

Anno, M., & Mori, T. (1985). *Anno's three little pigs.* London: Bodley Head.

Atwell, N. (1987). *In the middle: Reading, writing, and learning with adolescents.* Portsmouth, NH: Heinemann.

Atwell, N. (1998). *In the middle: New understandings about writing, reading and learning* (2nd ed.). Portsmouth, NH: Heinemann.

Ausubel, D. (1960). The use of advance organizers in the learning and retention of meaningful verbal material. *Journal of Educational Psychology, 51,* 267–272.

Avery, C. (1993). *And with a light touch.* Portsmouth, NH: Heinemann.

Baines, I., & Kunkel, A. (Eds.). (2000). *Going Bohemian: Activities that engage adolescents in the act of writing well.* Newark, DE: International Reading Association.

Baker, E. (2001). Approaches used to integrate literacy and technology. *Reading Onling,* 1–14. (http://readingonline.org/articles/baker/index.html)

Ball, D. (1994). *Emily Eyefinger and the lost treasure.* New York: Simon & Schuster for Young Readers.

Ball, J., & Airs, C. (1995). *Taking time to act: A guide to cross-curricula drama.* Portsmouth, NH: Heinemann.

The Bangles Recording Group. (1985). "Walk like an Egyptian" [in the album, *Different Light*], New York: Columbia Records.

Barone, D. (1999). *Resilient children: Stories of poverty, drug exposure, and literacy development.* Newark, DE: International Reading Association.

Bear, D., Invernizzi, M., Templeton, S., & Johnston, F. (2000). *Word their way: Word study for phonics, vocabulary, and spelling instruction* (2nd ed.). Upper Saddle River, NJ: Merrill/Prentice Hall.

Benson, G. (1991). *This poem doesn't rhyme.* London: Puffin.

Benson, G. (1994). *Does W trouble you?* London: Puffin.

Berghoff, B. (1995). *Inquiry curriculum from a semiotic perspective: First graders using multiple sign systems to learn.* Unpublished dissertation, Indiana University, Bloomington.

Berghoff, B., Egawa, K., Harste, J., & Hoonan, B. (2000). *Beyond reading and writing: Inquiry, curriculum, and multiple ways of knowing.* Urbana, IL: National Council of Teachers of English.

Binch, C. (1994). *Gregory Cool.* New York: Dial Books for Young Readers.

Biondo, S., Raphael, T., & Gavelek, J. (2000). *Mapping the possibilities of integrated literacy instruction* (http://www.readingonline.org/research/biondo/biondo.html).

Birge, E. (1966). *History of public school music in the United States.* Reston, VA: Music Educators National Conference. (Original work published 1928)

Blanchard, J. (1999). Introduction. In J. Blanchard (Ed.), *Educational computing in the schools: Technology, communication, and literacy* (pp. 1–4). New York: Haworth Press.

Blecher, S., & Jaffe, K. (1998). *Integrating in the arts: Widening the learning circle.* Portsmouth, NH: Heinemann.

Bloom, B. (1956). *Taxonomy of educational objectives: The classification of educational goals: Handbook 1, Cognitive domain.* New York: Longmans, Green.

Bloome, D., & Kinzer, C. K. Hard times or cosmetics? Changes in Literacy. Peabody Journal of Education, 341-375.

Bolter, J. (1998). Hypertext and the question of visual literacy. In D. Reinking, L. Labbo, M. McKenna, & R. Kieffer (Eds.), *Handbook of literacy and technology: Transformations in a post-typographic world* (pp. 3–13). Mahwah, NJ: Lawrence Erlbaum Associates.

Bond, P. (1999). *Firefly guide to space: A photographic journey through the universe.* Willowdale, Canada: Firefly Books.

Brett, J. (1987). *Goldilocks and the three bears* (Retold and illustrated). New York: Dodd Mead.

Brommer, G. (1995). *Aspects of visual art.* Glenview, IL: Crystal Productions. (http://www.crystalproductions.com)

Brown, M., & Jolly, R. (1999). *UNDP Human Development Report.* New York: United Nations Publications.

Brownlie, F., & King, J. (2000). *Learning in safe schools: Creating classrooms where all students belong.* Portland, ME: Stenhouse.

Bruce, B. C. (1997). Current issues and future directions. In J. Flood, S. B. Heath, & D. Lapp (Eds.), *Handbook of research on teaching literacy through the communicative and visual arts* (pp. 875–884). New York: Simon & Schuster Macmillan.

Buckingham, D. (1993). Introduction. In D. Buckingham (Ed.), *Reading audiences: Young people and the media* (pp. 1–23). Manchester, England: Manchester University Press.

Buehl, D. (2001). *Classroom strategies for interactive learning* (2nd ed.). Newark, DE: International Reading Association.

Bunchman, J., & Briggs, S. (1994). *Activities for creating pictures and poetry.* Worcester, MA: Davis.

Burnaford, G., Aprill, A., & Weiss, C. (2001). *Renaissance in the classroom: Arts integration and meaningful learning.* Mahwah, NJ: Lawrence Erlbaum Associates.

Buss, K., & Karnowski, L. (2000). *Reading and writing genres.* Newark, DE: International Reading Association.

Calkins, L. (1986). *The art of teaching writing.* Portsmouth, NH: Heinemann.

Calvert, S. (1999). *Children's journeys through the information age.* Boston: McGraw-Hill College.

Campbell, P., & Scott-Kassner, C. (1995). *Music in childhood: From preschool through elementary years.* New York: Schirmer.

Caney, S. (1980). *Steven Caney's America.* New York: Workman.

Capra, F. (Director). (1946) *It's a wonderful life* [Motion picture]. Encino, CA: Hal Roach Studios. (Re-released in 1986)

Carle, E. (1984). *The very hungry caterpillar.* New York: Putnam's Sons.

Carle, E. (1996). *The grouchy ladybug* (Revised ed.). New York: HarperCollins.

Carle, E. (1998). *You can make a collage: A very simple how to book.* Palo Alto, CA: Klutz Press.

Carle, E. (2000a). The Eric Carle Fan Club (E-mail: fanclub@eric-carle.com)

Carle, E. (2000b). Eric Carle: *Picture writer video.* Available from the Eric Carrle Store at http://www.eric-carle.com/pwriter.html

Cattagni, A., & Farris, E. (2001). Internet access in public schools and classrooms: 1994–2000. *Education Statistics Quarterly: Elementary and secondary education* [Electronic version]. Retreived August 21, 2001, from http://nces.ed.gov/pubs2001/quarterly/summer/q2-7.asp

Cecil, N., & Lauritzen, P. (1994). *Literacy and the arts for the integrated classroom: Alternative ways of knowing.* White Plains, NY: Longman.

CEO Forum. (1999). Professional development: A link to better learning [Electronic version]. Retrieved March 1, 1999, from http://www.ceoforum.org/report99/99report.pdf.

Chall, J. (1967). *Learning to read: The great debate.* New York: McGraw-Hill.

Chambers, A. (1990). *Booktalk.* London: The Bodley Head.

Char, C., & Forman, G. (1994). Interactive technology and the young child: A look to the future. In J. Wright & D. Shade (Eds.), *Young children: Active learners in a technological age* (pp. 167–177). Washington, DC: National Association for the Education of Young Children.

Charlesworth, R. (1992). *Understanding child development.* New York: Delmar.

Cherry, L. (1990). *The great kapok tree: A tale of the Amazon rain forest.* New York: Harcourt Brace.

Cherry, L. (1995). *The dragon and the unicorn.* San Diego: Harcourt Brace.

Chomsky, C. (1972). Stages in language development and reading exposure. *Harvard Educational Review, 42*(1), 1–33.

Clay, M. (1975). *What did I write?* Auckland, New Zealand: Heinemann.

Clay, M. (1993). *Reading recovery.* Portsmouth, NH: Heinemann.

CNET Help.com (http://www.help.com)

Cohle, D., & Towle, W. (2001). *Connecting reading and writing in the intermediate grades: A workshop approach.* Newark, DE: International Reading Association.

Colberg, J., Trimble, K., & Desberg, P. (Eds.). (1996). *The case for education: Contemporary approaches for using case methods.* Boston: Allyn & Bacon.

Colburn, L. (2000a). *An analysis of teacher change and required supports as technology is integrated into classroom instruction.* Unpublished doctoral dissertation, Vanderbilt University, Nashville, TN.

Colburn, L. (2000b, August). Integrating technology in your middle school classroom: Some hints from a successful process. *Reading Online, 4*(2). Retrieved August 16, 2002, from http://www.readingonline.org/electronic/Colburn/index/html

Collections of the Goodman Library. (2001). *Dances of the World* (Video no. 793.32/D195). (http://www.induce.edu/academic/library/Meiac/Video/Bib/vidbib_7html)

Coman, C. (1995). *What Jamie saw.* Arden, NC: Front Street, Inc.

Considine, D. (1987). Visual literacy and the curriculum: More to it than meets the eye. *Language Arts, 64*(6), 34–40.

Considine, D., & Haley, G. (1999). *Visual messages: Integrating imagery into instruction.* (2nd ed.). Englewood, CO: Teacher Ideas Press.

Considine, D., Haley, G., & Lacy, L. (1994). *Imagine that: Developing critical thinking and critical viewing through children's literature.* Englewood, CO: Teacher Ideas Press.

Cooke, G., Griffin, D., & Cox, M. (1997). *Teaching young children to draw: Imaginative approaches to representational drawing.* London: Falmer Press.

Cornett, C. (1999). *The arts as meaning makers: Integrating literature and the arts through the curriculum.* Upper Saddle River, NJ: Merrill.

Cowan, K. (2001). The arts and emergent literacy. *Primary Voices K–6, 9*(4), 11–17.

Cunningham, D. (1992). Beyond educational psychology: Steps toward an educational semiotic. *Educational Psychology Review, 4*(2), 165–193.

Cunningham, M. (1991). *The dancer and the dance: Merce Cunningham in conversation with Jacqueline Lesschaeve.* New York: Marion Boyars.

Cunningham, P. M., Hull, D. P., & Defee, M. (1991). Nonability grouped, multilevel instruction: A year in a first grade classroom. *Reading Teacher, 44,* 566–571.

A Curriculum of Peace [Themed issue]. (2000, May). *English Journal, 89*(5).

Dahl, K., Scharer, P., Lawson, L., & Grogan, P. (1999). Phonics instruction and student achievement in whole language first-grade classrooms. *Reading Research Quarterly, 3,* 312–341.

Daniels, H. (1994). *Literature circles: Voice and choice in the student-centered classroom.* Portland, ME: Stenhouse.

Desmond, R. (1997). TV viewing, reading and media literacy. In J. Flood, S. Heath, & D. Lapp, (Eds.). (1997). *Handbook of research on teaching literacy through the visual and communicative arts* (pp. 23–39). New York: Simon & Schuster Macmillan.

Dewey, J. (1913). *Interest and effort in education.* Boston: Riverside.

Dionisio, M. (1989). Write? Isn't this reading class? *The Reading Teacher, 36,* 746–749.

Disessa, A. (2000). *Changing minds.* Cambridge: MIT Press.

Doyle, W. (1990). Case methods in the education of teachers. *Teacher Education Quarterly, 17*(1), 7–15.

Drewe, S. (1996). *Creative dance: Enriching understanding.* Alberta, Canada: Detselig.

Durant, A. (1996). *Mouse party.* Cambridge, MA: Candlewick Press.

Dworkin, M. (1952). *Dewey on education.* New York: Teachers College Press.

Dyson, A. H. (1997). *Writing superheroes: Contemporary childhood, popular culture and classroom literacy.* New York: Teachers College Press.

Eagleton, M. B. (1999). The benefits and challenges of a student-designed school website. *Reading Online* [Electronic version] Retrieved June 1, 1999, from http://www.reading online.org/articles/eagleton/index.html

Eisner, E. (1978). Introduction. In E. Eisner (Ed.), *Reading, the arts, and the creation of meaning* (pp. 7–12). Reston, VA: National Art Education Association.

Eisner, E. W. (1991). What the arts taught me about education. In G. Willis & W. Schubert (Eds.), *Reflections from the heart of educational inquiry: Understanding curriculum and teaching through the arts* (pp. 34–48). Albany: State University of New York Press.

Eisner, E. (1992). The misunderstood role of the arts in human development. *Phi Delta Kappan, 7*(8), 591–595.

Eisner, E. (1995). Why the arts are marginalized in our schools. One more time. *On Common Ground, 5,* 5, 9.

Eisner, E. (1998). *The kind of schools we need: Personal essays.* Portsmouth, NH: Heinemann.

Elbow, P. (2000). *Everyone can write: Essays toward a hopeful theory of writing and teaching.* New York: Oxford University Press.

Elrich, A. (1985). *Cinderella.* New York: Dial Books for Young Readers.

Emory, P. (1986). *Reading and writing: Flip sides of the same coin.* Paper presented to the Maryland Writing Project Summer Teacher Institute, Baltimore, MD.

Epstein, S. (Ed.). (1999). *Adolescents and their music: If it's too loud, you're too old.* London: Falmer Press.

Ernst, K. (1994, January). Writing pictures, painting words: Writing in an artists' workshop. *Language Arts, 71,* 44–52.

Evans, K. (2001). *Literature discussion groups in the intermediate grades.* Newark, DE: International Reading Association.

Farstrup, A. E., & Myers, M. (Eds.). (1996). *Standards for the English language arts.* Urbana, IL: National Council of Teachers of English and Newark, DE: International Reading Association.

Fehlman, R. (1996). Viewing film and television as whole language instruction. *English Journal, 85*(2), 43–50.

Ferrington, G., & Anderson-Iman, L. (1996). Media literacy: Upfront and on-line. *Journal of Adolescent & Adult Literacy, 39*(8), 666–670.

Fisherkeller, J. (2000). "The writers are getting kind of desperate": Young adolescents, television, and literacy. *Journal of Adolescent & Adult Literacy, 43*(1), 596–606.

Flood, J., Heath, S., & Lapp, D. (Eds.). (1997). *Handbook of research on teaching literacy through the visual and communicative arts.* New York: Simon & Schuster Macmillan.

Flood, J., & Lapp, D. (1997–1998). Broadening conceptualizations of literacy: The visual and communicative arts. *The Reading Teacher, 51,* 342–344.

Flood, J., Lapp, D., & Wood, D. (1998, November). Viewing: The neglected communication process or "When what you see isn't what you get." *The Reading Teacher, 52*(3), 300–304.

Florian, D. (1987). *A winter day.* New York: Greenwillow Books.

Florian, D. (1999). *Winter eyes.* New York: Greenwillow Books.

Fountas, I., & Pinnell, G. (1996). *Guided reading.* Portsmouth, NH: Heinemann.

Fountas, I., & Pinnell, G. (2000). *Guided reading 3–6.* Portsmouth, NH: Heinemann.

Freedman, S., Flower, L., Hull, G., & Hayes, J. (1997). Ten years of research: Achievements of the National Center for the Study of Writing and Research. In J. Flood, S. B. Heath, & D. Lapp (Ed.), *Handbook of research on teaching literacy through the communicative and visual arts* (pp. 735–752). New York: Simon & Schuster Macmillan.

Galdone, P. (1984). *The three little pigs.* New York: Houghton Mifflin.

Gambrell, L., & Almasi, J. (Eds.). (1996). *Lively discussions! Fostering engaged reading.* Newark, DE: International Reading Association.

Gambrell, L., & Bates, R. (1984). Mental imagery and the comprehension monitoring performance of fourth and fifth grade poor readers. *Reading Research Quarterly, 21,* 454–464.

Gambrell, L., Kapinus, B., & Wilson, R. (1987). Using mental imagery and summarization to achieve independence in comprehension. *Journal of Reading, 30,* 638–642.

Garcia-Williams, R. (1995). *Like sisters on the home front.* New York: Lodestar Books.

Gardner, H. (1983). *Frames of mind: The theory of multiple intelligences.* New York: Basic Books.

Gardner, H. (1991). *The unschooled mind: How children think and how schools should teach.* New York: Basic Books.

Gardner, H. (1993). *Multiple intelligences: Theory into practice.* New York: Basic Books.

Gardner, H. (2000). Can technology exploit our many ways of knowing? In D. Gordon (Ed.), *The digital classroom: How technology is changing the way we teach and learn* (pp. 32–35). Cambridge, MA: Harvard Educational Letter.

Garvie, E. (1990). *Story as vehicle.* Clevedon, England: Multilingual Matters.

Gee, J. P. (1996). *Social linguistics and literacies: Ideology in discourses.* London: Taylor & Francis.

Gentry, J. (2000, November). A retrospective on invented spelling and a look forward. *The Reading Teacher, 54*(3), 318–332.

Gibbons, G. (1992). *Star gazers.* New York: Holiday House.

Gibbons, G. (1998). *Penguins.* New York: Holiday House.

Gilster, P. (1997). *Digital literacy.* New York: Wiley.

Goble, P. (1998). *Her seven brothers.* New York: Aladdin.

Goldberg, M. (2000, April). *The mirrored selves (Thanks Duke): Practicing professional development.* Paper presented at the annual meeting of the American Educational Research Association, New Orleans, LA.

Goldberg, M. (2001). *Arts and learning: An integrated approach to teaching and learning in multicultural and multilingual settings* (2nd ed.). Upper Saddle River, NJ: Merrill.

Goldberg, M., & Phillips, A. (1995). *Arts as education.* Cambridge, MA: Harvard Educational Review.

Goldberg, M., & Scott-Kassner, C. (in press). Instrumental outcomes of learning through the arts. In R. Colwell (Ed.). *Handbook on research in music education.* New York: Oxford University Press.

Goldsborough, R. (2000, October/November). Using the net to learn about the net. *Reading Today,* p. 14.

Goodman, K. (1986). *What's whole in whole language.* Portsmouth, NH: Heinemann.

Goodman, K. (1991). Revaluing readers and reading. In S. Stires (Ed.), *With promise: Redefining reading and writing for "special" students* (pp. 127–133). Portsmouth, NH: Heinemann.

Goodman, K. (1993). *Phonic phacts.* Portsmouth, NH: Heinemann.

Goodman, Y. (1986). Children coming to know literacy. In W. Teale & E. Sulzby (Eds.), *Emergent literacy: Writing and reading* (pp. 1–14). Norwood, NJ: Ablex.

Gordon, D. (Ed.). (2000). *The digital classroom: How technology is changing the way we teach and learn.* Cambridge, MA: Harvard Educational Letter.

Graves, D. (1983). *Writing: Teachers & children at work.* Exeter, NH: Heinemann.

Graves, D. (1984) *A researcher learns to write.* Portsmouth, NH: Heinemann.

Graves, D. (1991). All children can write. In S. Stires (Ed.), *With promise: Redefining reading and writing for "special" students* (pp. 115–125). Portsmouth, NH: Heinemann.

Graves, D., & Murray, D. (1980). Revision in the writer's workshop and in the classroom. *Journal of Education, 162,* 38–56.

Greene, M. (1995). *Releasing the imagination: Essays on education, the arts, and social change.* San Francisco: Jossey-Bass.

Greenfield, E. (1978). *Honey, I love.* New York: HarperCollins

Greenfield, E., & Little, L. (1987). *I can do it by myself.* New York: HarperCollins.

Grout, D. (1973). *A history of Western music* (Rev. ed.). New York: Norton.

Grout, D., & Palisca, C. (Eds.). (1988). *A history of Western music* (4th ed.). New York: Norton.

Grumet, M. (1991). Curriculum and the art of daily life. In G. Willis & W. Shubert (Eds.), *Reflections from the heart of educational inquiry: Understanding curriculum and teaching through the arts* (pp. 74–89). Albany: State University of New York Press.

Grumet, M. (1995). Scholae personae: Masks for meaning. In J. Gallop (Ed.), *Pedagogy: The question of impersonation* (pp. 36–45). Bloomington: Indiana University Press.

Guthrie, J. (1996). Educational contexts for engagement in literacy. *The Reading Teacher, 49,* 432–445.

Guthrie, J., & McCann, A. (1997). Characteristics of classrooms that promote motivations and strategies for learning. In J. Guthrie & A. Wigfield (Eds.), *Reading engagement: Motivating readers through integrated instruction.* Newark, DE: International Reading Association.

Guthrie, J., & Wigfield, A. (Eds.). (1997). *Reading engagement: Motivating readers through integrated instruction.* Newark, DE: International Reading Association.

Hamilton, M., & Weiss, M. (Beauty and the Beast Storytellers). (1990). *Children tell stories: A teaching guide.* Katonah, NY: Richard C. Owen.

Harrington, H., & Hodson, L. (1993, April). *Cases and teacher development.* Paper presented at the annual meeting of the American Educational Research Association, Atlanta, GA.

Harrington, H., Quinn-Learing, S., & Hodson, L. (1996). Written case analyses and critical reflection. *Teaching and Teacher Education, 12*(1), 25–37.

Harste, J. C. (1994). The sign systems. In R. Ruddell, M. Ruddell, & H. Singer (Eds.), *Theoretical models and processes of reading* (pp. 1220–1242). Newark, DE: International Reading Association.

Harste, J. C. (2000). Six points of departure. In B. Berghoff, K. A. Egawa, J. C. Harste, & B. T. Hoonan (2000). *Beyond reading and writing: Inquiry, curriculum, and multiple ways of knowing.* Urbana, IL: National Council of Teachers of English.

Harste, J., Short, K., & Burke, C. (1988). *Creating classroom authors.* Portsmouth, NH: Heinemann.

Hart, M. (1991). *Planet drum.* San Francisco: HarperSanFrancisco.

Harvey, S. (1998). *Nonfiction matters: Reading, writing, and research in grades 3–6*. Portland, ME: Stenhouse.

Hatchett, C. (1988). *The glow in the dark night sky book*. New York: Random House.

Hazen, B. (1992). *Who lost a shoe?* New York: Newbridge Communications.

Heinig, R. (1987). *Creative drama resource book*. Englewood Cliffs, NJ: Prentice-Hall.

Heinig, R. (1993). *Creative drama for the classroom teacher* (4th ed.). Boston: Allyn & Bacon.

Heinig, R. (1994). Reading, literature, and the dramatic arts. In C. Weaver, *Reading process and practice: From socio-psycholinguistics to whole language* (2nd ed., pp. 437–477). Portsmouth, NH: Heinemann.

Helfman, E. (2000). *Signs and symbols around the world*. Available from Backinprint.com

Heller, M. (1991). *Reading–writing connections: From theory to practice*. New York: Longman.

Hendrick, J. (Ed.). (1997). *First steps toward the Reggio Emelia way*. Upper Saddle River, NJ: Merrill/Prentice Hall.

Hobbs, R. (1997). Literacy for the information age. In J. Flood, S. Brice Heath, & D. Lapp (Eds.), *Research on teaching literacy through the visual and communicative arts* (pp. 7–14). New York: Simon & Schuster Macmillan.

Hobbs, R. (1998). The seven great debates in the media literacy movement. *Journal of Communication, 48*(1), 16–32.

Hoffer, C. (1990). Artistic intelligence and music education. In W. Moody (Ed.), *Artistic intelligence: Implications for education* (pp. 135–140). New York: Teachers College Press.

Hoffman, J. (1992). Critical reading and thinking across the curriculum. *Language Arts, 69*, 121–124.

Hoffman, M. (1991). *Amazing Grace*. New York: Dial.

Hofstetter, F. (2001, February 1). *The future's future*. Keynote address presented at the Project Director's annual meeting, Department of Education, Office of Special Education Programs, Washington, DC.

Hubbard, R. (1989). *Authors of pictures, draughtsmen of words*. Portsmouth, NH: Heinemann.

Hughes, M. (1996). *A handful of seeds*. New York: Orchard Books.

Hunt, G. (2001). Talking about reading. In P. Goodwin (Ed.), *The articulate classroom* (pp. 41–46). London: David Fulton.

Hunter, M. (1994). *Mastery teaching*. Thousand Oaks, CA: Corwin Press.

Hurd, R., & Cassidy, J. (1992). *Watercolor for the artistically undiscovered*. Palo Alto, CA: Klutz.

Jacobs, V., Goldberg, M., & Bennett, T. (1999, April). *Teaching core curriculum through the arts*. Paper presented at the annual meeting of the American Educational Research Association, Montreal, Canada.

Jalongo, M., & Stamp, L. (1997). *The arts in children's lives: Aesthetic education in early childhood*. Boston: Allyn & Bacon.

Jett-Simpson, M. (1989). Creative drama and story comprehension. In J. Stewig & S. Sebasta (Eds.), *Using literature in the elementary classroom* (pp. 91–109). Urbana, IL: National Council of Teachers of English.

Johnson, D., Johnson, R., & Holubec, E. (1990). *Cooperation in the classroom* (Rev. ed.). Edina, MN: Interaction.

Johnstone, K. (1979). *Impro*. New York: Theater Arts Books.

Jonassen, D. H., & Reeves, T. C. (1996). Learning with technology: Using computers as cognitive tools. In D. Jonassen (Ed.), *Handbook of research on educational communication and technology* (pp. 693–719.) New York: Scholastic.

Kalman, B. (1997). *Pioneer projects*. New York: Crabtree.

Kamil, M. L., & Lane, D. M. (1998). Researching the relationship between technology and literacy: An agenda for the 21st century. In D. Reinking, L. Labbo, M. McKenna, & R. Kieffer (Eds.), *Handbook of literacy and technology: Transformations in a post-typographic world* (pp. 323–342). Mahwah, NJ: Lawrence Erlbaum Associates.

Kamil, M., Mosenthal, P., Pearson, P., & Barr, R. (Eds.). (2000). *Handbook of reading research* (Vol. 3). Mahwah, NJ: Lawrence Erlbaum Associates.

Karchmer, R. A. (2001). Teachers on a journey: Thirteen teachers report how the Internet influences literacy and literacy instruction in their K–12 classrooms. *Reading Research Quarterly, 36*(4), 442–466.

Katz, L., & Cesarone, B. (Eds.). (1994). *Reflections on the Reggio Emelia approach.* Urbana, IL: ERIC Clearinghouse on Elementary and Early Childhood Education (ED 375 986).

Keeping schools and communities safe: What is the Department of Education doing to help Americans keep schools and communities safe? (http://www.ed.gove/offices/OESE/SDFS)

Kemp, A. (1997). *Abuse in the family: An introduction.* Monterey, CA: Brooks/Cole.

Kincheloe, J., & Steinberg, S. (1997). *Changing multiculturalism.* Philadelphia: Open University Press.

King, S. (2000). *On writing: A memoir of the craft.* New York: Scribner.

Kinzer, C., & Leander, K. (in press). Technology and the language arts: Implications of an expanded definition of literacy. In J. Flood, D. Lapp, J. M. Jensen, & J. R. Squire (Eds.), *Handbook of research on teaching the English language arts* (2nd ed). Mahwah, NJ: Lawrence Erlbaum Associates.

Kinzer, C. K., & Leu, D., Jr. (1997). The challenge of change: Exploring literacy and learning in electronic environments. *Language Arts, 74*(2), 126–136.

Kinzer, C., & Risko, V. (1998). Multimedia and enhanced learning: Transforming preservice teacher education In D. L. Labbo, M. McKenna, & R. Kieffer (Eds.), *Handbook of literacy and technology: Transformations in a post-typographic world* (pp. 185–202). Mahwah, NJ: Lawrence Erlbaum Associates.

Kist, W. (2000, May). Beginning to create the new literacy classroom: What does the new literacy look like? *Journal of Adolescent & Adult Literacy, 43*(8), 710–718.

Koshewa, A. (2001). Multiple cultures, multiple literacies. *Primary Voices K–6, 9*(4), 27–33.

Krupp, E. (1989). *The Big Dipper and you.* New York: William Morrow.

Kubey, R., & Baker, F. (1999, October 27). Has media literacy found a curricular foothold? *Education Week,* pp. 56–58.

Labbo, L. D. (1994, April). *The microcomputer and emergent literacy: A case study of computer-related literacy experiences at home.* Paper presented at the 39th International Reading Association Conference, Toronto, Canada.

Labbo, L. D. (1996). A semiotic analysis of young children's symbol making in a classroom computer center. *Reading Research Quarterly, 31*(4), 356–385.

Labbo, L. D., Eakle, A. & Montero, K. (in press). Digital language experience approach (D-LEA): Using digital photographs and creativity software as LEA innovation. *Reading Online.* (http://www.readingonline.org/default.asp)

Labbo, L. D., & Kuhn, M. (1998). Computers and emergent literacy: An examination of young children's computer-generated communicative symbol making. In D. R. Reinking, L. D. Labbo, M. C. McKenna, & R. Kieffer (Eds.), *Literacy for the 21st century: Technological transformations in a post-typographic world* (pp. 79–91). New York: Lawrence Erlbaum Associates.

Labbo, L. D., & Kuhn, M. (2000). Weaving chains of affect and cognition: A young child's understanding of CD-ROM talking books. *Journal of Literacy Research, 32*(2), pp. 187–210.

Langer, S. (1942). *Philosophy in a new key.* Cambridge, MA: Harvard University Press.

Langone, J. (1984). *Violence!—Our fastest growing public health problem.* Boston: Little, Brown.

Lear, E. (1968). *The Jumblies.* London: Chatto & Windus.

LeBaron, J., & Collier, C. (Eds.). (2001). *Technology in its place: Successful technology infusion in schools.* San Francisco: Jossey-Bass.

Leland, C., & Harste, J. (1994). Multiple ways of knowing: Curriculum in a new key. *Language Arts, 71,* 337–345.

Lemke, J. L. (1998). Metamedia literacy: Transforming meanings and media. In D. Reinking, L. D. Labbo, M. McKenna, & R. Keiffer (Eds.), *Handbook of literacy and technology: Transformations in a post-typographic world* (pp. 283–301). Mahwah, NJ: Lawrence Erlbaum Associates.

Leppert, R., & McLary, S. (Eds.). (1987). *Music and society: The politics of composition, performance, and reception.* Cambridge, England: Cambridge University Press.

Leu, D., Jr. (2000a). Literacy and technology: Deictic consequences for literacy education in an information age. In M. L. Kamil, P. Mosenthal, P. D. Pearson, & R. Barr (Eds.), *Handbook of Reading Research* (Vol. 3, pp. 743–770). Mahwah, NJ: Lawrence Erlbaum Associates.

Leu, D. Jr. (2000b, May). *New literacies for new times: Using Internet technologies.* Invited address presented to the Professors of Reading Teacher Educators, a Special Interest Group of the International Reading Association, at the annual meeting of the International Reading Association, Indianapolis, IN.

Leu, D., Jr. (2000c). Our children's future: Changing the focus of literacy and literacy instruction. *The Reading Teacher, 53*(5), 424–429.

Leu, D., Jr. (in press). The new literacies: Research on reading instruction with the Internet and other digital technologies. In J. Samuels & A. Farstrup (Eds.), *What research has to say about reading instruction.* Newark, DE: International Reading Association.

Leu, D., Jr., & Kinzer, C. (2000). The convergence of literacy instruction and networked technologies for information and communication. *Reading Research Quarterly, 35,* 108–127.

Leu, D., Jr., & Leu, D. (1997). *Teaching with the Internet: Lessons from the classroom.* Norwood, MA: Christopher-Gordon.

Leu, D., Jr., & Leu, D. (2000). *Teaching with the Internet: Lessons from the classroom* (3rd ed.). Norwood, MA: Christopher-Gordon.

Leu, D., Jr., Mallette, M., & Karchmer, R. (2001). New literacies, new technologies, and new realities: Toward an agenda for the literacy research community. *Reading Research and Instruction, 40,* 265–272.

Leveranz, D., & Tyner, K. (1996). What is media literacy? Two leading proponents offer an overview. *Media Spectrum, 23*(1), 10.

Levy, S. (2000, January 1). It's time to turn the last page. *Newsweek,* pp. 96–98.

Lockwood Summers, S. (1997). *Media alert! 200 activities to create media-savvy kids.* Castle Rock, CO: Hi Willow Research & Publishing.

Longley, L. (1999). Gaining the arts literacy advantage. *Educational Leadership, 57*(2), 71–74.

Lopez, B. (1986). *Arctic dreams.* New York: Bantam.

Lowenfeld, V., & Brittain, W. (1975). *Creative and mental growth* (5th ed.). New York: Macmillan.

Lowry, L. (1989). *Number the stars.* Boston: Houghton Mifflin.

Luke, A. (2000). Critical literacy in Australia: A matter of context and standpoint. *Journal of Adolescent and Adult Literacy, 43*(5), 448–461.

Luke, C. (2000a). Cyber-schooling and technological change: Multiliteracies for new times. In B. Cope & M. Kalantzis (Eds.), *Multiliteracies: Literacy learning and the design of social futures* (pp. 69–91). London: Routledge.

Luke, C. (2000b). New literacies in teacher education. *Journal of Adolescent & Adult Literacy, 43*(5), 424–435.

Lundeberg, M., Levin, B., & Harrington, H. (Eds.). (1999). *Who learns what from cases: The research base for teaching and learning with cases.* Mahwah, NJ: Lawrence Erlbaum Associates.

Maag, J. (1999). *Behavior management: From theoretical implications to practical applications.* San Diego: Singular.

Macaul, S., Giles, J. K., & Rodenberg, R. K. (1999). Intermediality in the classroom: Learners constructing meaning through deep viewing. In L. Semali & A. Watts Pailliotet (Eds.), *Intermediality: The teachers' handbook of critical media literacy* (pp. 53–74). Boulder, CO: Westview Press.

Macauley, D. (1975). *Pyramids.* New York: Houghton Mifflin.

Mallow, F., & Patterson, L. (1999). *Framing literacy.* Norwood, MA: Christopher-Gordon.

Martin, R. (1992). *The rough-face girl.* New York: Putnam's Sons.

Matthews, M., & Rainer, J. (2001). The quandaries of teachers and teacher educators in integrating literacy and mathematics. *Language Arts, 78*(4), 357–364.

Mayer, R. (1997). Multimedia learning: Are we asking the right questions? *Educational Psychologist, 32,* 1–19.

McBrien, J. (Ed.). (1999). *Media matters: Critical thinking in the information age.* Cincinnati, OH: South-Western Educational.

McCaslin, N. (2000). *Creative drama in the classroom and beyond* (7th ed.). New York: Longman/Addison Wesley.

McKenna, M. (2002). Hypertext. In B. Guzetti (Ed.), *Literacy in America: An encyclopedia.* Santa Barbara: ABC-CLIO.

McKenna, M., Stratton, B., McKenna, B., & Hanak, D. (2000, May). *Hot links to literacy: Websites that sizzle.* Retreived from http://www.reading.org

McMaster, J. (1998). "Doing" literature: Using drama to build literacy classrooms: The segue for a few struggling readers. *The Reading Teacher, 1*(7), 574–584.

McNiven, H., & McNiven, P. (1994). *Masks.* East Sussex, England: Wayland.

Merriam, A. (1964). *The anthropology of music.* Evanston, IL: Northwestern University.

Merseth, K. (1991). The early history of case-based instruction: Insights for teacher education. *Journal of Teacher Education, 42*(4), 243–249.

Messaris, P. (1997). Introduction. In J. Flood, S. Brice Heath, & D. Lapp (Eds.), *Research on teaching literacy through the visual and communicative arts* (pp. 3–5). New York: Simon & Schuster Macmillan.

Mikulecky, L., & Kirkley, J. R. (1998). Changing workplaces, changing classes: The new role of technology in workplace literacy. In D. Reinking, L. Labbo, M. McKenna, & R. Kieffer (Eds.), *Handbook of literacy and technology: Transformations in a post-typographic world* (pp. 303–320). Mahwah, NJ: Lawrence Erlbaum Associates.

Miller, B., & Kantrov, I. (1998). *A guide to facilitating cases in education.* Portsmouth, NH: Heinemann.

Moffett, J., & Wagner, B. (1992). *Student-centered language arts, K–12.* Portsmouth, NH: Heinemann.

Moje, E., & Wade, S. (1997). What case discussions reveal about teacher thinking. *Teaching and Teacher Education, 13*(7), 691–712.

Moje, E., Young, J., Readence, J., & Moore, D. (2000, February). Reinventing adolescent literacies for new times: Perennial and millennial issues. *Journal of Adolescent & Adult Literacy, 43*(5), 400–410.

Moline, S. (1995). *I see what you mean: Children at work with visual information.* Portland, ME: Stenhouse.

Moore, D., Beane, T., Birdyshaw, D., & Rycik, J (1999). Adolescent literacy: A position statement. *Journal of Adolescent & Adult Literacy, 43,* 97–112.

Moore, I. (1994). *A big day for little Jack.* Cambridge, MA: Candlewick Press.

Morgan, N., & Saxton, J. (1987). *Teaching drama: A mind of many wonders.* Portsmouth, NH: Heinemann.

Morine-Dershimer, G. (1996). What's in a case . . . and what comes out? In J. Colberg, K. Trimble, & P. Desberg (Eds.), *The case for education: Contemporary approaches for using case methods* (pp. 99–123). Boston: Allyn & Bacon.

Morrow, L. (1993). *Literacy development in the early years: Helping children read and write.* Boston: Allyn & Bacon.

Most, B. (1995). *If the dinosaurs came back.* San Diego: Harcourt Brace.

Munsch, R. (1980). *The paperbag princess.* Toronto, Canada: Annick Press.

Munsch, R. (1985). *Thomas's snowsuit.* Toronto: Annick Press.

Murray, D. (1982). *Learning by teaching.* Montclair, NJ: Boynton/Cook.

Murray, D. (1984). *Write to learn*. New York: Holt, Rinehart.

Murray, D. (1985). *A writer teaches writing* (2nd ed.). Boston: Houghton Mifflin.

Murray, D. (1989). *Expecting the unexpected*. Portsmouth, NH: Heinemann.

Murray, D. (2000). *Writing to deadline*. Portsmouth, NH: Heinemann.

Muspratt, S., Luke, A. & Freebody, P. (Eds.). (1998). *Constructing critical literacies*. Sydney: Allen & Unwin.

National Council for Accreditation of Teacher Education. (1997). *Technology and the new professional teacher: Preparing for the 21st century classroom*. Retrieved March 1, 1999, from http://www.ncate.org/projects/tech/TECH.HTM.

National Council of Teachers of English Elementary Section Steering Committee. (1996). Exploring language arts standards within a cycle of learning. *Language Arts, 73*(1), 10–13.

National Standards for Arts Education. (1994). Washington, DC: U.S. Department of Education, Office of Educational Statistics.

Neuman, S. (1991). *Literacy in the television age: The myth of the TV effect*. Norwood, NJ: Ablex.

The New London Group. (1996). A pedagogy of multiliteracies: Designing social futures. *Harvard Educational Review, 66*(1), 60–92.

The New London Group. (2000). *Multiliteracies: Literacy learning and the design of social futures*. London: Routledge.

Newkirk, T. (1982). Young writers as critical readers. In T. Newkirk & N. Atwell (Eds.), *Understanding writing: Ways of observing, learning, and teaching* (pp. 106–113). Portsmouth, NH: Heinemann.

Newkirk, T. (1985). Young writers as critical readers. *Language Arts, 59*, 451–457.

Newkirk, T. (1989). *More than stories: The range of children's writing*. Portsmouth, NH: Heinemann.

Newsweek [Themed Issue]. (1999, November 22).

Noddings, N. (2000). Foreword. In J. Richards & J. Gipe (Eds.), *Elementary literacy lessons: Cases and commentaries from the field* (pp. xv–xvi). Mahwah, NJ: Lawrence Erlbaum Associates.

Norton, D. (1997). *The effective teaching of language arts* (5th ed.). Columbus, OH: Merrill/Prentice Hall.

National Telecommunications and Information Association. (1999). *Falling through the Net: Defining the digital divide*. Washington, DC: U.S. Department of Commerce. Retrieved August 16, 2002, from http://www.ntia.doc.gov/ntiahome/fttn99/contents.html

Ogle, D. (1986). K-W-L: A teaching model that develops active reading of expository text. *The Reading Teacher, 39*, 564–570.

Oklo, C., & Hayes, R. (1996, April). *The impact of animation on CD-ROM books on students' reading behaviors and comprehension*. Paper presented at the annual meeting of the Council for Exceptional Children, Orlando, FL.

Olshansky, B. (1995, September). Picture this: An arts-based literacy program. *Educational Leadership, 53*(1), 44–47.

Oreck, B. (2000, April). *Artistic choices: How and why teachers use the arts in the classroom*. Paper presented at the annual meeting of the American Educational Research Association, New Orleans, LA.

Oreck, B., Baum, S., & Owen, S. (1999, April). *The development of teachers' skills and confidence in using the arts in the classroom*. Paper presented at the annual meeting of the American Educational Research Association, Montreal, Canada.

Pappas, C., Kiefer, B., & Levstik, L. (1999). *An integrated language perspective in the elementary school: An action approach* (3rd. ed). New York: Longman.

Paul, R., Binker, A., Jensen, K., & Kreklau, H. (1990a). *Critical thinking handbook: K–3 grades*. Sonoma, CA: Foundation for Critical Thinking.

Paul, R., Binker, A., Jensen, K., & Kreklau, H. (1990b). *Critical thinking handbook: 4th–6th grades*. Sonoma, CA: Foundation for Critical Thinking.

People in the History of Astronomy. (www.geocities.com/CapeCanaveral/Launchpad/4515/ History.html).

Piazza, C. (1999). *Multiple forms of literacy: Teaching literacy and the arts.* Upper Saddle River, NJ: Merrill/Prentice Hall.

Price, D. (1998). Explicit instruction at the point of use. *Language Arts, 76,* 19–26.

Primary Voices. (1994). [Themed Issue], *2*(1).

Putnam, R., & Borko, H. (2000). What do new views of knowledge and thinking have to say about research on teacher education? *Educational Researcher, 29*(1), 4–15.

Quin, R. & McMahon, M., (1992). Monitoring standards in media studies: Problems and strategies. *Australian Journal of Education, 37*(2), 182–197.

Rafferty, C. (1999, October). Literacy in the information age. *Educational Leadership, 57*(2), 22–25.

Raines, S., & Isbell, R. (1994). *Stories: Children's literature in early education.* Albany, NY: Delmar.

Raines, S., & Isbell, R. (1994). Stories, storytelling, creative dramatics, and puppetry. In *Stories: Children's literature in early education* (pp. 257–286). Albany, NY: Delmar.

Raphael, T. (1986). Teaching question answer relationship revisited. *The Reading Teacher, 39,* 516–555.

Raphael, T., Pardo, L., Highfield, K., & McMahon, S. (1997). *Book Club: A literature-based curriculum.* Newark, DE: International Reading Association.

Rasinski, T. (2000). Introduction. In T. Rasinski, N. Padak, B. Church, G. Fawcett, J. Hendershot, J. Henry, B. Moss, J. Peck, E. Pryor, & K. Roskos (Eds.), *Teaching comprehension and exploring multiple literacies: strategies from The Reading Teacher* (pp. 1–3). Newark, DE: International Reading Association.

Rasinski, T., & Padak, N. (2000). *Effective reading strategies: Teaching children who find reading difficult* (2nd ed.). Columbus, OH: Merrill.

Ratner, B. (Director). (2000). *The family man* [Motion picture]. Hollywood, CA: Universal Studios.

Redefining Literacy [Themed issue]. (1999). *Educational Leadership, 57*(2).

Reich, R. (1992). *The work of nations.* New York: Vintage Books.

Reinking, D. (1994). *Electronic text. Perspectives in reading No. 4.* Athens, GA: National Reading Research Center.

Reinking, D. (1998). Introduction: Synthesizing technological transformations of literacy in a post-typographic world. In D. Reinking, L. Labbo, M. McKenna, & R.Kieffer (Eds.), *Handbook of literacy and technology: Transformations in a post-typographic world* (pp. xi–xxx). Mahwah, NJ: Lawrence Erlbaum Associates.

Reinking, D., Labbo, L., McKenna, M.., & Kieffer, R. (Eds.). (1998). *Handbook of literacy and technology: Transformations in a post-typographic world.* Mahwah, NJ: Lawrence Erlbaum Associates.

Reinking, D., Mealey, D., & Ridgeway, V. (1993). Developing preservice teachers' conditional knowledge of content area strategies. *Journal of Reading, 36*(6), 458–469.

Richards, J. (2000, May). *Supporting urban elementary students' literacy learning through the arts: Preservice teachers' case quandaries and accomplishments.* Session presented at the annual meeting of the International Reading Association, Indianapolis, IN.

Richards, J. (2001, March). *Class notes, "What do you see?": A reading comprehension strategy for struggling readers.* Hattiesburg: University of Southern Mississippi.

Richards, J. (2002). Steps to independent writing (in The Reading/Writing Connection). In J. Gipe, *Multiple paths to literacy: Corrective reading techniques for the classroom teacher* (5th ed.). Upper Saddle River, NJ: Merrill/Prentice Hall.

Richards, J. (2003, January–March). Facts and feelings response diaries: Connecting efferently and aesthetically with informational text. *Reading and Writing Quarterly, 19*(10), 107–111.

Richards, J., & Gipe, J. (2000). *Elementary literacy lessons: Cases and commentaries from the field.* Mahwah, NJ: Lawrence Erlbaum Associates.

Richards, J., Gipe, J., & Necaise, M. (1994). Find the features and connect them. *The Reading Teacher, 48*(2), 187–188.

Richards, J., Moore, R., & Gipe, J. (2000, February). *Teaching for multiple literacies: Preservice teachers' case quandaries and accomplishments in three different early field programs.* Session presented at the annual meeting of the National Conference of Teachers of English Mid-Winter Assembly for Research, Seattle, WA.

Richards, J., Risko V., Camperell, K., Eanet, M., & Feldman, N. (1999). *Facilitating teaching cases: Techniques and approaches for promoting purposeful case discussions.* Symposium presented at the annual meeting of the College Reading Association, Hilton Head, SC.

Richardson, V., & Kile, R. S. (1999). The use of videocases in teacher education. In M. Lundeberg, B. Levin, & H. Harrington (Eds.), *Who learns from cases and how? The research base in teaching with cases* (pp. 121–136). Mahwah, NJ: Lawrence Erlbaum Associates.

Rief, L. (1992). *Seeking diversity.* Portsmouth, NH: Heinemann.

Rifkin, J. (1995). *The end of work: The decline of the global labor force and the dawn of the post-market era.* New York: Putnam's Sons.

Ringgold, F. (1991). *Tar beach.* New York: Crown.

Risko, V., & Alvarez, M. (1986). An investigation of poor readers' use of a thematic strategy to comprehend text. *Reading Research Quarterly, 21,* 298–316.

Robinson, F. (1961). *Effective study.* New York: Harper & Row.

Rose, M. (1995). *Possible lives: The promise of public education in America.* New York: Houghton Mifflin.

Rosen, E., Quesada, A., & Lockwood Summers, S. (1998). *Changing the world through media education.* Golden, CO: Just Think Foundation.

Rosen, M. (1946). *We're going on a bear hunt.* New York: Oxebury.

Rosenberg, H., & Prendergast, C. (1983). *Theatre for young people: A sense of occasion.* New York: Harcourt Brace Jovanovich College.

Rosenblatt, L. (1978). *The reader, the text, the poem: The transactional theory of the literary work.* Carbondale: Southern Illinois Press.

Ross, E., & Rowe, B. (1990). *An introduction to teaching the language arts.* Holt, Rinehart.

Routman, R. (1991). *Invitations: Changing as teachers and learners K–12.* Portsmouth, NH: Heinemann.

Routman, R. (1996). *Literacy at the crossroads.* Portsmouth, NH: Heinemann.

Routman, R. (2000). *Conversations: Strategies for teaching, learning, and evaluating.* Portsmouth, NH: Heinemann.

Rowe, D. W. (1994). *Preschoolers as authors: Literacy learning in the social world of the classroom.* Cresskill, NJ: Hampton Press.

Russell, M., & Plati, T. (2000). *Mode of administration effects on MCAS composition performance for grades four, eight, and ten* [Electronic version]. Chestnut Hill, MA: National Board on Educational Testing and Public Policy. Retrieved August 16, 2002, from http://nbetpp.bc.edu/reports.html

Sagan, J., & Sinton, N. (1993). *The expressive method of teaching art.* El Cerrito, CA: Institute for Creative and Artistic Development.

San Souci, R. (1989). *The talking eggs.* New York: Dial Books.

Santore, C. (1996). *Snow White.* New York: Parker Lane Press.

Schellaci, P. (1977, April). Roots on TV: It touched us all. *Media and Methods, 13*(8), 22–29. (ERIC Reproduction Document Service No. EJ 156 933)

Schneider, J., & Jackson, S. (2000). Process drama: A special space and place for writing. *The Reading Teacher, 54*(1), 38–51.

Schon, D. (Ed.). (1991). *The reflective turn: Case studies in and on educational practice.* New York: Teachers College Press.

Scieszka, J. (1989). *The true story of the Three Little Pigs by A. Wolf.* New York: Viking Kestrel.

Scott, D., & Villagrana, C. (1999). *Sketch to stretch.* Retrieved August 16, 2002, from http://www.rigby.com/teachers/sketch/htm

Sellers, D. (2001, September 17). *Nashville school superintendent: No new Macs.* MacCentral Online. Retrieved from http://maccentral.macworld.com/news/0109/sept17.shtml

Semali, L. M., & Fueyo, J. (2001). Transmediation as metaphor for new literacies in multimedia classrooms. *Reading Online.* Retrieved August 16, 2002, from http://www.readingonline.org/newliteracies/lit_index.asp?HREP=/newliteracies/semali2/index.html

Semali, L., & Hammett, L. (1999). In L. Semali & A. Watts Pailliot (Eds.), *Intermediality: The teachers' handbook of critical media literacy* (pp. 53–74). Boulder, CO: Westview Press.

Semali, L., & Watts Pailliot, A. (1999). Introduction: What is Intermediality and why study it in U.S. schools? In L. Semali and A.Watts Pailliot (Eds.), *Intermediality: The teachers' handbook of critical media literacy* (pp. 1–30). Boulder CO: Westview Press.

Shanahan, T. (Ed.). (1990). *Reading and writing together: New perspectives for the classroom.* Norwood, MA: Christsopher-Gordon.

Shanahan, T. (1997, September). Reading–writing relationships, thematic units, inquiry learning . . . in pursuit of effective integrated instruction. *The Reading Teacher, 51*(1), 12–19.

Sheldon, D. (1997). *Whale song.* New York: Puffin Pied Piper Books.

Short, K., & Burke, C. (1991). *Creating curriculum: Teachers and students as a community of learners.* Portsmouth, NH: Heinemann.

Short, K. & Harste, G., & Burke, C. (1996). *Creating classrooms for authors and inquirers.* Portsmouth, NH: Heinemann.

Short, K., Kauffman, G., & Kahn, L. (2000, October). "I just *need* to draw": Responding to literature across multiple sign systems. *The Reading Teacher, 54*(2), 160–171.

Short, K., Schroeder, J., Laird, J., Kauffman, G., Ferguson, M., & Crawford, K. (1996). *Learning together through inquiry.* York, ME: Stenhouse.

Shulman, J. (1992). *Case methods in teacher education* (pp. 1–30). New York: Teachers College Press.

Shulman, J. (1996). Tender feelings, hidden thoughts: Confronting bias, innocence, and racism through case discussions. In J. Colberg, K. Trimble, & P. Desberg (Eds.), *The case for education: Contemporary approaches for using case methods* (pp. 137–158). Boston: Allyn & Bacon.

Shulman, L. (1992). Toward a pedagogy of cases. In J. Shulman (Ed.), *Case methods in teacher education* (pp. 1–30). New York: Teachers College Press.

Siegel, M. G. (1984). *Reading as signification.* Unpublished doctoral dissertation, Indiana University, Bloomington.

Siegel, M. G. (1995). More than words: The generative power of transmediation for learning. *Canadian Journal of Education, 20*(4), 455–475.

Silverblatt, A., Ferry, J. & Finan, B. (1999). *Approaches to media literacy : A handbook.* Armonk, NY: M. E. Sharpe.

Silverman, R., & Welty, W. (1996). Teaching without a net: Using cases in teacher education. In J. Colberg, K. Trimble, & P. Desberg (Eds.), *The case for education: Contemporary approaches for using case methods* (pp. 159–171). Boston: Allyn & Bacon.

Silverstein, S. (1964). *The giving tree.* New York: Harper & Row.

Simmons, J., & Baines, J. (Eds.). (1998). *Language study in middle school, high school, and beyond: Views on enhancing the study of language.* Newark, DE: International Reading Association.

Simpson, P. (1993). *Language, ideology, and point of view.* London: Routledge.

Sis, P. (1996). *Starry messenger: Galileo Galilei.* New York: Farrar/Francis Foster.

Soderman, A., Gregory, K., & O'Neill, L. (1999). *Scaffolding emergent literacy: A child-centered approach for preschool through grade 5.* Englewood Cliffs, NJ: Prentice Hall.

Solley, B. (2000). *Writers' workshop: Reflections of eight middle school teachers.* Boston: Allyn & Bacon.

Spolin, V. (1983). *Improvisation in the theater.* Evanston, IL: Northwestern University Press.

Squires, M. (1992). *Video camcorder school: A practical guide to making great home videos.* Pleasantville, NY: Readers Digest.

Steel, J., Meredith, K., & Temple, C. (1998). *Methods for promoting critical thinking* (prepared for the Reading and Writing for Critical Thinking Project). Newark, DE: International Reading Association.

Steinberg, L. (1997). *You and your adolescent: A parent's guide for ages 10–20.* New York: Harper-Perennial Books.

Stilley, L., & Wolf, D. (1999). The art of observation: The place of visual thinking in science. In D. Wolf & D. Balick (Eds.), *Art works! Interdisciplinary learning powered by the arts* (pp. 78–97). Portsmouth, NH: Heinemann.

Stires, S. (1983). Real audiences and contexts for LD writers. *Academic Therapy, 18*(5), 53–63.

Stires, S. (1991). *With promise: Redefining reading and writing for "special" students.* Portsmouth, NH: Heinemann.

Stone, L. (1989). *Wetlands.* Vero Beach, FL: Rourke Enterprises.

Strunk, O. (1950). *Source readings in music history.* New York: Norton.

Sykes, G. (1992). Foreword. In J. Shulman (Ed.), *Case methods in teacher education* (pp. vii–ix). New York: Teachers College Press.

Sykes, G., & Bird, T. (1992). Teacher education and the case idea. *Review of Research in Education, 18,* 457–521.

Tammaro, T. (2001–2002, December–January). Art for your sake. *Navigator,* pp. 10–11.

Taylor, G. (1999, November). Reading, writing, arithmetic: Making connections. *Teaching Children Mathematics, 6*(3), 190–197.

Tell, C. (1999, October). Perspectives/Literacy—The pressure is on. *Educational Leadership, 57*(2), 7.

Temple, C., Nathan, R., Buris, N., & Temple, F. (1988). *The beginnings of writing.* Boston: Allyn & Bacon.

Thayer, H. S. (1981). *Meaning and action: A critical history of pragmatism.* Indianapolis, IN: Hackett.

Thayer, H. S. (1982). *Pragmatism: The classic writings.* Indianapolis, IN: Hackett.

Thoman, E. (1999). Skills and strategies for media education. *Educational Leadership, 56*(5), 50–54.

Tierney, R. J. (1990). Learning to connect reading and writing: Critical thinking through transactions with one's own subjectivity. In T. Shanahan (Ed.), *Reading and writing together: New perspectives for the classroom* (pp. 131–143). Norwood, MA: Christsopher-Gordon.

Topping, K. (1997). *Electronic literacy in school and home: A look into the future Reading Online.* Retrieved Decmeber 28, 1997, from http://www.readingonline.org/international/future/index.html

Trumble, K. (1999) *Cat mummies.* New York: Clarion Books.

Tyner, K. (1998). *Literacy in a digital world: Teaching and learning in the age of information.* Mahwah, NJ: Lawrence Erlbaum Associates.

Uchida, Y. (1971). *Journey to Topaz.* New York: Scribner.

U.S. Department of Education. (1999a). *Getting America's students ready for the 21st century: Meeting the technology literacy challenge.* Retrieved January 30, 1999, from http://www.ed.gov/Technology/Plan/NatTechPlan/

U.S. Department of Education. (1999b). *Teacher quality: A report on the preparation and qualifications of public school teachers* (USDE Publication No. NCES 1999-080). Washington, DC: U.S. Government Printing Office. Retrieved January 30, 1999, from http://nces.ed.gov/pubs99/1999080.htm

Valmont, W. J. (1995). *Creating videos for school use.* Boston: Allyn & Bacon.

Veenema, S., & Gardner, H. (1999, November 1/December 1). Multimedia and multiple intelligences. *The American Prospect, 7*(29). (Web site: http://www.prospect.org/printV29/veenema-s.html)

Verdi, G. (1869). *Aida* [Opera]. (CD available at www.Amazon.com)

Viorst, J. (1998). *Alexander who's not (Do you hear me? I mean it!) going to move.* New York: Aladdin Picture Books.

Vygotsky, L. (1986). Thought and language: Cambridge, MA: MIT Press.

Waber, B. (1972). *Ira sleeps over.* Boston: Houghton Mifflin.

Wachowiak, F. (1985). *Emphasis art: A qualitative arts program for elementary and middle schools* (4th ed.). New York: HarperCollins.

Wachowiak, F., & Clements, R. (1997). *Emphasis art: A qualitative arts program for elementary and middle schools* (6th ed.). New York: Addison-Wesley.

Wagner, B., & Thorne, B. (1990). *Drama as a learning medium* (Rev. ed.). London: Samuel French. (Originally published 1976 by National Education Association, Washington, DC)

Walt Disney. (1990). "Under the sea" from the sound track for *The little mermaid.* Burbank, CA: Mouse Works.

Walt Disney Home Video. (2000). *Fantasia.* Burbank, CA: Home Entertainment. (original movie produced in 1940).

Walt Disney Records. (2000). "Vamos" in *La Vida Mickey* (sung by Maya and the teen group, MDO). Burbank, CA: Author.

Walt Disney Studios. *Walt Disney's Masterpiece Cinderella.* Burbank, CA: Author.

Warner, M. (2001, March). Interdisciplinary team training for prospective middle school grade teachers. *Middle School Journal, 32*(4), 30–39.

Warschauer, M. (1999). *Electronic literacies: Language, culture, and power in online education.* Mahwah, NJ: Lawrence Erlbaum Associates.

Wasserman, S. (1994). Using cases to study teaching. *Phi Delta Kappan, 75*(8), 602–611.

Watson-Ellam, L. (1991). *Start with a story: Literature and learning in your classroom.* New York: Heinemann.

Watts Pailliotet, A. (1997). Questing toward cohesion: Connecting advertisements and classroom reading through visual literacy. In R. Griffin, J. Hunter, C. Schiffman, & W. Gibbs (Eds.), *VisionQuest: Journeys toward visual literacy* (pp. 33–41). State College, PA: International Visual Literacy Association.

Watts Pailliotet, A. (1998). Deep viewing: A critical look at texts. In S. Steinberg & J. Kincheloe (Eds.), *Unauthorized methods: Strategies for critical teaching* (pp. 123–136) New York: Routledge.

Watts Pailliotet, A. (2000, July). Welcome to new literacies. *Reading Online.* Retrieved August 28, 2000, from http://www.readingonline.org

Weaver, C. (1998). *Reading processes and practices: From socio-psycholinguistics to whole language* (2nd ed.). Portsmouth, NH: Heinemann.

Welty, W., Silverman, R., & Lyon, S. (1991). *Student outcomes from teaching with cases.* Unpublished manuscript, Pace University, Center for Case Studies in Teacher Education, White Plains, NY.

Wepner, S., Valmont, W., & Thurlow, R. (2000). *Linking literacy and technology: A guide for K–8 classrooms.* Newark, DE: International Reading Association.

Westreich, J. (2000). High-tech kids: Trailblazers or guinea pigs? In D. Gordon (Ed.), *The digital classroom: How technology is changing the way we teach and learn* (pp. 19–31). Cambridge, MA: Harvard Education Letter.

White, E. (1952). *Charlotte's web.* New York: HarperTrophy.

Whitin, P. (1996). Exploring visual response to literature. *Research in the Teaching of English, 30*(1), 114–141.

Williams, W. C. (1999, March). *Bibliography of the works of William Carlos Williams* (Prepared by Christopher MacGowan). New York: New Directions. (http://www.lit.kobe-u.ac.jp/~hishika/williams.htm)

Wolf, D., & Blalock, D. (1999). *Art works!: Interdisciplinary learning powered by the arts.* Portsmouth, NH: Heinemann.

Wolf, V. (1999). *Make lemonade.* New York: Holt.

Wood, A. (1984). *The napping house.* San Diego, CA: Harcourt Brace Jovanovich.

Wood, A. (1988). *Elbert's bad word.* San Diego, CA: Harcourt Brace Jovanovich.

Wood, A. (1993). *Rude giants.* San Diego: Harcourt Brace.

Wood, K., & Dickinson, T. (2000). *Promoting literacy in grades 4–9: A handbook for teachers and administrators.* Boston: Allyn & Bacon.

Worsnop, C. M. (1999a). *Assessing media work: Authentic assessment in media education.* Mississauga, Ontario, Canada: Wright Communications.

Worsnop, C. M. (1999b). *Screening images: Ideas for media education* (2nd ed.). Mississauga, Ontario, Canada: Wright. (Available through the Center for Media Literacy)

Wright, P. (1987). Reading and writing for electronic journals. In B. K. Britton & S. M. Glynn (Eds.), Executive control processes in reading (pp. 23–55). Hillsdale, NJ: Lawrence Erlbaum Associates.

Yolen, J. (1987). *Owl moon.* New York: Scholastic.

Yolen, J. (1988). In the artist's studio. *New Advocate, 1*(3), 148–154 (ERIC Reproduction Document Service No. EJ 374 850)

About the Authors

No one person can know everything about these new literacies. We
must collaborate and work together, contributing our expertise.
—Leu (2000b)

This book is the outcome of considerable collaboration between two teacher
educators who work in different educational contexts, hold contrasting
research interests, and have diverse teaching responsibilities. A common
thread, however, is that the authors have adopted broader conceptions of
literacy, and integrate multiple-literacy teaching into their undergraduate
and graduate curricula.

Janet C. Richards, a former K–6 classroom teacher, is a Professor of
Language and Literacy in the Division of Education and Psychology at the
University of Southern Mississippi, Long Beach, where she initiated and
supervises field-based literacy methods courses. Her research interests include devising reading comprehension and writing strategies and examining possible changes in preservice teachers' beliefs and cognitions as they
work in school settings. Her text entitled *Elementary Literacy Lessons: Cases
and Commentaries from the Field* (coauthored with Joan Gipe) was published
by Lawrence Erlbaum Associates in 2000.

Michael C. McKenna is a Professor of Reading Education at Georgia
Southern University, Savannah. He has written extensively on various dimensions of electronic text and issues related to using technology in literacy assessment. His text *Handbook of Literacy and Technology: Transformations
in a Post Typographical World* (coedited with David Reinking, Linda D. Labbo,
and Ron Kiefer) won an American Library Association award for an outstanding academic book in 1998.

Author Index

Note: Page number followed by *n* indicates footnote.

A

Airs, C., 82
Albers, P., xxv, 41, 43, 56, 150, 151, 152, 154, 155, 170, 171, 230, 231
Alcott, L., 184, 187, 188
Aliki, 194
Almasi, J., 110n
Altwerger, B., 215
Alvarez, M., 205
Alvermann, D. E., 20, 23, 32, 174, 177, 185, 186
Anderson, L., 138
Anderson-Iman, L., 173
Anno, M., 194
Aprill, A., 42n
Atwell, N., 101
Ausubel, D., 168, 202, 216, 225, 226
Avery, C., 106

B

Baines, I., 102n
Baines, J., 189
Baker, E., 126n
Baker, F., 174
Ball, D., 52
Ball, J., 82
Barone, D., 112n
Barr, R., 215
Bates, R., 196

Baum, S., 41, 42
Beane, T., 185
Bear, D., 108
Bennett, T., 42
Benson, G., 165
Berghoff, B., xxv, 17, 41, 47, 56, 151, 152, 157, 170, 171
Binch, C., 84, 122, 166, 167, 168, 169, 170
Binker, A., 214, 215
Biondo, S., 212n, 215
Bird, T., 4
Birdyshaw, D., 185
Birge, E., 60
Blalock, D., 43, 209
Blanchard, J., 125
Blecher, S., 41, 43
Bloom, B., 120n, 138
Bloome, D., 27
Bolter, J., 130
Bond, P., 193
Borko, H., 4
Brett, J., 83
Briggs, S., 193, 208
Brittain, W., 44
Brommer, G., 44
Brown, M., 27, 33
Brownlie, F., 112n
Bruce, B. C., 24, 27
Buckingham, D., 173
Buehl, D., 81, 91, 137, 163, 164, 176, 179, 196, 198, 200, 204

Bunchman, J., 193, 208
Buris, N., 108
Burke, C., 12, 179, 196, 200, 231
Burnaford, G., 42n
Buss, K., 165

C

Calkins, L., 105
Calvert, S., 149
Campbell, P., 57
Camperell, K., 4
Caney, S., 233
Capra, F., 185
Carle, E., 44
Cassidy, J., 193, 208
Cattagni, A., 20, 28
Cecil, N., 60, 61, 77, 80, 82, 99
Cesarone, B., 229n
Chall, J., 107
Chambers, A., 164
Char, C., 11
Charlesworth, R., 94
Cherry, L., 84, 195, 206, 216
Chomsky, C., 101
Clay, M., 101
Clements, R., 43, 44, 45
Cohle, D., 102n
Colberg, J., 4
Colburn, L., 28, 134
Collier, C., 126n
Coman, C., 113
Considine, D., 173, 174, 175
Cooke, G., 56
Cornett, C., 41, 42, 43, 80, 81, 99, 100
Cowan, K., 171
Cox, M., 56
Crawford, K., 210, 214, 215
Cunningham, D., 151
Cunningham, M., 57
Cunningham, P. M., 123

D

Dahl, K., 107
Daniels, H., 201
Defee, M., 123
Desberg, P., 4
Desmond, R., 172
Dewey, J., 210
Dickinson, T., 124

Dionisio, M., 102
Disessa, A., 20
Doyle, W., 3
Drewe, S., 73
Durant, A., 62, 63
Dworkin, M., 210
Dyson, A. H., 174

E

Eagleton, M. B., 30
Eakle, A., 11, 14, 16
Eanet, M., 4
Egawa, K., xxv, 17, 41, 47, 56, 152,
    157, 170, 171
Eisner, E. W., 13, 14, 41, 151
Elbow, P., 106
Elrich, A., 158
Emory, P., 102
Epstein, S., 189
Ernst, K., 41, 52, 53
Evans, K., 110n

F

Farris, E., 20, 28
Farstrup, A. E., 80, 107, 174
Fehlman, R., 174
Feldman, N., 4
Ferguson, M., 210, 214, 215
Ferrington, G., 173
Ferry, J., 23
Finan, B., 23
Fisherkeller, J., 179
Flood, J., 12, 41, 190
Flores, B., 215
Florian, D., 118
Flower, L., 101
Forman, G., 11
Fountas, I., 106
Freebody, P., 22, 32
Freedman, S., 101
Fueyo, J., 12, 14

G

Galdone, P., 42n
Gambrell, L., 110n, 196
Garcia-Williams, R., 113
Gardner, H., 14, 16, 17, 41, 42, 60, 80,
    84, 90, 151, 191, 201

Garvie, E., 164
Gavelek, J., 212n, 215
Gee, J. P., 22, 24
Gentry, J., 103n
Gibbons, G., 193, 208, 220
Giles, J. K., 174
Gilster, P., 12
Gipe, J., 4, 7, 9, 195, 263
Glass, P., 71
Goble, P., 219
Goldberg, M., 17, 42, 58, 60, 61
Goldsborough, R., 125
Goodman, K., 107, 108
Goodman, Y., 101
Gordon, D., 214
Graves, D., 102, 106, 108, 110, 123,
        124, 145, 187
Greene, M., 14, 41, 151
Greenfield, E., 118
Gregory, K., 178, 179
Griffin, D., 56
Grogan, P., 107
Grout, D., 59, 71
Grumet, M., 151
Guthrie, J., 211, 214, 231, 233

H

Hagood, M. C., 20, 23, 32, 174, 177,
        185, 186
Haley, G., 173, 174, 175
Hamilton, M., 81
Hammett, L., 12
Hanak, D., 130
Harrington, H., 4, 8
Harste, G., 196
Harste, J., xxv, 12, 17, 41, 47, 56, 76,
        117, 150, 151, 152, 155n,
        157, 170, 171, 179, 191, 200
Hart, M., 57
Harvey, S., 227, 228
Hatchett, C., 220
Hayes, J., 101
Hayes, R., 14
Hazen, B., 111
Heath, S., 41
Heinig, R., 80, 82
Helfman, E., 152n
Heller, M., 108
Hendrick, J., 229n
Highfield, K., 110n

Hobbs, R., xvii, 173, 174
Hodson, L., 4
Hoffer, C., 61
Hoffman, J., 137, 160
Hoffman, M., 115
Hofstetter, F., 20, 21
Holubec, E., 137
Hoonan, B., xxv, 17, 41, 47, 56, 152,
        157, 170, 171
Hubbard, R., 110
Hughes, M., 113
Hull, D. P., 123
Hull, G., 101
Hunt, G., 164
Hunter, M., 138
Hurd, R., 193, 208

I

Invernizzi, M., 108
Isbell, R., 82n, 101

J

Jackson, S., 82n
Jacobs, V., 42
Jaffe, K., 41, 43
Jalongo, M., 61
Jensen, K., 214, 215
Jett-Simpson, M., 81
Johnson, D., 137
Johnson, R., 137
Johnston, F., 108
Johnstone, K., 96
Jolly, R., 27, 33
Jonassen, D. H., 14, 17

K

Kahn, L., 150, 171
Kalman, B., 194
Kamil, M. L., 20, 215
Kantrov, I., 7
Kapinus, B., 196
Karchmer, R., 20, 35
Karnowski, L., 165
Katz, L., 229n
Kauffman, G., 150, 171, 210, 214, 215
Kemp, A., 111
Kiefer, B., 61, 211, 215, 233
Kieffer, R., 20, 263

Kile, R. S., 4
Kincheloe, J., 174
King, J., 112n
King, S., 106
Kinzer, C. K., 4, 12, 20, 23, 26, 27, 28, 30
Kirkley, J. R., 26, 27
Kist, W., 17
Koshewa, A., 171
Kreklau, H., 214, 215
Krupp, E., 219
Kubey, R., 174
Kuhn, M., 11, 14
Kunkel, A., 102n

L

Labbo, L. D., 11, 14, 16, 20, 263
Lacy, L., 173, 174
Laird, J., 210, 214, 215
Lane, D. M., 20
Langer, S., 151
Langone, J., 111
Lapp, D., 12, 41, 190
Lauritzen, P., 60, 61, 77, 80, 82, 99
Lawson, L., 107
Leander, K., 23
Lear, E., 164, 165
LeBaron, J., 126n
Leland, C., 47, 76, 117, 155n, 191
Lemke, J. L., 15
Leppert, R., 57
Leu, D., 6, 20, 128, 133, 134
Leu, D., Jr., xxii, 6, 12, 20, 23, 24, 26, 27, 28, 30, 35, 128, 133, 134, 263
Leveranz, D., 174
Levin, B., 8
Levstik, L., 61, 211, 215, 233
Levy, S., 125
Little, L., 118
Lockwood Summers, S., 175
Longley, L., 42
Lopez, B., 110
Lowenfeld, V., 44
Lowry, L., 105
Luke, A., 22, 32
Luke, C., 22, 30
Lundeberg, M., 8
Lyon, S., 3, 7

M

Maag, J., 186
Macaul, S., 174
Macauley, D., 193, 208
Mallette, M., 35
Mallow, F., 106
Martin, R., 158
Matthews, M., 212n
Mayer, R.
McBrien, J., 189
McCann, A., 211, 231
McCaslin, N., 82
McKenna, B., 130
McKenna, M., 20, 127, 130, 263
McLary, S., 57
McMahon, M., 172
McMahon, S., 110n
McMaster, J., 81, 89, 100
McNiven, H., 193
McNiven, P., 193
Mealey, D., 5
Meredith, K., 79
Merriam, A., 57, 58, 59
Merseth, K., 3, 4
Messaris, P., xxii
Mikulecky, L., 26, 27
Miller, B., 7
Moffett, J., 211
Moje, E., 8, 108, 185
Moline, S., 174
Montero, K., 11, 14, 16
Moody, W., 61
Moon, J. S., 20, 23, 32, 174, 177, 185
Moore, D., 108, 185
Moore, E.
Moore, I., 115
Moore, R., 4
Morgan, N., 82
Mori, T., 194
Morine-Dershimer, G., 7
Morrow, L., 101
Mosenthal, P., 215
Most, B., 143
Munsch, R., 47, 161
Murphy, S., 41, 43, 150, 151, 152, 156, 170, 171, 230, 231
Murray, D., 102, 104, 106
Muspratt, S., 22, 32
Myers, M., 80, 107, 174

N

Nathan, R., 108
Necaise, M., 195
Neuman, S., 174
Newkirk, T., 101, 102
Noddings, N., 4
Norton, D., 52

O

Ogle, D., 105, 200, 219, 226, 229, 230
Oklo, C., 14
Olshansky, B., 56
O'Neill, L., 178, 179
Oreck, B., 41, 42
Owen, S., 41, 42

P

Padak, N., 179, 191, 196, 200
Palisca, C., 59, 71
Pappas, C., 61, 211, 215, 233
Pardo, L., 110n
Patterson, L., 106
Paul, R., 214, 215
Pearson, P., 215
Phillips, A., 17
Piazza, C., 64, 76, 77, 78, 81
Pinnell, G., 106
Plati, T., 29
Prendergast, C., 80
Price, D., 107
Putnam, R., 4

Q

Quesada, A., 175
Quin, R., 172
Quinn-Learing, S., 4

R

Rafferty, C., xx
Rainer, J., 212n
Raines, S., 82n, 101
Raphael, T., 110n, 121, 212n, 215
Rasinski, T., 10, 179, 191, 196, 200
Ratner, B., 185
Readence, J., 108, 185

Reeves, T. C., 14, 17
Reich, R., 26
Reinking, D., 5, 20, 24, 126, 263
Richards, J., 4, 7, 9, 43, 131, 135, 195, 263
Richardson, V., 4
Ridgeway, V., 5
Rief, L., 106
Rifkin, J., 26
Ringgold, F., 217
Risko, V., 205
Robinson, F., 135, 136, 138
Rodenberg, R. K., 174
Rose, M., 114
Rosen, E., 174
Rosen, M., 66
Rosenberg, H., 80
Rosenblatt, L., 43
Ross, E., 101
Routman, R., 101, 104, 105, 106, 107, 124, 227, 228
Rowe, B., 101
Rowe, D. W., 12
Russell, M., 29
Rycik, J., 185

S

Sagan, J., 50
San Souci, R., 84, 162, 163, 164, 165, 166
Santore, C., 42n
Saxton, J., 82
Scharer, P., 107
Schellaci, P., 193
Schneider, J., 82n
Schon, D., 3
Schroeder, J., 210, 214, 215
Scieszka, J., 105
Scott, D., 179, 200
Scott-Kassner, C., 57, 58, 60
Sellers, D., 28
Semali, L. M., 12, 14, 173
Shanahan, T., 12, 214
Sheldon, D., 47, 48
Short, K., 12, 150, 171, 179, 196, 200, 210, 214, 215, 231
Shulman, J., xviii, xix, 3, 7, 9
Shulman, L., xviii, xix, 5
Siegel, M. G., 151
Silverblatt, A., 23

Silverman, R., 3, 7
Silverstein, S., 45n
Simmons, J., 189
Simpson, P., 153, 154
Sinton, N., 50
Sis, P., 219
Soderman, A., 178, 179
Solley, B., 124
Sosniack, L., 138
Spolin, V., 82
Squires, M., 193
Stamp, L., 61
Steel, J., 79
Steinberg, L., 186
Steinberg, S., 174
Stilley, L., 209
Stires, S., 105, 124
Stone, L., 227
Stratton, B., 130
Strunk, O., 57
Sykes, G., 4, 5

T

Tammaro, T., 44
Taylor, G., 158, 160, 200, 216
Tell, C., 10, 90
Temple, C., 79, 108
Temple, F., 108
Templeton, S., 108
Thayer, H. S., 150
Thoman, E., 173, 174
Thorne, B., 82
Thurlow, R., 128
Tierney, R. J., 12, 17
Topping, K., 20
Towle, W., 102n
Trimble, K., 4
Trumble, K., 223
Tyner, K., 22, 23, 174

U

Uchida, Y., 105

V

Valmont, W., 128, 175
Veenema, S., 16
Verdi, G., 71
Villagrana, C., 179, 200
Viost, J., 94, 95
Vygotsky, L., 54, 121, 174

W

Waber, B., 198, 199, 201, 202
Wachowiak, F., 43, 44, 45
Wade, S., 8
Wagner, B., 82, 211
Warner, M., 212n
Warschauer, M., 20, 23
Wasserman, S., 9
Watson-Ellam, L., 83
Watts Pailliotet, A., 173, 174
Weaver, C., 82
Weiss, C., 42n
Weiss, M., 81
Welty, W., 3, 7
Wepner, S., 128
Westreich, J., 90, 133, 214
White, E., 48
Whitin, P., 56
Wigfield, A., 233
Williams, W. C., 47
Wilson, R., 196
Wolf, D., 43, 209
Wolf, V., 113
Wood, A., 119n
Wood, D., 190
Wood, K., 124
Worsnop, C. M., 175
Wright, P., 13

Y

Yolen, J., 44, 47
Young, J., 108, 185

Subject Index

Note: Page number followed by *n* indicates footnote.

A

Abstract art
  artists, 237, 238, 240, 241
  visual-arts/reading lessons, 46
Abuse in the Family (Kemp), 111
Activities for Creating Pictures and Poetry
      (Bunchman/Briggs), 193, 208
Adolescents and Their Music (Epstein),
      189
Advance organizer
  defined, 235
  multiple literacies–inquiry integra-
      tion, 225–226, 231
  music–dance reading lessons, 72–75
  thematic organizer, 205
  viewing–representing–content read-
      ing, 202–206
Aesthetic reading
  defined, 235
  visual-arts/reading lessons, 43
Aesthetic stances, 43
Aesthetic value
  music–dance reading lessons, 58,
      63–64, 75
  visual-arts/reading lessons, 42, 43
Africa, 59, 62, 193
A History of Western Music
      (Grout/Palisca), 59n.2
Aida (Verdi)
  defined, 235
  music–dance reading lessons, 71

Akhnaten (Glass)
  defined, 235
  music–dance reading lessons, 71
Alaska, 106
Alexander, Patti, 143–144, 166–167
*Alexander, Who's Not (Do You Hear Me? I
      Mean It!) Going to Move*
      (Viorst), 94–95
Amazing Grace (Hoffman), 115
A Medieval Feast (Aliki), 194
Andrews, Marci, 184
*An Integrated Language Perspective in the
      Elementary School* (Pappas et
      al.), 61, 215, 233
Anno's Three Little Pigs (Anno/Mori),
      194
Arctic Dreams (Lopez), 110
Artistic Intelligence (Moody), 61
Arts and Learning (Goldberg), 61
Arts As Education (Goldberg/Phillips),
      17
Arts as Meaning Makers (Cornett), 43,
      99–100
Arts in Children's Lives, The (Jalongo/
      Stamp), 61
*Art Works! Interdisciplinary Learning
      Powered by the Arts*
      (Wolf/Blalock), 43, 209
Assessing Media Work (Worsnop), 175
Astronomy, 219–223
Auding
  defined, 235

visual-arts/reading lessons, 48
Austin, Terri, 51–52, 91–92, 97,
        132–134
Australia
    oral maps, 59–60, 62
    popular-culture texts, 172
Authenticity
    electronic symbol making, 16
    Internet technologies, 20
    multiple literacies–inquiry integra-
        tion, 228
    viewing–representing–content read-
        ing, 194
    visual-arts/reading lessons, 44
A Winter Day (Florian), 118

B

Bangles, The, 69, 70
Bathhurst, Angelique, 215–216
Beethoven, Ludwig van (1770–1827)
    romantic composer, 241
    Romantic Movement, 235
Begoray, Deborah, 161–162, 221–223
Berlioz, Hector (1803–1869), 235, 241
Beyond Reading and Writing (Berghoff
        et al.), 17, 170, 171
Big Day for Little Jack (Moore), 115–117
Big Dipper and You, The (Krupp), 219
Blachowicz, Camille, 136–138
Bliss, Charles, 235
Bliss symbol board
    defined, 235
    viewing–representing–content read-
        ing, 190
Bloem, Patricia, 111–113, 117–118
Bloom, Benjamin, 120n.13, 235
Bloom's Taxonomy
    defined, 235
    reading–writing–computer technol-
        ogy, 138
    reading–writing integration, 120
Body movement, 46, 48, *see also* Music–
        dance–reading lessons
Book Club (Pardo et al.), 110n.4
Breland, Karen, 135–136
Brown, Melinda, 139–140
Build a Literate Classroom (Graves),
        123–124

C

Caldecott Medal
    defined, 235
    multiple literacies–inquiry integra-
        tion, 219
Calder, Alexander (1898–1976), 239
Canada
    popular-culture texts, 172
    thematic unit, 216
Carr, Kathryn Chapman, 47–48,
        218–219
Case method, *see* Teaching cases
Case Methods in Teacher Education
        (Shulman), 9
Cat Mummies (Trumble), 223
CD–ROM resources
    reading–writing–computer technol-
        ogy, 136, 138–139
    semiotics integration, 165
Center for Media Literacy, 175
Cézanne, Paul (1839–1906), 240
Chagall, Marc (1887–1985)
    surrealism, 235
    visual-arts/reading lessons, 44
*Changing the World Through Media Edu-
        cation* (Lockwood Summers
        et al.), 175
Charlotte's Web (White), 48–49
    Child development
    domains of, 93–94
    writing literacy, 107–108
*Children's Journeys Through the Informa-
        tion Age* (Calvert), 149
Chopin, Frédéric (1810–1849), 241
Choral reading, 66, 67, 68
Choreographer
    defined, 235
    music–dance reading lessons, 59
Church Altar, The (Herbert), 241
Cinderella (Walt Disney), 159
Cinquain
    defined, 236
    music–dance reading lessons, 75, 79
    reading–writing integration, 122
Clark, Janice, 87–88
Clarke, David, 73, 165–166, 217–218
Cognition
    child development, 94

electronic symbol making, 12, 13,
  14–17
Cognitive tools
  defined, 236
  electronic symbol making, 14–16
Collaboration
  dramatic-arts/reading lessons, 81, 98
  electronic symbol making, 16
  multiple literacies–inquiry integra-
    tion, 211, 213–214,
    230–231
  reading–writing integration, 103, 105
  visual-arts/reading lessons, 42, 50
Collages
  defined, 236
  visual-arts/reading lessons, 44
Colors, 156–157
Communication formats, 165–166
Communication systems, semiotics,
    151–152, 157, 162–163, 164,
    165–166, *see also* Multiple
    communication systems
Communicative literacy
  defined, 236
  electronic symbol making, 12–13
  Internet technologies, 19–20,
    22–23, 24–25, 35–36
  music–dance reading lessons, 57–60
  reading–writing integration, 102
  visual-arts/reading lessons, 42–43,
    44, 48
Comprehension facilitation
  dramatic-arts/reading lessons, 81
  reading–writing integration, 101,
    102, 103
  visual-arts/reading lessons, 43, 44, 48
Concept maps, 200
Conditional knowledge
  defined, 236
  teaching cases, 5
*Connecting Reading and Writing in the
    Intermediate Grades*
    (Cohle/Towle), 102n.1
Connections Log, 215
Constructivism, 211
Content-reading lesson defined, 236, *see
    also* Dramatic-arts/reading les-
    sons; Media/popular-culture/
    content reading; Music–dance–
    reading lessons; Viewing–rep-
    resenting–content reading;
    Visual-arts/reading lessons
Conversations (Routman), 228
Cooper, Victoria, 131–132
Cosgrove, Mary Ellen, 200–202
Creating Videos for School Use (Valmont),
    175
Creative Behavior (Sagan/Sinton), 50
Creative Drama for the Classroom Teacher
    (Heinig), 82
*Creative Drama in the Classroom and
    Beyond* (McCaslin), 82
Critical literacy
  defined, 236
  Internet technologies, 22, 23,
    25–26, 32, 35
Critical thinking
  media/popular-culture/content
    reading, 188
  multiple literacies–inquiry integra-
    tion, 210–211, 214
Critical Thinking Handbook (Paul et al.),
    214
Critical viewing
  defined, 236
  media/popular-culture/content
    reading, 178–179
Cubism, 238, 240
Cultural diversity, 22–23, 24, 32–33
Cumbest, Christina, 66–67

D

Daniels, Kelly, 219–220
da Vinci, Leonardo (1452–1519)
  Last Supper, The, 236
  media/popular-culture/content
    reading, 179
  Mona Lisa, 236
Day-books, 104
Debussy, Claude (1862–1918), 236
Degas, Edgar (1834–1917), 236
  impressionism, 238
  visual-arts/reading lessons, 44
Deixis
  defined, 236
  Internet technologies, 30–31
Desktop publishing, 134–135
Dewey, John, 210

Dialogue journals
  defined, 236
  reading–writing integration, 104
Diamante
  defined, 236–237
  music–dance reading lessons, 75, 78
Diebenkorn, Richard (b. 1922)
  "Ocean Park," 237
  visual-arts/reading lessons, 44
Different Light (The Bangles), 69, 70
Digital Classroom, The (Gordon), 214
Digital divide, 27
Digital literacy
  defined, 237
  electronic symbol making, 12–13
Digital video disk (DVD)
  defined, 237
  music–dance reading lessons, 76
Dioramas
  defined, 237
  visual-arts/reading lessons, 42
Discourse
  defined, 237
  dramatic-arts/reading lessons, 81
  electronic symbol making, 12
  Internet technologies, 29–30
Discovery Channel: Planet Earth, 229
Docents
  defined, 237
  visual-arts/reading lessons, 44
Does W Trouble You? (Benson), 165
Dragon and the Unicorn, The (Cherry),
    195
Dramatic-arts/reading lessons
  case 6.1, 83
  case 6.1 commentaries, 84–87
  case 6.1 inquiries, 84
  case 6.2, 87–88
  case 6.2 commentaries, 88–91
  case 6.2 inquiries, 88
  case 6.3, 91
  case 6.3 commentaries, 91–94
  case 6.3 inquiries, 91
  case 6.4, 94–95
  case 6.4 commentaries, 95–97
  case 6.4 inquiries, 95
  analytic inquiry, 98–99
  benefits of, 81
  child development domains, 93–94
  collaboration, 81, 98
  comprehension facilitation, 81

discourse knowledge, 81
emergent readers, 81
group management, 83–87, 91–94
guided imagery, 91
historical context, 80
improvisation, 81
learning buddies, 90
listening skills, 81
metacognitive knowledge, 81
multiple literacies, 80, 93
overview, 80–81
portfolios, 90
practical application, 98–99
professional development, 81–82, 98
professional standards, 80–81
quotation excerpts, 80
Readers Theatre, 81–82
reading resources, 82, 83, 84, 89,
    99–100
reflections, 89–90, 93, 98
shape poem, 98
syntactic knowledge, 81
teacher preparation, 94–97
Web site resources, 80–81
Drill-and-practice
  defined, 237
  electronic symbol making, 16, 17
  reading–writing–computer technol-
      ogy, 129
DVD, *see* Digital video disk (DVD)

E

EdTech (listserv), 128
Educational Leadership, 107
Effective Study (Robinson), 135n.3
Effective Teaching of Language Arts, The
    (Norton), 52
Efferent reading
  defined, 237
  visual-arts/reading lessons, 43
Efferent stances, 43
Egypt
  multiple literacies–inquiry integra-
      tion, 223–226
  music–dance reading lessons, 68–71
  visual-arts/reading lessons, 52–54
Elbert's Bad Word (Wood), 119n.10
Electronic symbol making, *see also*
        Internet technologies; Reading–
        writing–computer technology

audience anticipation, 15
authenticity, 16
cognition, 12, 13, 14–17
cognitive tools, 14–16
collaboration, 14–16
communicative literacy, 12–13
computer-related multimedia, 10–11, 12–17
computer tools, 14–16
curriculum interdependence, 12, 13
curriculum symbiosis, 12, 13
defined, 13, 237
digital literacy, 12–13
discourse participation, 12
drawing tools, 15
drill-and-practice, 16, 17
empowerment, 12, 16, 17
introduction, 10–11
learning styles, 16
letter-stamp-pad tool, 14–15, 16
listening skills, 12, 13
literacy ability shift, 12, 13
literacy conceptualization, 11–12, 17
literacy reconceptualization, 12–13, 17
meaning construction, 13–14, 16
media convergence, 15–16
multimedia composing, 14–17
multiple sign systems, 11–17
new literacies, 12
overview, xviii, 11
photography, 13–16
quotation excerpts, 10
reading literacy, 11–12, 13
reading resources, 17
reflections, 15
semiotics, 13–14, 16–17
sound effects, 15–16
speaking skills, 12, 13
teaching implications, 16–17
theoretical framework, 13–14, 16–17
whole-language, 12
writing literacy, 11–12, 13
Electronic text
defined, 237
reading–writing–computer technology, 126–127
Elementary Literacy Lessons (Richards/Gipe), 9, 263
Emergent literacy learner
defined, 237

media/popular-culture/content reading, 178–179
music–dance reading lessons, 63–64
Emergent readers
defined, 237
dramatic-arts/reading lessons, 81
Emily Eyefinger and the Lost Treasure (Ball), 52
Empowerment
electronic symbol making, 12, 16, 17
Internet technologies, 28
English Journal, 115
ERIC (Educational Research Information Clearinghouse), 54, 122, 175
Expression enhancement, *see also* Communicative literacy music–dance reading lessons, 57–60
reading–writing integration, 102, 103, 104
visual-arts/reading lessons, 41–42
Expressionism, 240, 241, 243

F

Family Man, The (Ratner), 185
Fandom
defined, 237
media/popular-culture/content reading, 185
Fantasia (Walt Disney), 193
Feminist perspective
defined, 237
Internet technologies, 23
Film, 178, 185
Firefly Guide to Space (Bond), 193
First Steps toward the Reggio Emelia Way (Hendrick), 229n.5
Fischman, Bruce, 178–179
Flexibility, 212
Florida, 42
Folklórico Ballet
defined, 237
music–dance reading lessons, 62
Fore, Trudy, 226–227
Framing Literacy (Mallow/Patterson), 106
Free expression, 45–46, 47
Frescos
mural contrast, 240
visual-arts/reading lessons, 44

G

Galilei, Galileo, 219
Gaugin, Paul (1848–1903), 240
Genesio, Margaret Humadi, 52–53
Ghana, 60
Giving Tree, The (Silverstein), 45n.7
Glass, Philip (b. 1937)
    Akhnaten, 71, 235
    minimalism, 238
    music–dance reading lessons, 71
Globalization, 19, 22–23, 24, 26–28,
    35
Glow in the Dark Night Sky Book, The
    (Hatchett), 220
Goals 2000: The Educate America Act,
    41
Gobert, Mary, 53–54, 225–226
Going Bohemian (Baines/Kunkel),
    102n.2
Goldilocks and the Three Bears (Brett), 83
Graphic organizers
    media/popular-culture/content
        reading, 179
    viewing–representing–content read-
        ing, 200
Great Kapok Tree, The (Cherry), 84, 206,
    216
Green, Jennifer, 45–46
Gregory, Cecil, 202–203
Gregory Cool (Binch), 84, 166–170
Grisham, Dana, 181–182
Grouchy Ladybug, The (Carle), 44
Group discussions, 7
Group feedback, 105
Group management
    dramatic-arts/reading lessons,
        83–87, 91–94
    music–dance reading lessons, 63,
        64–65, 66
Grove Dictionary of Art, The (Grove Dic-
    tionaries, Inc.), 44n.6
"Guernica" (Picasso), 178
Guided imagery
    defined, 238
    dramatic-arts/reading lessons, 91
    semiotics integration, 163–164
Guided Reading (Fountas/Pinnell), 106
Guillot, Karen Parker, 84–85

H

Haiku
    defined, 238
    music–dance reading lessons, 75, 78
    reading–writing integration, 122
Hall, John, 52
Handbook of Literacy and Technology
    (McKenna et al.), 263
Handbook of Reading Research (Kamil et
    al.), 215
Handful of Seeds (Hughes), 113
Handspring Visor, 24
Harden, Michael, 177
Herbert, George, 241
Her Seven Brothers (Goble), 219, 220
Holism, 210–211
Honey, I Love (Greenfield), 118
Hunt, George, 70–71, 134–135, 163–165
Hypertext
    defined, 238
    reading–writing–computer technol-
        ogy, 127

I

I Can Do It by Myself (Greenfield/Little),
    118
I-Chart
    defined, 238
    reading–writing–computer technol-
        ogy, 137
    semiotics integration, 160
If the Dinosaurs Came Back (Most), 143
Image text
    defined, 238
    viewing–representing–content read-
        ing, 190–191
Impressionism
    artists, 236, 238, 239, 241
    defined, 238
    visual-arts/reading lessons, 44
Improvisation
    defined, 238
    dramatic-arts/reading lessons, 81
Information and communication tech-
    nologies (ICT)
    defined, 238

Internet technologies, 18, 19, 20, 21–25, 26–28, 30–35
Integrated learning system (ILS), 129, 148
Integrating in the Arts (Blecher/Jaffee), 43
International Reading Association (IRA), 106–107, 109, 130, 155, 174, 185
Internet technologies, *see also* Reading–writing–computer technology
  analytic inquiry, 19, 33, 34–35
  authenticity, 20
  commercial context, 22, 23, 26
  communicative literacy, 19–20, 22–23, 24–25, 35–36
  critical literacy, 22, 23, 25–26, 32, 35
  cultural diversity, 22–23, 24, 32–33
  decision-making, 26, 28
  defined, 238
  deixis, 30–31
  digital divide, 27
  discourse knowledge, 29–30
  economic context, 22, 23, 26–28
  empowerment, 28
  feminist perspective, 23
  globalization, 19, 22–23, 24, 26–28, 35
  Handspring Visor, 24
  information access, 19–20, 25, 27, 29, 30, 33–34
  information and communication technologies (ICT), 18, 19, 20, 21–25, 26–28, 30–35
  information evaluation, 22, 23, 25, 29, 32, 33–34
  Internet defined, 238
  learning styles, 31–32, 34
  learning transformation, 19–21, 29–31, 33–34, 35–36
  linguistic diversity, 22–23, 24, 32–33
  listserv, 34
  literacy conceptualization, 18–19, 36
  literacy reconceptualization, 19–21, 29–31, 35–36
  meaning construction, 34–35
  media literacy, 22, 23, 25–26, 32, 35
  metacognitive knowledge, 29–30
  Microsoft, 24

mp3, 31
multiple literacies, 21, 22–23, 24–26, 35
new literacies, 18, 19–20, 35–36
new literacy characteristics, 23–25, 30–31, 33–34
new literacy perspectives, 21–23
new literacy principles, 25–35, 36–37
  organizational implications, 26–28
  overview, xviii, 18, 21
  Palm Pilot, 24
  PDA (personal digital assistant), 24
  pdf (portable document format), 31
  political context, 22, 23, 28
  popular-culture interpretations, 23
  postmodernism, 23
  print media, 30
  professional development, 28–29, 30
  professional role, 30
  professional standards, 29
  reading literacy, 18–20, 22–23, 24–25, 29–30, 35–36
  reading–writing–computer technology, 130
  research transformation, 20–21, 24–25, 31, 32, 35
  search engine, 31
  sociocultural perspective, 22, 31–33
  strategic knowledge, 34–35
  student preparation, 19, 20–21, 27–29, 30, 32, 33–34, 35, 36
  syntactic knowledge, 29–30
  teaching transformation, 20–21, 24–25, 28–29, 30, 31, 33–34, 35–36
  theoretical development, 21–22, 25–35
  word processor, 24
  workplace implications, 26–28
  World Wide Web component, 238, 243
  World Wide Web distinction, 130
  writing literacy, 19–20, 22–23, 24–25, 29–30, 35–36
Invitations (Routman), 106
Ira Sleeps Over (Waber), 198–199, 201–202
It's a Wonderful Life (Capra), 185

J

Jackdaw, *see* Realia
Jacobs, Eli, 111
Jigsaw groups
    defined, 238
    viewing–representing–content reading, 204
Journal of Adolescent and Adult Literacy, 175
Journals
    dialogue journal, 104, 236
    media/popular-culture/content reading, 179
    reading response journal, 104
    reading–writing integration, 103–104, 118–122
    sketch journal, 179
Journey to Topaz (Uchida), 105
Jumblies, The (Lear), 164–165

K

Kandinsky, Wassily (1866–1944)
    abstract art, 238
    postimpressionism, 238
    visual-arts/reading lessons, 44
Keyboarding, 131–135
Khedive
    defined, 238
    music–dance reading lessons, 71
Klee, Paul (1879–1940)
    cubism, 238
    surrealism, 238
    visual-arts/reading lessons, 44
K-W-L
    defined, 239
    multiple literacies–inquiry integration, 219, 226–231
    reading–writing integration, 105
    viewing–representing–content reading, 200
K-W-L Plus
    defined, 239
    viewing–representing–content reading, 200

L

Lane, Cassandra, 198–199

Language Study in Middle School, High School, and Beyond (Simmons/ Baines), 189
Latin America, 216
Learning buddies, 90
Learning disabilities
    reading–writing integration, 108
    viewing–representing–content reading, 190–191
Learning in Safe Schools (Brownlie/ King), 112n.8
Learning logs
    reading–writing integration, 104
    visual-arts/reading lessons, 53–54
Learning styles
    electronic symbol making, 16
    Internet technologies, 31–32, 34
    multiple literacies–inquiry integration, 213
    music–dance reading lessons, 63–64
    reading–writing integration, 108
    viewing–representing–content reading, 195–198
    visual-arts/reading lessons, 50
Learning Together Through Inquiry (Paul et al.), 215
LeBlanc, Beth, 179–180
Lenski, Davis, 85–87
Letort, Brook, 68–69, 223–224
Like Sisters on the Home Front (Garcia–Williams), 113
Linearity, 151
Linguistic diversity, 22–23, 24, 32–33
Linking Literacy and Technology (Wepner et al.), 128
Listening skills
    dramatic-arts/reading lessons, 81
    electronic symbol making, 12, 13
    music–dance reading lessons, 64, 65, 66
    visual-arts/reading lessons, 48
Listserv
    defined, 239
    Internet technologies, 34
    reading–writing–computer technology, 128, 130, 147
Liszt, Franz (1811–1886), 239
Literacy and the Arts for the Integrated Classroom (Cecil/Laritzen), 61, 77, 82, 99

Literacy at the Crossroads (Routman), 107, 124

Literature Discussion Groups in the Inter-mediate Grades (Evans), 110n.6

Literature logs, 104

Little Mermaid, The (Walt Disney), 72

Little Women (Alcott), 184, 187–188

Lively Discussions! Fostering Engaged Reading (Gambrell/Almasi), 110n.5

Lloyd, Carol, 68, 224–225

Local area network (LAN), 128

M

Make Lemonade (Wolf), 113

Manet, Édourard (1832–1883)
  impressionism, 238, 239
  visual-arts/reading lessons, 44

Mapping the Possibilities of Integrated Literacy Instruction (Biondo et al.), 212n.1

Masks (McNiven/McNiven), 193

Massachusetts, 3

Mastery Teaching (Hunter), 138n.4

McClain, Anita, 121–122

McCullough, Peggy, 67

McKenna, Kathleen, 116–117, 138–139, 220–221

Meaning construction
  electronic symbol making, 13, 14, 16
  Internet technologies, 34–35
  media/popular-culture/content reading, 179
  reading–writing integration, 102, 108
  semiotics integration, 151–154

Media Alert! 200 Activities to Create Media–Savvy Kids (Lockwood Summers), 175

Media literacy, Internet technologies, 22, 23, 25–26, 32, 35

Media Matters (McBrien), 189

Media/popular-culture/content reading
  case 10.1, 177
  case 10.1 commentaries, 177–179
  case 10.1 inquiries, 177
  case 10.2, 179–180
  case 10.2 commentaries, 181–184
  case 10.2 inquiries, 180
  case 10.3, 184
  case 10.3 commentaries, 185–188

  case 10.3 inquiries, 184, 187
  advocacy, 172–173
  analytic inquiry, 188–189
  Australia, 172
  benefits of, 173–174
  Canada, 172
  critical thinking, 188
  critical viewing, 178–179
  emergent literacy learner, 178–179
  fandom, 185
  film, 178, 185
  graphic organizers, 179
  meaning construction, 179
  model artwork, 178
  music, 177–179
  overview, 172–174
  Pokemon, 179–184
  popular-culture text, 172, 240
  practical application, 188–189
  principles of, 173
  professional development, 174–176, 188
  professional standards, 174, 185
  quotation excerpts, 172
  reading resources, 175, 177, 178, 184, 189
  reflections, 179, 188
  Renaissance, 179
  sketch journals, 179
  story maps, 179
  video production, 175
  visual organizers, 179
  Web site resources, 175, 179, 184
  zine, 176

Mendelssohn, Felix (1809–1847), 239, 241

Meneses, Mariela, 94–95

Metacognition
  defined, 239
  reading–writing integration, 104

Metacognitive
  defined, 239
  dramatic-arts/reading lessons, 81
  Internet technologies, 29–30

Metaphors
  defined, 239
  reading–writing–computer technology, 147
  semiotics integration, 157

Mexico, 59

Microsoft, 24

Miller, Sharon, 113–115, 159–161, 182–184

Minilessons, 105

Minimalism
  composers, 238
  defined, 239

Mobiles
  Calder, Alexander (1898–1976), 239
  defined, 239
  visual-arts/reading lessons, 42, 43
  Web site resources, 239

Monet, Claude (1840–1926)
  impressionism, 238, 239, 241
  "Impression Sunrise," 239
  visual-arts/reading lessons, 239

Morales, Cynthia, 48–49

Morse, Timothy, 167–168, 185–186

Mouse Party (Durant), 62–63

Mp3
  defined, 239
  Internet technologies, 31

Moving Picture Experts Group (MPEG), 239

Multimedia video cases, 4

Multiple communication systems
  multiple literacies–inquiry integration, 214
  semiotics integration, 162–163, 165–166
  viewing–representing–content reading, 191–192

Multiple Forms of Literacy (Piazza), 76, 77–78

Multiple intelligences
  defined, 239
  music–dance reading lessons, 60
  viewing–representing–content reading, 191, 201
  visual-arts/reading lessons, 41–42

Multiple literacies
  defined, 240
  dramatic-arts/reading lessons, 80, 93
  Internet technologies, 21, 22–23, 24–26, 35
  music–dance reading lessons, 72, 74
  reading–writing–computer technology, 134
  research inspiration, xvii
  research objectives, xvii
  semiotics integration, 159, 165
  visual-arts/reading lessons, 41–42

Multiple literacies–inquiry integration
  case 12.1, 215–216
  case 12.1 commentaries, 217–219
  case 12.1 inquiries, 216
  case 12.2, 219–220
  case 12.2 commentaries, 220–223
  case 12.2 inquiries, 220
  case 12.3, 223–224
  case 12.3 commentaries, 224–226
  case 12.3 inquiries, 224
  case 12.4, 226–227
  case 12.4 commentaries, 227–231
  case 12.4 inquiries, 227
  advance organizer, 225–226, 231
  analytic inquiry, 231–233
  Astronomy, 219–223
  authenticity, 228
  Caldecott Medal, 219
  Canada, 216
  collaboration, 211, 213–214, 230–231
  Connections Log, 215
  constructivism, 211
  critical thinking, 210–211, 214
  Egypt, 223–226
  flexibility, 212
  holism, 210–211
  K-W-L, 219, 226–231
  language arts, 210–211
  Latin America, 216
  learning objectives, 213
  learning styles, 213
  multiple communication systems, 214
  multiple literacies, 226
  overview, 210–214
  planning map, 213–214
  practical application, 231–233
  professional development, 211, 214–215, 231
  professional standards, 211, 213
  project design, 213
  quotation excerpts, 210
  reading resources, 214–215, 217, 219–220, 223, 227, 228, 231, 233
  realia, 229, 232
  reflections, 231
  Reggio Emelia Approach, 229–230
  resource assembly, 212–213
  science, 210–211

semiotic systems, 211
social studies, 210–211
subject coverage, 219–223
teacher role, 211–214
team teaching, 216, 218–219
thematic unit, 212, 215–219,
224–226
time constraints, 215–219
time management, 213–214
Venn diagram, 216
Web site resources, 219, 220, 229
wetlands, 226–231
Multiple semiotic systems, *see*
Semiotics integration
Multiple sign systems
electronic symbol making, 11–17
music–dance reading lessons, 73
semiotics integration, 157–162,
165, 166–170
Munch, Edvard (1863–1944)
expressionism, 240
media/popular-culture/content
reading, 178
Murals
defined, 240
fresco contrast, 240
viewing–representing–content reading, 194
visual-arts/reading lessons, 42, 43,
44, 48–52
Music
media/popular-culture/content
reading, 177–179
semiotics integration, 163, 165–166
visual-arts/reading lessons, 48
Musical chairs activity, 202–206
Music–dance–reading lessons
case 5.1, 62–63
case 5.1 commentaries, 63–66
case 5.1 inquiries, 63
case 5.2, 66–67
case 5.2 commentaries, 67–68
case 5.2 inquiries, 67, 68
case 5.3, 68–69
case 5.3 commentaries, 70–71
case 5.3 inquiries, 69
case 5.4, 72
case 5.4 commentaries, 73–75
case 5.4 inquiries, 72
advance organizer, 72–75
aesthetic value, 58, 63–64, 75

Africa, 59, 62
analytic inquiry, 61, 76–77
Australia, 59–60, 62
choral reading, 66, 67, 68
choreographers, 59
cinquain, 75, 79
communicative literacy, 57–60
diamante, 75, 78
digital video disk (DVD), 76
disciplinary function, 58–59
educational function, 60
emergent literacy learner, 63–64
expression enhancement, 57–60
familiar melodies, 64
Folklórico Ballet, 62
functions of, 57–58
Ghana, 60
group management, 63, 64–65, 66
haiku, 75, 78
Khedive, 71
learning styles, 63–64
learning transformation, 60
listening skills, 64, 65, 66
literacy function, 59–60
Mexico, 59
multiple intelligences, 60
multiple literacies, 72, 74
multiple sign systems, 73
overview, 57–60
poetry, 65, 75, 78–79
practical application, 76–77
professional development, 61–62,
75–76
program music, 59
pyramid music, 68–71
quotation excerpts, 57
rants, 62
reading resources, 61, 77–78
reflections, 73, 75–76
rhythm instruments, 64, 65–66, 68
romantic composers, 62
sign systems, 60, 70, 73
student participation, 63, 66, 67,
68, 70, 71
symbolic representation, 58–59
syntax, 60
tanka, 75, 78
tape-recordings, 67, 70, 71
teacher modeling, 74
therapeutic value, 58
video production, 70

video resources, 74
"World Premiere Party," 70
Music Educators National Conference,
    80–81

N

Napping House, The (Wood), 119n.11
National Council for the Accreditation
    of Teacher Education
    (NCATE), 29
National Council of Teachers of Eng-
    lish (NCTE), 106–107, 109,
    155, 174
National Science Teachers Association,
    229
National Standards for Arts Education
    (1994), 41–42, 46, 80–81
National Writing Project (NWP),
    108–109
Native American study, 135–139
*New Grove Dictionary of Music and Musi-
    cians* (Sadie/Tyrell), 59n.2
New Jersey, 3
New literacies, *see also* Internet tech-
    nologies
    defined, 240
    electronic symbol making, 12
New London Group, 22–23, 24
New Mexico, 42
Newsweek, 107
New York Times, 82
Noe, Katherine Schlick, 227–229
Nonfiction Matters (Harvey), 228
Nonlinearity
    reading–writing–computer technol-
        ogy, 127
    reading–writing integration, 103
Nonstructured–nonprocess writing,
    103–104, 105
Number the Stars (Lowry), 105

O

On Writing (King), 106
Oral maps, 59–60, 62
Oral text
    defined, 240
    semiotics integration, 165

viewing–representing–content read-
    ing, 190–191
Oreck, Barry, 49–51, 95–97
Osterman, Jane, 119–121, 199–200
Owl Moon (Yolen), 47

P

Palm Pilot, 24
Paperbag Princess, The (Munsch), 161
Papier-mâché
    defined, 240
    visual-arts/reading lessons, 42, 50
    Web site resources, 240
Park, Kristy, 118–119
Patterson (Williams), 243
Payne, Carol, 65–66
PDA (personal digital assistant)
    defined, 240
    Internet technologies, 24
Pdf (portable document format)
    defined, 240
    Internet technologies, 31
Peirce, Charles Sanders, 150
Penguins (Gibbons), 193, 208
People in the History of Astronomy, 219
Percival, Jane, 140–142, 168–170,
    186–188, 229–231
Perez, Katherine, 142–143
Personal development, 109–110
Phonic Phacts (Goodman), 107
Phonics, 107
Photography
    electronic symbol making, 13–16
    viewing–representing–content read-
        ing, 193, 194
Picasso, Pablo (1881–1973)
    abstract art, 240
    cubism, 240
    media/popular-culture/content
        reading, 178
    visual-arts/reading lessons, 44
Picture Writer (Carle), 44
Pioneer Projects (Kalman), 194
Planning map, 213–214
Poetry, *see also* Cinquain; Diamante;
        Haiku; Shape poem; Tanka
    dramatic-arts/reading lessons, 98
    music–dance reading lessons, 65,
        75, 78–79

reading–writing integration, 113,
115–118, 122
semiotics integration, 162–163,
164–166
visual-arts/reading lessons, 45–47
Pointillism
defined, 240
Seurat, George (1859–1891), 240
visual-arts/reading lessons, 44
Pokemon, 179–184
Political context
Internet technologies, 22, 23, 28
reading–writing integration, 107
Popular-culture interpretations, 23
Popular Culture in the Classroom
(Alvermann et al.), 177
Popular-culture media, xvii
Popular-culture text, *see* Media/popular-
culture/content reading
Portfolios, 90
Possible Lives (Rose), 114
Postimpressionism
artists, 238, 240
defined, 240
visual-arts/reading lessons, 44
Postmodernism, 23
Primary Voices K–6, 215
Print media, 30
Print text, 190–191
Process logs, 104
Professional development
Internet technologies, 28–29, 30
media/popular-culture/content
reading, 174–176, 188
multiple literacies–inquiry integration, 211, 214–215, 231
music–dance reading lessons,
61–62, 75–76
reading–writing–computer technology, 128–130, 147
reading–writing integration, 106,
108–109, 122
semiotics integration, 154–155,
156–157, 170
viewing–representing–content reading, 192–194, 206
visual-arts/reading lessons, 41,
43–44, 54
Professional standards
dramatic-arts/reading lessons,
80–81

Internet technologies, 29
media/popular-culture/content
reading, 174, 185
multiple literacies–inquiry integration, 211, 213
reading–writing integration,
106–107
semiotics integration, 155
teaching cases, 4
visual-arts/reading lessons, 41, 42
Program music, 59
Promoting Literacy in Grades 4–9
(Wood/Dickinson), 124
Pyramid (Macaulay), 193, 208
Pyramid music, 68–71
Pyramids
multiple literacies–inquiry integration, 225–226
visual-arts/reading lessons, 52–54

Q

Question–Answer Relationships
(QARs)
defined, 240
reading–writing integration, 121
Quiocho, Alice, 63–65, 74–75

R

Rants
defined, 241
music–dance reading lessons, 62
Rasinski, Timothy, 146–147, 196–197
Readers Theatre
defined, 241
dramatic-arts/reading lessons,
81–82
viewing–representing–content reading, 200
Reading Engagement (Guthrie/Wigfield),
233
Reading Online, 175
Reading Process and Practice (Weaver),
82
Reading resources, *see also* CD–ROM
resources; Video resources;
World Wide Web resources
electronic symbol making, 17

media/popular-culture/content reading, 175, 177, 178, 184, 189
multiple literacies–inquiry integration, 214–215, 217, 219–220, 223, 227, 228, 231, 233
music–dance reading lessons, 61, 77–78
reading–writing–computer technology, 128, 143, 149
reading–writing integration, 104–105, 106, 107, 110, 111, 113, 114, 115, 118, 119, 123–124
semiotics integration, 152, 156, 157–158, 161, 162, 164–165, 166, 170, 171
teaching cases, 8–9
viewing–representing–content reading, 193, 195, 198, 206, 208–209
visual-arts/reading lessons, 43, 44, 47–48, 50, 56
Reading response journal, 104
Reading Teacher, The, 89, 175, 214
Reading Teachers (RT) (listserv), 130
Reading–writing–computer technology, *see also* Internet technologies
case 8.1, 131–132
case 8.1 commentaries, 132–135
case 8.1 inquiries, 132
case 8.2, 135–136
case 8.2 commentaries, 136–139
case 8.2 inquiries, 136
case 8.3, 139–140
case 8.3 commentaries, 140–143
case 8.3 inquiries, 140
case 8.4, 143–144
case 8.4 commentaries, 145–147
case 8.4 inquiries, 144
analytic inquiry, 148
benefits of, 125–127
Bloom's Taxonomy, 138
CD–ROM, 136, 138–139
computer utilization, 139–143
desktop publishing, 134–135
drill-and-practice, 129
EdTech, 128
electronic text distinctions, 126–127
hypertext, 127

I-Chart, 137
integrated learning system (ILS), 129, 148
Internet, 130
keyboarding, 131–135
listserv, 128, 130, 147
local area network (LAN), 128
metaphors, 147
multiple literacies, 134
Native American study, 135–139
nonlinearity, 127
overview, 125–127
practical application, 129–130, 148
professional development, 128–130, 147
quotation excerpts, 125
reading resources, 128, 143, 149
Reading Teachers (RT), 130
reflections, 126–127, 147
semantic maps, 131
semiotic systems, 141
server failure, 143–147
S(PH)QR strategy, 138–139
SQ3R strategy, 135–139
teacher preparation, 144, 146–147
teacher utilities, 129, 130
teaching transformation, 127
tutorials, 129
Web site resources, 128, 130
word processor, 129, 134–135
World Wide Web, 130
Reading–writing integration
case 7.1, 111
case 7.1 commentaries, 111–115
case 7.1 inquiries, 111
case 7.2, 115–116
case 7.2 commentaries, 116–118
case 7.2 inquiries, 116
case 7.3, 118–119
case 7.3 commentaries, 119–122
case 7.3 inquiries, 119
Alaska, 106
analytic inquiry, 107, 122–123
benefits of, 101–102
Bloom's Taxonomy, 120
child development, 107–108
cinquain, 122
collaboration, 103, 105
communicative literacy, 102
comprehension facilitation, 101, 102, 103

day-books, 104
dialogue journals, 104
expression enhancement, 102, 103, 104
group feedback, 105
haiku, 122
journals, 103–104, 118–122
K-W-L, 105
learning disabilities, 108
learning logs, 104
learning styles, 108
literature logs, 104
meaning construction, 102, 108
metacognition, 104
minilessons, 105
nonlinearity, 103
nonstructured–nonprocess writing, 103–104, 105
overview, 101–105
personal development, 109–110
phonics, 107
poetry, 113, 115–118, 122
political context, 107
practical application, 107–108, 122–123
process logs, 104
process similarity, 102–103
professional development, 106, 108–109, 122
professional standards, 106–107
Question–Answer Relationships (QARs), 121
quotation excerpts, 101
reading resources, 104–105, 106, 107, 110, 111, 113, 114, 115, 118, 119, 123–124
reading response journal, 104
recursive process, 103
reflections, 104, 122
sequencing, 102
story features, 111
structured–process writing, 103, 104–105
student conferences, 105
student preparation, 102
syntax, 101
teacher conferences, 108–109
viewpoints, 101–102, 104–105
violence, 111–115
Web site resources, 108–109, 110, 112n.7, 113, 122n.14

whole-language, 107
Reagan, Bill, 83–84
Realia
  defined, 241
  multiple literacies–inquiry integration, 229, 232
Recursive process, 103
Reflections
  media/popular-culture/content reading, 179, 188
  multiple literacies–inquiry integration, 231
  music–dance reading lessons, 73, 75–76
  reading–writing–computer technology, 126–127, 147
  reading–writing integration, 104, 122
  semiotics integration, 170
  teaching cases, 7
  viewing–representing–content reading, 206
  visual-arts/reading lessons, 44, 50, 54
Reflections on the Reggio Emelia Approach (Katz/Cesarone), 229n.4
Reggio Emelia Approach, 229–230
Renaissance
  defined, 241
  media/popular–culture/content reading, 179
Renaissance in the Classroom (Burnaford et al.), 42n.2
Renoir, Pierre Auguste (1841–1919)
  impressionism, 238
  visual-arts/reading lessons, 44
Resilient Children (Barone), 112n.9
Rhythm instruments, 64, 65–66, 68
Risko, Victoria J., 204–206
Romantic composers
  composers, 235, 239, 241
  defined, 241
  music–dance reading lessons, 62
Romantic Movement, 235
Roots (Haley), 193
Rothko, Mark (1903–1970)
  abstract expressionism, 241
  visual-arts/reading lessons, 44
Rough-Face Girl, The (Martin), 157–159
Rude Giants (Wood), 119n.12, 120

S

Scaffolding Emergent Literacy (Soderman et al.), 178–179
Scary Movie, 178
Schubert, Franz (1797–1828), 241
Schumann, Robert (1810–1856), 241
Schussler, Deborah, 197–198, 203–204
Sconyers, Alison, 195–196
"Scream, The" (Munch), 178
Screening Images (Worsnop), 175
Search engine
    defined, 241
    Internet technologies, 31
Seeking Diversity (Rief), 106
Selin, Ann-Sofie, 89–91, 145–146
Semantic maps, 131
Semantic webs, 200
Semaphore
    defined, 241
    viewing–representing–content reading, 191
Semiotics integration
    case 9.1, 157–159
    case 9.1 commentaries, 159–162
    case 9.1 inquiries, 159
    case 9.2, 162–163
    case 9.2 commentaries, 163–166
    case 9.2 inquiries, 163
    case 9.3, 166–167
    case 9.3 commentaries, 167–170
    case 9.3 inquiries, 167
    analytic inquiry, 170–171
    CD–ROM, 165
    colors, 156–157
    communication formats, 165–166
    communication systems, 151–152, 157, 162–163, 164, 165–166
    component connections, 151
    component relationships, 150–151
    electronic symbol making, 13–14, 16–17
    guided imagery, 163–164
    I-Chart, 160
    interpretant, 150–151
    linearity, 151
    meaning construction, 151–154
    metaphors, 157
    multiple communication systems, 162–163, 165–166
    multiple literacies, 159, 165
    multiple semiotic systems, 162–165, 166–170
    multiple sign systems, 157–162, 165, 166–170
    music, 163, 165–166
    object, 150–151
    oral text, 165
    overview, 150–156
    poetry, 162–163, 164–166
    practical application, 170–171
    principles of, 152–154
    professional development, 154–155, 156–157, 170
    professional standards, 155
    quotation excerpts, 150
    reading resources, 152, 156, 157–158, 161, 162, 164–165, 166, 170, 171
    reflections, 170
    research contribution, xxii
    semiotics defined, 13, 241
    semiotic systems, 152–157, 162–165, 166–170
    sign, 150–151
    sign systems, 151–156, 157–162, 165, 166–170
    similes, 157
    theoretical components, 150–151
    Tobago, 166–170
    Venn diagram, 160
    video resources, 159
Semiotic systems
    defined, 241
    multiple literacies–inquiry integration, 211
    reading–writing–computer technology, 141
    research inspiration, xvii
    semiotics integration, 152–157, 162–165, 166–170
    visual-arts/reading lessons, 41–42
Sequencing
    reading–writing integration, 102
    viewing–representing–content reading, 194
Seurat, George (1859–1891), 240
Shape poem
    defined, 241
    dramatic-arts/reading lessons, 98
Shaw, Larisa, 157–159

Signs and Symbols Around the World (Helfman), 152n.1
Sign systems, *see also* Multiple sign systems
  defined, 241
  electronic symbol making, 11–17
  music–dance reading lessons, 60, 70, 73
  research contribution, xxii
  semiotics integration, 151–156, 157–162, 165, 166–170
Simile, *see* Metaphor
Simulation
  defined, 242
  viewing–representing–content reading, 202
Sketch journals, 179
Sketch–to–Stretch, 196–197, 200
Smith, Patricia, 88–89
Snow White (Santore), 42n.3
Social psychology defined, 242
Sociocultural perspective
  defined, 242
  Internet technologies, 22, 31–33
Sontag, Patrice, 91
Spatial intelligence
  defined, 242
  viewing–representing–content reading, 201
Spiers, Joni, 115–116, 162–163
SQ3R strategy
  defined, 242
  reading–writing–computer technology, 135–139
S(PH)QR modification, 138–139
Standards for the English Language Arts (1996), 80, 155, 174
Star Gazers (Gibbons), 220
Starry Messenger (Sis), 219
Starry Night (van Gogh), 55
Start With a Story (Watson–Ellam), 83
Stetzer, Jay, 46–47, 177–178
Steven Caney's Kids America (Caney), 233
Stokes, Amy, 72
Stories (Raines/Isbell), 82n.1
Story features
  defined, 242
  reading–writing integration, 111
Story maps
  media/popular-culture/content reading, 179

viewing–representing–content reading, 198, 200
Strategic knowledge, 34–35
Streaming defined, 242
Structured–process writing, 103, 104–105
Student conferences, 105
Student preparation
  Internet technologies, 19, 20–21, 27–29, 30, 32, 33–34, 35, 36
  reading–writing integration, 102
Sunflowers (van Gogh), 157
Surrealism, 235, 238
Syntactic
  defined, 242
  dramatic-arts/reading lessons, 81
  Internet technologies, 29–30
Syntax
  defined, 242
  music–dance reading lessons, 60
  reading–writing integration, 101

T

Ta'i Chi
  defined, 242
  visual-arts/reading lessons, 46
  Web site resources, 242
Taking Time to Act (Ball), 82
Talking Eggs, The (San Souci), 84, 162–166
Tanka
  defined, 242
  music–dance reading lessons, 75, 78
Tape-recordings, 67, 70, 71
Tar Beach (Ringgold), 217
Taxonomy of Educational Objectives (Bloom), 120n.13
Teacher conferences, 108–109
Teacher modeling
  music–dance reading lessons, 74
  visual-arts/reading lessons, 46–47, 48, 51
Teacher preparation
  dramatic-arts/reading lessons, 94–97
  reading–writing–computer technology, 144, 146–147
Teacher utilities
  defined, 242

reading–writing–computer technology, 129, 130
Teaching cases
    analysis of, 7
    authoring guidelines, 5–7
    authoring process, 5
    benefits of, 4
    case method, 3
    case method defined, 235
    conditional knowledge, 5
    exemplary attributes, 4–5
    group discussions, 7
    historical context, 3
    introduction, 3–4
    Massachusetts, 3
    multimedia video cases, 4
    New Jersey, 3
    overview, xvii–xviii
    professional standards, 4
    quotation excerpts, 3
    reading resources, 8–9
    reflections, 7
    summary, 8
Teaching With the Internet (Leu/Leu), 6,
    128
Teaching Young Children to Draw (Cooke
    et al.), 56
Team teaching
    defined, 242
    multiple literacies–inquiry integration, 216, 218–219
Technology in its Place (LeBaron/Collier), 126n.1
Telling Pieces (Albers/Murphy), 43, 152,
    156, 170, 171, 231
Tena, Jose, 237
Thematic organizer, 205
Thematic unit
    defined, 243
    multiple literacies–inquiry integration, 212, 215–219,
        224–226
This Poem Doesn't Rhyme (Benson), 165
Thomas's Snowsuit (Munsch), 47
Three Little Pigs, The (Galdone), 42n.4
Time constraints, 215–219
Time line defined, 243
Time management, 213–214
Tobago, 166–170
Transactional voice
    defined, 243

viewing–representing–content reading, 192
Transmediation
    defined, 243
    visual-arts/reading lessons, 47
Triche, Paula, 92–94
*True Story of the Three Little Pigs by A.
    Wolf, The* (Scieszka), 105
Trust, 51–52
Tutorials
    defined, 243
    reading–writing–computer technology, 129

U

Useforge, Renee, 70

V

Vanaman, Deneen, 62–63
van Gogh, Vincent (1853–1890)
    expressionism, 243
    postimpressionism, 238
    semiotics integration, 157
    Starry Night, 55
    Sunflowers, 157
    visual-arts/reading lessons, 44
Venn diagram
    multiple literacies–inquiry integration, 216
    semiotics integration, 160
    viewing–representing–content reading, 200
Verdi, Giuseppe
    Aida, 71, 235
    music–dance reading lessons, 71,
        235
Very Hungry Caterpillar, The (Carle), 44
Video Camcorder School (Squires), 193
Video production
    media/popular-culture/content
        reading, 175
    music–dance reading lessons, 70
    teaching cases, 4
    viewing–representing–content reading, 193–194
Video resources, *see also* CD–ROM resources; Reading resources;
    World Wide Web resources

music–dance reading lessons, 74
semiotics integration, 159
viewing–representing–content reading, 193
visual-arts/reading lessons, 44
Viewing–representing–content reading
case 11.1, 195
case 11.1 commentaries, 196–198
case 11.1 inquiries, 195–196
case 11.2, 198–199
case 11.2 commentaries, 199–202
case 11.2 inquiries, 199
case 11.3, 202–203
case 11.3 commentaries, 203–206
case 11.3 inquiries, 203
advance organizer, 202–206
analytic inquiry, 207–208
authenticity, 194
Bliss symbol boards, 190
concept maps, 200
graphic organizers, 200
image text, 190–191
Jigsaw, 204
K-W-L, 200
K-W-L Plus, 200
learning disabilities, 190–191
learning styles, 195–198
multiple communication systems, 191–192
multiple intelligences, 191, 201
murals, 194
musical chairs activity, 202–206
oral text, 190–191
overview, 190–192
photography, 193, 194
practical application, 207–208
print text, 190–191
professional development, 192–194, 206
quotation excerpts, 190
Readers Theatre, 200
reading resources, 193, 195, 198, 206, 208–209
reflections, 206
semantic webs, 200
semaphore, 191
sequencing, 194
simulation, 202
Sketch-to-Stretch, 196–197, 200
social studies integration, 191–192
spatial intelligence, 201

story maps, 198, 200
thematic organizer, 205
transactional voice, 192
Venn diagram, 200
video production, 193–194
video resources, 193
viewing defined, 243
Viewpoints, 101–102, 104–105
Violence, 111–115
*Violence–Our Fastest Growing Public
   Health Problem* (Langone), 111
Visual-arts/reading lessons
case 4.1, 45–46
case 4.1 commentaries, 46–48
case 4.1 inquiries, 46
case 4.2, 48–49
case 4.2 commentaries, 49–52
case 4.2 inquiries, 49
case 4.3, 52
case 4.3 commentaries, 52–54
case 4.3 inquiries, 52
aesthetic stances, 43
aesthetic value, 42, 43
analytic inquiry, 51–52, 54–56
auding, 48
authenticity, 44
benefits of, 41–43
body movement, 46, 48
class presentations, 43
collaboration, 42, 50
collages, 44
communicative literacy, 42–43, 44, 48
comprehension facilitation, 43, 44, 48
content–reading lessons, 43
dioramas, 42
docents, 44
efferent stances, 43
expression enhancement, 41–42
free expression, 45–46, 47
frescos, 44
impressionism, 44
learning enhancement, 41–42, 48, 54
learning logs, 53–54
learning styles, 50
listening skills, 48
mobiles, 42, 43
multiple intelligences, 41–42
multiple literacies, 41–42

murals, 42, 43, 44, 48–52
music, 48
overview, 41–43
papier-mâché, 42, 50
poetry, 45–47
pointillism, 44
postimpressionism, 44
power dynamics, 42
practical application, 54–56
professional development, 41,
     43–44, 54
professional standards, 41, 42
pyramids, 52–54
quotation excerpts, 41
reading literacy, 42, 43, 48
reading resources, 43, 44, 47–48,
     50, 56
recall facilitation, 43
reflections, 44, 50, 54
semiotic systems, 41–42
Ta'i Chi, 46
teacher modeling, 46–47, 48, 51
transmediation, 47
trust-building, 51–52
video resources, 44
warm-up activities, 50
Web site resources, 42, 44, 54
writing literacy, 42, 43, 48
Visual Messages (Considine/Haley), 175
Visual organizers, 179

W

Walt Disney, 72, 159, 193
Washington, 42
Watercolor for the Artistically Undiscovered
     (Hurd/Cassidy), 193, 208
Ways of knowing defined, 243
We're Going on a Bear Hunt (Rosen),
     66–67
Wetlands, 226–231
Wetlands (Stone), 227
Whale Song (Sheldon), 47, 48
What Jamie Saw (Coman), 113
What's Whole in Whole Language (Good-
     man), 107
Who Learns What From Cases and How?
     (Lundeberg et al.), 8
Whole-language

electronic symbol making, 12
reading–writing integration, 107
Who Lost a Shoe? (Hazen), 111, 115
Williams, William Carlos (1883–1963)
     Patterson, 243
     visual-arts/reading lessons, 47
Winfrey, Oprah, 110
Winter Eyes (Florian), 118
Wisconsin, 42
With Promise (Stires), 124
Word processor
     defined, 243
     Internet technologies, 24
     reading–writing–computer technol-
          ogy, 129, 134–135
"World Premiere Party," 70
World Wide Web
     defined, 243
     Internet component, 238, 243
     Internet distinction, 130
World Wide Web resources, *see also*
          CD–ROM resources; Reading
          resources; Video resources
     dramatic-arts/reading lessons, 80–81
     media/popular-culture/content
          reading, 175, 179, 184
     mobiles, 239
     multiple literacies–inquiry integra-
          tion, 219, 220, 229
     papier-mâché, 240
     reading–writing–computer technol-
          ogy, 128, 130
     reading–writing integration,
          108–109, 110, 112n.7,
          113, 122n.14
     Ta'i Chi, 242
     visual-arts/reading lessons, 42, 44, 54
Writer's Workshop (Solley), 124

Y

You Can Make a Collage (Carle), 44

Z

Zine
     defined, 243
     media/popular-culture/content
          reading, 176